CW00543751

Popular education
and
social movements
in
Scotland today

Popular education and social movements in Scotland today

Edited by
Jim Crowther, Ian Martin and Mae Shaw

NIACE
THE NATIONAL ORGANISATION
FOR ADULT LEARNING

Thanks to Dorothy Halliday of the Portland Desktop, Edinburgh for typing the manuscript

Published by the National Institute of Adult Continuing Education
(England and Wales)
21 De Montfort Street, Leicester, LE1 7GE
Company registration no. 2603322
Charity registration no. 1002775

First published 1999
© NIACE

All rights reserved. No reproduction, copy or transmission of this publication may be
made without the written permission of the publishers, save in accordance with the
provisions of the Copyright, Designs and Patents Act 1988, or under the terms of any
licence permitting limited copying issued by the Copyright Licencing Agency.

CATALOGUING IN PUBLICATION DATA
A CIP record for this title is available from the British Library
ISBN 1 86201 041 2

Typeset by The Midlands Book Typesetting Company, Loughborough
Cover design by Boldface, London EC1
Printed in Great Britain by Antony Rowe Ltd

Contents

Section 3: Social and cultural action

Section 4: Struggles in practice

Foreword

I welcome this book with warmth, surprise and more than a little envy.

There have been times in the last thirty years when I have despaired of radical politics and adult education in Britain. Mired in constitutionalism, saturated in paternalism and often surrounded by popular indifference, it's not surprising that the thought has formed itself: I could be doing something more productive with my time. The brave challenges seemed to have had no effect, left no mark, gone unheard.

But some wonderful things have happened in the last year. The people of Britain voted overwhelmingly for something different, a change for the better; and the people of Scotland voted decisively for a degree of self-government and a parliament with tax-varying powers. The politicians in Northern Ireland have continued the search for a common road to peace. These changes constitute the start of an irreversible process.

And elsewhere, under the surface, things have really been shifting. It is a shift in the direction of self-determination of small nations and ordinary people. It is a shift in the direction of international communication and collaboration. This is the wider context in which to read a new book that, in my opinion, is going to be important and inspirational.

In their choice of a title, the editors have captured and connected three crucial themes: first, Scottish action-reflection in recent years has been mould-breaking and instructive, possibly even paradigmatic; second, the idea of popular education, in challenging both the old paternalism and the new vocationalism, has much to contribute to a re-visioning of what learning, teaching and living are all about; third, social movements, animated by passionate commitment, argument and creativity, do have an impact on political, social and economic structures. This book tackles these themes theoretically, historically and practically, with reference to concrete experience – both Scottish and international.

In these pages Scotland and her multicultural peoples claim their place as insubordinate citizens and equals on a wider stage. And they have things to say that must be heard beyond Scotland.

Colin Kirkwood

1 Introductory essay: popular education and social movements in Scotland today

Ian Martin

The growth of movements which have as their aim the creation of a better social order is not less important than the process of education itself. In some ways, it is more important, for such movements create the background of aspiration and endeavour which is the foundation of more directly educational work, and suggest the questions for which men and women seek in study to find an answer. (Ministry of Reconstruction (1919)Final Report of the Adult Education Committee)

The threat of a good example

This book began as one idea and became another idea – bigger, more complex, more problematic, and far more promising. In retrospect, it now seems clear that this was essentially a move from negative to positive, from an account of the educational possibilities of Scotland's rejection of Thatcherite conservatism to an exploration of the opportunities presented by the prospect of democratic renewal in Scotland. In some ways, however, the resources for reconstruction are the same as they were for resistance – it is simply that they can now be deployed in a more positive, hopeful and creative way. This, of course, reflects changes in the political context: in particular, the election of a Labour government in May 1997 and subsequently the overwhelming vote in the Referendum that followed in favour of a Scottish Parliament and a significant degree of self-government.

The experience of preparing this book represents a defining feature of popular education: it is always contextual and contingent, reflecting and responding to changing circumstances and, in particular, the changing relationship between the formal politics of state and the informal politics of social movements in civil society. The essence of the argument presented here is that the 'popular' is located within the dialectic between the political culture of the state and the cultural politics of communities, and the potential of a 'popular education' is to catalyse this dialectic, to make it work. For a variety of reasons outlined below and considered more fully in the chapters that follow, Scotland today is a peculiarly rich and suggestive context in which to examine the changing relationship between popular education, social movements and social change. On the other hand, although the nature of popular education is such that its argument must be worked out in terms of the specificities of particular historical, cultural and material conditions, the force of the account presented here is neither merely parochial nor idiosyncratic.

Other societies are now facing similar choices in striking the balance between, for instance, market and democratic definitions of citizenship, competition and co-operation, difference and solidarity, rights and responsibilities. The outcome of the choices they make remains open and undecided – and the prospects for human well being deeply ambivalent. Can Scotland today pose the threat of a good example?

Scotland: mirror and lens

In the era of globalisation, the Scottish experience is not only generalisable but may also be to some degree – and this is a more ambitious claim – paradigmatic. This book suggests that Scotland today is in some significant ways a microcosm of wider processes now at work in many other societies. As such, Scotland is both a mirror reflecting these processes and a lens through which to examine them. In this sense, the focus on Scotland enhances rather than diminishes the wider relevance of this book because Scotland today is a case in point rather than simply a case study.

As a mirror, Scotland reflects the shifting boundaries between the state, the market and civil society, and confronts what some would perceive as a growing crisis in the legitimacy of the liberal democratic nation state itself as historically constituted (eg Held, 1995; Nairn, 1997). This crisis has both internal and external dimensions. Internally, it points to the growing disjunction between the politics of civil society and the politics of the state. This is perhaps particularly apparent in the case of relatively small countries which have been dominated by larger and more powerful neighbours. The present demand is for greater democracy and autonomy in order to facilitate a new kind of settlement between the cultural formation of the nation and the political formation of the state. But the mirror must be reflexive as well as reflective: the people of Scotland have to look at themselves and ask what kind of democratic citizenship they want. Externally, the globalisation of capital and the growing power of transnational corporations seem increasingly to threaten the very idea of national sovereignty and pose in very stark terms the contradiction between market and democratic notions of freedom.

As a lens, Scotland provides an opportunity to see the beginnings of what could be a new kind of democracy at work – and popular education, as several of the contributions to this book demonstrate, has always been about the struggle to extend democracy. What Scotland has done, in effect, is to contradict the mantra of neo-liberal conservatism that 'There is no alternative'. In rejecting the hegemony of resignation in this way, it has opened up the opportunity to renew democracy by developing a more pluralistic and participative political culture. Indeed, some would argue that – especially if the widely canvassed demand for an equal gender balance in the new Scottish Parliament is met – Scotland has the opportunity to become one of the most democratic societies in Europe. But the Parliament is not simply a new national political institution; it must also become the symbol of the possibility of a new settlement between the state and civil society. This is what makes the Scottish case so interesting and instructive.

In terms of the paradigmatic nature of the contemporary Scottish experience, it is worth making some preliminary points. The global restructuring of capital produces universal problems as well as possibilities (for some), but these – and the balance between them – are played out in particular contexts. This process of economic restructuring, which often rides rough shod over national and political boundaries, urgently demands new ways of thinking about democracy and the nature of citizenship in a free society – as distinct from a 'free' market. As capital goes global, it undermines the sovereignty (at any rate, as traditionally understood) of the nation state and, simultaneously, exerts similar pressures everywhere to maximise profit and cut back on public expenditure. The same processes are at work in the logic of the globalised market and its familiar euphemisms, whether accomplished through the 'modernisation' of the welfare state in the rich world or 'structural adjustment' programmes in the poor world – the costs of which, in both contexts, are primarily borne by those who can least afford them, mainly poor women.

This, in turn, begins to reconfigure the relationship between the state and civil society, generating new social movements (or resuscitating old ones) in response to policy change. At the same time, a tension is set up between competing discourses of democracy: the new discourse of the 'liberal competition state' versus the old discourse of the 'democratic safety state'. These discourses are based on the contested claims of an essentially economistic definition of democracy coupled with a citizenship of consumption and 'choice' in the market place, on the one hand, and a more inclusive and essentially moral definition of democracy coupled with a citizenship based on the balance between social rights and responsibilities, on the other. Education, and particularly the current rhetoric of 'lifelong learning', mean very different things in each case. And 'education for citizenship' is, of course, a key site of contest between them. It should be emphasised that these processes are global, but they are acted out locally. The connections between the global and the local are well understood by capital; they therefore need also to be well understood by those who do not take its side.

In many parts of Eastern Europe the collapse of the totalitarian communist state and the command economy has opened the floodgates to the stark inequalities of untrammelled market forces as well as the ugly flowering of vicious and exclusive forms of nationalism. Elsewhere, however, the picture is less grim. In Scotland, for instance, the current restructuring of the political (as distinct from welfare) state is partly the outcome of pressures exerted not by capital but by social movements in civil society – often in direct opposition to state policies. In this context, the challenge is to construct a reinvigorated national democracy based on an inclusive notion of citizenship – that is, to renew politics rather than abandon it. Democratic renewal in Scotland, however, will depend on a new kind of relationship between the state and civil society. It is the argument of this book that popular education has a crucial part to play in catalysing this relationship.

Popular education: an emergent paradigm

Popular education is not a term which has been widely used in either the Scottish or UK contexts. Nevertheless, the idea of a 'popular' education, ie an education that is rooted in the interests, aspirations and struggles of ordinary people, is implicit in the history of radical adult education in both Scotland and the UK as a whole (Chapter 2: Jim Crowther). This book seeks to make its role and significance explicit, by inserting it purposefully into the contemporary debate about the relationship between education and social change. It is the idea of being self-consciously on the side of, ie committed in a partisan and broadly political way, that distinguishes popular education from other forms of education. This book argues for an education that is on the side of democratic renewal in Scotland by giving voice to excluded, exploited and subordinated groups and forging in solidarity with them a common project of inclusive citizenship. Its argument therefore has to start from what is in danger of impeding this process, conceived as a popular project – a project of the people.

Perhaps the clearest way of illustrating the distinctive positioning of popular education in these terms is to reproduce in full the statement of definition and purpose agreed by the recently formed Popular Education Forum for Scotland:

Popular education
Popular education is understood to be popular, as distinct from merely populist, in the sense that:

- it is rooted in the real interests and struggles of ordinary people
- it is overtly political and critical of the *status quo*
- it is committed to progressive social and political change.

Popular education is based on a clear analysis of the nature of inequality, exploitation and oppression and is informed by an equally clear political purpose. This has nothing to do with helping the 'disadvantaged' or the management of poverty; it has everything to do with the struggle for a more just and egalitarian social order.

The process of popular education has the following general characteristics:

- its curriculum comes out of the concrete experience and material interests of people in communities of resistance and struggle

- its pedagogy is collective, focused primarily on group as distinct from individual learning and development
- it attempts, wherever possible, to forge a direct link between education and social action.

Linking the local and the global

Although the term has come to be associated with relatively recent developments in Latin America, it has strong resonances with both the radical tradition in British adult education and the distinctively Scottish interest in promoting democratic access to the exploration of ideas and to the debate about what counts as worthwhile knowledge.

Popular education seeks to connect the local and the global. In every context it proceeds from specific, localised forms of education and action, but it deliberately sets out to foster international solidarity by making these local struggles part of the wider international struggle for justice and peace.

The purpose of the Popular Education Forum for Scotland

In the short-term, the purpose of the Forum is to:

- bring together people in Scotland with an existing interest in and commitment to popular education
- begin to forge active links and solidarity at both national and international levels.

In the longer-term, the Forum seeks to:

- catalyse action by linking local activists, workers and politically committed academics
- produce and provide educational resources for social and political action
- reassert and reinvigorate adult and community education's role as an integral part of progressive social movements.

It should be emphasised that although this statement has been endorsed by a group of committed activists, the contributors to this book do not necessarily subscribe to it in every particular. In fact, there is debate among them about, for instance, the relationship between the state and civil society and consequently about the nature and purpose of popular education and social movements. Nevertheless, the statement does reflect the general idea of popular education that frames this collection of papers. In this respect, it should be noted that in recent years the majority of the Scottish electorate has consistently expressed a stubborn attachment to broadly left-of-centre politics, including a strong degree of residual collectivism and a belief that public life should be so ordered as to demonstrate that there is, indeed, such a thing as society. As such, the idea of popular education is paradigmatic in the sense that it offers a way of bringing together a range of related positions and practices that reflect a general conceptual and ideological coherence within the contemporary Scottish context.

It is the sense that the learner should be regarded as an active citizen in a democracy that is at the heart of popular education, and explains its central concern with challenging and changing whatever gets in the way of this. Popular education, then, is at the sharp end of the long tradition of the 'adult education of engagement' in which students are treated as committed partners in learning *because* they are active and responsible citizens in a democratic society. This tradition has the following characteristics:

> the view that adults bring something which derives both from their experience of adult life and from their status as citizens to the educational process; that adult education is based on a dialogue rather than a mere transmission of knowledge and skill; that education is not only for personal development and advancement but also for social advancement; that adult education constructs knowledge and does not merely pass it on; that adult education has a dialectical and organic relationship with social movements (Jackson, 1995).

Popular adult education, then, cannot be neutral. It is true, of course, that no education is neutral in the sense that it always reflects particular values and serves particular interests. Indeed, this is by now a truism – but it is also one that is frequently forgotten, or conveniently set aside. What is distinctive about popular education is that it is quite explicit about the political purpose and the ideological commitment that inform it.

In some important respects, popular education seeks to reverse the ways in which education usually works. For example, it derives its curriculum, ie the systematic organisation of educational content and methods, primarily from the interests, aspirations and lived experience of its students rather than the expertise of the teacher, the demands of the discipline or the imperatives of policy. In this sense and put rather crudely, it is a 'bottom-up' rather than a 'top-down' process, ie worked *up* from people's concrete experience of social reality. In this way, it seeks to counter what Raymond Williams called the 'selective tradition' which is tacitly but actively at work throughout the traditional curriculum (Chapter 14: Elspeth King). Like all educational orthodoxies, this process of epistemological filtering of what is worth knowing and learning is, as Jane Thompson (1997) remarks, almost invariably a 'highly particular (ie dead, white, male, middle class and European) selection of knowledge and culture confirmed as truth'.

Moreover, the utility and efficacy of the 'knowledge from below' that is the hallmark of popular education is defined primarily in collective rather than individual terms. In this sense, popular education is informed by an egalitarian rather than a meritocratic ethic. This reflects a particular kind of analysis of inequality and understanding of the dialectic of agency (the possibility of freedom) and structure (the reality of constraint) within the common experience of its constituent communities of interest – often communities of resistance and struggle. This kind of analysis is required in order to make sense of the world as it is, but the aim of popular education is also to change that world for the better, ie in the interests of the poor, the exploited, the marginalised and the excluded. And for popular education, this is where the real struggle for democracy as a way of life and a way of living must begin.

As a way of thinking about and 'doing' education, popular education sharpens and enriches the standard vocabulary and rhetoric of adult and community education because it starts from the collective experience and interests of ordinary people. For example, it stretches and activates the discourse of lifelong learning to the idea of learning for living in order to live a different kind of life, of experiential learning to learning from experience in order to change reality, of social capital and community capacity building to reasserting social purpose and forging solidarity as a common political project. The learner is socially located and recognised as an activist. In engaging with social movements, therefore, popular education seeks to make the educative elements of people's collective experience, ie what they learn in the process of social and political action, more systematically educational (Chapter 22: Lorraine Dick). This suggests, incidentally, that educators are more often part of the problem than part of the solution – or, at any rate, that they cannot be part of the solution until they see how they can compound the problem: 'Adult educators often overlook the learning dimension that is integral to social life, so intent are they on constructing "education" ' (Foley, 1994). In this sense, popular education positions itself as the ally of progressive social movements – as distinct from much 'provided education' which is so often used to service, sometimes to suppress, them.

It is important to note the ambivalence of popular education's relationship to the state. Where the state is minimal and frequently repressive, as in many parts of Latin America (Chapter 4: Liam Kane), popular education is essentially the educational dimension and the educational resource for the 'popular movement', the movement of the poor and dispossessed. This movement is often against the state (ie protecting the interests of its members, who are defined essentially in class terms because they are materially poor, powerless and exploited), but it may also, at the same time, be a surrogate for the state (ie providing its members with services). Indeed, faced with an authoritarian central state, the popular movement may be concerned to 'reinvent or expand the public space of civil society' in order to secure a basic degree of freedom from state coercion and control (Miller, 1997). In some ways, this reflects the early history of the radical tradition in British adult education which placed a high premium on independence from an expanding and, in its view, predatory state as the only real guarantee against incorporation within it (Silver, 1965). In contrast to this, it may be noted that the Scandinavian folk high school movement managed to develop as a beneficiary of state sponsorship and yet remain independent of state control. In the contemporary Western European and North American contexts, however, the configuration tends to be different. Popular struggles may be both for and against the state. But, as the role of the state changes (eg in the current restructuring of welfare), so new spaces for popular education are opened up in the reconfigured relationship between the state, the market and civil society. In the contemporary British context, for instance, this process of moving into the spaces created by the contradictions and unintended outcomes of policy is particularly evident in relation to 'care in the community' and the resistance of both disabled people and carers to accepting the consequences of this arbitrary redrawing of the boundaries between public and personal responsibilities. Popular education often operates within the creative possibilities of this gap between the intentions and outcomes of policy (Chapter 24: Margaret Beveridge).

Finally, it must be noted that although popular adult education played an important part in the development of social democracy and, ultimately, in securing the civil, political and social rights of citizenship enshrined in the post-war settlement, this legacy of social democracy is now under threat:

> The process of globalisation is a tremendous challenge to democracy itself and to the notion of adult and popular education as fundamental for a democratic society. The fact that adult education and training are increasingly governed by the goals of labour market policies makes it necessary to consider the traditional links between adult education, national community, democracy and civil society. Historically, it is within the framework of the nation state that the fight for freedom and equality, democracy and human rights has been won. The national struggles for freedom in the twentieth century were fought in the belief that democracy, human rights and social justice are central elements in the establishment of the sovereign state. (Korsgaard, 1997)

The question is: how can popular adult education contribute to the defence and, indeed, the extension of social democracy and the rights of citizenship in face of the powerful economic, political and ideological forces now ranged against them?

Social movements and social change

The focus on the relationship between popular education, social movements and social change suggests that although the state may provide education, people also learn a great deal directly from their own autonomous civic and voluntary activity outside the state in civil society. Through their direct and significant experience of the 'generalisation of politics' (Hall, 1996) in everyday life, people

– often united in communities of struggle – learn to connect the personal and the political. Historically, civil society constituted the social and political terrain, independent of government, on which the people (however defined) struggled to expand their freedoms. In this sense, it embodied and articulated 'a category of liberty characterising the public space where the citizens acted politically' (Korsgaard, 1997). Today civil society is usually understood to refer to those (still extensive) areas of social and 'civic' life and voluntary association which remain relatively autonomous, ie unregulated by the institutions of the state. The point, however, is that although the distinction is vital and the differences are real, the boundaries between the state and civil society are both permeable and shifting, and the relationship is often a symbiotic one. Indeed, in historical terms, it could be argued that societies are most resourceful and dynamic when the relationship between social movements in civil society and the institutions of the state is relatively open and dynamic (Jackson, 1997).

By social movements is meant movements of people in civil society which cohere around issues and identities which they themselves define as significant. Welton (1993) identifies three general characteristics of such social movements: they articulate a 'collective identity', ie their members subscribe to a 'cause' which is common and is expressed collectively in the 'movement'; they exist in an 'antagonistic relation to an opposed group' (or interest), ie they are 'for' something because they are 'against' something; they have a 'normative orienta-tion', ie they embody a mobilising ethic, moral code or set of beliefs which reflects shared values and purposes. In the chapters of this book social move-ment activity is fairly broadly defined to include movements of working class people, women, the poor and dispossessed, trade unionists, environmentalists and disabled people as well as the struggles of minority ethnic and faith com-munities, land use and land rights campaigners, social and cultural action groups, and a variety of issue-based groups of local activists. It is necessary, of course, to make a clear distinction between what, in terms of this account, would be considered 'good' and 'bad' social movements. This book unambiguously takes the side of those movements which are socially and politically progressive in the sense that they are concerned to challenge inequality, exclusion and discrimination and to be part of the historic struggle for democracy and social justice (Chapter 7: Tom Steele).

Such movements are autonomous in the sense that they control their own affairs, and they are active largely outside the structures of the state. On the other hand, they may make demands and exert pressure in ways which help to shape the policies of the state and influence the politics of social democracy (Chapter 3: Lindsay Paterson). Indeed, many social movements are formed in response to the workings of the institutions of the state or the market and a common feature of much social movement activity is its oppositional or, in some way, alternative nature. In this sense, social movements are reactive, ie they exist in reaction to something else and they are generated and sustained in their dialectical relation to this: 'It is the interaction between movements and the forces they contest that shapes their development' (Barker, 1996).

Social movements may seem to be the epiphenomena of social life because the nature of their concerns and activities often makes them appear to be multiple and shifting, and they move in and out of alignment with each other. Fundamentally, however, underneath this impression of being diverse, fragmented and ephemeral, they reflect and express universal concerns and ask abiding questions. They do so in two distinct but often related ways. On the one hand, as already noted, many progressive social movements express a 'dissenting vocation' (Miliband, 1989) in the sense that they attempt to develop an alternative power base from which to challenge the powers that be and change the *status quo*. At the same time, however, a primary concern may be to present an essentially moral critique of the world as it is and to propose an alternative or prefigurative vision of the world as it might be (Chapter 10: David Fisher). The contemporary activity of most progressive social movements contains both oppositional and alternative elements, and the balance between them continually changes.

Such an account of progressive social movements suggests, as EP Thompson argued, that they may, over time, come to embody a 'moral economy' which expresses a generally held view among people both inside the movement and outside it in the wider community about what is right and wrong, or legitimate and illegitimate in terms of, say, government action or policy. This moral or counter-hegemonic work may, in turn, become the 'common sense of an era' (Clegg, 1996), ie what is generally assumed to be 'right' and is therefore taken for granted. This may help to explain, for example, the widespread opposition to – and the even more widespread sense of unease about – the Poll Tax: most people simply felt, instinctively, that it was 'wrong', and not just in Scotland. In terms of the relationship between social movements and social change, therefore, perhaps the crucial point is that social movements help to prepare people for change (or for resistance to change) by challenging (or confirming) the ways in which they think and feel and act politically. In this sense, they are intrinsically educative (Chapter 20: Helen Martin and Cathy McCormack).

Having characterised social movements in a general way, four particular points now need to be made about what, in linking them with popular education, may be called the 'curriculum' of social movements:

- First, social movements ask big, universal questions about what it means to be human. In educational terms, therefore, social movements are agents of what Freire (1972) calls 'ontological vocation'. It is in this sense that, despite their apparently fluid and erratic character, they are the 'carriers of historical projects of importance to all people' embodying fundamental questions about, for example, the relationship between men and women, human beings and the environment, master and servant (Gustavsson, 1997). This is precisely why social movements are often so deeply and disturbingly subversive – and it is also why the cultural politics of civil society tend to raise much more profound and existential questions than the essentially pragmatic politics of the state.

- Second, social movements, whatever their immediate concerns and preoccupations, propose a more rounded and holistic idea of what it means to be human than the reductionist materialism of either the political right or left. Thus, for example, the significance many social movements ascribe to culture, spirituality and the environment as crucial dimensions of human experience. This implies a relational understanding, ie a sense of the interconnectedness, of learning and living which applies both to relations between people and to people's relationship to the wider environment. It is in this sense that Welton (1993) argues that the agenda of progressive social movements constitutes a 'social ecology'.

- Third, the idea of social ecology suggests that social movements question, in some fundamental ways, the claims of the 'system world' over those of the 'life world'. In Habermasian terms, the former is the world of money (the market) and power (the state) in which people strive to *have* whereas the latter is the world of uncoerced human relationships and creativity in which people seek to *be*. In the older language of Tonnies, social movements are creatures of *gemeinschaft* rather than *gesellschaft,* and their rationality is organic rather than instrumental. It should be emphasised, however, that this does not necessarily imply other-worldliness; on the contrary, many contemporary social movements are actively attempting to change the world as it is – rather than escape from it (see Welton, 1995).

- Implicit in this is the fourth point: social movements seek to reassert the centrality of human agency, the capacity of people to choose – and to act to make a difference. As Crowther and Shaw (1997) put it, 'movements move people'. This is not a naive engagement, but it is a determined one. Perhaps the one thing all social movements would agree upon is that there is always an alternative – and alternatives are wrought by human action. The constraints of structure are, after all, the products of the agency of human beings who have chosen to act – or not to act – in particular ways. In their actions, therefore, social movements raise moral issues, questions about the 'good life'. To ask and answer such questions has consequences, and these have to be understood and accepted.

Social movements, then, are active at the intermediate level of social reality – indeed, it might be argued that in some respects they constitute it – of collective identities or communities of interest. These exist between the micro and immediate relations of the individual (the object of most educational intervention) and the macro structures and processes of society and the state as a whole.

In this sense, social movements mediate what C Wright Mills (1970) calls the 'personal troubles of milieu' and the 'public issues of structure'. In doing so, they bring together the personal and political dimensions of people's experience – thus directly challenging the 'central animus of neo-conservative politics [in which] the division between the personal and the political had to be zealously maintained' (Welton, 1993).

It is worth emphasising that social movement activity generates both social capital and intellectual capital (Chapter 21: John Dickie). In their membership of social movements, people develop social cohesion and solidarity. They do so through their direct participation in sustaining the bonds of affiliation and collective action which, in turn, 'establish networks, norms and social trust and facilitate co-ordination and co-operation for mutual benefit' (Putnam, 1995). Consequently, social movement activity suggests that any attempt to reconstruct social cohesion should reflect the intrinsic value placed on human relationships and reciprocity (and address the stark inequalities which undermine them) – as distinct from the instrumental imperatives of the cash nexus as reflected, for example, in the crude certainties of the 'human resource development' model of adult education and training (Chapter 17: Mick McGrath). In addition, it must be recognised that not only do people learn through their engagement in social movements but that these movements actually make and disseminate new knowledge and understanding through their activity. It is in this sense that they constitute 'epistemological communities', the creators and carriers of alternative kinds of knowledge and culture, which may challenge many of the shibboleths of modernity (Chapter 19: Eurig Scandrett). As such, the activity of social movements is rightly characterised by Eyerman and Jamison (1991) as 'cognitive praxis'.

In social movements, therefore, people act collectively to assert their agency within the constraints of structure – often beginning by learning that the first lesson of freedom is to understand the reality of *un*freedom. Belief in the possibility of freedom and in the necessity to fight for it is fundamental. This is where the struggle for democracy begins, and it is where popular education is at work in ordinary people's lives:

> The history of social movements is a history of people operating in the cracks of superstructures. Of using the energies generated at the margins of systems and organisations. Of exercising considerable imagination, critical thinking, subversion and undutiful behaviour to de-stabilise and de-construct the authority of the inevitable. All of them ways of 'taking back control' based on the inter-relationship between consciousness and courage, between theory and practice. Taking back control and joining with others in collective action to achieve change is at the root of concepts like participation and democracy. It finds its impetus in human agency and can transform people's lives. (Thompson, 1997)

The reference to social movements in the title of this book, therefore, indicates the level and locus of popular education's engagement with people. It should be emphasised that in order to understand this, and to work with it, requires both a modernist account of the significance of 'old' social movements (based essentially around the politics of class and the social relations of production), which continue to be reproduced and reinforced in the process of economic globalisation, and a postmodernist account of the significance of 'new' social movements (based on the politics of identity and difference), which helps to explain how the effects of late modernity are inscribed in people's lived experience. Moreover, in thinking about the relationship between popular education, social movements and social change, the distinction between 'old' and 'new' movements should not be overstated. As categories of affiliation and collective action, they are certainly distinct, but they are not mutually exclusive and the boundaries between them are often fluid and permeable. For example, members of the 'old' trade union movement may well be key actors in 'new' movements (Chapter 8: Robert Duncan) – and, in any case, the politics of production is not always easily separable from the politics of consumption. Both old and new movements have a crucial contribution to make to social, political and economic change.

The focus on social movements, therefore, suggests the need to accommodate new ways of understanding contemporary social reality. In particular, it points to the significance of cultural politics within civil society as a key site of popular struggle and resistance. It also emphasises the need to modernise – but not to abandon – traditional forms of class analysis (Harvey, 1993). In this respect, it should be noted that popular education today must recognise the impoverishment and excluding logic of a version of the radical tradition in adult education which got locked into a reductionist and overdetermined account of class (see Westwood, 1992). At the same time, however, it must also avoid the real danger of loss of collective social and political purpose that is implicit in some postmodern celebrations of identity and assertions of difference. In the condition of late modernity there has certainly been a generalisation of politics, but this has often been an unstable and incoherent politics. The question, therefore, is how can popular education help to transform these 'symptoms of resistance' (Gilroy, 1987) into a common struggle for social justice?

In their relations to the state, social movements within civil society are both proactive and reactive. They are proactive in the sense that they make new demands upon the state, eg for improved services, more freedoms, more inclusive forms of citizenship; they are reactive in the sense that they mobilise opposition, protest and resistance to some state policies – ranging from the possessive individualism of the new right to the authoritarian collectivism of the old left. It is important, however, to recognise how, particularly in the context of globalisation, state policy is now combining with the demands of the market to reconfigure these sites of struggle and thus the terrain of both social movements and popular education. As yet, the outcomes of this process in Scotland remain open. The recent history of some social movements indicates a basic choice between a reconstructed public life based on a new kind of democratic politics or a retreat into personalism – in effect, opting out of the business of citizenship (Chapter 5: Jean Barr). In these terms, it is no exaggeration to say that the present conjuncture in Scotland is historic because any inclusive notion of democratic citizenship is predicated on finding new ways of reconciling the competing claims of the system world and the life world.

The argument of this book is that the educational implications of all this can only be worked out and worked through in a genuinely popular process, and that this process has to equip people for democracy as a way of life. In Scotland today, then, what is the potential for linking popular education and social movements in the struggle to renew democracy and forge a new and inclusive notion of citizenship? The answer to this question must begin by recognising that we are all diminished by the exclusion of the 'other' (see Stuart and Thomson, 1995). In this respect, the politics of the disability movement begins to show us the promise of this new kind of politics (Chapter 12: Margaret Petrie and Mae Shaw) and popular education has much to learn from the politics of disability, as both an inspiration and a resource, in seeking to forge a new and inclusive kind of democracy in Scotland. Perhaps the essential point to make is that some of the 'new' social movements present society with clear moral and, indeed, ontological choices. These go well beyond the emphasis of the 'old' movements on material inequality and what Ralph Miliband (1989) calls the 'injuries of class'. The latter remain central to any socially progressive agenda because they prevent people from reaching their full potential as human beings and citizens, but, ultimately, the 're-membering' of society and the body politic is a moral and spiritual project as well as a material and political task (Chapter 16: Alastair McIntosh). The new politics must therefore find ways to embrace both the reality of difference and the necessity of common purpose. But the opportunity to do this has to be seized and made. It will not simply happen.

In terms of the argument of this book, it is crucial to avoid both false dichotomies and simplistic distinctions. Just as the state is a contradictory formation, so too are social movements. Some of them, as already noted, are far from progressive, let alone emancipatory – bent, as they are, upon sustaining deeply entrenched patterns of privilege and subordination. Making the connection between popular education and social movements, therefore, means making choices – political choices and, ultimately, moral choices. In some significant ways, however, the activities of progressive social movements prefigure a new and genuinely popular kind of politics (Chapter 13: Isobel McPhail). The opportunity to enact this new kind of politics – or to democratise democracy – is now at hand in Scotland, and the claim of this book is that popular education has a central role to play in the process.

Scotland today: from democratic deficit to democratic renewal

These are early days, and consequently the argument that popular education has a vital and distinctive contribution to make to the renewal of democracy in Scotland must be somewhat tentative. But it is crucial that this argument is made because the process of reaching a new settlement between the state and civil society is a highly ambivalent one. The outcomes can be negative, violent and repressive, as in many parts of Eastern Europe where, as already noted, the virtual collapse of the state has led to the worst kinds of nationalism, racism and, in some cases, the obscenities of 'ethnic cleansing'. On the other hand, the outcomes can potentially be positive, reflecting the renegotiation and reconstruction of national and cultural identity as the basis for a new kind of engagement with the world at large. The argument is speculative because the outcomes are as yet undecided and the process unfinished. This is precisely why popular education is central to the task of democratic renewal.

It must be emphasised, however, that in seeking to build a new democracy, Scotland is not starting from scratch. The Gramscian distinction between long-term organic change and short-term conjunctural change suggests that Scottish people today need to have a sense not only of their own history but also of themselves in history as active agents in the present conjuncture (Chapter 18: Vernon Galloway). In this respect, it is important to note that since its settlement with the British state in the Act of Union of 1707 Scotland has retained a relatively high degree of civil and cultural autonomy. This has actively sustained both its strong sense of national identity and a vital tradition of civic politics (eg see Brown *et al*, 1996; Paterson, 1994). Of particular significance is the fact that Scots have kept control over their own distinctive national institutions of the church, the law and education – all of which are quite different from those of the rest of the United Kingdom. In consequence, there has always been some tension between Scottish civil society and the British state, including resistance to any form of incorporation which would mean ceding control over its own ways of doing certain things. In recent years this has been particularly evident in widespread opposition to various attempts at the 'reform' of education – which is, of course, both a key agent of social reproduction and a crucial marker of cultural identity.

Underneath this pattern of political behaviour, then, is the insistent and persistent belief among most Scots that somehow they are different. Often it is difficult to pin down this sense of difference in any precise or agreed way – a consequence of which is that it has tended to be expressed negatively in terms of opposition to perceived stereotypes of 'Englishness'. This superficial expression of difference, however, belies something of much more substance and significance. As Ralph Miliband (1994), taking an explicitly socialist position, argues:

> ... in all societies, there are ... enduring and diverse currents of
> thought, sentiment, and practice, and some of them at least constitute
> important sources of resistance to the domination of society by the impera-
> tives and values of capitalism – for instance, resistance emanating from
> labour and socialist movements, from social movements based on race,
> ethnicity, gender, fighting against super-exploitation; and resistance to
> capitalist values and practices also derives from religious or traditional
> modes of thought.

It is worth pointing to three particular dimensions of the social and political
capital that is built into contemporary Scottish culture and society. First, in
recent years there has been a remarkable bourgeoning of genuinely popular
interest in issues of Scottish culture and identity. This informal cultural politics
is partly, at least, a reaction against what many Scots have increasingly come to
regard as the alien and alienating formal politics of the British state. Its curriculum of learning and activity encompasses language and literature (including the 'Gaelic renaissance' of recent years) as well as music and dance. In this
way, many Scots are actively expressing and reconstructing their national cultural
identity as different and distinctive: they are interested in themselves. Second, in
doing so, they draw upon the mobilising power of myth. There is undoubtedly,
for example, a stubborn belief, rooted in a powerful mythology, that Scotland is
historically and culturally a more democratic, egalitarian and open society than
England. The empirical basis for this mythification of Scottish history and
culture may well be disputed. For example, the democratic myth often seems
to mask an essentially meritocratic reality. The point is, however, that this does
not reduce the power of such myths or the tenacity with which they are held
(Chapter 11: Sue Mansfield). Indeed, it could be argued that precisely the
opposite is the case: the social construction of the myth is always more potent
than the empirical reality of the fact. Or, to put it another way, the facts feed
the myths just enough to sustain and reinvigorate them. Democratic church
governance, the meritocratic 'lad o' pairts' (albeit never a lass), relatively open
(if highly gendered) access to higher education, 'democratic intellectualism',
Red Clydeside – they all do their work in the Scottish psyche. And it is certainly
true to say that in their antipathy to the politics of the new right, many Scots
built up this mythology until it assumed almost counter-hegemonic propor-
tions. Third, and perhaps most significantly, in this process of cultural renewal
Scots draw upon very real and distinctively democratic traditions of intellectual
enquiry and public debate (Chapter 6: Murdo Macdonald) as well as spiritual
discipline.

Nevertheless, if these dimensions of difference are to become resources
for popular education, it is necessary to confront their ambivalence: to expose
the consequences of sexism and gender-blind accounts; to confront the
deeply ingrained conservatism of some parts of Scotland's traditional civic

establishment; to understand why the characteristic seriousness of the Scots about the idea of education is matched by the deep-seated unease many of them feel towards the reality of it; to recognise the inherent dangers of ignorance, arrogance, complacency and parochialism; to resist exclusive and reductionist definitions of identity. In this sense, the problematic of the 'popular' has to be honestly confronted in any popular education which seeks to work up its curriculum from the lived experience of people in Scottish communities.

So what are the key dimensions of the challenge of moving from resistance to reconstruction and what part has popular education to play in this process? Essentially, the argument is that the politics of the state and the politics of civil society have become divorced. In this sense, democracy has been experienced as deficiency. The key challenge facing Scotland today is therefore to construct a new settlement between the state and civil society based on a more active and inclusive concept of citizenship. However, to make and sustain this claim, it is necessary to understand the problems that must be faced in seeking to transform the overwhelmingly negative experience of the democratic deficit into the positive prospect of democratic renewal. This has to be a critical as well as a creative process if it is to prevent the new Scottish state simply replicating the old British state.

> If realising our freedom partly depends on the society and culture in which we live, then we exercise a fuller freedom if we can help determine the shape of this society and culture. And this we can do only through instruments of common decision. This means that the political institutions in which we live may themselves be a crucial part of what is necessary to realise our identity as free beings. (Taylor, 1985)

The idea of a 'democratic deficit' can be used as a metaphor to describe three key aspects of Scotland's recent political experience within the British state, and these help to define an agenda for popular education in the process of democratic renewal. In this respect, it is important to note that the recent experience of the politics of the new right, especially in the guise of Thatcherism, exposed rather than created the problems and unresolved issues implicit in the democratic deficit – which was psychic (ie something people in Scotland experienced existentially) as well as institutional (ie something they had done to them, as it were). The three key aspects are as follows:

● First, there is the obvious sense in which the idea of the democratic deficit describes the experience of the failure of representative democracy and of the Scots' increasing sense of being disenfranchised within the politics of the British state. Throughout the last two decades the majority of the Scottish electorate consistently voted against the political programme of the new right and opposed the main thrust of its social policies in relation, for example, to educational reform, the restructuring of the welfare state, privatisation, the emasculation of local government and the imposition of 'quangocracy' – and, most famously of all, the Poll Tax, that archetypal symbol of the politics of possessive individualism and the project of remoralisation that was implicit in it. In short, the politics of Scotland was effectively silenced in the politics of the British state. Consequently, according to McCrone (1992), 'Thatcher became, quite unwittingly, the midwife of Scottish Home Rule'. It is also worth noting, of course, that Mrs Thatcher successfully used precisely the same idea of the democratic deficit to justify the curbing of trade union power and the restructuring of local government.

• Second, the democratic deficit describes some of the ways in which many people have in recent years come to feel excluded from the internal political process within Scotland itself. In some parts of the country, for instance, particularly the industrialised central belt (long dominated by the Labour Party), the paternalism, complacency and, in some cases, the evident corruption of traditional Labourism has been experienced as the very antithesis of democracy.

• Both these dimensions of the democratic deficit help to explain the third, which can be described as moral or ideological. This is difficult to define – but perhaps all the more real for that. It is the sense in which Scotland's rejection of the new right seemed to express in negative terms something more positive, ie a different kind of moral vision of itself as an 'imagined community' with common and communal interests – informed by a residual collectivism (as reflected, for example, in the support in the recent Referendum for tax-varying powers of the new Scottish Parliament).

Of course, until the Referendum on devolution, the experience of the democratic deficit, in all its dimensions, tended to be expressed in oppositional terms, ie against other things which were perceived to be in some way alien or repressive. In this respect, it is worth noting that although at the last general election Scotland voted overwhelmingly for Labour, more recent evidence seems to suggest that there is some hostility to much of what 'New Labour' stands for. The challenge is therefore to find some way of doing politics differently. This is a task for a popular civic education – which is not simply about how to be a citizen but rather about deciding what being a citizen in the new Scotland should mean.

There is, of course, a double danger here: of expectations that are simultaneously too high and too low. What is needed now, therefore, is to construct a new kind of politics by assimilating some of the social and cultural capital generated in the politics of Scottish civil society back into the politics of the state – at all levels (local, regional, national and supra-national). The point to emphasise here is that the activity of progressive social movements in Scotland should not be understood as a rejection of the state but rather a struggle to reconfigure the relationship between the state and civil society in a new, more equitable and democratic way. In this sense, the option taken in Scotland has been for 'voice' rather than 'exit'. But this option for 'voice' has been highly conditional, and the challenge now is to transform it into active and unambiguous 'loyalty'. So the burden of expectation on the new politics is great, and moves towards greater political autonomy must be seen as the beginning rather than the end of the process of democratic renewal.

Perhaps the crucial point is that the new politics of the state needs to be constructed in ways which strengthen civil society and political life *outside* the state. Indeed, the democratic state must learn how to foster the civic autonomy of communities – rather than seek, as all too often in the past, to co-opt and incorporate them. This is as much an educational as a political task. All the questions, problems and challenges implicit in the idea of the democratic deficit need to be articulated, addressed and worked through in a curriculum of popular civic education. Such a curriculum cannot be civic (in the sense of preparing people for a new kind of citizenship) unless and until it is a popular curriculum, ie one which addresses the real experience and concerns of ordinary people and actively draws upon these as resources for educational work in communities. How is this to be done? Although it is not what this book was originally intended to be about, it is a question the book raises and one that it may help to answer. In the end, what we have to ask is: what have Scottish people learned from their experience of political struggle and what resources for reconstruction have they accumulated in that process?

In seeking answers to such questions, it must, of course, be emphasised that the new Scottish Parliament will have to work in a context which is not new – indeed, a context in which most of the old interests and institutions of the political, business and civic establishment will remain intact. There is already evidence of resistance to change – for instance, in the retreat of some of the major political parties from the principle, widely endorsed before the Referendum, of ensuring gender balance and equity in representation in the Scottish Parliament. In addition, the arrangements for the selection of candidates and voting procedures indicate that the new parliament is likely to be dominated by the old political parties – even if they have to learn the lessons of coalition government. The element of proportional representation to be introduced will do nothing to break this down. And, of course, no amount of local political autonomy is likely to thwart the economic logic of globalisation and the threat inherent in it to any kind of democratic national politics.

Democracy is a continuing and active process, not simply the outcome of political activity which becomes institutionalised in particular ways. In other words, the Referendum was no more than the first step in the continuing struggle to create a new kind of democracy in Scotland. The main impetus for this struggle must continue to come, as it has in the past, from Scottish civil society, eg in ensuring that the policy making process is as open, democratic and accessible as possible (because it is probable that the legislative process will not be). The debate must therefore be as much about processes as it is about structures if new ways of doing politics are to be found (Chapter 15: Alice Brown). Moreover, the prospect of coalition government requires a kind of democracy and citizenship mature and active enough to combine a pluralistic form of politics with sufficient consensus to articulate in policy terms a work-able degree of strategic agreement and common purpose. Apart from anything else, it is worth remembering that the Scottish Parliament, ironically perhaps, could give the Conservative Party a new and unfamiliar voice in Scottish politics. Any attempt to do politics differently will therefore demand a high level of political and democratic literacy – and one which, it is hoped, will be based not on a narrow and exclusive nationalism but rather on a positive and expansive sense of national identity. In this process, it must be expected that the relationship between the politics of the state and the politics of civil society will remain conditional, sometimes contradictory. The political chemistry is likely to be complex and unpredictable (see Paterson, 1998). For example, the fact that many Scots – some no doubt encouraged by the unapologetic socialism of the the left wing of the Scottish National Party – are as ambivalent about the policies of New Labour as they are about the politics of old Labour suggests that the relationship between civil society and the state will remain fiercely contested in some respects.

Two hundred years ago popular adult education became a key agent in the long struggle to democratise the British state. This is what the 'really useful knowledge' tradition was essentially about (Johnson, 1979). It now needs to be reinvented in Scotland and reinserted into its history as the catalyst – or, indeed, the agent of the dialectic – between the cultural politics of civil society and the political culture of the state. This will require not only more representative and participative political processes and procedures but also structures which enable and encourage civil society to continue to act upon the state in order to change it. Jane Thompson gives a vivid impression of how a stronger political voice for women, for example, could ensure a 'more gender-balanced agenda' that might eventually help to shift the parameters of traditional politics in decisive ways:

> In practice this would mean transforming the culture of existing political institutions and decision making bodies – not simply to make them more women-friendly and reflective of women's issues, but in order to reconstitute some of the assumptions about what counts as political concerns – from a women's point of view. This would provoke many more debates – and in turn policies – about environmental issues, community concerns, child care, women's employment rights, reproductive and health rights, and issues concerning violence against women, for example, than is currently on the agendas of most malestream political parties. (Thompson, 1997)

It is as well to be quite clear about what this argues *against*: first, the simplistic arithmetic of 'additive' politics which can never, by definition, be transformative; second, a notion of consensus which stands in the way of openness, transparency and debate; third, the dumbed down democracy of the focus group and the sound bite.

The logic of this argument is that the new politics in Scotland will mean learning to understand and respect difference because this is the only realistic basis on which to define (and delimit) common purpose. Consequently, doing politics differently will mean struggling towards the difficult goal of achieving solidarity in difference. This implies a kind of democracy which recognises that political support is always contingent and that dissent is an essential characteristic of active citizenship (Paterson, 1997, 1998; Allen, 1992). To use the current jargon, community capacity building for democratic citizenship must include (and, if necessary, enhance) the communal capacity to say no. In the end, this is the only way to keep democracy alive and to guarantee the continuing possibility of democratic change.

This book therefore argues that popular education must provide ways of articulating and engaging positively with the reality of diversity, ie the fact that there are different kinds of Scottishness (Chapter 23: Rowena Arshad). Indeed, as Paulo Freire states, the idea of difference is implicit in the idea of democracy:

> I don't believe in unanimity. Democracy is the confrontation with differences and the necessity to overcome antagonisms . . . We cannot wait till God comes to solve this problem. It is not his task. It is our task to look for justice, not to collapse us all into one . . . [but to discover] how it is possible for us to grow together in the differences: to get unity in diversity. (quoted in Kirkwood, 1998)

This is one of the essential ways in which popular education in Scotland today must be 'popular': in listening to and articulating voices which have been silenced and excluded in what many minority groups have experienced as a disabling and discriminating society (Chapter 9: Elinor Kelly and Bashir Maan). Popular education must therefore seek to demonstrate that identity is multiple and dynamic rather than monolithic and static (as the Gaels in Scotland have long insisted) and to celebrate and respect diversity. This means actively countering the processes of exclusion and marginalisation that diminish us all if the peoples of Scotland are to be offered a new and genuinely inclusive citizenship. In this respect, we have much to learn in the common struggle for majority rights from specific struggles for minority rights, as several of the chapters in this book demonstrate.

Consequently, any popular education for democratic renewal in Scotland must start from the real and systematic inequalities that currently exclude many of its people from anything more than a nominal notion of citizenship. It should also be recognised not only that many 'new' social movements have not been genuinely popular at all but also that much fashionable postmodern 'theorising' about them may well impede effective political action (see Demaine and Entwistle, 1996). On the other hand, the actual experience of some of these movements can help in this task. Above all, what a genuinely inclusive popular education has to address is the reality of *un*popular issues. The struggle for the rights of minority and marginalised groups is an integral part of the wider struggle for social justice.

This is one of the crucial senses in which popular education now needs to become more genuinely 'popular', ie of and for *all* the peoples of Scotland. In effect, what the idea of an active and inclusive democracy requires is a concerted movement from a 'customary' towards a 'conventionalist' view of the national community and its relationship to the politics of the state (Yeatman, 1994). This entails a process in which the idea of the nation as an 'imagined community' is actively reconstructed through policy in order simultaneously to celebrate diversity and promote solidarity – rather than being assumed as an historical given which is inherited and preserved on the basis of some vague and increasingly untenable claim to kinship. Such a process demands a commitment to the kind of dialogue which has always been part not only of the philosophy and pedagogy of popular education but also of the distinctively Scottish traditions of 'democratic intellectualism' and 'common sense' (see Davie, 1991). If democracy is to become a way of life, then – in a fundamental sense – we must learn to make it up as we go along.

Conclusion

The real challenges and problems implicit in this account must not be underestimated. Apart from anything else, the discourse of difference often assumes an equivalence about issues of power and control which provides cover for all manner of elisions and evasions about structural inequalities (Chapter 25: Jane Meagher). It can also lead to a debilitating moral relativism (Meekosha, 1993). It is therefore as well to reassert the uncompromisingly materialist analysis explicit in the Popular Education Forum for Scotland statement quoted earlier because, as Ralph Miliband (1994) puts it, 'there can be no true citizenship without a rough equality of condition'. In the end, democracy and citizenship must be material realities before they can become political possibilities. Similarly, this materialist analysis must make the connections in the popular education curriculum between the local and global. If, in the long run, the aim is to renew democracy, it will be essential to understand the international forces that now stand in the way of this, and to link the local and the global by working towards horizontal alliances across national cultures and political boundaries which are committed to an alternative, oppositional and popular process of 'globalisation from below' (Eade, 1997). In this respect, the rich world has much to learn from the poor world and its more socialised and genuinely civic traditions of popular adult education. These recognise that real citizenship is forged and real social capital is consolidated within civil society. This is where the 'learning society' must learn to be a society.

Popular education offers one way of understanding and engaging with the problems and possibilities presented by the unfinished business of democratic renewal, and beginning to work towards a broader vision of a transnational 'cosmopolitan democracy' that binds the pluralistic politics of the international community into a common moral commitment to democracy as a way of life (Held, 1995). There is now a unique opportunity to begin to do this in Scotland. Although it is the product of a specific context and conjuncture, it reflects global processes of challenge and change. The Scottish case will therefore be observed with interest in many other parts of the world. Ultimately, making the connections between social movements and social change is an educational project as well as a moral purpose – and it is always and inevitably a political struggle. This book is offered as a resource for what Raymond Williams called that 'journey of hope':

> The dynamic moment is . . . in the difficult business of gaining confidence in our own energies and capacities. It is only in the shared belief and insistence that there are practical alternatives that the balance of forces and chances begins to alter. Once the inevitabilities are challenged, we begin gathering our resources for a journey of hope. If there are no easy answers, there are still available and discoverable hard answers, and it is these we can now learn to make and share. (Williams, 1983)

References

Allen, G (1992) 'Active citizenship' in Allen, G and Martin, I (eds) *Education and Community: The Politics of Practice*, London, Cassell, pp 130–144.

Barker, C (1996) 'What is to be done? contrasting activists' visions in community protest' in Barker and Kennedy, P (eds), *To Make Another World: Studies in Protest and Collective Action*, Aldershot, Avebury, pp 25–44.

Brown, A, McCrone, D and Paterson, L (1996) *Politics and Society in Scotland*, London, Macmillan.

Clegg, (1996) 'From women's movement to feminisms' in Barker, C and Kennedy, P (eds), *To Make Another World: Studies in Protest and Collective Action*, Aldershot, Avebury, pp 45–68.

Crowther, J and Shaw, M (1997) 'Social movements and the education of desire', *Community Development Journal*, 32 (3), pp 266–279.

Davie, G (1991) *The Scottish Enlightenment and Other Essays*, Edinburgh, Edinburgh University Press.

Demaine, J and Entwistle, H (eds) (1996) *Beyond Communitarianism: Citizenship, Politics and Education*, London, Macmillan.

Eade, D (1997) *Development and Patronage*, Oxford, Oxfam.

Eyerman, R and Jamison, A (1991) *Social Movements: A Cognitive Approach*, Oxford, Polity Press.

Foley, G (1994) 'Adult education and capitalist reorganisation', *Studies in the Education of Adults*, 26 (2), pp 121–143.

Freire, P (1972) *Pedagogy of the Oppressed*, Harmondsworth, Penguin.

Gilroy, P (1987) *There Ain't No Black in the Union Jack*, London, Hutchinson.

Gustavsson, B (1997) 'Lifelong learning reconsidered' in Walters, S (ed), *Globalisation, Adult Education and Training: Impacts and Issues*, Leicester, NIACE, pp 237–249.

Hall, S (1996) 'The meaning of New Times' in Morley, D and Chen, K-H (eds), *Stuart Hall: Critical Dialogues in Cultural Studies*, London, Routledge, pp 223–237.

Harvey, D (1993) 'Class relations, social justice and the politics of difference' in Squires, J (ed), *Principled Positions: Postmodernism and the Rediscovery of Value*, London, Lawrence and Wishart, pp 85–120.

Held, D (1995) *Democracy and the Global Order: From the Modern State to Cosmopolitan Governance*, Cambridge, Polity Press.

Jackson, K (1995) 'Popular education and the state: a new look at the community debate' in Mayo, M and Thompson, J (eds), *Adult Learning, Critical Intelligence and Social Change*, Leicester, NIACE, pp 82–96.

Jackson, K (1997) 'The state, civil society and the economy: adult education in Britain' in Walters, S (ed), *Globalisation, Adult Education and Training: Impacts and Issues*, Leicester, NIACE, pp 47–56.

Johnson, R (1979) '"Really useful knowledge": radical education and working class culture, 1790–1848' in Clarke, J, Crichter, C and Johnson, R (eds), *Working-Class Culture: Studies in History and Theory*, London, Hutchinson, pp 75–102.

Kirkwood, C (1998) 'Challenging education, creating alliances: the legacy of Paulo Freire in the new Scotland', *Scottish Journal of Community Work and Development*, 3, pp 53–67.

Korsgaard, O (1997) 'The impact of globalisation on adult education' in Walters, S (ed), *Globalisation, Adult Education and Training: Impacts and Issues*, Leicester, NIACE, pp 15–26.

McCrone, D (1992) *Understanding Scotland: The Sociology of a Stateless Nation*, London, Routledge.

Meekosha, H (1993) 'The bodies politic: equality, difference and community practice' in Butcher, H, Glen, A, Henderson, P and Smith, J (eds), *Community and Public Policy*, London, Pluto Press/Community Development Foundation, pp 49–72.

Miliband, R (1989) *Divided Societies*, Oxford, Oxford University Press.

Miliband, R (1994) *Socialism for a Sceptical Age*, London, Polity Press.

Miller, C (1997) 'The theory and practice of social movements', *Community Development Journal*, 32 (3), pp 289–294.

Ministry of Reconstruction (1919) *Final Report of the Adult Education Committee*, Cmnd. 321, London, HMSO.

Nairn, T (1997) 'Sovereignty after the Election', *New Left Review*, 224, pp 3–18.

Paterson, L (1994) *The Autonomy of Modern Scotland*, Edinburgh, Edinburgh University Press.

Paterson, L (1997) 'Scotland and democracy', *Concept*, 7 (3), pp 4–6.

Paterson, L (1998) 'The Scottish parliament and Scottish civil society: which side will education be on?', *Political Quarterly*, 69 (3), pp 224–233.

Putnam, R (1995) 'Bowling alone: America's declining social capital', *Journal of Democracy*, 6 (1), pp 65–78.

Silver, H (1965) *The Concept of Popular Education*, London, McGibbon and Kee.

Stuart, M and Thomson, A (eds) (1995) *Engaging with Difference: The 'Other' in Adult Education*, Leicester, NIACE.

Taylor, C (1985) *Philosophical Papers (Volume 2): Philosophy and the Human Sciences*, Cambridge, Cambridge University Press.

Thompson, J (1997) *Words in Edgeways: Radical Learning for Social Change*, Leicester, NIACE.

Welton, M (1993) 'Social revolutionary learning: the new social movements as learning sites', *Adult Education Quarterly*, 43 (3), pp 152–164.

Welton, M (ed) (1995) *In Defense of the Lifeworld: Critical Perspectives on Adult Learning* Albany, State University of New York Press.

Westwood, S (1992) 'When class became community: radicalism in adult education' in Rattansi, A and Reeder, D (eds), *Rethinking Radical Education*, London, Lawrence and Wishart.

Williams, R (1983) *Towards 2000*, Harmondsworth, Penguin.

Wright Mills, C (1970) *The Sociological Imagination*, Harmondsworth, Penguin.

Yeatman (1994) *Postmodern Revisionings of the Political*, London, Routledge.

Section 1:

Theorising popular education and social movements

2 Popular education and the struggle for democracy

Jim Crowther

This account is not so much a history of popular education as an attempt to locate popular education in history. It offers a historical argument about the nature of popular education and the shifting sites of struggle in which it has developed over time. Popular education has deep roots in the history of radical adult education. An important and consistent feature of its development has been the contribution it has made to the struggle for the extension of democracy and the rights of citizenship. The chapter argues that much can be learnt from the neglected role of popular education in the history of radical adult education for continuing struggles for democracy and social justice in the present and the future. In particular, the prospect of democratic renewal in Scotland today opens up a new conjuncture in which popular education can play a significant role. What is needed now is to understand how to make the most of this opportunity. It is time, once again, to insert popular education into history.

Nineteenth century roots: education by 'collision'

'In a large town the influences which educate a man against his will are almost incessant.' So noted the Committee on Public Libraries in 1849, going on to suggest that the consequences of social and political action led to 'exercising the minds of the labouring classes' better than any school instruction. What marked this period off from earlier periods in the history of British adult education was the role of popular movements as educative forces; they provided a motive and stimulus for 'disciplined action and an adherence to principle' on a scale hitherto unseen (Dobbs, 1919).

The late eighteenth and early nineteenth centuries involved 'collisions' of several kinds: reason and science clashed with the traditional authority of the church and the establishment; the new discipline needed for factory life conflicted with folk customs; poverty and destitution visibly jarred with opulence and wealth; the expansion of urban living created friction with traditional patterns of rural life; the state sought to suppress the proliferation of radical groups seeking political freedoms. Above all, the newly emerging working class which was culturally, politically and economically growing in consciousness and confidence as a class collided with the dominant order of society (see Thompson, 1968). It was through such 'collisions' that popular organisations taught themselves about the nature and causes of exploitation and injustice – as well as what could be done about them.

The growth of radical movements between 1790 and 1850 provided opportunities for independent forms of popular education to develop (Simon, 1974). In Scotland dissenting groups like the Friends of the People, Corresponding Societies, Working Men's Associations, and the later Owenite community experiments and Chartist agitations all contributed to learning through active engagement in a process of social and political struggle. The People's Charter – with its demand for parliamentary reform and the extension of the franchise – was the first mass movement with a large working class constituency. These radical organisations and movements also nurtured educational activities to generate popular support amongst those outside the immediate struggle. Wright (1953) argues that Chartism in Scotland took a more overtly educational and peaceful route than that of the more explicit class struggle espoused by the northern Chartists in England. Owenite communities included education as a vital component of their work – their slogan was, after all, 'educate, educate and educate'. The Owenite movement was significant in New Lanark and Chartist and co-operative organisations existed in major industrial cities in the central belt of Scotland and as far north as Aberdeen, Elgin and Banff (Wilson, 1970).

The struggle for political rights was grounded in the material exploitation and grievances of ordinary people. It was conditions at work, in communities and in the home which fuelled discontent and which the popular movements sought to remedy. Consequently, the 'curriculum' of popular struggles was 'practical and wide' (Johnson, 1993). Provided education, in contrast, was more concerned with social control, narrow instrumentalism or moral rescue. Popular movements gave rise to a conviction and consciousness that education could involve 'acting and educating against the status quo' (Silver, 1965).

A fundamental characteristic of popular education was its refusal to separate education from politics. This did not involve a simplistic assertion of ideology over reason, experimentation and argument. Instead, radicals wanted a curriculum which opened up debate rather than closed it down. Critical knowledges were 'knowledges calculated to make you free' (Johnson, 1993) which would involve challenging power, vested interests and traditional understandings of common sense. What this needed was the welding of education to a social purpose. 'Really useful knowledge' was practical in the radical sense that it was aimed at people changing rather than adapting to prevailing conditions. As such, it was a guide to social and political action for a better world. In this process, the experience of everyday life was an important resource but one that had to be critically 'tested' and hardened through debate, study and action. From this perspective, to separate education from politics was at best misguided and naive, at worst manipulative and deceitful.

Recognising the complex relationship between education and politics in this way had two important implications. First, the process of political struggle was itself educative. The 'collisions' encountered in such struggles generated a curriculum for developing critical consciousness. Second, control of educational resources determined what and whose purposes were served. 'Really useful knowledge' could only come about through systematic efforts by working class people to develop their own independent forms of education.

Working class self-education

The demand for working class self-education during the late nineteenth and early twentieth centuries accompanied the growth of socialism as an ideological and political force – a movement in which class struggle would be educative and which, in turn, self-education would foster and support. This was a movement of the working class and therefore represented a significant development in terms of popular adult education as workers' education. But to achieve this, education had to be independent from the state. In Scotland the demand for this particular kind of independent working class education was led by John MacLean, an extraordinarily active and energetic populariser of Marxist ideas. And, like their counterparts in England and Wales, the Scottish Labour Colleges were to be controlled by committees reflecting the interests of the working class and financed by subscriptions from the trade union movement. In terms of curriculum, the emphasis was on understanding Marxism as a way for workers to further their interests as a class (MacLean, 1978).

The Labour Colleges represented a significant attempt by the labour movement to create their own independent educational provision based on a class analysis of exploitation within capitalist society. An important continuity with the popular education of the beginning of the nineteenth century was the focus on material inequality. 'Collisions' at the point of production had to be reinforced by systematic study of capitalism from the point of view of workers. The strength of the Labour Colleges lay in the attempt to institutionalise a radical form of education which could create critically conscious and militant workers. During the 1920s they provided the only successful large-scale attempt to involve working class people in adult education in Scotland (see Bryant, 1984). But the experiment was short-lived.

The purist position of the Labour Colleges on the issue of independence from the state meant they had to depend entirely on financial support from the labour movement – primarily the trade unions. After the collapse of the General Strike in 1926 working class militancy waned and the trade unions supporting the Labour Colleges demanded a less radical curriculum. As the subsequent accommodation between the state and the labour movement developed, so the Labour Colleges became increasingly isolated and out of touch with their wider constituency in the working class as a whole. Moreover, the increasing significance of the Workers' Educational Association (WEA) in the late 1920s and 1930s began to put additional pressure on the Labour Colleges.

In contrast to the Labour Colleges movement, the WEA, founded in 1903, was committed to the development of university level education for working class people and aimed to educate the leaders of the labour movement into the kind of understanding and wisdom this required. Its curriculum was liberal in the best sense of being open, critical and wide-ranging – and support for the WEA grew. It was precisely this political openness which attracted the criticism of the Labour Colleges. However, the accusation of 'class collaborationism' they levelled at the WEA tended to oversimplify the reality (Brown, 1980). For example, many WEA tutors were able to develop the kind of political economy within the curriculum which the Labour Colleges would have supported and, indeed, in some cases the tutors employed by both organisations were the same. In maintaining their stance on 'independence', however, the Labour Colleges rejected any potential there might be in working 'in and against' the state.

In terms of curriculum, the Labour Colleges were also selective in a way which limited their potential. The commitment to Marxism certainly introduced into the curriculum a body of 'really useful knowledge' which challenged the intellectual justification for private control over the means of production. From this perspective, economic equality by means of the socialisation of production was a necessary precondition for political equality. However, the status of this knowledge as 'scientific socialism' put Marxism on a pedestal as an undisputed truth. In the end, the Labour Colleges came to be trapped by the limitations of their own highly economistic version of Marxism, their uncompromisingly directive pedagogy and the general reductionism of their analysis. The logic implicit in the development of the Labour Colleges meant that the appeal of and constituency for this particular kind of adult education was always going to be limited to a relatively narrow section of organised labour – white, male and working class – an elite vanguard of the class rather than the wider membership. This prevented them from engaging effectively with the realities of social and economic change, and they gradually lost touch with the real currents of working class life.

To be genuinely popular, therefore, this form of self-education needed to broaden its appeal. In this sense, the focus on workers in production was both a strength and a limitation. On the one hand, it developed adult education for working class people on the basis of their role in the process of production, promoting class consciousness and building industrial organisation. On the other hand, its neglect of sources of power and oppression outside of production limited its scope and appeal – and eventually its relevance (see Westwood, 1992). It was in the subsequent turn towards cultural politics that the possibility for generating a wider social base for popular education was recreated.

The turn to cultural politics

In the period immediately after the Second World War an important shift in the focus of radical adult education developed. The 'socialist humanism' that characterised the disparate activities of some dissident left intellectuals working in the field of adult education involved a reconceptualisation of Marxism away from economism towards a Marxian analysis and approach which shifted the focus towards the previously neglected realm of culture and consciousness. This movement opened up the opportunity to extend popular education into the politics of everyday life including, but not reducible to, the sphere of production. This proved to be fertile ground for radical and creative educators.

Raymond Williams, a significant figure in this process of extending the base of popular education, and for many years a WEA tutor, was engaged in an intellectual reworking of the terrain of culture. His distinction between high culture and 'culture as ordinary' broadened the focus of what later came to be known as cultural studies. Working class culture for Williams was principally about the 'collective idea' and the patterns of behaviour, values, beliefs and institutions to which it gave rise. Unless this was critically exposed and explored, validated and enabled to flourish, it was subject to colonisation by the basic 'individualist idea' of middle class culture. Williams' concern with how meanings were produced shifted attention from the arena of material production towards the communications industry and the politics of representation in literature, art, film, drama, television and everyday life. In educational work cultural analysis drew particular attention to the construction of the curriculum and the selective tradition which informs it – that is, the process in which knowledge and power come together to legitimate and delegitimate meanings. This served to dilute, exclude or reappropriate the culture of subordinate groups and classes. In Williams' view therefore cultural politics, rather than being secondary to economic and political struggle, was central to it. As Steele (1997) puts it, cultural struggle is politics by other means.

For EP Thompson, another key thinker working in adult education at this time, experience was a central (yet neglected) category of Marxist analysis. Marx's axiom that 'social being determines consciousness' was, as Thompson (1978) argued, an indication of the importance of the ideas and expectations within which social being is reproduced: 'Experience arises spontaneously within social being, but it does not arrive without thought; it arises because men and women . . . are rational, and they think about what is happening to themselves and their world.'

Adult education for Thompson was always a resource for progressive social change. 'Cultural studies' – through subjects like English literature and social history – was a way of critically interrogating the experiences of life. In his teaching the clash of argument was a constant aim in order to develop a popular, critical consciousness. He defined his own purpose in terms of 'making revolutionaries', but this was not to be restricted to an intellectual vanguard of the working class. His interest in a democratic culture and society was also expressed in his concern to bring together both intellectual rigour and life itself. A creative dialectic between education and experience was necessary to avoid both anti-intellectualism and arid intellectualism. Thompson's famous remark in *The Making of the English Working Class* (a book that came out of his work with WEA students in West Yorkshire) that he was seeking to rescue 'the poor stockinger, the Luddite cropper, the obsolete hand-loom weaver, the utopian artisan . . . from the infinite condescension of posterity' (Thompson, 1968) provided an inspiration and approach which encouraged others to discover the 'hidden histories' of oppressed groups and peoples.

In Gramscian terms this shift in focus opened up the terrain of civil society as a site of struggle. It is in civil society, Gramsci argues, that the 'social glue' of hegemony which binds people to the dominant order is created. Hegemonic power is created through a diverse range of institutions and private organisa-tions in civil society – the family, the media, voluntary organisations, the church, trade unions and so on. These institutions generate meanings which we use to make sense of experience. When they are internalised as 'natural' and expressed as 'common sense', the process of hegemonic contol 'saturates experience'. In reality, of course, common sense is inconsistent and incoherent precisely because it reinforces and reflects the wider contradictions of society. Working on these contradictions can provide a basis for arriving at 'good sense' – that is, a more critical understanding of society in order to change it. Consequently, civil society is not only the bulwark of the established order but also its Achilles' heel in that hegemony is a process which has constantly to be remade and is therefore always susceptible to contestation and challenge.

In deterministic versions of Marxism the transition to socialism is seen as a historic inevitability which will eventually emerge from the contradictions of capitalism. As a consequence, the role of education as a force for progressive change is relatively insignificant. The turn towards cultural struggle, however, reasserted the dialectic between 'social being and consciousness'. Material conditions may set limits within which action occurs, but these can be altered in the process of struggle. From this perspective, popular education as cultural struggle can contribute towards both the shaping of consciousness and the ability of people to change their circumstances. Rather than waiting for history to happen, popular education is inserted into the process of making it. Cultural work therefore opens up a 'new' site of struggle to make power visible and to create a more open, equal and democratic society. Consequently, popular educa-tion involves an expanded notion of democracy which connects with the politics of everyday life. What this implies is a more dynamic and inclusive form of adult education attuned to popular experience.

For popular education to contribute towards social change it has to connect with the forces that move people to act. It has to be joined to the cultural roots which sustain it – and which it, in turn, can help to sustain. Ironically, however, as Steele (1995) points out, cultural studies as a discipline which grew out of the work of radical adult educators subsequently became cocooned within the academy and an impenetrable discourse of high theory. This, in effect, left the original project of popular adult education in a time warp, the 'selective tradition' having filtered out the radical message and reinterpreted it. In the current context, however, the emergence of new social movements provides an opportunity once again to ground popular education in social interests and forces struggling for change.

New social movements

> If you want flowers you must have flowers, roots and all, unless you are satisfied, as many people are satisfied, with flowers made from paper and tinsel. And if you want education you must not cut it off from the social interests in which it has its living and perennial sources. (Tawney quoted in Jackson, 1995)

The roots and social interests to which Tawney refers are constantly being reshaped and reconstituted. This process offers new opportunities for popular education. In recent years new social movements have emerged rooted in contemporary culture representing new social interests and actors and generating new 'collisions'. This is the context of the current stage in the dialectics of popular education.

The term 'new social movements' refers to movements which emerged in the 1960s (eg the women's liberation movement, the peace and disarmament movement, the green movement, local and urban movements and the student movement) – not all of which were, in fact, so new (Miliband, 1989). One of their defining features was their exclusion from – and often their rejection of – 'mainstream' politics and the old movement of labour. Dissatisfied with the marginalisation of their interests in formal political processes, they inspired direct forms of popular protest and social action. Generally, the problems and concerns they addressed moved the key site of struggle away from production and the economy towards reproduction and consumption, from the state to civil society. Direct resistance to state policies was also a catalyst for some of these movements. Many of them mobilised people to act by focusing on 'single issues' which opened up wider concerns about the nature of society. For example, the women's movement and feminist theory raised crucial questions about the nature of power within patriarchal capitalism. In doing so, they extended the sphere of politics and provided possibilities for the radicalisation of 'selective values' rather than universal ones (see Welton, 1993).

This raises epistemological as well as political questions. One of the major aims of new social movements is to challenge dominant knowledge by generating counter-information. They also create their own versions of 'really useful knowledge' which can galvanise and legitimate action for change. According to Eyerman and Jamison (1991), the defining characteristic of these movements is their 'cognitive praxis' in that they create conditions in which new and critical knowledges emerge. One of the ways in which this occurs is by recognising and validating the tacit knowledge acquired in everyday life. Tacit knowledge is implicit in what we do and think – 'what we know but do not say' (Wainright, 1994). Social movements of this kind provide the space for their members to share and broaden their tacit knowledge and then to act upon it. This can generate local sites of struggle such as those created by the women's peace movement at Greenham Common, various forms of environmental action, the Anti-Poll Tax campaign, direct action against further motorway construction and 'reclaim the road' campaigns. Moreover, in thinking globally and acting locally, connections can be made between such local action and national and, indeed, international struggles.

Social movements have played an important part in stretching our imagination about alternative ways of living. To use William Morris's eloquent phrase, they are essentially about 'educating desire' because they open up questions about what we value and how we want to live. By seeing the world as it is and how it might be, social movements are intrinsically utopian. In this sense, utopia's proper role is to stir the imagination and challenge comfortable habits – a place to be desired rather than 'a place which does not exist' (Bauman, 1976). Social conformism, as Gramsci understood, is at its deepest when hegemonic ideas are internalised as common sense. Social movements inject critique, vision and imagination into what we have learnt to take for granted.

It is also necessary, however, to recognise the weaknesses of social movements. First, they have a tendency to ebb and flow with changing social conditions and, almost by definition, they lack the institutionalised base and the resources required for sustained, organised action. Second, they have been predominantly middle class movements. Consequently, they have failed to involve a wide cross-section of working class people. Finally, not all of them are progressive: some have evolved simply to defend privileged positions against threatening developments (eg aspects of the current men's movement); different ideological positions within movements can lead to progressive or reactionary politics (eg the fracturing between 'old' and 'new' feminisms); some movements seek to achieve a less rather than a more open society (eg the growth of neo-fascist movements). Nevertheless, precisely because old and new movements draw on different sources of power and mobilise different constituencies, making alliances between them can enhance the potential for a more widespread project of social change. If popular education is to make a significant impact, then a key challenge will be to build the links between them.

Learning the lessons of history

The lesson of historical analysis is that, if popular education is to be authentically popular, it needs to connect with both old and new social movements. It must be rooted in people's experiences and aspirations as both workers (ie in the sphere of production and the 'old' movements of labour) and as citizens (ie in the sphere of reproduction and consumption, as reflected in the new social movements). It is the argument here that reconstructing popular education as part of both a cultural and a political struggle may be at once the means and the outcome of this. As Gramsci enjoined, we must not allow the 'pessimism of the intellect' to overwhelm the 'optimism of the will'. We certainly have to recognise that there are real difficulties in making alliances between the politics of old and new movements. For example, the history of the labour movement has been a deeply ambivalent one: all too often it has embodied racism, sexism and prejudice against minority interests. Indeed, it was partly their experience of exclusion which generated new social movements in the first place. Issues of identity and difference based, for instance, on gender, 'race', disability and sexuality are crucial aspects of popular experience which have been systematically marginalised or ignored in the traditional labour agenda. Consequently, for many groups and interests, the labour movement has been part of the problem rather than part of the solution.

New social movements, on the other hand, have sought to demonstrate the importance of connecting the personal with the political. Whilst old movements are considered to have paid insufficient attention to personal experience by concentrating almost exclusively on wider political and economic objectives, a criticism of some of the new social movements is that they neglect the wider political dimension by focusing too narrowly on the significance of personal experience and interpersonal relationships. What really matters therefore is that we learn to locate personal experience within a framework of collective interests, and recognise the relationship between them.

The potential, therefore, for change through alliances remains significant. On the one hand, new social movements mobilise people to act and give voice to concerns which formal political processes tend to ignore, suppress or dilute. By challenging conventional thinking and ways of working, new social movements can create opportunities for the personal to be transformed into the political. But, in doing so, they cannot draw upon the same working class constituency as the traditional labour movement – nor its endurance. The labour movement has survived for well over a century and it has successfully withstood continued attempts to undermine it. In the end, as Miliband (1989) argues, the success of the new social movements is ultimately predicated on the success of the old. Ways have to be found to build alliances between them in order to pursue what are, fundamentally, common interests. Popular education has, potentially, an active role to play in this process.

In the contemporary context, it is perhaps in reconstructing the discourse of citizenship that this potential for popular education to develop alliances between old and new movements has the best prospect of success. Traditionally, the labour movement has defined citizenship primarily in terms of economic and political rights. This struggle is essentially conducted at the point of production and in the wider political process. New social movements, on the other hand, have often rejected this polititical process because it has excluded their interests and they have demanded the right to define their own problems and to develop their own organisational forms in order to get their voice heard. This has frequently involved a politics of protest and direct action which is, in itself, a form of active citizenship. The active citizen, in this sense, is the dissenting citizen, demanding to be directly involved 'in politics' – as subject rather than object (see Crowther and Shaw, 1997). The challenge posed by the new movements is therefore not only about the substance of policy but also about the nature of the political process. These movements demand – and in some cases prefigure – a new kind of politics. It is the argument of this paper that in Scotland there is now a unique opportunity for the potential strengths of both old and new social movements to combine for common ends.

Conclusion

> It may be that radical education always depends, minimally, on widespread political excitement, and especially the expectation of major social change . . . . (Johnson, 1993)

There are grounds for claiming that we are witnessing such a prospect in Scotland today. As Paterson (1997) argues, the results of the General Election in May 1997 witnessed the collapse of the Conservative vote across Scotland amongst both men and women, across the age range and in all social classes with the exception of professional and managerial occupational groups. Scotland and Wales now have no Conservative MPs at all. What is more, in September 1997 the Yes:Yes vote in the Referendum on devolution endorsed the proposal for a Scottish Parliament (74.3 per cent support) with tax varying powers (63.5 per cent support).

The significance of the Referendum vote in particular needs to be grasped. Two key points follow from it. First, it seems that the electorate wants a decisive change in the way Scotland is governed. During the Thatcher-Major administrations the experience of a 'democratic deficit' in Scotland was exacerbated by deeply unpopular measures such as the Poll Tax, water privatisation, cuts in health care and education, the imposition of testing in primary schools and the systematic assault on local authorities – all carried out by a central government without a popular mandate. Second, the Referendum vote on tax varying powers for the Scottish Parliament contradicts the conventional wisdom that people simply vote in a narrowly self-interested way and consequently against the possibility of paying higher taxes for improved public services. It seems that the Scottish people have voted for a different and better kind of society more in tune with their collective values and aspirations.

An important lesson to be learnt from the history of popular education has been the link between popular aspirations and the wider conjunctures in which they emerge. The concern to improve the material circumstances of the worst off should be central to the popular education project in Scotland today. This will require a new kind of politics based on a new kind of relationship between the state and civil society. It is essential that both old and new social movements consider how they can contribute to a process of democratic renewal which must go well beyond formal political processes if it is to have any significant impact on redistributing wealth and power. Of course, this aspiration increasingly has international dimensions. In a global economy, for example, the power of multinational companies is often greater than that of national governments. We therefore need to understand the economic as well as the political dimensions of citizenship because, to be citizens in society, we also need to be citizens at work.

Popular participation in more active forms of politics must become central to the process of democratic renewal in Scotland. In this respect, the lesson to be learnt from the new social movements is that direct and participative ways to 'be in politics' can generate and mobilise new interests and forces in unprecedented ways. Indeed, the direct politics of these movements is one of the most significant ways in which the demand for a new kind of politics has been expressed in Scotland, especially through the systematic campaigning both by women for equal representation in the new parliament (eg see Brown *et al*, 1996) and specific groups in civil society such as the Scottish Civic Assembly (incidentally, but significantly, initiated by the Scottish Trade Union Congress), Scotland Forward and Charter 88. Moreover, as Paterson (1997) suggests, active citizenship implies scepticism as well as commitment. Popular education should therefore enable people to engage actively and critically in the new political process as well as the tensions it will inevitably create between the new state and civil society in Scotland.

Both the process and prospect of democratic renewal in Scotland provide a unique opportunity to apply the lessons learnt from the history of popular education in a new context. In particular, there is the possibility of popular education contributing towards a different kind of relationship between the political culture of the new Scottish state and the experience of people in Scottish communities. As this paper has argued, the history of popular education is closely entwined with the history of the struggle for democracy. Both these histories are entering a new phase in Scotland. There is now 'widespread political excitement' – even the 'expectation of major social change'. To fulfil this sense of excitement and expectation is not only a political challenge, it is also an urgent educational task. Popular education has a part to play in this process. It is time, once again to demonstrate, as William Lovett the Chartist organiser put it some 150 years ago, that 'The franchise is the best schoolmaster'.

References

Bauman, Z (1976) *Socialism: The Active Utopia*, London, Allen and Unwin.

Brown, A, McCrone, D and Paterson, L (1996) *Politics and Society in Scotland*, Basingstoke, Macmillan.

Brown, G (1980) 'Independence and incorporation: the Labour College movement and the Workers' Educational Association before the Second World War' in Thompson, J (ed), *Adult Education for a Change*, London, Hutchinson, pp 109–125.

Bryant, I (1984) *Radicals and Respectables: The Adult Education Experience in Scotland*, Edinburgh, Scottish Institute of Adult Education.

Crowther, J and Shaw, M (1997) 'Social movements and the education of desire', *Community Development Journal*, 32 (3), pp 266–279.

Dobbs, A E (1919) *Education and Social Movements, 1700–1850*, London, Longman, Green & Co.

Eyerman, R and Jamison, A (1991) *Social Movements: A Cognitive Approach*, Cambridge, Polity Press.

Jackson, K (1995) 'Popular education and the state: a new look at the community debate' in Mayo, M and Thompson, J (eds), *Adult Learning, Critical Intelligence and Social Change*, Leicester, NIACE, pp 182–203.

Johnson, R (1993) 'Really useful knowledge, 1790–1850' in Thorpe, M, Edwards, R, and Hanson, A (eds) *Culture and Processes of Adult Learning*, London, Routledge, Open University, pp 17–29.

Maclean, J (1978) *In the Rapids of Revolution*, London, Alison and Busby.

Miliband, R (1989) *Divided Societies*, Oxford, Oxford University Press.

Paterson, L (1997) 'Scotland and democracy', *Concept*, 7 (3), pp 4–6.

Silver, H (1965) *The Concept of Popular Education*, London, Macgibbon and Kee.

Simon, B (1974) *Education and the Labour Movement*, London, Lawrence and Wishart.

Steele, T (1995) 'Cultural struggle or identity politics: can there still be a popular education?' in Mayo, M and Thompson, J (eds), *Adult Learning, Critical Intelligence and Social Change*, Leicester, NIACE, pp 47–57.

Steele, T (1997) 'Marginal occupations: adult education, cultural studies and social renewal', *Scottish Journal of Adult and Continuing Education*, 4 (1), pp 21–36.

Thompson, E P (1968) *The Making of the English Working Class*, Harmondsworth, Penguin.

Thompson, E P (1978) *The Poverty of Theory*, London, Merlin Press.

Wainwright, H (1994) *Arguments for a New Left*, London, Blackwell.

Westwood, S (1992) 'When class became community: radicalism in adult education' in Rattansi, A and Reeder, D (eds), *Rethinking Radical Education*, London, Lawrence and Wishart, pp 222–248.

Welton, M (1993) 'Social revolutionary learning: the new social movements as learning sites', *Adult Education Quarterly*, 43 (3), pp 152–164.

Wilson, A (1970) *The Chartist Movement in Scotland*, Manchester, Manchester University Press.

Wright, L C (1953) *Scottish Chartism*, Edinburgh, Oliver and Boyd.

3 Social movements and the politics of educational change

Lindsay Paterson

This chapter focuses on the complex relationship between social movements and the state. Whilst recognising the problems of defining social movements, it argues that there are significant differences between 'old' and 'new' movements. The latter have emerged partly as a reaction to their perceived exclusion from mainstream left politics, and their critique of class as a 'mobilising category' has led to an engagement with the 'politics of difference' which rejects universalism as untenable. However, whilst the absence of a coherent organising principle has offered new possibilities, it has also produced problems. On the one hand, challenges to the truth claims of particular kinds of knowledge offer space for radical education to take place even within state sponsored education. On the other hand, precisely because of the relativism which is implicit in this position, some universalistic principles have to be rediscovered to distinguish between 'good' and 'bad' social movements. The forms of the state need to be renewed to reflect a more complex social reality, but the state itself nevertheless retains an essential function, acting 'above society' in promoting common welfare. The new social movements have expanded our understanding of politics to include cultural action in civil society. They offer new ways of thinking and acting which can contribute to the process of democratic renewal in Scotland – a process which can itself be seen, in part at least, as an outcome of sustained social movement activity.

Introduction

This chapter outlines a general account of social movements in order to offer a framework for discussion. Some of the educational implications are drawn out by way of examples, but the chapter does not deal exclusively with education.

The core of the argument is this. Social movements have, by now, provided an unanswerable critique of what has been called the 'old' politics – a critique of the styles of radicalism which dominated socialist and communist parties until, at least, the 1950s – styles that could be summed up in the word 'statist'. Social movements also have some impressive achievements to their credit – achievements not only of radicalising people (what feminism has called 'consciousness raising') but also of social reform, often achieved by non-statist means. But social movements are not enough: indeed, unfettered enthusiasm for social movements poses some serious threats to any coherent programme of radical social action. The state remains an essential means of democratic reform, and yet the more radical tendencies in current social movements still regard the state with great suspicion.

Social movements and modernist socialism

Social movements in their current form are usually seen as dating from the 1960s (a point to which I return later): the best-known examples are the women's movement, movements arguing for the rights of gays and lesbians, the environmental movement, and the anti-racist movement (Pierson, 1991; Sassoon, 1996; Wainwright, 1994).

Any attempt to define social movements precisely would fail because they are enormously diverse, and because they have changed their character over time. There have always been social movements, even before the era of democracy and mass political parties. For example, in Scotland in the eighteenth and nineteenth centuries, a frequent means by which the concerns of the weak and the poor were brought to the attention of policy makers was by riots and other types of organised protest (Breitenbach, 1993; Logue, 1979; Sher, 1982). Early in the twentieth century, the pre-eminent forms of social movement in Scotland were the trade unions and the various movements for women's suffrage, each to some extent agitating for reform outwith the structures of formal politics.

But the 'new social movements' – which are the main topic of this chapter – can be distinguished from their predecessors by three characteristics:

- they have rejected, in some measure, the 'old' politics of parties (and of earlier social movements) on the grounds that these have ossified as vehicles for radical change
- they have insisted on autonomous organisation, partly because of that same rejection of older movements, but partly also on principled grounds: for example, segments of the women's movement have organised autonomously because any other way would have involved ceding some influence on the movement to other institutions
- they have not believed, either in theory or in practice, that their demands could be subsumed into some greater whole of mass politics: for example, it was not possible to claim that women's movement demands could be straightforwardly aligned with those of the labour movement.

What were they up against? Obviously, on the one hand, they confronted what many saw as an essentially unreformed capitalism, based in fundamental ways on patriarchy and on an ecologically disastrous industrialism. In the states of Western Europe and North America, this social order was also intrinsically racist, insofar as it was based on the exploitation either of immigrant labour or of dependent ex-colonies in the southern parts of the world. That much was agreed, but could also be agreed by many quite conventional reformist politicians – figures such as Willy Brandt of the West German Social Democratic

Party or Richard Crossman of the British Labour Party or Palmiro Togliatti of the Italian Communist Party. The question for the social movements was how to replace these exploitative systems by means that did not fall into what they saw as the ineffective politics of the parties which a Brandt or a Crossman or a Togliatti represented. So the main political impact of the social movements was on leftist thinking, because the established leftist parties were the only other serious option on offer for social reform.

It is useful to see the social movements' critique of leftist politics as relating to four elements of what can be called 'modernist socialism'. These elements have been adapted from Ernesto Laclau (1996), and can be summarised as follows.

The first point is a claim by the old versions of socialist politics that society is homogeneous, working according to one set of laws, and based on a small set of organising principles. The most obvious instance of this theory is the crude Marxist one – that society can be fully understood in terms of the relationship between the means of production and the social infrastructure of production. In education, the claim by the old radicalism was that schools and other agencies serve a class society and industrial capitalism, even while claiming to be universal. For example, James D Young in his recent book on Scottish radicalism provides an explicitly political quotation from the radical educationalist AS Neill, writing in 1936 with CW Thomson:

> Our schools are conditioned and regulated by the State. The State is a capitalist, imperialist State, apparently ruled by a sham democracy, but in reality by the minority, who hold the power and the wealth. The schools must not teach anything that might be subversive of the State. (Young, 1996)

But although that kind of view is most obvious in Marxism, it pervaded old styles of social democracy as well – notably, in Britain, the Fabians. For example, RH Tawney drew a parallel between a selective system of education and the class character of capitalist society: a selective system 'does more than any other single cause, other than capitalism itself, to perpetuate the division of the nation into classes' (Tawney, 1931).

Second, there is the claim of old socialist politics that the social order can be known and understood if you have the right scientific point of view: that is, there is a way of obtaining infallible revolutionary knowledge. AS Neill, for example, would subscribe to this: despite being a product of the Scottish education system himself, he is happy to claim an insight into the hypocrisies of Scottish democracy which, presumably, the children whom he teaches and their parents do not automatically have. So too would many social democrats. The British Fabian tradition would even claim that there is a scientific way of understanding the processes of society. As Hilary Wainwright argues:

> The assumption that all the knowledge necessary to a socialist transforma-
> tion of society can be codified, turned into an overview of society and
> drawn upon in a single, more or less democratic process, underlies the
> reforming and revolutionary ambitions of . . . Fabianism and . . . Leninism.
> (Wainwright, 1994)

Third, there is the claim that there is a single force for change which can
develop the knowledge that allows it to understand the workings of capitalist
society. This force was, in classical Marxist accounts, the working class, or possibly the leading party of the working class. Social democrats had a similar view
of their own party.

Finally, there is the belief that the leading force for change can not only
reform society, but reconstruct it on a wholly new foundation – fundamental
change that leaves everything different. This view is well-known from the old
communist left. But we find it among most gradualists as well. Here is a quotation from TH Marshall, the eminent social philosopher who was close to the
Labour Party, writing in 1964:

> In the twentieth century, citizenship and the capitalist class system have
> been at war . . . The expansion of social rights is no longer merely an
> attempt to abate the obvious nuisance of destitution in the lowest ranks of
> society . . . It is no longer content to raise the floor-level in the basement
> of the social edifice, leaving the superstructure as it was. It has begun to
> remodel the whole building. (quoted in Giddens, 1994)

In this connection, education can serve revolutionary ends. In the hands of the
Marxists of the Labour Colleges (such as John Maclean) between the two
world wars, education was explicitly about equipping people to understand the
capitalist system in order to overthrow it (see Simon, 1990). But, although the
social democrats would not have subscribed to this view, and would have seen
the extension of education as a good in its own right, they too placed enormous
faith in the effects which universal enlightenment would have in building a
new society. For example, Tony Crosland argued that comprehensive schools
would pave the way for a classless society – a point which, as Harold Entwistle
(1977) observes, was being made half a century earlier by Gramsci.

Critique of modernist politics

The social movements have developed a critique of each of these four elements
of modernist socialism, a critique that has become so much part of the new
politics of our society as to be apparently now unanswerable. I will refer to this
critique as the social movements' philosophy. If there is one pervading principle
of this philosophy, it is that universalism is untenable (Laclau, 1996): there are
no universal principles that are valid for all time and in all places. The belief in

that was a legacy of the Enlightenment which has had to be abandoned in the face of the failures of the various projects derived from the Enlightenment – liberalism as well as socialism – to achieve utopia (although the Enlightenment also produced views on the provisional nature of truth which would fit quite well with the new philosophy). For social reformers, the main reason for rejecting universalism is that it is believed to lead to totalitarianism, either of the Stalinist sort or the statist centralism which Fabian social democracy has produced.

First, society does not have just one organising principle. There are multiple identities and intentions, which cannot be reduced to each other. Here is one way of putting it, from the literary critic Cairns Craig:

> core cultures are . . . by definition, abnormal, since cores are few and peripheries many. Cultural analysis has operated largely through the application of values which are themselves the cultural consequences of core conditions, highlighting integrity, unity, coherence, sustained develop-ment. But those are not in fact cultural values: they are the application to culture of the structural values required, within a certain pattern of the world economy, if a nation is going to maintain its core position. (Craig, 1996)

Thus, in education, whatever may be true of the claims by AS Neill and others that schools perpetuate a class-based society, there are other dimensions of exclusion or even oppression which are not reducible to class, for example sexism and racism. In the words of Stuart Hall: 'Class cannot serve as a . . . mobilising category through which all the diverse social interests and identities of people can be reconciled and represented' (Hall, 1992). This is the reason why the new social movements are sometimes referred to as engaging in the 'politics of difference'.

The second claim is that there are no privileged vantage points. A fully scientific knowledge about society is not available. Different social experiences lead to different types of knowledge. Thus Hall in fact adds to the quotation just given that class cannot be a unifying 'discursive device' any more than it can be a unifying principle of political organisation. As Hilary Wainwright (1994) points out, the social knowledge that has been developed in the women's movement gives a different understanding of society to that which was tradition-ally developed by socialist theorists. Three key elements of this approach to knowledge could be mentioned:

- it is based on experience as much as theory
- it acknowledges emotions as a source of knowledge, not just reason
- it accepts that all knowledge is unavoidably fallible.

In education, two quite different implications of this can be discerned. On the one hand, it accords respect to the knowledge which people develop for themselves, and in that sense is consistent with the practice of a strand of the old workers' education (in other words, the strand that saw workers' education as being about workers' educating themselves, rather than the strand which saw it as the workers' being educated by the Marxist teacher who already knows the answers). On the other hand, the acceptance that knowledge is fallible also seems to open space for radical education to take place even within state-sponsored education: if all knowledge is fallible, then the same is true even of the knowledge which the dominant social order claims, and so astute radicals can find spaces to insert their own ideas and practices.

Third, despite the importance of these points about social reality and social knowledge, the most obvious characteristic of the social movements is that they would deny that there is a single revolutionary force. Whatever may be the continuing impact of politics based on social class, there can be equally effective interventions based on gender or race, for example. As Donald Sassoon says, linking this point with the first one about there being no social totality: 'People never have a single identity and much of the struggle of politics consists in attempts to privilege a particular identity at the expense of others' (Sassoon, 1996). In education, then, the social forces that might be conducive towards change are not only class-based ones. Feminism, for instance, has an influence on change independent of class.

Fourth, there can be no fundamental overthrow of society. If society has no single foundation (such as the character of the ownership of the means of production), then there is no question of revolutionising it in a fundamental way. That does not mean that radical change is impossible. It means simply that we cannot talk about revolutionising the entire basis of society. It would be possible to have a revolution in one dimension, but for nothing much to change in another. For example, the reforms to secondary education in Scotland between the 1920s and the 1940s did have an impact on social mobility between social classes (Payne, 1987; Heath, 1990), but did not have much effect at all on women's chances relative to men of the same class. But then, since the 1970s, we have had a revolution in women's expectations and experience without there having been much change in social class inequalities (Burnhill and McPherson, 1984; Gray *et al*, 1983; Paterson, 1995).

Achievements of social movements

With this critique of old socialist politics, the social movements have secured some impressive achievements. The intellectual critique which I have just outlined of modernist socialism is now widely agreed, and in the realm of debate could be said to have been the main impact of the new social movements. People who try to reduce revolutionary or reformist politics to one dimension (class struggle) in which one agent (the working class) is the dominant actor now seem quaintly old-fashioned.

Linked with that intellectual success is the impact which the new social movements have had on people's political self-confidence: 'consciousness raising' has brought into active politics a greater variety of people (even while the overall level of formal political activity has dropped). Indeed, by defining politics more broadly, the social movements have also involved people in political action in a variety of forums that, in the old accounts, would not be recognised as central to the struggle. In education, we could readily cite here recent campaigning over school closures or the resistance to primary school national testing in Scotland in 1991–92.

That example reminds us, however, that whatever may be the new character of social movements since the 1960s, they do share some features with much older organisations and campaigns. People were agitating for schools in the 1920s, and were linking that to the rebuilding of society. For example, Jennie Lee writes about her grandfather and his generation at the beginning of the century in south Fife: 'members of school boards, pressing for free books, better schools, free secondary education, maintenance grants for all' (Lee, 1963). There have also always been social movements that have resisted being incorporated by the dominant labour movement – for example, the rent strikes on Clydeside during the 1914–18 War, and the land raids in the western Highlands and the islands immediately after both World Wars.

But what the post-1960s wave of social movements has achieved is to help us remember these earlier episodes as significant stages in social reform. Esther Breitenbach has argued that what had to be overcome for the earlier history to be remembered as politics was:

> a conceptual framework that construes political activity as being of a certain kind, and political organisation taking certain forms . . . typically the ways in which men have acted and organised. (Breitenbach, 1993)

Summing up such points, the sociologist Alberto Melucci argues that:

> Mobilisations and whole movements certainly do disappear. But the pessimistic view fails to understand that a great deal of important activity takes place during the invisibility stage. The submerged networks of social movements are laboratories of experience. (Melucci, 1989)

Moreover, because social movements have always been around, and because new social movements are now some three decades old, they have in fact had an enduring effect even on mildly reformist parties. Donald Sassoon points out that, since the 1960s, the new social movements have brought new ideas to the social democratic parties. For example, feminism has had an impact on these parties throughout Europe and North America, but the source of the feminist ideas has, first of all, been outside the parties themselves, in the women's movement (Sassoon, 1996). The impact was being felt in earlier eras too, however. For example, one of the main ways in which the idea of comprehensive secondary education was accepted by the Labour Party in Britain was the New Education Fellowship, the organisation which promoted child-centred methods from the 1920s onwards (Darling, 1994; Paterson, 1996). Among its prominent members were radical dissidents such as AS Neill, but also prominent people in or close to the Labour Party, such as RH Tawney, AD Lindsay (the Scot who founded Keele University), and William Boyd of the Education Department at Glasgow University.

Very recently, in Scotland, the social movements have also had a now widely recognised impact on the debate about self-government. The main forum in which that has happened has been the Constitutional Convention. It was set up in 1989 as an attempt to find an agreed scheme for a Scottish Parliament following the 1987 general election in which the Conservative Party had won power again while losing 11 of its 21 Scottish seats. The Convention grouped a variety of civic bodies with the Labour Party and the Liberal Democrats, and the proposals it eventually produced have formed the basis for the 1997 Labour government's scheme for a Scottish Parliament (Scottish Constitutional Convention, 1995).

The Convention proposed, for example, that the Scottish executive be scrutinised by powerful committees of elected members (on the lines of the US Congressional Committees), that there would be far more pre-legislative consultation than at present, and that the electoral system should not only be proportional as between the parties but should also secure a much higher presence than at present of representatives who are women or who come from minority ethnic groups. These radical ideas were introduced mainly by the civic movements in the Convention, not by the parties (Brown *et al*, 1996). For example, the proposal on gender balance came from the Women's Committee of the Scottish Trades Union Congress (a much more consensual body than the TUC is in England (Aitken, 1997)). The ideas on committee structures and on consultation were influenced by the Scottish branch of Charter 88. The debate about Scotland's governing system, then, has influenced, and been influenced by, the new thinking and practice of social movements.

Critique of social movements

So the impact of social movements has been impressive. They seem to have given us a new way of thinking and acting, a way which can have an impact on politics through the pragmatism which (for example) the women's movement has always shown, but which at the same time can pose radical intellectual challenges to both the dominant society and the older ways of radical politics.

However, unalloyed enthusiasm for social movements is not a sufficient basis for social reform. This critique in fact draws on the social movements' philosophy, which is not always respected consistently by social movements themselves. Despite the radical potential of the social movements' philosophy, each particular movement does have a tendency to slip into a new fundamentalism which would be as oppressive as the old fundamentalism of old socialism.

There is both a pragmatic and a philosophical point here. The pragmatic point is that, as numerous social democratic parties have found, the new social movements do not provide politics with easily identifiable enemies. In the words of Donald Sassoon:

> The two key issues of the new politics – ecology and feminism – do not target a small group of easily identifiable enemies like the capitalists . . . Which political party could expect wide popularity in singling out 'consumers' or 'men' as the opponent to beat? (Sassoon, 1996)

In other words – and this is the philosophical version of the point – the main lesson from the social movements is that all essentialism is mistaken (Barth, 1969; Brown *et al*, 1996; Laclau, 1996). Another way of putting this is that so-called 'identity' politics can be inimical to pluralism (Mercer, 1996). There are no polar opposites any more. If a social movement does try to act as if there were polar opposites – for example, as if men and women were indeed essentially different – then it would come up against the same limitations (and maybe horrors) as the old type of socialism did (Segal, 1987).

One particular reason to be wary of the claims of the new social movements is that they tend to be as dominated by middle class activists as almost any other social organisation. It is one of the most consistent findings of political science that the middle class makes up the vast majority of social activists, however defined (Smith, 1994). That, in itself, is not necessarily a bad thing, nor does it necessarily impose a limitation of perspective. But – if we are to be consistent with the social movements' own philosophy – it should lead us to be somewhat wary of claims from any particular movement that it holds the key to social explanation and political action. If experience shapes knowledge, then organisations mainly staffed by people with one type of experience may not be able to speak authentically on behalf of people with different experience.

Beyond this fairly narrow point, however, is a much broader point about what counts as an acceptable social movement. Enthusiasm for social movements tends to forget about the nasty ones. What about new social movements of the Right, such as anti-abortion groups, anti-immigration groups, and religious fundamentalists? Gregor McLennan asks 'why is it that only *progressive* [movements] are typically included as component new social movements within the politics of difference?' (McLennan, 1995).

Ernesto Laclau argues from this, not that all social movements are equally acceptable, but that one of the tenets of the social movements' philosophy must be modified: not all points of view are equally valid, because 'if particularism is the only valid principle, I have to accept the rights to self-determination of all kinds of reactionary groups' (Laclau, 1996). So we have to rediscover some universalistic principles after all, even though we thought we had rejected them in our rejection of old-style socialism. If we reject the politics of 'identity' as a threat to pluralism, then it is not enough to assert instead a politics of 'difference'. The only kinds of demands by a minority group that can succeed permanently are those aligning that group's claims with some principles which apply to all groups in the society, including the currently privileged: for example 'the right of everybody to have access to good schools, or live a decent life, or participate in the public space of citizenship' (Laclau, 1996).

Social movements and the state

This point about universalism brings us to the last set of comments on the social movements, all relating to their connection to the state – to their influence on it, and to the state's conditioning of them.

The social movements themselves are highly dependent on the state, despite their own rhetoric of autonomy. Alice Brown (1991) has argued that this was noticed in Britain with the advent of the Thatcher government, when restrictions on public expenditure suddenly made many social movements face up to their dependence on support from – especially – local government. Hilary Wainwright gives some examples: the social movements have

> produced many new institutions and ways of living, though their sustainability has depended, ironically, on social democracy – the very political strategy they were often initiated against. These institutions [included] women's centres of various kinds, innovation in health care, extensions of adult education, radical cultural centres. (Wainwright, 1994)

In any case, the biggest impact which the social movements have had has been on the welfare state – not just on socialist movements (as mentioned earlier) but on social policy itself. For example, claims that Scottish education is unchanged since the days of AS Neill at the turn of the century are simply not plausible. We can trace a thread from the child-centred campaigning in the New Education Fellowship to the child-centred philosophies of the school guidance system, and then we can record from surveys and other research that young people have noticed the improvement (Paterson, 1997b). They have enjoyed their time at school to an increasing extent, and have felt that their teachers valued them as individuals. That is not to say that further reform is not needed. It is simply to point to the enormous changes which have affected the education of children, and even to some extent of adults.

Insofar as it is possible to isolate explanations of these and similar democratising changes, we might say that educational expansion as such came about primarily because of pressure from social democratic parties (and in some countries communist ones), allying themselves with those industrialists and others who believed that social reform was necessary to stave off fundamental revolution. In that sense, the radical social movements were marginal. But the form which the expansion has taken has been heavily influenced by thinking in the social movements (see Ball, 1990; Williams, 1961).

The final point is, then, that the state that is characteristic of broadly liberal democracies is necessary after all. Not only is it the most effective means by which relatively powerless groups can influence politics. It is also the only known way in which basic rights can be guaranteed – including the right to engage in social movements at all (Paterson, 1997a). The problem with unalloyed enthusiasm for civic activism is that it is not always a good thing. Pierson (1991) notes that citizenship depends on the state for its very existence – for legal guarantees of rights, or, more positively, for action to counter the actual inequalities of power which individual citizens or individual bodies in civil society experience (see also Hills, 1993). Attempts to counter this concern by the values of 'civic republicanism' or 'civic virtue' are not plausible (Hall, 1995; Seligman, 1995). Even if it were possible to imagine a society in which a sense of civic duty was so pervasive that no one exploited anyone else, the objection would remain that getting there would require an inconceivable exercise in totalitarianism. We have to live with 'moderated hypocrisy', a phrase which John Hall (1995) draws from the thinking of the Enlightenment Scots. What matters is not how people are, but how they behave. The welfare state could be said to be a monument to that principle: unlike its revolutionary rivals, it did not seek to change people (although its long-term effects might have been to do that), but rather sought to counter, by means of collective action, the worst things which people do.

So some 'centre' does have to continue to act, above society, to sanction equal rights, to counteract inequalities and to promote common welfare (McLennan, 1995). Laclau makes the point that the fact that the state represents particular interests at any given moment does not prove that it must always represent only one particular interest (Laclau, 1996). The very reason we are debating social movements in Scotland today is an illustration of these points. It is a discussion in the context of a wider debate about renewing the forms of the state in Scotland, and of how that renewal might help to promote a new type of democracy (Paterson, 1997a). Despite some rhetoric of the self-government movement, it is not at all, mostly, a debate about abolishing the Scottish state altogether.

In conclusion, we can say that social movements have radicalised left-wing politics in an irrevocable way. They have also indelibly marked our understanding of society and of the political sources of social change. But they have not done away with the universalistic concept of social rights themselves. And the social movements have not disposed of the need for a strong state, to guarantee these rights, and to provide the resources and the education without which most people would simply have no realistic access to their rights at all.

References

Aitken, K (1997) *The Bairns o' Adam: The Story of the STUC*, Edinburgh, Polygon.

Ball, S (1990) *Politics and Policy Making in Education*, London, Routledge.

Barth, F (1969) *Ethnic Groups and Boundaries*, Bergen, Scandinavian University Books.

Breitenbach, E (1993) 'Out of sight, out of mind? The history of women in Scottish politics', *Scottish Affairs*, 2, pp 58–70.

Brown, A (1991) 'Thatcher's legacy for women', *Radical Scotland*, 50, pp 10–12.

Brown, A, McCrone, D and Paterson, L (1996) *Politics and Society in Scotland*, London, Macmillan.

Burnhill, P and McPherson, A (1984) 'Careers and gender: the expectations of able Scottish school leavers in 1971 and 1981' in Acker, S and Warren, D (eds), *Is Higher Education Fair to Women?*, London, Society for Research in Higher Education, pp 83–114.

Craig, C (1996) *Out of History*, Edinburgh, Polygon.

Darling, J (1994) *Child-Centred Education and its Critics*, London, Paul Chapman.

Entwistle, H (1977) *Class, Culture and Education*, London, Methuen.

Giddens, A (1994) *Beyond Left and Right*, Cambridge, Polity.

Gray, J, McPherson, A and Raffe, D (1983) *Reconstructions of Secondary Education: Theory, Myth and Practice since the War*, London, Routledge and Kegan Paul.

Hall, J A (1995) 'In search of civil society' in Hall, J A (ed), *Civil Society*, Cambridge, Polity, pp 1–31.

Hall, S (1992) 'The question of cultural identity' in Hall, S (ed), *Modernity and its Futures*, Cambridge, Polity, pp 273–316.

Heath, A (1990) 'Educational reform and changes in the stratification process in Great Britain' in Leschinsky, A and Mayer, K U (eds), *The Comprehensive School Experiment Revisited: Evidence from Western Europe*, Frankfurt, Verlag Peter Lang, pp 92–110.

Hills, J (1993) *The Future of Welfare: A Guide to the Debate*, York, Joseph Rowntree Foundation.

Laclau, E (1996) *Emancipation(s)*, London, Verso.

Lee, J (1963) *This Great Journey: A Volume of Autobiography 1904–45*, London, MacGibbon and Kee.

Logue, K J (1979) *Popular Disturbances in Scotland, 1780–1815*, Edinburgh, John Donald.

McLennan, G (1995) *Pluralism*, Milton Keynes, Open University Press.

Melucci, A (1989) *Nomads of the Present*, London, Hutchinson Radius.

Mercer, K (1996) 'Welcome to the jungle: identity and diversity in postmodern politics' in Rutherford, J (ed), *Identity: Community, Culture and Difference*, London, Lawrence and Wishart, pp 43–71.

Paterson, L (1995) 'Social origins of under-achievement among school-leavers' in Dawtrey, L, Holland, J, Hammer, M, and Sheldon, S (eds), *Equality and Inequality in Education Policy*, Milton Keynes, Open University Press, pp 77–92.

Paterson, L (1996) 'Liberation or control: what are the Scottish educational traditions in the twentieth century?' in Devine, T M and Finlay, R J (eds), *Scotland in the Twentieth Century*, Edinburgh, Edinburgh University Press, pp 230–249.

Paterson, L (1997a) 'Scottish autonomy and the future of the welfare state', *Scottish Affairs*, 19, pp 55–73.

Paterson, L (1997b) 'Individual autonomy and comprehensive education', *British Educational Research Journal*, 23 (3), pp 315–327

Payne, G (1987) *Employment and Opportunity*, London, Macmillan.

Pierson, C (1991) *Beyond the Welfare State?*, Cambridge, Polity.

Sassoon, D (1996) *One Hundred Years of Socialism*, London, I B Tauris.

Scottish Constitutional Convention (1995) *Scotland's Parliament, Scotland's Right*, Edinburgh, Scottish Constitutional Convention.

Segal, L (1987) *Is the Future Female?*, London, Virago.

Sher, R B (1982) 'Moderates, managers and popular politics in mid-eighteenth century Edinburgh' in Dwyer, J, Mason, R A and Murdoch, A (eds), *New Perspectives on the Politics and Culture of Early Modern Scotland*, Edinburgh, John Donald.

Simon, B (ed) (1990) *The Search for Enlightenment*, London, Lawrence & Wishart.

Seligman, A B (1995) 'Animadversions upon civil society and civic virtue in the last decade of the twentieth century' in Hall, J A (ed), *Civil Society*, Cambridge, Polity, pp 200–223.

Smith, D H (1994) 'Determinants of voluntary association participation and volunteering: a literature review', *Nonprofit and Voluntary Sector Quarterly*, 23 (3), pp 243–263.

Tawney, R H (1931[1973]) *Equality*, reprinted in Silver, H (ed) *Equal Opportunity in Education,* London, Methuen, pp 51–55.

Wainwright, H (1994) *Arguments for a New Left*, Oxford, Blackwell.

Williams, R (1961) *The Long Revolution*, Harmondsworth, Penguin.

Young, J D (1996) *The Very Bastards of Creation*, Glasgow, Clydeside Press.

4 Learning from popular education in Latin America

Liam Kane

This is an uncompromisingly class-based and materialist analysis which openly eschews professional 'neutrality' and draws its inspiration from popular education in Latin America. A symbiotic link between popular movements and popular education is crucial to the essentially political orientation of popular education. The argument is both comparative and contextual in that it seeks to identify convergences and divergences between Latin America and Scotland. Particular attention is paid to the dialectic between the state and civil society and the place of progressive social movements within it. The prospect of a Scottish Parliament may present opportunities for the development of popular education involving people as active 'subjects' in the process of social and political change. This, however, demands a clear understanding of the opportunities and threats presented by the present conjuncture.

What is educación popular?

The current appeal of the term 'popular education' owes much to the experience of *educación popular* in Latin America which, over the last 30 years, has proved inspirational to radical educators throughout the world. Taking account of the different social and political contexts, this chapter attempts to examine the nature of popular education in Latin America, evaluate its successes and failures and speculate on what lessons, if any, it may hold for Scotland today.

Firstly, in Spanish and Portuguese the word *popular* has connotations which are frequently lost in translation. It means 'of the people', the people being the working class, the unemployed, the *campesinos* or 'peasants', the 'poor' and sometimes even the lower middle class. It excludes and stands in contradistinction to the well-off middle class and the rich. Trade unions, neighbourhood associations, peasant associations, women's groups, co-operatives, human rights groups – all would be referred to as *popular* organisations. It is even common to talk of the *popular* as opposed to the 'established' church. Sometimes *popular* communicates the idea of 'working in the interests of' as opposed to 'composed of' the popular classes. Thus, for example, a human rights group campaigning on behalf of landless peasants would also be considered a popular organisation, even though its main activists were sympathetic middle class lawyers. A 'popular movement' is either a single organisation operating on a grand scale, such as the Brazilian *Movimento dos Sem Terra* (the 'Landless People's Movement'), or a collective noun for all popular organisations existing within one particular region or country. It should be noted that while sociologists increasingly talk of 'new social movements' to describe actors operating outside conventional politics, 'social' says little about the class-based nature of 'popular' organisations. Rooted in a class analysis of society, *educación popular* seeks to develop an educational practice which serves and promotes the interests of the popular classes.

Throughout Latin America, popular education was inspired by the Brazilian experience of the early 1960s when, in the course of struggling to bring about social change, popular organisations themselves identified the need for an alternative education, one which was related to their experience and under their control. In Brazil it is still within the framework of the popular movement that popular education takes place, where 'the movement is the school'. However, throughout Latin America the strength of the popular movement varies in time and place, with some variation as to whether the popular movement stimulates popular education or the other way round. In either case, 'first world' attempts to emulate the Latin American experience often seem unaware of this symbiotic relationship between popular education and the popular movement. Whilst some of the theory and practice of popular education is already familiar to Western practitioners, it is worth highlighting the main points and drawing attention, in particular, to what it is *not*.

Much of what Paulo Freire espoused in his earlier work is still relevant today, despite enlightening critiques of his notion of knowledge transfer (Lovett *et al*, 1983) or the vagueness of his thinking (Youngman, 1986; Taylor, 1993). All education is political and it either sides with the oppressed or, by default, the oppressors; popular education promotes action and reflection, encouraging people to be 'subjects' rather than 'objects' of change; its values are collectivist and it aims at empowering groups (as distinct from individuals); it promotes 'bottom-up' rather than 'top-down' development. It eschews any concept of left wing 'banking' education (where the educator seeks to 'deposit' knowledge into the mind of the passive learner), but it has, on the whole, a clear socialist bias in that it is underpinned by the values of equality and collectivism. A strictly socialist definition would be inaccurate, however. There are various interpretations of popular education, and the least politically developed could simply be based on the desire for a 'better deal for the oppressed' under capitalism.

In terms of practice, it is worth highlighting the following points:

- Popular education is not simply about teaching literacy skills.
- Its starting point is the immediate interests and concerns of a group – the 'generative' issues – and it then branches out to wider political considerations.
- The methodology of post-literacy popular education has fired the imagination of many northern radical educators. Drama, artwork, allegory, song –

the whole of popular culture is invoked to engage groups in analysis and discussion.

- Popular culture (in the sense of the total system of beliefs and values of the popular classes) is highly valued and respected, but is neither romanticised nor uncritically accepted because oppressive ideology has also been internalised by the oppressed.

- In recent years popular education has tended to develop areas of specialism, eg popular education for women, refugees, human rights and ethnic minorities. It is, however, important to emphasise that each would seek to promote an understanding of how different issues interconnect and form part of a wider social reality.

- Funding for popular education has generally come from a plethora of 'Non-Governmental Organisations' (NGOs), some indigenous to Latin America and some from abroad (eg Oxfam, Christian Aid and Scottish Catholic International Aid Fund). Many popular educators are based in independent, NGO-funded popular education centres which provide support to a range of popular organisations.

- Finally, 'popular education' means different things to different people and at times it has been reduced to a de-politicised, if not outright reactionary, technicism in which 'popular' simply means that the target group is the poorest sector. Reactionary governments, the military, right-wing evangelists, drug barons and even the CIA have all claimed to be involved in popular education! To avoid confusion, 'authentic' popular education has constantly to reassert its political orientation.

The Latin American context

After a colonial history which included slavery, mass exploitation and genocide, Latin America today is a kaleidoscope of ethnicities and cultures in which the dominance of European, African, indigenous American or *mestizo* ('mixed' ethnicity or culture) influence varies from place to place. At one extreme, while maintaining aspects of a nationalist culture, wealthy elites will characteristically have much in common with their counterparts in the United States, many being graduates of its universities or military academies. At the other extreme, Indian groups, now worse off than before the arrival of the first *conquistadors*, doughtily defend their culture against local and global capitalism. In a variety of regional and national contexts the interplay between local (sometimes rival) elites, foreign states or investors and the economically and culturally 'oppressed' is the background against which the struggle for change is played out and, accordingly, the practice of popular education expresses itself in numerous different ways.

At times only the use of severe repression has enabled those who have power to keep control. In this context popular education has operated under two different sets of circumstances. In the first, it is forced to work within the ideological constraints imposed by the oppressors, in which case it is usually driven underground or disguised as something else. While people will always find a way to struggle against oppression – and there are many examples of this (see Archer and Costello, 1990) – there is no doubt that the potential for popular education in such circumstances is extremely limited. By contrast, in other cases, as in El Salvador in the 1980s when guerrilla opposition constructed 'liberated zones' in the midst of a radicalised population, popular education can thrive relatively free of constraint (Pearce, 1986; López Vigil, 1995).

Most often, however, popular education has operated in a political context in which, though considered 'subversive', it is tolerated, albeit to varying degrees and with periodic clamp-downs. At one extreme, it may be on a permanent state of alert, liable to be on the receiving end of repression if it goes too far, as happened in Argentina in the 1970s (Puiggrós, 1994). In the middle ground, where governments claim more liberal credentials, there is a 'dialectical relationship' between popular education and the state. The state allows popular education to operate, but will try to limit its effectiveness, while popular education's critique of the state can also bring about reform. Currently, Brazil and Ecuador show how both quantitative and qualitative changes in state-run adult education have come about in response to a popular education critique. In this liberal context, as well as effecting change at the local level, popular education can fulfil a nation-wide role, taking advantage of the inadequacies of formal adult education. Further to the left there have been 'populist' governments which claim to be on the side of 'the people' but still maintain a top-down, pro-capitalist position. Whilst this continues to impose constraints, it also constitutes a 'window of opportunity' in which the tone of public debate is receptive to a popular education discourse. It was under just such a populist government – that of João Goulart (1963–64) – that Freire was able to carry out his earlier work in Brazil. (As only literate people had the vote, Goulart courted the peasantry and encouraged the spread of literacy in order to retain power. In the end, he was seen as too radical and was ousted in a military coup which also sent Freire into exile.) In Nicaragua as well as Cuba and Grenada, Latin America also provides examples of revolutionary societies which saw nation-wide popular education as a crucial part of their development. The image of 40,000 enthusiastic volunteers from the towns going out to teach literacy to *campesinos* and to encourage participation in the making of a new society is a tremendous inspiration to anyone interested in education for change (Arnove, 1986).

Towards the end of the 1990s, however, there is considerable confusion and debate about what is happening in Latin America. There has been a clear shift away from the era of dictatorship and civil war towards an albeit fragile 'democracy' and peace. It has been argued (Cubitt, 1995) that this owes much to the efforts of popular movements, in which popular education played its part. However, there has been little structural, economic change: neo-liberalism still dominates the politics of the region and the poor are now worse off than ever before. There is disorientation on the left, firstly as a consequence of the failure to bring about real, revolutionary change (an important moment being the Sandinista defeat in the 1990 Nicaraguan elections) and, secondly at an ideological level, through the postmodernist attack on 'grand-narrative' theories of change, particularly Marxism. Popular education is not immune from such disorientation and the excitement and promise of the 1960s and 1970s have now been tempered by an acceptance that education, on its own, has been unable to change the world in any radical way. Its role is currently under scrutiny and there is much debate about future directions, particularly regarding the extent to which it should remain outside the state or embark on constructive engagement with it. In this climate of uncertainty, debate about such concepts as class, community, identity and difference are as common in Latin America as they are here.

Scotland and Latin America: a comparison

In trying to assess the relevance of *educación popular* to Scotland it is important to examine the differences between the two contexts. It can be argued that since there is less absolute poverty in Scotland than there is in Latin America, 'oppression' is not as widespread and the sense of urgency regarding social change is weaker. Whilst this may be true, there is no denying the existence of social inequality in Scotland. Freire (1983) talks of the 'Third World' within the 'First World' and recent studies in the United Kingdom point to increasing polarisation and social inequality (eg Rowntree, 1995). Consequently, economic injustice has become more visible. Illiteracy is much higher in Latin America and many adults can be attracted to education with 'literacy' as the carrot (though what actually constitutes 'literacy' is subject to debate). However, it is wrong to equate popular education with literacy, even though, given the worldwide fame of Freire's earlier work, this is often what happens. What is important is 'reading the world' – trying to interpret the social forces influencing our lives – and that is as relevant in Scotland as Latin America.

Given the link between popular education and social movements, it is important to consider the nature of these movements in each context and how they relate to both the state and civil society. Whilst European and Latin American movements have certain elements in common – they operate outside conventional politics, they are more participatory and less authoritarian than conventional institutions – there are significant differences. It is commonly argued, however, that, in comparison with Latin America, in Western Europe 'the state's penetration of civil society has been far greater and . . . the welfare functions of the state have been much more effectively established' (Slater, 1985). In addition, the concerns of European social movements are generally seen to respond to a post-industrial society and project post-materialist values. They attempt to 'democratise democracy' (Slater, 1985) and 'extend the political space available to citizens, bringing into the public realm the concerns of everyday life and of the personal' (Hellman, 1992). If they have a defined social base, 'it is among the educated middle classes who have the time and income to organise and agitate'. However,

> the basic issue for most communities and associations in Latin America remains how to consume enough to survive, and material demands remain paramount for the great majority of social movements. It is mainly the lower or 'popular' classes which mobilise for reasons of work, wages, services and housing. (Foweraker, 1995)

In comparison to Europe, therefore, where social movements are seen as occupying and expanding this 'public sphere' within civil society, in Latin America social movements organise primarily against the state. The state has, in fact, either prevented the development of civil society (by failing to provide basic services or respect human rights, for example) or, through a variety of 'development plans' it has been the main cause of major social problems, such as rampant urbanisation or massive inequality. An important consequence of this cultural difference is that, whereas in Latin America people perceive the need to take matters into their own hands, in so-called advanced 'democracies' established political institutions (such as parliament, local authorities and political parties) are considered the appropriate agents of change. Consequently, the potential power of mass political activity is undermined. There is little in Scotland which can be directly compared with the popular movements of Latin America. Broad-based campaigns have some similarities (the Anti-Poll Tax campaign comes to mind) and there are fragmented grassroots organisations working for local change but there is no coherent mass, organised activity in which the grassroots are the 'subjects' of change. The problem is that, given dependency on the state to bring about change, since poverty has increased in the last 18 years, it has led to a widespread sense of powerlessness. This contrasts with the dynamism and hope springing from involvement in popular movements in Latin America. Indeed, Latin American popular educators visiting the UK frequently point to what they perceive as 'apathy' to be a major difference between the two 'cultures'.

With greater resources than its counterparts in the Third World, the state in our 'democracy' is seen as the natural provider, both able and expected to organise basic welfare services, including education. There is currently no serious, large-scale attempt to organise 'alternative' education outside the state. In Latin America, however, since state provision of education is limited, popular education has been able to occupy a vacuum which does not exist in Scotland. Furthermore whilst Scotland – and indeed the UK – does have its own history of organised, independent radical education (Westwood, 1992), it has effectively faded away since the 1950s following important debates regarding the wisdom of engaging with the state, the very issue that is actively under discussion in Latin America today. In the current political conjuncture, the prospect of resurrecting such a radical tradition – disengaged from the 'old', class-based workers' movements to which it was tied historically – might well seem a difficult challenge.

What counter-hegemonic forces exist in Scotland with which popular education could engage? Groups campaigning for basic material demands are the most likely equivalent of 'popular organisations' and would certainly seem to be an important target. I am not aware of any systematic research into either the extent or potential collective strength of such groups but it is a piece of work crying out to be done. Trade unions are another possibility, though most of the educational work they do tends to be focused on issues of negotiation with management and is directed at representatives only – as opposed to mass membership (Field, 1988). At the time of writing, the Labour Party has just spent its first few months in power. Before that, while it was the largest organised opposition to the policies of the Conservative government, it would be difficult to argue that it was, in any sense, involved or even interested in popular education. The Labour leadership wanted, as it has in the past, leaders to lead and members to follow. It has at times actively intervened to argue against mass participation (as in the Poll Tax campaign). It seems to me, therefore, that the idea of people as 'subjects' of change (as opposed to passive occasional voters) remains something far removed from the collective consciousness of the Labour Party. This hierarchical straitjacket would also be typical of most centre-left parties in Latin America with the notable exception of the Workers Party in Brazil which grew organically out of the Brazilian popular movement's attempt to influence conventional politics as one (and only one) method of bringing about social change. Finally, in Scotland, there is nationalist and – recently triumphant – devolutionist opposition to what is seen as 'English' hegemony. Though there are some overtones of class consciousness here, the appeal is to 'the Scottish people'; there is seldom any discussion of Scottish class differences. The campaign to bring about a Scottish Parliament, in my view, could not be classified as a popular movement – at any rate, not in the Latin American sense.

Lessons for Scotland from the Latin American experience

While it would be wrong to romanticise popular education in Latin America, it can stimulate creative thinking and provide insights into our own practice. Highlighting both strengths and deficiencies, the following section attempts to draw lessons from Latin America with particular reference to the conceptualisation of popular education itself, its relationship to the social and political context – in particular, the role of the state – and the methodological concerns of educational practice.

There are similarities between Scottish and Latin American conceptualisations of popular education but there are also important distinctions. In Latin America, the political nature of popular education is much more sharply defined and the commitment to 'side with the oppressed' is more openly spelled out – although there is some debate regarding the precise explanation of oppression, with a variety of humanist and Marxist interpretations competing (Youngman, 1986). Whilst the concept of politically committed education is not new to Scotland either, it certainly needs resuscitation, given the dominance of Conservative policy and ideology in recent years. Its presence within mainstream Scottish (or British) education is marginal whereas political 'neutrality' and uncritical vocationalism are now sacrosanct. The clarity of political purpose in Latin America can bring its own problems, however, and popular educators are sometimes accused of encouraging discussion of political issues at the expense of the more immediately-held concerns of grassroots organisations (Archer and Costello, 1990). While this is clearly a danger, and should serve as a warning to the more enthusiastic political agitators, such disregard for a group's 'culture' would, in fact, constitute bad popular education by definition.

Because it can start from any 'generative' theme but connect with so many different issues, the Latin American experience also demonstrates the relevance of popular education to all educators of adults, no matter what their point of contact with learners is. Translated into a Scottish context, where formal learning opportunities for adults are much more widespread, the lesson is that popular education should not be considered the sole domain of community education. Given prior political commitment to progressive social change, anyone involved in adult education could learn from the philosophy and practice of popular education: health workers, training officers, trade union representatives, housing officials, campaigners, subject-based community educators (artists, local historians, linguists, flower arrangers and so on) and even university and further education lecturers. All of these work under constraints, but their curriculum, at least, provides opportunities for engaging in popular education.

Above all, in Latin America popular education is understood as the intellectual property of grassroots movements working for change rather than being the preserve of professional educators. As part of such movements, popular education can undoubtedly improve the quality of people's lives and bolster attempts to secure economic and political change, particularly at the local level. In this respect, it has had a profound effect on thinking about issues of 'development' and nowadays any NGO worth its salt promotes popular education in all its projects, even though ostensibly the focus may be health, housing or income generation. In this context, the notion of people as 'subjects' of change has a very real meaning in Latin America. This experience offers a powerful challenge to radical education in Scotland where most work is carried out within the state and/or in isolated projects. The Latin American example suggests that we look outside the formal sector, seek out organisations already engaged in action for change and promote educational work within them, effectively trying to build a popular movement from below. Given the omnipresence of the state, this is no easy task and is somewhat back-to-front when compared with the Latin American experience, where popular education emerged from the movement. It is precisely what has been recommended by Latin American popular educators, however, who, on visiting Scotland, are impressed by the projects they see but dismayed by their isolation from any wider movement. This is now beginning to be recognised within Scotland itself – as the publication of this book suggests. It is also a concern of Scottish Education and Action for Development (SEAD). While conditions may not be conducive to massive, Latin American-style popular movements, it is not unrealistic to consider taking small steps in that direction. The recently formed Popular Education Forum for Scotland is a promising development and its current research into the level of grassroots activity throughout Scotland should provide a clearer picture of the available social spaces – both inside and outside the state sector – in which popular education might operate.

With all its variety, then, Latin America is a valuable backdrop for understanding, in general terms, the dialectic between popular education and the state. This can stimulate new insights into the Scottish experience and even offer useful tools of political analysis. The concept of 'populism', for example, well entrenched in Latin American discourse, is helpful in identifying a particular type of relationship between state and people. A 'populist' regime (whether national or local) is a curious mixture. On the one hand, it appears radical, claims to be on the side of the poor (though it appeals to all classes) and can point to welfarist policies to back up its claims. Accordingly, it creates a climate in which the radical discourse of popular education can reverberate. Simultaneously, however, it is inherently conservative, and uses radical rhetoric to diffuse and co-opt genuinely popular movements and is perfectly capable of authoritarianism in order to keep power. In their struggles with the state at various levels, therefore, popular movements have learned to be alert to the existence and dangers of populism. Foweraker (1995) argues that, provided this awareness exists, movements can still make tactical gains against the state even within a statist strategy of co-option.

Though seldom referred to, 'populism' would be useful in identifying a particular practice in Scotland as well. Most obviously, it could apply to the more notorious Labour councils whose political malpractice contrasts with the radicalism of their stated intentions. Before its demise, Strathclyde Regional Council claimed to promote 'community empowerment', a stated goal being that there would be 'evidence that the community exert influence over the public policy agenda' and that there would be 'local leadership which as far as possible reflects the views of local people' (Strathclyde Regional Council, 1993).

In Glasgow, however, grassroots activists in Easterhouse, themselves inspired by the example of popular education in Nicaragua, talked of constant attempts at the co-option of assertive community councils – even resorting to gerrymandering. Funded and organised by local authorities, the Community Education Service itself is not immune and 'radical' authorities have even funded projects explicitly claiming to be Freirian. The City of Edinburgh Council supports the Adult Learning Project in the Gorgie-Dalry district of the city, for example. When a real Latin American-style popular movement briefly emerged in Scotland, however (the Anti-Poll Tax campaign), it stood in direct opposition to local authorities. Since the authorities both administered the Poll Tax and pursued non-payers, they were obviously opposed to this particular grassroots activism. Councils applied their financial and political pressure. In spite of its Freirian philosophy, even the Adult Learning Project felt unable to work with the campaigners. Other projects which did engage with the campaign (such as the Unemployed Workers' Centre in Edinburgh) were closed down. Clearly, then, the issue of state support for popular education and grassroots change is complex. An awareness of the concept of populism, with both its dangers and opportunities, is a useful intellectual tool for popular educators wrestling with these issues.

The context in which popular education operates has clearly a crucial bearing on its outcome. In Latin America, in terms of revolutionising social relations and developing 'subjects' who participate in change, it has been most successful in liberated zones (or even self-regulated refugee 'camps') where mass participation was effectively the only means of survival. Economic and political isolation limited its potential although, as liberated zones negotiated reintegration into a national state, the experience of undiluted 'participatory democracy' enabled grassroots organisations to continue to campaign for change. Revolutionary governments also create the conditions for a massive impact: they have a clear vision of education's importance in social change; they can integrate the work of different government departments in the attempt to promote popular education; they can allocate financial resources and mobilise the media to support their work; and, in a genuinely revolutionary conjuncture, the mass of the population both desires change and feels there is an opportunity to bring it about. But problems persist. To what extent will any government really promote genuine critical thinking when this might be used against itself? In Nicaragua, there were many complaints that the literacy primers used in the nation-wide campaigns were really 'banking education' of a different kind, the purpose being to raise support for the Sandinista government rather than to encourage people to become agents of change. Attempts at government-led radical popular education eventually petered out for two reasons: first, external pressures caused by United States aggression, in which popular educators were a prime target of the Contras; second, because of internal pressures such as a lack of suitably trained educators and the tendency to fall back into traditional educational practice. However, the persistence to this day of many active grassroots organisations suggests that earlier attempts at popular education have had a long-term effect.

As for other contexts, it is clear that popular education has been most effective when there is at least a 'window of opportunity' in which to operate, as opposed to struggling under the constraints of authoritarianism or repression. It has been argued, however, that in these circumstances, successful popular education (and the ensuing grassroots pressure on the ruling class) can provoke a political crisis and the return of authoritarianism, as happened in the wake of Freire's work when the Goulart government was overthrown (Torres, 1990). It is equally arguable, however, that it could tip the balance the other way and lead to radical change: the debate is as much about political analysis as it is about education.

Latin America shows that popular education can make progress when the context is right for it. This is a timely lesson for Scotland. After 18 years of Conservative rule, Labour came back to power and the 'Yes-Yes' vote was cast for a Scottish Parliament. I have little faith that, left to their own devices, either the British government or a Scottish Parliament would be willing or able to effect substantial social change in favour of the 'oppressed'. However, they are likely to be – I hope – more 'populist' than their predecessors and more empathetic with popular aspirations. There is an expectation of change throughout the country (though clear attempts have been made to dampen it down) and this is an opportune time for grassroots organisations – and those seeking support for radical education – to apply pressure on the state. In the next few years the strength of 'popular' organisation could be decisive in determining the kind of change a Scottish Parliament can bring about. It is important to encourage such organisation, not least because powerful business interests are already at work to maintain an essentially conservative agenda.

Whether within authoritarian, liberal, populist or even revolutionary political climates, Latin America shows that there are always constraints on how effective popular education can be. The lesson is twofold. First, it is important to clarify the constraints (and opportunities) existing at any particular time and consider how these affect the potential for change. This process of 'conjunctural analysis' is a regular feature of popular education programmes in Latin America and, with practice, develops impressive analytical skills in the people involved. Second, having identified the constraints, the task is then to work hard, and imaginatively, to minimise their effects. As already discussed, the major constraint in Scotland is the lack of a clearly identifiable popular movement and the creation of such a movement is the biggest challenge for the immediate future. Although the many movements in Latin America can be inspirational and serve as examples of what can be done, some aspects of the Scottish context may well be so different that Latin American models have little to offer. The contradiction experienced by educators working 'in and against' the state has been examined much more fully in Europe (see Mayo and Thompson, 1995) where Gramsci's notion of civil society as a 'site of struggle' has become a key concept in radical adult education. Indeed, as popular struggles now begin to win more 'social space' after decades of 'independence', Gramsci's ideas are attracting increasing interest in Latin America where the popular education movement is beginning to examine the extent to which it should remain outside the state.

The practice of popular education

The methodology of Latin American popular education has attracted international interest and offers a rich source of 'pedagogical tools' or 'participatory techniques', many of which have been translated into English and are already used effectively in a variety of Scottish and British settings. More than a collection of techniques, however, the methodology is a philosophical framework for attempting to interpret and act on social reality. The Central American popular education network, *Alforja*, is particularly emphatic about the difference between 'methodology' and 'technique', constantly promoting in its training what is now widely known as the 'Concept of a Dialectical Methodology' (CDM). It is ironic that popular education produces some complex terminology and, though it can be a struggle to come to terms with this particular piece of jargon, it is worth a closer look. The question of translation also requires serious thought. The explanations which follow are based on a fairly literal translation of the Spanish original, but a serious attempt to promote the ideas to a wider public in Scotland would require systematic cultural as well as linguistic translation. This is a task for a large group rather than a solitary author.

The CDM is a theoretical framework which urges educator and activists to think dialectically, to consider the interplay between different – and, indeed, conflicting – social forces at any moment in time. This is seen as helpful to educators in at least three important ways. First is the belief that:

> social practice is the source, test and ultimate end of the process of knowing, the principle which invalidates action emanating from preconceived, abstract theories: the application of such theories to reality merely becomes mechanical and laboured. (Antillón, 1991)

In other words, when working with popular organisations, activist-educators should not set out with preplanned programmes of what groups ought to do but rather should find out what is already being done and make that the starting point for analysis. Essentially, this is a dialectic between action and reflection. Second, we must see social change as a dynamic process in which the actions and practices of participants interact with context – the history, place and political conjuncture of which they are part. Groups should therefore be encouraged to analyse their context from an historical perspective to better determine appropriate action to take. Third, while reality exists as a totality, its dimensions are multiple, complex and contradictory, and human relationships take place in many contexts – at work, home, church and in struggle, for example. In practice, groups are encouraged to bring to the surface – not conceal – these complexities and contradictions, in order better to understand their social reality.

It is within this understanding that the 'pedagogical tools' previously mentioned are used to put the CDM into practice. 'Triple Self Diagnosis' (IMDEC, 1991), for example, is a useful activity in 'theorising from practice'. It is particularly appropriate for the earlier stages of organisation because it encourages groups to analyse what they think they are doing, what they actually do, and the context in which they operate. They then examine the dialectical relationship between these three areas and search for inconsistencies and contradictions. In thinking about conjunctural analysis, a useful analogy is to see 'reality' as a piece of music played over a hi-fi system, the complex 'dialectics of conjuncture' being captured in the graphics equaliser. One dial might represent the influence of politics, for example, whilst others represent economic, historical or cultural influences, or the strength of the popular movement. Discussion of the synthesised 'music' revolves around how high each dial is turned up and which dials need to be 'tuned', in which direction, to improve the final symphony (Nuñez, 1993).

There are many 'participative techniques' from Latin American practice which can help to galvanise group discussion on a variety of issues. A few of my own favourites are 'Statues' (participants build a human statue which expresses their perception of a particular issue), 'Sociodramas' (participants act out a brief sketch reflecting their concerns and explore different options for action) and 'Drawing' (one group graphically presents its perception of an issue for others to 'decode'). Initially these may require some effort – and adaptation – but they seldom disappoint. While accounts of these particular techniques are already published in English (eg Arnold et al, 1994), others are as yet only available in Spanish or Portuguese, the seminal source being Bustillos and Vargas (1993) *Técnicas Participativas para la Educación Popular.*

Whilst being ready to learn from problems in Latin America, however, it is important to guard against both the deliberate co-option of the methodology (Kidd and Kumar, 1981) and the assumption that 'participatory techniques' and popular education are one and the same thing. Techniques are only tools and can be employed for reactionary as well as progressive ends. With this in mind, the recently formed Popular Education Forum for Scotland has done well to produce a working definition of popular education and insist that groups interested in joining it should be in broad sympathy with its basic political principles.

The organisational structures of popular education in Latin America also provide food for thought. Independent of the state and funded by NGOs, there is a vast array of 'support centres' which exist to give different kinds of assistance to different types of popular organisation. These centres come in many shapes and sizes – for example, the Women's Network in Brazil, the Integral Corporation for Social and Cultural Development in Colombia, the Ecuadorian Institute of Popular Education, Research and Promotion (CEAAL, 1993). They vary considerably in size (from two to 30 full-time staff). Some have expertise in a specific area while others work with many different organisations. Some may even only work with one, operating, in effect, as its educational wing. While it may be more difficult to organise a network of independent centres in Scotland – the question of funding is an obvious concern – it is a model worthy of consideration. It is not dissimilar to that of the Development Education Centres (DEC) spread throughout the UK. Indeed, the DEC in Oxford already employs a 'popular educator' and PODER, a group of activists in Easterhouse in Glasgow, is aspiring to this model already. The development of this initiative will be worth watching. Its success could be an inspiration to others.

The specific support provided by popular education centres varies but a key element, from which much could be learnt, is the training of activists in the principles and methodology of popular education. For example, the Mexican Institute of Community Development runs a School of Methodology attended by activists from popular organisations throughout the country. Four times a year they participate in a week-long workshop, going back to their organisations in between to test out the methodology in practice. Not only does this enable key activists (and their organisations) to become more effective, but the act of bringing together different organisations itself contributes to the strengthening of the wider popular movement. In addition, the recording and documentation of workshop discussions provide useful educational materials for a wider audience as well as an on-going historical analysis of an evolving popular movement.

Conclusion

Scottish educators, activists and grassroots organisations will develop their own indigenous forms of popular education appropriate to Scotland today. Latin America is a source of inspiration, but the influence of the social and political context needs always to be borne in mind. It is important, moreover, not to romanticise the Latin American experience and to learn from its limitations as well as its achievements. Nevertheless, I believe that radical educators in Scotland have much to learn from Latin America both in understanding the relationship between popular education and society and in improving their day-to-day educational practice.

Perhaps the greatest challenge from Latin America is that it forces us to think of popular education in terms of its relationship to a popular movement. The long-term aim of radical, 'popular' education in Scotland should be to contribute to the building of just such a movement. The time is right, many are willing and the Popular Education Forum for Scotland has already made a start. *Adelante!*

References

Antillón, R (1991) *Cuáles Son Los Elementos Esenciales de la CMD*, Mexico, Instituto Mexicano para el Desarrollo Comunitario.

Archer, D and Costello, P (1990) *Literacy and Power: The Latin American Background*, London, Earthscan.

Arnold, R, Barndt, D and Burke, B (1994) *A New Weave: Popular Education in Canada & Central America*, Canada, Cuso and Oise.

Arnove, R F (1986) *Education and Revolution in Nicaragua*, New York, Praeger.

Beecham, D (1995) 'Credit where it's due?' *Socialist Worker Review*, June.

Boal, A (1992) *Games for Actors and Non-Actors*, London, Routledge.

Bustillos, G and Vargas, L (1993) *Técnicas Participativas para la Educación Popular*, Mexico, Instituto Mexicano para el Desarrollo Comunitario.

CEAAL (1993) *Nuestras Prácticas . . . Perfil y Perspectivas de la Formación de Educadores Populares en América Latina*, Mexico, Consejo de Educacion de Adultos de America Latina / Instituto Mexicano para el Desarrollo Comunitario.

Cubitt, T (1995) *Latin American Society*, Harlow, Longman.

Escobar, A and Alvarez, S E (1992) *The Making of Social Movements in Latin America*, Oxford, Westview Press.

Field, J (1988) 'Workers' education and the crisis of British trade unionism' in Lovett, T (ed) *Radical Approaches to Adult Education,* London, Routledge, pp 224–241.

Foweraker, J (1995) *Theorizing Social Movements*, London, Pluto Press.

Freire, P (1983) 'You have the Third World inside you: conversation with Paulo Freire', *Convergence* 16 (4), pp 32–38.

Hellman, J A (1992) 'The study of new social movements in Latin America and the question of autonomy' in Escobar, A and Alvarez, S E (eds), *The Making of Social Movements in Latin America: Identity, Strategy and Democracy*, Oxford, Westview Press, pp 52–61.

IMDEC (1991) *Escuela Metodológica Nacional: Partir de La Práctica: Primer Taller*, Mexico, Instituto Mexicano para el Desarrollo Comunitario.

Kidd, R and Kumar, K (1981) 'Co-opting Freire: a critical analysis of pseudo–Freirian education', *Economic and Political Weekly*, 16, pp 27–36.

López Vigil, J I (1995) *Rebel Radio*, London, Latin American Bureau.

Lovett, T, Clark, C and Kilmurray, A (1983) *Adult Education and Community Action*, London, Croom Helm.

Mayo, M and Thompson, J (eds) (1995) *Adult Learning, Critical Intelligence and Social Change*, Leicester, NIACE .

Nuñez, C H (1993) 'Permiso para pensar . . . educación popular: propuesta y debate', *América Libre,* 2, Buenos Aires, Abril-Mayo Liberarte, pp 47–61.

Pearce, J (1986) *The Promised Land*, London, Latin American Bureau.

Puiggrós, A (1994) 'Politics, praxis and the personal: an Argentine assessment' in McLaren, P and Lankshear, C (eds), *Politics of Liberation: Paths from Freire*, London, Routledge, pp 154–172.

Rowntree, J (1995) *Inquiry into Income and Wealth* (Foundation Income and Wealth Inquiry Group), York, Joseph Rowntree Foundation.

Slater, D (ed) (1985) *New Social Movements and the State in Latin America,* USA, Foris.

Strathclyde Regional Council (1993) *The Social Strategy for the Nineties,* Glasgow, Strathclyde Regional Council.

Taylor, P V (1993) *Texts of Paulo Freire,* Buckingham, Open University Press.

Torres, C (1990) 'Adult education and popular education in Latin America: implications for a radical approach to comparative education', *International Journal of Lifelong Education,* 9 (4), pp 271–288.

Westwood, S (1992) 'When class became community: radicalism in adult education' in Rattansi, A and Reeder, D (eds), *Rethinking Radical Education: Essays in Honour of Brian Simon,* London, Lawrence and Wishart, pp 222–248.

Youngman, F (1986) *Adult Education and Socialist Pedagogy,* London, Routledge.

5 Women, adult education and really useful knowledge

Jean Barr

Radical adult education constitutes a crucial, if always precarious, space for the generation of the 'knowledge from below' which is needed to sustain and reinvigorate democratic life. In many ways, this space has been closed down by recent developments in policy and practice, ranging from the retreat into personalism to the hegemony of technical rationality. Too many feminists have withdrawn into the academy or the counsellor's chair. On the other hand, novel political and material conditions present new possibilities as well as problems. In seeking to revive the radical project in adult education today, we have much to learn from the theory and practice of feminist adult educators who successfully combine a dual commitment to personal development and social change. The argument is supported by reference to the author's practical experience in women's education and women's studies in the west of Scotand.

The current context of adult education

Historically there has been a tension between adult education's mission in servicing social movements committed to social justice goals and its role in servicing the economy and state. Over time the latter has become predominant and has led to increasing professionalisation and bureaucratisation. As a result, much adult education practice is instrumental and unaware of its social and economic location and effects. This failure to locate our educational practice within wider social and economic processes is now critical as the processes of economic, cultural and workplace restructuring are having an increasing effect on our own work as adult educators (see Foley and Morris, 1995).

At a time of global change, most workers, including teachers, are being turned more and more into narrow technicians with 'competences'. Their work is being radically restructured precisely to exclude wider social, political and cultural understandings and engagements. In such a context, the danger is that adult and community educators become simply the deliverers of the prescriptions of politicians and business interests.

Adult learning is now a major area of government policy. The past 15 years have seen more legislation relating to adult education and training than the previous 50. The agenda is clear, set by continuing government rhetoric that Britain needs a highly skilled, flexible workforce to be competitive in the world market. Vocationalism, 'enterprise skills' and accreditation are leaving other aspects of adult learning out in the cold. And research indicates that after nearly 20 years of New Right individualism, the notion of the social purpose of adult education is giving way amongst practitioners to notions of 'widening the market' where students are viewed as consumers and adult education as a commodity (see Benn and Fieldhouse, 1995).

Some practitioners, however, believe that the current social and cultural context offers new possibilities for developing a radical agenda for adult education. Sallie Westwood, for example, maintains that the prevalent emphasis on individualism, in which 'the private is more and more privileged and the public realm of culture and society denuded', actually presents the 'opportunity for [adult education] to become, in part, a space for alternative traditions where other discourses can be maintained and where a diversity of cultures can thrive' (Westwood, 1989). Some adult educators, speaking for the British radical tradition, have called on members of the adult education community to put the politics of resistance and transformation back on the agenda (eg Johnson, 1988; Thompson, 1993). Others try to ensure that adult education's past traditions of engagement with particular social groups and movements should not become part of our 'forgotten memory' (Alexander, 1994). It is that project which defines this article.

I regard adult education as both a cultural and intellectual project. As such − a kind of public dialogue − it has the radically democratic development of knowledge at its heart. This entails the engagement of many excluded and progressive 'publics' in the generation of knowledge. It means foregrounding the question which was so important in the informal education of the women's movement: whose knowledge? And it means seeing adult education's current task primarily in intellectual and cultural terms rather than institutional and organisational terms. This way of seeing adult education − that is, in terms of its critical and creative role within the wider culture − may fit uneasily with current policy priorities. Nevertheless, those of us who have chosen adult education as our field (rather than fallen into it by accident) will probably want to replace a pedagogy in which the concept of 'catching up' is the key idea with a pedagogy through politics in which public debate on matters of concern to citizens is the central purpose. Such a pedagogy points to the future rather than the past. It is about new meanings and knowledge and its emphasis is on the conditions and means through which these can be developed − rather than on simply increasing access to existing knowledge. As David Alexander has commented, it is precisely in allying itself with the development of socially critical and mature cultural understandings and with the grasp and production of 'really useful knowledge' as defined by different social groups and movements (rather than experts) that adult education in Britain has earned its reputation as a democratising force (Alexander, 1994).

The past 20 years have been a period of great uncertainty − even struggle − over the means by which adult education is to be understood, defined and regulated. This is particularly true of women's education. Adult education research in Britain is still stubbornly gender blind – with some notable exceptions (eg Keddie, 1981; Thompson, 1983; McGivney, 1993; Ball, 1992; Aird, 1985; Taking Liberties Collective, 1989). There are few studies of feminist-influenced programmes and few studies of adult education practice carried out from a feminist perspective or informed by feminist ideas and research methodologies. This is probably due to the tendency of educational research to explain educational privilege primarily in class terms. However, the dearth of research is also due to the fact that women working in feminist women's adult education in its heyday in the 1970s and 1980s in programmes designed by feminist women for women have largely failed to document their work. The reasons are understandable. Most of it took place outside formal institutions and in the least well-resourced adult education sector (the Workers' Educational Association (WEA) and local authority and extra-mural provision) and was carried out by part-time tutors with little time or resources to write and theorise about their work.

Yet that period was notable in that it marked a historical moment when a 'space of enunciation', in which women named the world in their own terms, was carved out and when many and varied (feminist-inspired) groups coexisted in productive tension with one another. Towards the end of this period Jane Thompson was to write that women's education/women's studies had made the transition from a precarious to a permanent marginality (Thompson, 1983). Thompson also stressed that women's studies did not arise simply through a rational awareness of sexism in existing bodies of knowledge but was brought into existence by political movements which continue to struggle for legitimacy.

I want to outline some of the main features of this moment as I now see it. I do so for two reasons: first, because of the dearth of research already noted; second, because it offers a model of adult education which emphasises the active creation of new knowledge.

Women's education and really useful knowledge

Women's studies as it developed in the 1970s was a direct consequence of the re-emergence of feminism and the development of the Women's Liberation Movement which was a seedbed of many radical educational activities – study groups, conferences, newsletters, consciousness raising. It developed primarily as a strategy for social change specifically aimed at ending women's oppression. Significantly, whilst in the USA the strongest women's studies networks were developed in higher education, in Britain, to a significant degree, women's studies grew up and acquired its distinctive methods and approaches in adult education (see McNeill, 1987) – that is to say, in the least well resourced, most marginal sector of education and the only one in which women were in the majority. Nell Keddie has described British adult education (as it was then) as a women's education service, studented by women, serviced by women – and run by men (Keddie, 1981).

Adult education, before the sweeping changes of the last 20 years, seemed to many British feminists a fruitful place to carry out the educational work inspired by the Women's Liberation Movement. Many were attracted by its rhetoric of empowerment and by its non-hierarchical ways of organising. Adult education's involvement in social change provided a space for tutors to experiment and develop their work. The moral and political ground occupied by adult education in the 1970s and, to a degree, the early 1980s made it possible to have, and occasionally to win, the argument for resources (see Westwood and Thomas, 1992; O'Rourke and Croft, 1994).

Small groups of feminists exploited the rhetoric of adult education to establish a base for women's studies and for different kinds of women's education from the usual diet of, on the one hand, subjects related to their domestic role and, on the other, 'selective admission to a system of knowledge which is defined, theorised and controlled by men' (Blundell, 1992). This flowering of women's education and women's studies is an example of the growth of new 'epistemological communities', engaged in the creation of new (really useful) knowledges (see Nelson, 1990; 1993). The hybrid term 'women's education/ women's studies', which was often used, signalled a central feature of the development: it was not purely the creation of academic critique. It was diverse, changing and multi-faceted, concerned as much with the environment of educational work – creches, context and timetabling – as with its content and pedagogy.

Adult women's education/women's studies had many of the features of a popular education movement. Influenced by different feminisms, much of it took place in local neighbourhoods. Alliances were built between working class communities and community groups and with the women's health, trades union and peace movements, as well as with the wider women's movement.

Learning through active engagement with groups has been central to feminist pedagogic practice. Through consciousness raising groups, women (ideally) shared understandings and learned both to respect each other's knowledge and to construct their own. They 'made visible what had been rendered invisible' (Luttrell, 1989). Most such groups were fairly general but some focused on specialist areas such as health or science (eg see Brighton Women and Science Group, 1980). Self-help health groups, in particular, produced a kind of knowledge about medical phenomena different from that provided by medical science and its experts – knowledge and skills which drew on women's own experiences and needs (see Bell, 1994).

Women's education as it developed in adult education thus challenged in concrete, practical ways the notion of disembodied knowledge, recognising that knowledge is not neutral but always socially situated. There is no 'God's eye view' – no 'knowledge from nowhere' (Haraway, 1989). By taking an explicitly partisan approach to knowledge, it revalued the place of experience in its generation. It was, in short, a thoroughly political process which self-consciously acknowledged the need for gender politics in adult education and feminist politics in knowledge production (see McNeill, 1987). Questions concerning the relationship between theory and practice were to the fore: who and what is adult education for? and what is really useful knowledge? It was fired by a belief in the possibility of personal and social change. The capacity to engage in self critique, to challenge usually taken for granted ways of feeling and thinking and to locate their source in social organisation and relations was central to the collective sharing and analysis of experience.

Making a difference: women's education in the west of Scotland

The following historical case study of women's adult education is offered in the hope of contributing to our self-understanding as adult educators, not to wallow in the past but to point to the future. In remembering, we come back to the things that matter. Such remembering doesn't stay in the past. It can transform the present.

Throughout the 1980s I was District Secretary of the West of Scotland District of the Workers' Educational Association (WEA). For much of this time there were only two female WEA District Secretaries in the UK (out of a total of 21) and both were in Scotland. My district had an already established tradition of women's education. This stretched back to Jean McCrindle's collaborative work with the Cooperative Movement in the 1960s and her pioneering 'women's studies' classes held in the afternoons for working class women in Lanarkshire. These classes even provided childcare – an aspect of provision which was not enshrined in WEA national policy until some years later.

From the mid-1970s, women's studies courses were mounted by the district in Areas for Priority Treatment (APTs) using money released by the then new Strathclyde Region in line with its social deprivation strategy. They were developed by tutors who were also involved in the women's movement in the west of Scotland at the time. These tutors drew many of their ideas and educational practices from their experiences in campaigning and consciousness raising groups and from the workshop-based conferences which were then a fairly regular feature of feminists' lives.

It was women's education/women's studies, *not* 'education for the disadvantaged', in which they were engaged. It was also a form of women's education which was defined as much in terms of class as gender. Groups focused on themes: the family, welfare, employment and sexuality, for example. Curricula developed out of the women's own lives, making connections with literature, the law and social and historical studies.

In all of this work, personal experience was central. But 'sharing experiences' was not the point or the purpose. Ideally, dialogue – rather than simply discussion – was what mattered. People involved in discussion share knowledge they already have, often in a series of monologues. In contrast, those involved in dialogue help each other examine their experience of the world, develop more complex understandings and, through identifying and clarifying problems and new questions to be asked, they actually create knowledge (see Allman, 1987).

Another important feature of this work in the West of Scotland District was the women's dayschools which were organised to bring women together from different areas. These generated many of the groups with which the district worked for the remainder of the 1970s. 'Awaydays' were started – whole groups of women or members of different groups going to a residential adult education college in the country for day or weekend workshops. Most of these groups met in large housing schemes – in nursery schools, community centres and, later, unemployed workers' centres and 'Family Centres'. From being initially discussion groups, some developed into drama groups or writers' and readers' groups; some provided a stepping stone into other forms of education or into various kinds of community and political action.

By the mid-1980s there was a growth in self-defence classes and in practically focused courses in, for example, women's health and assertiveness training – reflecting the growing trend towards finding private and personal solutions to what were essentially public and political problems. By this time, with a few exceptions, the social change coupled with personal development agenda of this work had given way to personal development goals. Tutors began requesting training in counselling skills. I remember worrying that the educational point of the tutors' work was becoming subordinated to a counselling role and that relationships based on solidarity, trust and friendship were in danger of being replaced by professionalised notions of counselling.

Counselling had indeed become institutionalised in Britain in the 1980s, in health and social services as well as education. This growing faith in counsellors coincided with a waning of belief in politics and social movements as forces for change. Some commentators suggested that it signified a new strategy of social control – a means of achieving discipline through self-discipline (see Foucault, 1979; Fairclough, 1989). And feminism itself fragmented, with 'therapeutic' and 'cultural' feminism taking greater hold. Thatcherism effectively forced the most political forms of British feminism – socialist and radical feminism – underground.

Now, in the late 1990s, there is very little of the radical kind of women's education left and few written testimonies to it exist. Women's studies as a field of academic study is now fairly well entrenched in the academy, but it has tenuous and often incidental links with grassroots feminist politics. The demands of 'professionalism' are powerful for all academics – including feminists. Tensions have developed between women's studies (explicitly feminist, with its distinctive methodology and subject areas) and women's education, masking the latter's feminist antecedents and increasingly concentrating on assertiveness training, access, new opportunities and vocational preparation courses (see O'Rourke and Croft, 1994). The two strands which used to coexist in adult education – women's studies and women's education – provided feminist scholarship more generally with a dynamic intellectual community which was not primarily academic but was constituted by a much wider educational, cultural and political project. Crucially, this was defined to a significant degree by pressures 'from below' rather than by educational priorities set 'from above'.

What has been referred to as the 'epistemological debate' has now been underway within academic feminism for the last decade and a half (eg see Rose, 1994; Harding, 1991). A basic aim of that debate is to contribute to the expansion of democracy in the production of knowledge and its basic premise is that knowledge should be useful to those who produce it. But that dialogue about knowledge has so far been conducted at a highly abstract level amongst a small group of feminist academics and scholars. And yet it is implicit in such dialogue that there will be little progress towards the goal of 'really useful knowledge' until abstract debates about knowledge are brought down to earth and practical spaces opened up for democratic knowledge making.

> If we wish to empower diverse voices, we would do better . . . to shift strategy . . . to the messier, more slippery, practical struggle to create institutions and communities that will not permit some groups of people to make determinations about reality for all. (Bordo, 1990)

It is precisely such a practical space for the democratic development of knowledge which was opened up by women's education/women's studies as this developed within British adult education during the 1970s and early 1980s. Central to it was an emphasis on women as agents and makers of knowledge and the insight that *what* we learn is influenced by *how* we learn. Perhaps even more important was its insistence that if we are to develop more inclusive practices of knowledge making, we need to abandon once and for all the prevalent individualistic and heroic notion (and myth) of knowledge development which is enshrined in our education system. We need to acknowledge the part played by social processes and collective change in the development of knowledge – as well as by non-rational factors.

Redefining enlightenment: the education of desire

Adult education and feminism are enlightenment projects. Both rest on the belief that people can develop better understandings and knowledge of themselves and their social world and that they can act to transform them. Both recognise that knowledge and 'reason' are human practices, rooted in the judgements of fallible inquirers. As such, they are subject to contestation. Donna

Haraway maintains that struggles over what counts as rational accounts of the world are struggles over how to 'see' (Haraway, 1989; 1991). Women's education/women's studies and its new constituencies constitute just such a struggle and challenge within adult education, promoting learning which does not privilege expert academic knowledge or prize intellectual over emotional understanding.

Tom Steele argues that adult education has traditionally invoked a mode of thinking which is imaginative and forward-looking (even utopian) as well as critical. It has embraced a collective project which concerns, crucially, what William Morris called the 'education of desire' (Steele, 1995). The same is true of feminism. Through imagining how things might be otherwise, adult education and feminism can stimulate both the desire and the will for a different way of living. From this vantage point we can begin to seek transformation of the present. I believe that feminism and adult education are now more vital than ever in identifying and opening up spaces where such challenging and imaginative thinking (and desiring) can be formed – where, that is, alternative visions for democratic social change can take root and grow.

In looking back on a particular period of women's adult education, the point is not to urge a return to some past golden age of adult education. It never existed. It has long been recognised that old traditions of radical adult education, rooted in a male working class and based on the impulse to enlighten according to the radical educator's definitions of reality, simply will not do. It has to be recognised, too, that there are several women's movements with diverse aims and varying power. These movements, though virtually ignored by the media (and much adult education), have mobilised way beyond the women's liberation groups of the 1970s. In so doing, they have created new national and international networks which have become a focus for much new learning. Many women, particularly the poorest amongst them, faced with new and extreme circumstances, have had to learn fast and intensively. Some women's groups and networks have grown out of a basic need to survive in the face of 'flexibility' and the dominance of market forces. Their starting point may not have been a desire to be women in new and challenging ways (a key impulse of the women's movement of the 1970s) and yet they have often found themselves doing and thinking the unimaginable. This is true for many community-based women's groups in Scotland. It is also true in Mexico, Peru, Brazil, Nicaragua and South Africa where many thousands of women, unable to care for their families, have mobilised around prices, basic social needs, schools and sanitation. In so doing, they have redefined the 'political' and created a new space in the public sphere of politics (see Rowbotham, 1997).

Where is adult education in all this? There is clearly plenty of space for 'popular education' if what we mean by this is starting from the problems, experiences and social position of excluded majorities, working from their lived experiences to develop the new meanings and new knowledge which are needed to deal creatively and critically with their lives. That space which radical adult education traditionally inhabited, where the democratic control and development of knowledge are pursued as an ideal of citizenship, may be shrinking. But new opportunities may also be developing.

Adult education and the global production of knowledge

Michael Gibbons and colleagues have argued that the production of knowledge is now characterised by greater transdisciplinarity. It is produced in a wider arena, including government think tanks and commercial organisations, and is critically dependent on global communications and electronics. This encourages scientists, amongst others, to be less interested in solving basic problems and more interested in the market. This sort of knowledge production is more widely distributed and open ended – but, left to the market, it is also likely to enhance global inequalities (Gibbons *et al*, 1994). Working class women, for instance, are unlikely to be participating in this emerging nexus of knowledge creation linked to markets – except as nimble fingers for the manufacture of electronics components in the sweatshop factories of Asia.

Adult education has been the focus of a great deal of government attention in recent years precisely because it can be a means of promoting conformity and flexibility in a rapidly changing world. But, as the kind of women's education I have described indicates, adult education can also be a means by which people deal creatively and critically with the world in order to change it (see Mayo, 1995). It must be stressed that the forgetting of such traditions and practices amongst those engaged in the education of adults has gone hand in glove with a professionalised ideology of individualism. This unreflective 'common sense' amongst adult educators has helped pave the way for what is now occurring in adult and continuing education – its thorough overhaul and shift in power and control in favour of employers and business interests and, in the case of my own sphere of work in university adult education, its absorption into the mainstream (see Thompson, 1993; Barr, 1996).

Nevertheless, present social and cultural conditions may indeed favour a return of the old, creative space adult education once inhabited. As an intellectual and cultural project which has always recognised the social interests involved in the development of knowledge, adult education could be at the cutting edge of the far reaching intellectual change which some commentators are heralding (see Gibbons *et al*, 1994; Scott, 1995).

Such changes in knowledge production as are purportedly taking place – for example, its wider distribution, open-endedness and transdisciplinarity – in some ways fit in very well indeed with adult education. Adult education's radical practices and engagements with marginalised groups and progressive social movements recognise the dependence of knowledge on the social conditions of its production and it has never overly respected knowledge/discipline boundaries. Its cultural territory could, indeed, be extended in the present historical circumstances. But if it is to do this, it will have to struggle with the dominant instrumental values which are oiling the wheels of the new forms of knowledge production and which, left to the market, will enhance rather than diminish global inequalities.

A personal journey

When I studied philosophy I saw it as dealing with universal questions. Minds met other minds on equal terms, and the messy, fleshy concerns of everyday life could be transcended. I now regard such a disembodied notion of philosophy as nonsense, and I also feel an increasing desire to bring the intellectual and personal aspects of my life more closely together. I retain my attachment to philosophy, but I do not believe that I am simply a dutiful daughter who has learned her lessons well.

What I now regard as an important legacy from my experience of the women's movement and of the educational work which arose out of it was learning a new notion of 'rigour'. The kind of rigour which infused women's education/women's studies was the opposite of the safe, self-censoring – and always ready to censor – puritanism I learned from my philosophy training. According to this, the right to speak seemed to require the assertion of oneself as a kind of super-consciousness with an overview of everything that had been thought or written up until now. In the sort of women's education I have described, on the contrary, everything is brought in (life stories, jokes, dreams, improvisations, free writing, group poems) to undo the often prohibitive learning which many girls and women – as well as many men – have acquired from their past educational experiences. But this is a recent acknowledgement. For much of my life I have been wedded to a narrow notion of 'theory' and accorded far too much respect, I now believe, to the theory produced by academics, including academic feminists. I have overprivileged academic and abstract knowledge and undervalued knowledge born of experience and emotional understanding. The trouble with the knowledge produced by academics is that it is likely to denigrate – deem as not-knowledge – the other knowledges of students. In an academic context 'expert knowledge' always wins.

For many of us, myself included, the hardest thing of all is to find a voice – not the voice of super-conscious self-assertion speaking from a position of overview (the voice of my philosophy undergraduate days, the voice from nowhere) but a voice which 'in summoning the resources of the place we come from can speak with eloquence of and for that place' (Kuhn, 1995). I now see the task and promise of adult education as lying precisely in helping identify and open up spaces where such a summoning up of resources can take place – where, that is, what has been called 'responsible knowledge' can take root and grow (Haraway, 1989). My continuing choice of adult education as my field is fuelled by the will and desire to transcend the divide and heal the breach between different ways of knowing and forms of knowledge which are usually separated off in our culture: knowledge 'from above' and knowledge 'from below', expert and lay knowledge, academic and everyday knowledge, cerebral and emotional understanding.

I have learned from adult educators like Paulo Freire that education can only be liberating if knowledge is viewed as a field in which everyone has a part to play in its development. And I have learned from the women's movement and from my own teaching and research that striving for knowledge contained in books is of limited value if it is not connected to people's aspirations for knowledge about how to live in the world. It was that aspiration which took me into philosophy in the first place. Yet what I learned there was how to become smart in book knowledge, to indulge in philosophy's overestimation of the power of thinking and its centrality to human life – and to forget my original goal.

I have also moved from a belief in the potentially transformative power of adult education to a belief in a more modest project. This involves enabling the articulation of 'views from below' – not because they offer truer, more accurate accounts of the world but because they increase the possibilities of knowledge, especially knowledge which is useful to those who generate it. As Lynn Nelson puts it:

> Knowledge will never be complete but the experiences and stories that have in their claim to universality excluded and mystified other experiences and knowledges . . . in reflecting the experiences of privileged men . . . have been partial in terms of what it was or is possible to know in given historical, social and cultural contexts. (Nelson, 1993)

To borrow an expression from bell hooks, adult education – with all its limitations – remains a 'location of possibility' where 'we [can] collectively imagine ways to move beyond boundaries, to transgress. This is education as the practice of freedom' (hooks, 1994).

References

Aird, E (1985) 'A different perspective: change in women's education' in Women's Educational Advisory Committe *Breaking Our Silence*, London, WEA.

Alexander, D (1994) 'The education of adults in Scotland: democracy and curriculum', *Studies in the Education of Adults*, 26 (1), pp 31–49.

Allman, P (1987) 'Paulo Freire's educational approach' in Allen, G, Bastiani, J, Martin, I and Richards, K (eds), *Community Education: An Agenda for Educational Reform*, Milton Keynes, Open University Press, pp 214–37.

Ball, W (1992) 'Critical social research, adult education and anti-racist feminist praxis', *Studies in the Education of Adults*, 24 (1), pp 1–25.

Barr, J (1996) 'The SHEFC Review of Continuing Education', *International Journal of Lifelong Education*, 15 (6), pp 471–79.

Bell, S (1994) 'Translating science to people', *Women's Studies International Forum*, 17 (1), pp 9–18.

Benn, R and Fieldhouse, R (1995) 'Notions of community for university continuing education', *UACE Pre-Conference Papers 1995*.

Blundell, S (1992) 'Gender and the curriculum in adult education', *International Journal of Lifelong Education*, 11 (3), pp 199–216.

Bordo, S (1990) 'Feminism, postmodernism and gender scepticism' in Nicholson, L (ed), *Feminism and Postmodernism*, New York and London, Routledge, pp 133–156.

Brighton Women and Science Group (1980) *Alice Through the Microscope: The Power of Science over Women's Lives*, London, Virago.

Fairclough, J (1989) *Language and Power*, London, Longman.

Foley, G and Morris, R (1995) 'The history and political economy of Australian adult education' in Foley, G (ed), *Understanding Adult Education and Training*, St Leonards, New South Wales, Allen and Unwin, pp 108–120.

Foucault, M (1979) *Discipline and Punish*, New York, Vintage Books.

Gibbons, M, Limoges, C, Nowotny, H, Schwartzman, S, Scott, P and Trow, M (1994) *The New Production of Knowledge: The Dynamics of Science and Research in Contemporary Societies*, London, Sage.

Haraway, D (1989) *Primate Visions*, London, Routledge.

Haraway, D (1991) 'The contest for primate nature: daughters of manthehunter in the field' in Haraway D, *Simians, Cyborgs and Women*, London, Free Association Books, pp 81–108.

Harding, S (1991) *Whose Science? Whose Knowledge?*, Milton Keynes, Open University Press.

hooks, b (1994) *Teaching to Transgress: Education as the Practice of Freedom*, New York, Routledge.

Johnson, R (1988) 'Really useful knowledge, 1790–1850' in Lovett T (ed), *Radical Approaches to Adult Education,* London, Routledge, pp 3–34.

Keddie, N (1981) *Adult Education: A Women's Service*, Unpublished.

Kuhn, A (1995) *Family Secrets: Acts of Memory and Imagination*, London, Verso.

Luttrell, W (1989) 'Working class women's ways of knowing: effects of gender, race and class', *Sociology of Education,* 62, pp 33–46.

Mayo, M (1995) 'Adult education for change in the nineties and beyond: towards a critical review of the changing context' in Mayo, M and Thompson, J (eds), *Adult Learning, Critical Intelligence and Social Change*, Leicester, NIACE, pp 5–17.

McGivney, V (1993) *Women, Education and Training*, Leicester, NIACE.

McNeill, M (ed) (1987) *Gender and Expertise*, London, Free Association Books.

Nelson, L (1990) *Who Knows: From Quine to Feminist Empiricism*, Philadelphia, Temple University Press.

Nelson, L (1993) 'Epistemological communities' in Alcoff, L and Potter, E (eds), *Feminist Epistemologies*, London, Routledge, pp 121–159.

O'Rourke, R and Croft, A (1994) 'Through the wall: adult education, social change and new university subjects', *1994 SCUTREA Conference Papers*, pp 87–90.

Rose, H (1994) *Love, Power and Knowledge: Towards a Feminist Transformation of the Sciences*, Cambridge, Polity.

Rowbotham, S (1997) 'Real women of the real world', *Guardian*, 19 April.

Scott, P (1995) *The Meanings of Mass Higher Education*, Milton Keynes, SRHE/Open University Press.

Steele, T (1995) 'Cultural struggle or identity politics: can there still be a "popular" education?' in Mayo, M and Thompson, J (eds), *Adult Learning, Critical Intelligence and Social Change*, Leicester, NIACE, pp 47–57.

Taking Liberties Collective (1989) *Learning the Hard Way: Women's Oppression in Men's Education*, Basingstoke, MacMillan.

Thompson, J (1983) *Learning Liberation: Women's Responses to Men's Education*, London, Croom Helm.

Thompson, J (1993) 'Learning, liberation and maturity: an open letter to whoever's left', *Adults Learning*, 4 (9), p 44.

Westwood, S (1989) 'Enterprise culture and the restructuring of British adult education: an exploration', *Adults Learning*, 1 (1), pp 8–9.

Westwood, S and Thomas, J (eds) (1992) *The Politics of Adult Education*, Leicester, NIACE.

6 The significance of the Scottish generalist tradition

Murdo Macdonald

This chapter draws upon the generalist tradition characterised in the work of the contemporary Scottish philosopher George Davie and exemplified in the work of the polymath Patrick Geddes. This tradition is driven by the conviction that the pursuit (and reification) of specialised, expert knowledge without recognition of the importance of the context and connections within which specialisation takes place is an educational and social disaster. The Scottish generalist tradition can be of great value not only to an understanding of history, but also to the general conduct of contemporary civic life at all levels. The politics of knowledge must be understood in order to address the current context in which the pressure towards increasingly specialist forms of knowledge leads to fragmentation and, ultimately, social ignorance and disintegration. Generalism is, in short, a key guarantor of democracy.

The generalist tradition

We live in a culture in which both knowledge and society itself are fragmented. Most of us are – or will be, or have been – specialists in one field or another, and specialism is clearly of great value. But we all know that on its own, specialism is not enough. The social anthropologist Gregory Bateson said, 'Break the pattern which connects the items of learning and you necessarily destroy all quality' (Bateson, 1979). Bateson was responding to the compartmentalisation of knowledge which is reflected in the structure of society and which is even more advanced today than it was when he was writing in the 1970s.

It is interesting to reflect on the compartments of knowledge. Even when we are trying to break out of them as when we talk about networking or interdisciplinarity, we find ourselves doing so in specialised networking focus groups and specialist interdisciplinary seminars. But there is another way to approach knowledge and society and it is a way which is inherently more critical than the specialist approach. It is also an approach which was taken for granted at one time in Scotland and is still strong here. This approach is the 'generalist tradition' of this chapter's title.

In a recent interview, the Italian architect Giancarlo De Carlo said:

Here in Scotland, in Scottish culture, from what I have read and I have studied, I think you have one educational pillar which is very important. It is what you call generalism. I think this is peculiar to Scotland, this idea that you have to have a general view of something in order to understand it. Specialisation, specialists, I consider in a way to be an accident of our present time. (quoted in Wilson, 1994)

Such comprehensive vision has an increasingly obvious relevance today as we face problems of pollution and ecological depredation on the one hand and educational impoverishment on the other. Both these problems stem from a crudely industrialised culture which 'specialises' in production, neglecting not only environmental consequences, but also the broad educational needs of those who work in that society. Instead of enabling the development of a broad appreciation of the context within which we live and work, only narrow knowledge, which can be seen to have immediate and usually short-term relevance to this or that, is valued.

George Davie: the democratic intellect

An exploration of the generalist tradition is that of George Davie. In the entry devoted to him in *Chambers Scottish Biographical Dictionary*, Davie is described as a pioneer in studies of the Scottish Enlightenment. This is an apt description and his two volumes of essays on the Scottish Enlightenment (1991) give emphasis to it. Yet he is most widely known for his seminal work, *The Democratic Intellect: Scotland and her Universities in the Nineteenth Century* (1961), which began the process of linking the intellectual traditions of the Scottish Enlightenment to those of today. Here, and in its sequel, *The Crisis of the Democratic Intellect: The Problem of Generalism and Specialisation in Twentieth Century Scotland* (1986), he demonstrated with skill, humour and historical grasp, the need to reassess and to value anew the generalist tradition of education in Scotland, a tradition in which philosophy played a key role. His work has provided a philosophical underpinning for the widely recognised need for interdisciplinarity both in our institutions of learning and in wider educational practice. It has also been recognised as a significant commentary on the relationship between the expert and the wider community. It has become a reference point for the discussion of cultural thought in Scotland, straddling, as it does, the fields of education, history, philosophy and politics.

Since the publication of *The Democratic Intellect* in 1961 Davie has been recognised as a key educational theorist whose exposition of the Scots generalist tradition in education can be of great value not only to an understanding of history but also to contemporary practice, at all levels. His explorations have drawn attention to the civic and educational power generated when, as a matter of course, one area of thought or expertise or activity is illuminated by another and vice versa. Davie's work has attracted widespread interest. Illustrative of this are the comments of the novelist James Kelman, who writes with reference to Davie's discussion of the views of the eighteenth century cultural activist Andrew Fletcher of Saltoun:

He argued that an educational system devoted to the production of specialists would result in a situation where none of the educated community would be fit to govern the nation, given that being fit to govern the national entails the capacity for decision making in general contexts. This capacity involves the power of judgement and critical evaluation; it is developed more potently by the ability to see beyond the limits of your own discipline. If the educational system is to thrust groups of people into separate compartments then none will be equipped to take the wide view necessary. No longer does it become possible for the poet to discuss methodology with sculptors and electricians. Reasoning devices like mathematics, logic and intuition stagnate, this being abetted by the decline in subjects thought to be impractical, eg philosophy, the classics, the study of languages and other cultures, those very subjects which encourage a general approach to the world. In this scenario actual knowledge itself becomes at a premium, cut off from those who are not 'specialising'. And gradually the majority of men and women and children become divorced from those areas where 'experts' reign supreme. What remains is not only repugnant but disastrous . . . At the root of the matter is the segmentation of knowledge, the push for individual disciplines to keep themselves to themselves. (Kelman, 1990)

A key notion to take from Davie's ideas is that the expert's knowledge is inherently incomplete. In short, the narrow focus of the specialised expert creates blindspots. The point about a generalist approach such as democratic intellectualism is not that non-experts have a right to scrutinise the work of the expert, but that the work of the expert is only complete in the light of such scrutiny. It is not, therefore, an attack on experts. Rather the reverse, for the expert is valued as part of a community but it is recognised that his or her value as an expert can only be fully realised if it is accepted that blindspots within that expert view are an inevitability. Thus, others in the community, by virtue of their lack of expertise (which gives them a different perspective from that of the expert), have a responsibility to comment on these blindspots. By the same token, such comments may reveal blindspots in the view of the commentator, which are again open to the scrutiny of the community (of which, of course, all experts are themselves part).

Conveniently enough, the events surrounding James Kelman's winning of the prestigious Booker Prize for literature in 1994 provide interesting examples of the blindspots of experts and the desirability of a generalist perspective. These blindspots were particularly impressive among London critics. Indeed, there was a tendency even in the friendly media to stereotype Kelman as a kind of exotic Glaswegian hard man who had spontaneously started writing novels. This stereotype, incidentally, takes us right back to the image of Robert Burns as a 'heav'n-taught ploughman' – but that's another story, although not entirely because Burns (like Kelman) is himself part of this generalist tradition. The point here is that Kelman's work as a novelist is just one expression of a generalist philosophical commitment which was never even mentioned by these critics. The reason perhaps was that in our modern specialised world if you are a novelist no one is prepared to accept that you can be anything else.

Scotland has a long history of people refusing to observe these boundaries, particularly with respect to what one might call the everyday right to philosophy which Kelman takes to himself. In the prologue to *The Crisis of the Democratic Intellect*, George Davie comments:

> It used to be noted that visitors to Scotland without a taste for metaphysics were liable to be nonplussed by the questions publicly debated, because of the tendency for arguments about mundane matters to develop into arguments about first principles and for ordinary problems about material things to turn into rarefied problems about the relation of matter to mind. Commenting caustically on this situation, Dr Johnson remarked that Scotland was the only country in the civilised world in which the advance of learning had not been accompanied by a corresponding advance in the material quality of life, while William Cobbett, putting the same thing from a rather different point of view, spoke of the Scots as having the absurd idea that the way to improve the condition of the working man was not to give him 'bacon' with a small 'b' but 'Bacon' with a big 'b'. The facts, as thus stated, were not disputed by the Scots, many of whom, indeed, had a certain sympathy with these criticisms; but generation after generation, a core of Scottish orthodoxy composed of persons of the most varied status and points of view, nevertheless held to the opinion that their country had got its priorities right. The opposing course was considered by them to be a distortion of human nature which, though perhaps making things easier in the short turn, would be in the long run disastrous to the quality of life. (Davie, 1986)

One thing that is being said here is that the act of questioning is fundamental to the quality of life. It is in this spirit that, in introducing George Davie's *The Scottish Enlightenment and Other Essays (1991)*, James Kelman formulates the following set of questions:

> Do people have the fundamental right to freedom? By what authority does one person, or group of people, control another? Is there a case for assuming responsibility over the social and spiritual life of other adults? When does 'teaching' become colonisation? Can one culture ever be 'better' than another? Is the attempt to deny your right to exploit me 'unconstitutional'?

He goes on:

> Davie assembles a coherent picture of a continuous intellectual movement
> in Scotland, a genuinely democratic movement. But the ultimate chal-
> lenge of his work seems to me to lie in the context he sets this picture,
> which is his theory of knowledge . . .

Patrick Geddes: place, folk and work

Another thinker of relevance here is Patrick Geddes who grew up in a
nineteenth century Scottish culture which took generalist views for granted as
its starting point. Geddes was a polymath who distinguished himself both within
Scotland and internationally as an ecologist, a botanist, a theorist of cities, an
advocate of the arts, a community activist, a publisher, a town planner and an
educator. He was born in Ballater in Aberdeenshire in 1854 and spent most of
his childhood in Perth. For most of his career the Outlook Tower in Edinburgh
was his base for international activities, particularly in India and Palestine. He
died at the Scots College he had founded in Montpellier in the South of
France in April 1932. These 77 years saw a life of extraordinary vitality, variety
and interest. On the one hand – as a scientist – he studied evolution with TH
Huxley in London where he came into direct contact with Darwin. Later in
that city he was one of the founders of the Sociological Society. On the other
hand – as a cultural activist – in Edinburgh he was a moving force behind the
Celtic Revival in literature and the visual arts making common cause with,
among others, the Glasgow architect Charles Rennie Mackintosh and the great
collector and editor of Gaelic texts, Alexander Carmichael. As a student, both
from a scientific and a cultural perspective, he was drawn to France where he
studied biology in Paris and Brittany and absorbed the sociology of Comte and
the anarchist politics of French geographers such as his friend Elisee Reclus.
He embarked on all this in the spirit of the Auld Alliance between France and
Scotland which had, as Geddes was well aware, remained an active political and
cultural force from the time of Joan of Arc to the Jacobite wars.

Geddes's relationship with mainstream academia was always uneasy and he
never took a formal degree. Nevertheless, in 1888 he was appointed Professor
of Botany at University College, Dundee. Thirty years later he became the first
Professor of Civics and Sociology at the University of Bombay, a university
which he had himself helped to found. But he is often thought of today
primarily as a pioneer of community sensitive town planning and as a theorist
of the relations between city and region. Indeed, it has been the planners who
have kept his name alive within academic teaching (Hall, 1988) for Geddes
carried out some of the first studies on the conservation and regeneration of
urban environments in, among other places, the Old Town of Edinburgh,
Jerusalem, Dunfermline and Dublin, as well as developing an evolutionary

analysis of the growth and decline of cities which was adopted (and adapted) by his disciple Lewis Mumford in *The Culture of Cities* (1938).

In 1897, as a direct practical response to the Ottoman Empire's persecution of Armenians, Geddes and his wife Anna undertook short-term but effective planning and relief work in Cyprus (see Boardman, 1978). This involvement in the cultures of the Middle East was to gain its fullest expression in his proposals in the 1920s for a Hebrew University in Jerusalem. From 1914 onwards a series of major planning studies was carried out in India, of which the architectural historian Norma Evenson has written:

> Unlike the British engineers who had directed most municipal public works in India, Geddes had a sympathetic appreciation for Indian townscape. His common sense approach was . . . difficult to fault. He approached his investigations with receptivity to the local scene, seeking to understand the nature of the Indian settlement and making no attempt to impose a foreign conception of urban environment. (Evenson, 1988; see also Tyrwhitt, 1947)

This approach can be seen in illustrations which show the Geddes plan for the development of an area of an Indian town versus the municipal plan. The municipal plan is based on imposing an alien grid of streets. Geddes's plan is sensitive to the local building pattern and is centred on the planting of a tree, the creation of a community space. In one of his Indian reports he summed up his philosophy of planning as follows:

> Town planning is not mere place planning, nor even work planning. If it is to be successful it must be folk planning. This means that its task is not to coerce people into new places against their association, wishes and interest – as we find bad schemes trying to do. Instead its task is to find the right places for each sort of people; places where they will really flourish. To give people in fact the same care that we give when transplanting flowers, instead of harsh evictions and arbitrary instructions to 'move on', delivered in the manner of officious amateur policemen. (quoted in Tyrwhitt, 1947)

This statement is all the more remarkable to the reader of today when one reflects that it was first published in 1915, before the urban disasters of the twentieth century to which it seems to refer had happened. It is worth noting here the echo of John Stuart Blackie's comment with respect to the Highland Clearances:

> I lay it down as an axiom of social science, that all changes affecting the welfare and comfort of large classes of men ought to be made not hastily and in the way of sharp revolution, but gradually, moderately and with great tenderness; and this especially when the sufferers by any such social changes are not to be the few rich and prosperous, but the many poor and industrious of the land. (Blackie, 1882)

There is a prophetic quality to much of Geddes's writing whether on planning or ecology. However, the reality is not that Geddes saw the future, but that he understood the present. And the problems he saw in his present of planning, of ecology, of education, of loss of culture and skills, are now so prominent that they cannot be avoided by any of us.

Thus one doesn't have to look far for examples of Geddes's generalism. Everywhere in his work one area of thought brings illumination to another and vice versa. One can cite his interdisciplinary systematisation of knowledge in the Outlook Tower. Or again, one can note his firm insistence on understanding history *and* myth, ecology *and* town planning, art *and* science, all in the context of both local community and international links. Despite his pragmatic approach to education, which was exemplified by his pioneering interdisciplinary Summer Meetings in Edinburgh, his interest in a wide range of subjects is often interpreted as a maverick tendency or a proneness to dilettantism. This is to misunderstand the generalist cultural context to which I have drawn attention. George Davie's friend Hugh MacDiarmid endorsed Geddes's generalism as follows:

> . . . his constant effort was to help people to think for themselves and to think round the whole circle, not in scraps and bits. He knew that watertight compartments are useful only to a sinking ship and traversed all the boundaries of separate subjects. (MacDiarmid, 1966)

In an attempt to reclaim generalism for the modern period, Geddes tried to define sociology as *the* generalist discipline – able to give context to all others. He failed in this (or, perhaps, sociology failed in this), but it can be noted that this contextualising role is precisely the role that philosophy occupied in the Scottish university curriculum in the nineteenth century. Thus, this notion of one discipline providing a general context was inherent to the educational culture in which Geddes was brought up.

But in twentieth century Britain generalism has become a kind of thought crime. Geddes the generalist has thus dropped out of historical sight and so well has this particular thought crime been policed that when CP Snow wrote his 'The two cultures' article for the *New Statesman and Nation* in 1956 it generated a great deal of interest because the points he was making seemed so new. Yet all he did in this article was to draw attention to the educational split between the arts and the sciences. Snow was only beginning to scratch the surface of the epistemological and social problems that generalism addresses. These have been systematically obscured by overspecialisation in all fields.

Thus, Geddes must be seen as an ecologist of the mind, to use another of Gregory Bateson's phrases, as well as an ecologist of the planet (Bateson, 1973) and the complement to Geddes the environmentalist can be seen to be Geddes the educator. Like Bateson, throughout his life Geddes resisted the fragmentation of knowledge consequent on misguided notions of specialisation in education. But – as in the case of George Davie – this was not, of course, a denial of the value of specialisation; rather it was an assertion that specialisation without the recognition of the importance of the context within which that specialisation takes place, was a social disaster.

Conclusion: the challenge of democratic intellectualism

I have drawn attention to the importance of generalism both as a societal and an epistemological process. I have also drawn attention to a philosophically developed description of generalism: democratic intellectualism. This is a way of seeing different areas of knowledge and activities in relation to one another, the key to the process being the recognition that any approach will have its blindspots and, in relation to the whole, will need the illumination of those blindspots that other areas of knowledge may provide. The question for educators (and, indeed, for everyone else) is how to create a set of activities for the generation and communication of knowledge which can facilitate such mutual illumination of blindspots, whether within an individual, a group or an entire culture.

To end with another quote from Giancarlo de Carlo, 'I think we should go back to the idea of the general view and in Scotland you have a good grounding in this approach . . .' (quoted in Wilson, 1994). That is reassuring to know, but the pressing practical question is, how can one make use of this grounding in generalism when the ultimate tools of specialist fragmentation – local government reorganisation, short-term contracts and a few little dods of Lottery funding – are, in so many areas of our lives at present, supposed to be adequate to the needs of society?

References

Bateson, G (1973) *Steps to an Ecology of Mind*, London, Paladin.
Bateson, G (1979) *Mind and Nature: A Necessary Unity*, London, Wildwood House.
Blackie, J S (1882) *Altavona: Fact and Fiction from my Life in the Highlands*, Edinburgh, David Douglas.
Boardman, P (1978) *The Worlds of Patrick Geddes*, London, Routledge.
Davie, G (1961) *The Democratic Intellect: Scotland and her Universities in the Nineteenth Century,* Edinburgh, Edinburgh University Press.
Davie, G (1986) *The Crisis of the Democratic Intellect: The Problem of Generalism and Specialisation in Twentieth Century Scotland,* Edinburgh, Polygon.
Davie, G (1991) *The Scottish Enlightenment and other Essays,* Edinburgh, Polygon.
Evenson, N (1988) *The Indian Metropolis,* Newhaven, Yale University Press.
Hall, P (1988) *Cities of Tomorrow,* Oxford, Blackwell.

Kelman, J (1990) 'A reading from Noam Chomsky and the Scottish tradition in the philosophy of common sense', *Edinburgh Review*, 84, pp 46–76.

MacDiarmid, H (1966) *The Company I've Kept,* London, Hutchinson.

Mumford, L (1938) *The Culture of Cities*, London, Secker and Warburg.

Snow, C P (1956) 'The two cultures', *New Statesman and Nation,* 6 October.

Tyrwhitt, J (ed) (1947) *Patrick Geddes in India*, London, Lund Humphries.

Wilson, P (1994) Interview in Newsletter No 1, *Edinburgh City of Architecture Bid.*

Section 2:

Historical perspectives

7 With 'real feeling and just sense': rehistoricising popular education

Tom Steele

Popular education is a construct which emerges out of particular historical, cultural and material conditions. In this sense, as the history of popular education movements in Western Europe demonstrates, it is always contextual and contingent – taking distinctive forms in different times and places. What is more, it can be a deeply ambivalent formation: managed from above as an instrument of control or forged from below as an agent of emancipation. Nevertheless, the dynamics of progressive social movements are continuously recreating civil life and, in this process, popular education is 'constantly reinventing itself'. As part of the historic 'project of equity and social justice', there is now as much need as ever for a popular education movement – as well as a unique opportunity to reconstitute it within the struggle for democratic renewal in Scotland today.

Introduction

Modern education is an intervention into what we understand from our everyday life-world and customary experience – often experienced as an irruption, sundering and dislocation. This fracturing may be even more intense when it arrives in peasant communities in the hands of the impassioned popular educator brandishing the torch of enlightenment and, all too frequently, the message in a bottle. We professionals assume that education is a good thing – it is after all how we make our living – and it has been a good thing for us. For those of us from working class families it has fundamentally changed our lives – it is our ladder of opportunity into the middle class. Through it we have ridden the rainbow of culture and taste denied to our families. Our bookshelves sigh with the weight of knowledge, but we pursue endlessly a wisdom that each new book seems to promise yet deny us. Somehow the wisdom we seek seems to be back there, behind or beyond us, locked up in a different kind of life. We have forsaken life for the book and we imagine a rich life lived by simple people for whom education is a mere distraction from the contemplation of deeper truths. WB Yeats caught this mood in his poem *The Fisherman* where he imagined writing a poem for this 'wise and simple man' contrasting him with the urban sophisticates with whom the poet constantly came in contact. In the context of the 'beating down of the wise/And great Art beaten down' he would imagine:

A man who does not exist,
A man who is but a dream;
And cried, 'Before I am old
I shall have written him one
Poem maybe as cold
And passionate as the dawn'.

This is of course a modern romance, the Romance of Modernism, the paradox at the heart of the modernist project, but it would be foolish to dismiss it as mere romanticism because it is a valuation of that otherness that lies beyond the pale of the expert. For adult educators the recognition that 'customary knowledge', as EP Thompson put it, has to be valued and carefully negotiated in any formal learning situation, should be uppermost. Thompson's appraisal of the Romantic tradition has always been explicit as was revealed in his book, *Witness against the Beast: Blake and the Moral Law* (Thompson, 1993), a study of the poet William Blake. Thompson, who spent 17 years as an adult educator in the Department of Extra Mural Studies in the University of Leeds, was never convinced that everything that passed in the name of education was an undisputed good. He developed his reasons at the height of the student revolt in 1968, when he returned to Leeds from his new post at Warwick 'Business University' to give the Albert Mansbridge Memorial Lecture in his former department, saying that 'in most areas throughout the nineteenth century, the educated universe was so saturated with class responses that it demanded an active rejection and disposal of the language, customs and traditions of received popular culture'. As a consequence, he continued, education was for many indistinguishable from social control:

> and this entailed too often, a repression or denial of the validity of the life experience of the pupils as expressed in uncouth dialect or in traditional cultural forms. Hence education and received experience were at odds with each other. And those working men who by their own efforts broke into the educated culture found themselves at once in the same place of tension, in which education brought with it the danger of the rejection of their fellows and self-distrust. (Thompson, 1968a)

Thompson's *The Making of the English Working Class* was, in large part, the culmination of exploring this tension with his adult students in the West Riding of Yorkshire and dedicated to two of those class members. In his Mansbridge lecture he revealed something of his motivation and method by a longish quotation from Book XII of Wordsworth's *The Prelude*:

When I began to enquire,
To watch and question those I met, and held
Familiar talk with them, the lonely roads
Were Schools to me in which I daily read

With most delight the passions of mankind,
There saw into the depths of human souls,
Souls that appear to have no depths at all
To vulgar eyes. And now convinced at heart
How little that to which alone we give
The name of education hath to do
With real feeling and just sense . . .

The idea that 'real feeling and just sense' should be immanent properties of uneducated folk would be scornfully dismissed by contemporary postmodernist intellectuals, who would refer Thompson to the implications of his own phrase about the ideologically saturated educational universe. Yet another side of postmodernism would value his attention to the 'otherness' of this culture. Lift any postmodern stone and the unreconstructed modernist crawls out.

If the idea of 'education' can be seen to contain a nostalgia for its absent Other, what about its partner in the formula, 'popular education'? The 'popular' is one of the slipperiest of terms and not at all self-evident. As Stuart Hall notes, 'the people' is very much a construction rather than a given.

> The people are not always back there, where they have always been, their culture untouched, their liberties and their instincts intact . . . as if, if only we can 'discover' them and bring them back on stage, they will always stand up in the right, appointed place and be counted'. (Hall, 1981)

Mrs Thatcher, Hall reminds us, relied on a rhetoric of populism to legitimate her deeply reactionary 'reforms', as when she declared: 'We have to limit the power of the trade unions because that is what the people want'. Hall argues that there is, consequently, no fixed subject called 'the people' and no fixed content to the category of 'popular culture', but, if it is to make any sense, the idea of popular culture has to be organised around the central contradiction of the popular forces versus the power bloc. This is the terrain of what Gramsci called the cultural struggle. We need, therefore, to rehistoricise the term and chart the material context of its historical emergence as a concept.

The idea of 'popular culture' makes its appearance in the late eighteenth century as opposed to 'learned culture' first formulated by the German writer JG Herder. The 'popular' here was discovered by the intellectual upper classes for whom it indicated everything they thought they were not: the 'other' of the 'sophisticated, natural, simple, instinctive, irrational and rooted in the local soil' (Burke, 1981). Politically, Burke argues, the importance of the discovery of popular culture was that 'it fitted into and legitimated the movements of national liberation which erupted all over Europe in the early nineteenth century'. So it belonged to a quite specific historical period and was born in the context of distinct material struggles. 'Popular culture', therefore, began to be constructed as a potent material force in the context of the struggle for national identity of the formerly subjected people, or folk, in what became the independent states of Greece, Serbia, Belgium, Poland, Finland and Czechoslovakia. Not surprisingly, the Scots, the Irish, the Welsh and the Bretons developed strongly popular or folk cultures and 'transitions' from this time, in opposition to their imperialist masters in what became for them, a newly invented term, a 'nationalist' struggle.

In English, which is mostly a historically developed amalgam of old German and Norman French, something of a distinction developed between the idea of *popular* culture and *folk* culture which has interesting political ramifications. For example, the instinctive, irrational and natural elements such as rootedness in the soil came to be more identified with 'folk' rather than 'popular' culture. More worryingly, the 'folk' came to be associated with blood kinship and *race* (a similarly constructed totality of the nineteenth century: the Irish, Scots, Welsh and Bretons, for example, rediscovered the Celt within, even though this same Celt had for millennia been intermarried with Saxon, Jew, Asian and African and as often as not had black hair and non-freckled skin). The 'folkish' connoted the country, the peasantry, tradition and rustic simplicity. The 'folk', which hinted at brooding Scandinavian forests and Germanic stolidity, pre-existed modernity and the Enlightenment and belonged to a timeless past.

In contrast 'popular' culture came to be associated with the modernising moment of the Enlightenment, as integral to a technologised urban way of life. The 'people' more often lived in towns and worked in industries; there were popular revolutions, something the folk would never do; popular entertainments replaced folk traditions; popular music was quite the opposite of folk music. The idea of folk education never became popular. Indeed, to some it seemed oxymoronic and, while the term popular came to be associated with enjoyment, 'folkish' always connoted something rather serious. It may be that I've laboured this difference too much, but it's clear that the two terms are not simply interchangeable and may conceal deeper ideological differences.

However, as Stuart Hall noted, popular education can just as easily have a negative connotation: 'Capital had a stake in the culture of the popular classes because the constitution of a whole new social order around capital required a more or less continuous, if intermittent, process of re-education' (Hall, 1981). Thus popular education could be motivated both by the desire to enable or empower the people and its opposite, to reinforce hegemony over them.

Popular education

Popular education first appears properly as a social formation in the late eighteenth and early nineteenth century, manifested as largely autonomous, often self-help public activities located in social movements, nationalist movements, workers and socialist movements. It was also often associated with non-conformist religious groups. Popular education in the earlier part of the century also designated attempts by liberal and radical intellectuals to mount programmes of public education, usually popularising science and in many cases history and culture.

The science-popularising movement was usually a charitable form of public service by university professors and industrialists in the Enlightenment tradition. Often covertly anti-clerical, in France and some other European countries, this form of popular education was supported by radical freemasonry. It led to a multitude of associations for the popularisation of science in the metropolitan capitals of Europe, culminating in Britain in the Mechanics Institutes. These sometimes became centres for self-help education by the artisan class but also led to the foundation of Technical Schools in the late nineteenth century.

As an example of popular adult education, the Mechanics Institutes can be read in various ways. In his seminal work, *The Concept of Popular Education* (1965), Harold Silver notes at least three political responses to them. Not surprisingly, Tories saw mainly danger and catastrophe. An article in *Blackwood's Magazine* of 1827 asserted 'whenever the lower orders of any great state have obtained a smattering of knowledge, they have generally used it to produce national ruin' (quoted in Silver, 1965). The Liberal Whigs under Brougham, adopting what Silver calls 'the rescue motive', promoted the institutes but only so long as they eschewed political education. The Owenite proto-socialist movement was openly sceptical of the Whigs' idea of 'useful knowledge' and aimed instead for democratic control. William Cobbett, for example, contributed his five pounds to the Mechanics Institutes as a sign of his 'attachment to the *working classes* of the community' but adjured them 'not to be *humbugged*, which you most certainly will be, if you suffer any body but REAL MECHANICS to have anything to do in managing the concern' (quoted in Silver, 1965). Thus, according to contemporary ideological perspectives, popular education signified alternatively political subversion, a means of class harmonisation, or democratic emancipation.

The popularisation of science became integral to the growing working class demand for 'really useful knowledge' or knowledge not just suitable for vocational purposes for skilled workers but a critique of superstitious and irrational forms of thought. Liberal scientists and wealthy philanthropists occasionally acknowledged this demand and offered public lectures and courses in scientific and technical instruction, but universities did not themselves contribute until later in the century, in part because they themselves had only rudimentary facilities for scientific education. Alongside was a related demand for cultural and historical education, often led by associations for the promotion of higher education of women, which resulted in more systematic courses in the history, traditions, culture and language of the 'nation'. Newly reconstructed ideas of the nation began to appear which resulted in the creation of 'national literatures' and written histories of what previously had been only regional, folkish or half-formed popular entities.

Another feature of popular education was, increasingly, a demand for a 'scientific' understanding of society, which related Darwinian ideas of natural evolution to social progress. In France, especially, the origins and growth of a positivist social science, inspired by Auguste Comte and Emile Durkheim, fuelled popular belief in an 'objective' approach to social problems. In truth, this perspective was held by petit-bourgeois businessmen and fostered by the anti-clerical masonic organisations under the leadership of the *Grand Orient* but, as we shall see, it was adopted by many libertarian skilled workers who, politically, did not want to be associated with the Marxist Workers' International (Donzelot, 1991; Elwitt, 1982; Hayward, 1961, 1963; Steele, 1997).

European forms of popular education

By the late nineteenth century many of the informal initiatives in popular education of the earlier part of the century had developed into three main formations: University Extension, the Folk High School and the *Universités Populaires*. Also associated were the *volksheims*, university settlements, people's palaces, Spanish 'rationalist' schools and a variety of other national developments (Steele, 1992).

The most influential form of popular education was university extension. Founded by the Scot, James Stuart, Cambridge University Extension held its first classes in 1874 after exploratory classes were given for the Ladies' Educational Associations of Liverpool, Manchester, Sheffield and Leeds (Harrison, 1961). Undertaken largely as a mission to the industrial north by liberal intellectuals, who had been under the tutelage of such men as John Ruskin and TH Green, university extension was the most pedagogically advanced and systematic form of adult popular education then devised. As the first systematic engagement of universities in extra-mural work, it had enormous influence over Northern Europe, especially in the larger towns of Germany, Austria, Holland and Scandinavia, and North America. It also inspired the Modern Universities movement which led to the founding of university colleges in the northern industrial towns where the classes were first held and, in turn, became the civic redbrick universities. These adopted a significantly different organisational model from Oxford and Cambridge, in that they eschewed the mediaeval college-based system and instead organised their teaching through new disciplinary departments, loosely grouped into faculties. Newly established departments of English and languages and the embryonic social science departments, often chaired by former university extension lecturers with a determined belief in social relevance, further marked their conceptual distance from the 'ancient' universities.

In contrast, the Folk High Schools originated in Denmark in 1864 under the leadership of a Lutheran pastor called Gruntvicg, in opposition to German annexations of Danish territory. They were rural-based, residential and concentrated on the creation of folk-national identity among small farmers. At times fiercely anti-Enlightenment, they were both religious and traditional. As a social movement, however, the folk high schools were highly democratic and sociable. Concentrating on life skills, they relied on residential courses of three or six months rather than university extension's weekly classes. The schools were also privately owned, entirely open and refused examinations. The folk high school was common in Scandinavia and German-speaking Europe but not emulated in southern Europe. In England, it became the model for a number of residential adult education settlements like Woodbridge and Fircroft.

A quite different model, the *universités populaires*, originated in Paris in late 1890s, the inspiration of Georges Deherme, an anarchist printer. In the period following the upheavals of the Dreyfus affair, they multiplied rapidly, especially in the provinces, where they were often associated with radical, anti-clerical freemasonry and the trade unionist *bourses de travail*. Politically socialist or anarchist/libertarian (depending on local affiliations) and independent of the moribund French universities, the movement was emulated in southern Europe, particularly in Italy and Spain. More politically radical than the folk high schools and university extension and deeply sceptical of clericalism in any guise, especially Catholicism, this was primarily an urban workers' movement. With the exception of the followers of Comtean social science, intellectuals were treated with a degree of scepticism. In Spain a related but separate development were the anarchist Rational Schools, mainly in Catalonia and Andalusia, which was again ardently anti-clerical and anti-Catholic. In metropolitan centres university intellectuals were involved in setting up Workers' Athenaeums not unlike university settlements and *Casas del Pueblo* whose main function was social rather than educational (Tiana-Ferrer, 1996).

Significantly, without the backing of the universities, in France the *universités populaires* rapidly lost a great deal of their spontaneous early radicalism and became sociable workers' clubs. In Italy they did not succeed in moving beyond a diet of popular lectures. In 1916, for instance, Antonio Gramsci several times attacked the popular universities in the left press as having no understanding of the different needs and background of people who had not been through secondary school. They merely aped, he argued, the curricula of existing bourgeois universities. In an unsigned editorial in the socialist newspaper *Avanti!*, considering the need for a workers' cultural association, Gramsci dismissed the popular university in Turin with savagery:

> It is best not to speak of the Popular University. It has never been alive, it has never functioned so as to respond to a real need. Its origin is bourgeois and it is based on a vague and confused criterion of spiritual humanitarianism. It has the same effectiveness as charitable institutions which believe that with a bowl of soup they can satisfy the physical needs of wretches who cannot appease their hunger and who move the tender hearts of their superiors to pity. (Gramsci, 1985)

Gramsci argued that the Turin proletariat should dispense with all bourgeois cultural props and create its own specifically class-based institution. He argued that this was now a world historical moment when the proletariat should recognise 'that the complexity of its life lacks a necessary organ and creates it, with its strength, with its good will, for its own ends' (Gramsci, 1985). Compared with Italy's backwardness, he claimed that both England and Germany had contained powerful organs of proletarian and socialist culture and named the Fabian Society, when it belonged to the Second International, as its exemplar. For Gramsci the value of the Fabian Society was in offering a forum for thorough and popular discussion of the moral and economic problems affecting the working class and also that it had moved a large part of the English intellectual and university world into this work.

By the turn of the century all forms had to some extent intermarried. For example, in Vienna the *volkshochschule*, inspired by both English university extension and French positivist thought, were centres of scientific enlightenment which were pedagogically far in advance of the University of Vienna, still languishing under Hapsburg obscurantism. In Denmark itself by the mid-1890s the folk high schools had also begun to incorporate extension-type work; although, according to a contemporary report, 'they take no part in the gratuitous instruction given to artisans and workmen in the towns. It is the students of Copenhagen who have here set the example and taken up a work, which undoubtedly has much more in common with the English undertaking' (Povlsen, 1894). In turn, British university extension had recognised the value of residential and sociable forms by inaugurating annual international summer schools (first introduced into Britain by Patrick Geddes at Edinburgh).

In an example of what Marriott perceptively calls 'rhetorical convergence' many educational self-help groups in central and eastern Europe demanded 'university extension' from the universities, often gaining the support of liberal intellectuals. The name university extension seemed to offer legitimacy to their activities although exactly what was 'extended' was not the same in all cases (Marriott, 1992; Steele, 1992). In many cases these were distinctly political movements for workers' or national rights. In Czechoslovakia, for example, the leading intellectual in the movement for university extension, the sociologist and philosopher TG Masaryk, became the first president of independent Czechoslovakia. In Poland, the demand for popular education was integral to the workers' movement which, in the absence of a developed middle class, itself led the nationalist cause.

Although the name 'popular education' never gained currency in Britain, the European popular university movements may well have stimulated the demand for an independent *workers'* educational movement. The European developments had occurred roughly contemporaneously with the rupturing of the newly organised Labour movement from the Liberal Party and the formation of the Independent Labour Party, in which political education was already a prominent feature. Educationally, the most important development was the Workers' Educational Association (WEA) founded in 1903 and, following the strike of students at Ruskin College in 1909, the more politically partisan Labour Colleges and Plebs League. As a consequence therefore of the rise of the workers' and socialist movements of the late nineteenth century, it is clear that the forms of popular education which had arisen earlier in the century acquired a much more overtly political character and the ideal of objective or neutral education associated with the universities declined. Even the Workers' Educational Association, which otherwise espoused these ideals, refused to be subsumed under university extension and adopted a more independent form of organisation. Marriott notes that, 'In effect the WEA set about re-politicising adult education in line with changed circumstances' (Marriott, 1992).

Conclusion

It may be possible to draw a number of related conclusions from this short account of popular education in Europe. In the first place, it is clear that a great deal of nineteenth century popular education was closely linked to social movements – socialist, workers', nationalist and feminist. Second, it was nearly always linked to demands for university or higher education denied to the working classes and women – particularly in science and 'culture'. These demands were often related to struggles for identity – national, class, gender or significant minority. Third, there were nearly always associated groups of liberal or radical intellectuals concerned with extending culture and democracy who wished either to promote class harmony or, more rarely, to promote class struggle. A fourth conclusion is that the demand for popular education leads to a revaluation of and modernisation of universities themselves which in some cases effectively leads to the modern university system in terms of syllabus and curriculum. New subjects of knowledge – such as English studies, social science, industrial relations, cultural studies and women's studies – owe their origins in whole or part to popular education movements. From this it might be concluded that contextually, popular education is part of the overall *modernising* movement within Western society which has founded the modern nation states, the welfare state and democratic institutions. Beyond that popular education has reinvigorated, even to some extent recreated, *civil life* by stimulating the growth of voluntary democratic movements informed by current thinking on scientific, social, cultural and political matters.

Was popular education, therefore, simply a conjunctural phenomenon linked to the development of modern industrial states, which was aimed at a backward peasantry and rapidly organising working class? If this is the case, then is there any need for it now?

In the late twentieth century there is an awesome array of educational or training paraphernalia aimed at adults from Job Seekers training programmes to

Access routes into higher education. Guidance systems (the new gatekeepers?) funnel adults into vocational 'pathways' in further education and the 'new' universities. Distance learning systems which utilise the media and information technology now allow learning freely into the home. Public service broadcasting is education in the broadest sense and offers virtually a home-learning service. The Internet has made universal knowledge instantly available − if you have the technology. So who needs popular education?

One thing which is certain is that many of the institutions which have historically been linked to popular education are finding it increasingly difficult to provide it. Government policy has dragged university adult education (now called continuing education) into the mainstream, professionalised it and refocused it *away* from its extra-mural origins to the internal institutional needs of the universities. During the period of resource-starved expansion insisted on by the Tory administration in the late 1980s and early 1990s adult students suddenly became highly visible and were targeted to fill quotas. In other respects, the older adult education curriculum has been narrowed to fit accreditation schemes for which, if there were equity for part-time students, there *may* be an identifiable demand. Subjects of knowledge have fossilised, education has become instrumentalist and oriented towards a short-term and under-resourced vocationalism. The demise of community education in the local authorities is leaving a vacuum which now threatens the partnership with universities, and Access schemes, painfully developed over 20 years, have to scramble for funds or have already been scrapped.

Perhaps these are merely the more obvious signs of the postmodernist era that a generation of ageing radicals finds hard to accept. Have we witnessed the end of politics now? Is the grand narrative of socialism simply an archaeological relic? Is there nothing to learn except how to make the capitalist system work a little better, equip yourself with a variety of transferable skills to ease into the exploitable niches the market opens up? Does citizenship education mean learning your duties only and not making a fuss about rights? Since economic and social affairs are now so complex, should they not be left to the experts? Has democracy been tried and found wanting? Shouldn't we just shut up and mind our own business?

Well, as the result of the 1997 General Election and the Referendum in Scotland showed, of course not! Popular education is constantly reinventing itself and the experts do not always recognise it when they see it. We need humility in the face of the wisdom that comes from customary experience and struggle. We no longer bear messages in a bottle but if the universities and the education they provide are worth something it must lie in the tools of the trade − scholarship, rigorous argumentation and reasonable discussion, committed but reflexive enquiry, systematic bodies of knowledge and, not least, excellent teachers. What a revitalised popular education must do is put these things at the disposal of the many who are excluded from them and renew the project of social justice and equity which has still to be completed.

References

Burke, P (1981) 'The discovery of popular culture' in Samuel, R (ed), *History and Socialist Theory*, London, Routledge & Kegan Paul, pp 216–226.

Donzelot, J (1991) 'The mobilization of society' in Burchill, G Gordon, C and Miller, P (eds), *The Foucault Effect*, London, Harvester, pp 169–179.

Elwitt, S (1982) 'Education and the social question: the *universités populaires* in late nineteenth century France', *History of Education Quarterly*, Spring, pp 55–69.

Gramsci, A (1985) *Selections from Cultural Writings*, Forgacs, D and Nowell-Smith, G (eds), London, Lawrence and Wishart.

Hall, S (1981) 'Notes on deconstructing the popular' in Samuel, R (ed), *People's History and Socialist Theory*, London, Routledge & Kegan Paul, pp 227–240.

Harrison, J F C (1961) *Learning and Living 1790–1960*, London, Routledge & Kegan Paul.

Hayward, J E S (1961) 'The cooperative origins, rise and collapse of the *universités populaires*', *Archive Internationales de Sociologie et la Cooperation*, 9, pp 3–17.

Hayward, J E S (1963) 'Educational pressure groups and the indoctrination of the radical ideology of solidarism, 1895–1914', *International Review of Social History*, VIII, pp 1–17.

Marriott, S (1992) 'The popular universities in Europe, 1890 to 1920: what was being popularised?' in Hake, B and Marriott, S (eds), *Adult Education Between Cultures: Encounters and Identities in European Adult Education since 1890*, Leeds, Leeds Studies in Adult Education, pp 86–112.

Povlsen, A (1894) 'Report on the Danish Folk High Schools', *University Extension Gazette*, September, pp 146–149.

Silver, H (1965) *The Concept of Popular Education*, London, Macgibbon and Kee.

Steele, T (1992) 'A science for democracy: the growth of university extension in Europe 1890–1920' in Hake, B and Marriott, S (eds), *Adult Education Between Cultures: Encounters and Identities in European Adult Education since 1890*, Leeds, Leeds Studies in Adult Education, pp 61–85.

Steele, T (1997) 'French radical freemasonry, scientific positivism and the rise of the universités populaires' in Hake, B J and Steele, T (eds), *Intellectuals, Activists and Reformers: Studies of Social, Cultural and Educational Reform Movements 1890–1930*, Leeds, Leeds Studies in Continuing Education, Cross-Cultural Studies in the Education of Adults.

Thompson, E P (1968a) *Education and Experience*, Fifth Mansbridge Memorial Lecture, Leeds, Leeds University Press.

Thompson, E P (1968a) *The Making of the English Working Class,* Harmondsworth, Penguin.

Thompson, E P (1993) *Witness against the Beast: Blake and the Moral Law*, London, Routledge.

Tiana-Ferrer, A (1996) 'University extension and the popular university in Spain at the turn of the century: An educational strategy for social reform' in Hake, B, Steele, T and Tiana, A (eds), *Masters, Missionaries and Militants: Studies of Social Movements and Popular Education in Europe 1890–1939*, Leeds, Leeds Studies in Continuing Education, pp 13–38.

8   A critical history of the Workers' Educational Association in Scotland, 1905-1993

Robert Duncan

This account of the history of the Workers' Educational Association (WEA) in Scotland, covering the period from its formation in 1905 to its reorganisation from three district associations into one national body in 1993, fills an important gap in the existing literature. It examines the tensions between the Association's commitment to both liberal educational values and social purpose objectives, and the difficulties of managing this dualism in an often indifferent and at times hostile policy context. In addition, in the earlier part of its history it faced competition with the more radical, Marxist Scottish Labour College movement. In Scotland, unlike England and Wales, the WEA was never granted Responsible Body status as a provider of adult education – in effect making its development heavily dependent on collaboration with the universities, local authorities and trade unions. In the pre-war period, its purpose and programme were closely identifed with the causes of 'old' social movements and the politics of class; in more recent times, the impact of 'new' social movements, especially the women's movement, has been evident in both the content and methods of its educational work.

The WEA approach: some defining characteristics

The provision and control of adult working class education in twentieth century Britain has been, and arguably remains, an ideological and political battlefield. The controversy surrounding it is addressed in a growing historiography (Brown, 1980; Fieldhouse, 1996; Lewis, 1993; Lovett, 1988; Mayo and Thompson, 1995; Simon, 1990) although few scholarly accounts of its manifestations in the Scottish context have been published to date (see Duncan, 1992).

This chapter examines the Scottish case in which the issues raised by education by and for individual workers, members of the organised working class, trade unions and the labour movement have been highly contested. Focusing on the role of the Workers' Educational Association (WEA) as a key agency in adult and worker education, the intention is to demonstrate how the WEA in Scotland has contributed to, and been influenced by, progressive social movements. As a voluntary and worker education movement in its own right, the WEA's history in Scotland will be reviewed and the character, policy and parameters of its work critically examined.

Founded in 1903 in Oxford as a partnership between the worlds of aspiring labour and the universities, the WEA was from the start a campaigning body aiming to achieve working class access to the broad stream of higher learning. As will be seen, its early history in Scotland reflected that rationale, although subsequent developments, particularly from the 1970s, revealed a very different emphasis.

The main thrust of the WEA's struggle to advance the educational interests of adult workers was essentially dualistic: it involved, on the one hand, personal enrichment and a greater understanding of the modern world derived from learning as a liberal pursuit, and, on the other, social purpose, whereby workers could gain a heightened awareness of social and political affairs and equip themselves for active and effective citizenship through informed democratic participation in trade unions, co-operative societies, political parties and other working class organisations. In deciding and determining curricular priorities at any time, it is not surprising that the tensions inherent in this dualism were bound to be problematic as, for example, between the promotion of personal growth goals and more radical collective empowerment and solidarist objectives. The meaning and implications of the WEA mission to promote social purpose education and, indeed, its role in the public and political domain were to prove a source of conflicting interpretation both within and beyond the association itself (Doyle, 1986). To grasp the complexity and context of this tension requires brief preliminary explanation.

As a voluntary organisation, with members and branches organised as a democratic community of learners, the WEA has operated at various levels. It has embodied a propagandist role, to arouse demand and recruit for adult and worker education; an organising role, as facilitator and provider of courses and programmes; and a campaigning, pressure group and interventionist role at a wider policy level in the political arena. Further, in its approach to the curriculum and in its public profile, the WEA has maintained a consistently non-sectarian stance in politics and religion and, while careful to avoid identification with any political party, it has sought to develop formal and informal links with the broad labour and trade union movement in the cause of worker education. It has, also, from the outset, insisted on a non-doctrinaire approach to teaching and learning, advocating and practising an open, robust form of critical intellectual enquiry, rejecting dogmatism as a negation of the educational process. Armed with this approach, it has usually been possible for the resourceful tutor to handle the most sensitive and politically controversial subjects, to challenge orthodoxy and even selectively to plant some seeds of subversion.

Nevertheless, by adopting this non-dogmatic stance and by seeking to align itself with the central and local state and the universities in a sustained effort to gain full recognition for liberal adult and worker education, the WEA, from 1908 onwards, was subject to constant attack from the Marxist Plebs League and the Labour College movement for independent working class education (Brown, 1980; Armstrong, 1988). From 1916 Scottish Labour College activists and from 1921 the National Council of Labour Colleges consistently denounced the WEA as a class collaborationist organisation. In contrast to the apparently ambiguous WEA commitment to the emancipation of labour, the Scottish Labour College project had a hegemonic mission to create and implant a socialist counter-culture, relying solely upon the support and resources of an insurgent labour movement. Its whole effort involved the political education of class conscious workers in the principles and practice of the struggle for socialism. Its approach to education was thoroughly propagandist and fundamentalist. Further, it propounded the crude, formalist and reductionist argument which meant that it was impossible to negotiate meaningful reforms or concessions from the capitalist state (Brown, 1980).

As a pressure group the WEA made an early and consistent choice to reject the revolutionary road to change. Instead, its ideological parameters might usefully be characterised as liberal pluralist, embodying a pragmatic, reformist but non-deferential approach to the established authorities, preferring to work with various allies in the labour movement and elsewhere to mobilise, lobby and negotiate for substantial, incremental resourcing of educational provision for the majority. Over the years, this approach has been reflected in the character and conduct of the leading figures in the WEA voluntary movement in Scotland, who have come mainly from activists and officers in the Labour Party and the co-operative and trade union movements. Whether labourist, social democratic or democratic socialist, they have tended to belong to the aspiring 'labour aristocracy' and lower professional intelligentsia, exhibiting a strong adherence to the value of education for self-improvement, active citizenship and social purpose.

The Scottish context

In England, the WEA received direct grant aid from the Board of Education as well as funding from local educational authorities and the university sector. Consequently, it was able to grow rapidly within a few years, with thousands of members, a proliferation of local branches and a large programme of academic classes throughout the country (Jennings, 1979; Fieldhouse, 1996). In Scotland, however, the WEA pattern of development was markedly different, and it was much slower to take root. Here no 'golden stream' of central and local state funding was made available to help launch and sustain it. Its expansion was also hampered by administrative regulations, an absence of policy and official indifference at Scottish Education Department (SED) level, and by a penny-pinching mentality within the rates-conscious school boards before 1918. Statutory and providing powers for adult education were to continue throughout in the hands of the SED and local authority sector, and until the 1920s neither was easily persuaded to extend its remit beyond compulsory day schooling for children and vocational evening continuation classes for young workers. WEA claims for support were also hindered by the official view that demand for further education at or below university level was unproven and that university education in Scotland was, in any case, accessible to deserving young men and women from all social backgrounds.

Moreover, the Scottish universities were also denied Responsible Body status and the accompanying state grants to provide extra-mural classes either on their own account or jointly with the WEA. However, in 1924, AD Lindsay, a Christian Socialist and professor of moral philosophy, was instrumental in persuading Glasgow University to form a joint committee on the Oxford model of university-WEA representation, with attendant funding to provide educational programmes (Shearer, 1976). The other Scottish universities followed suit and, by the end of the 1920s, this partnership with the higher education sector made possible the provision of classes stimulated by WEA demand.

The WEA continued to press for changes in SED regulations in order to give recognition to adult education as a separately funded category. When this was eventually achieved in 1934, more local authorities became receptive to collaboration with the WEA in sponsoring and arranging courses. Nevertheless, until relationships were formally renegotiated in the 1960s and 1970s, the WEA in Scotland was set in a dependent and unequal partnership with the local authorities and the universities.

Whereas local branches, with direct funding support, multiplied and flourished south of the border, in Scotland, from the 1930s, the number of branches and student groups remained around 20 to 25, reaching a peak of 42 in the wartime 1940s. It should be emphasised that the WEA in Scotland had the services of only one full-time organising secretary from 1919 until the formation of the three districts in 1947 and it did not receive core grants from the SED for administrative support before the 1950s. All this time, it was unable to employ more than one tutor organiser to help generate programmes and support the voluntary movement grouped in various local branches. That so much was achieved between the 1920s and 1960s in promoting the WEA on the ground in the main urban and rural centres in Scotland must therefore be attributed, for the most part, to the labours of committed voluntary activists.

The WEA achievement in Scotland

Having outlined the poor relation and marginal status of the WEA in Scotland for the greater part of its existence, it is now in order to assess the nature of its achievement as a pioneering and campaigning body.

Despite barriers to recognition, modest progress was made between 1905 and 1919, when the WEA Scottish Council was formally constituted. Due to voluntary and material support from trades councils, local trade union branches and co-operative societies and the enthusiastic leadership of a small core of socially-conscious academics (notably A Darroch, Professor of Education at

Edinburgh University, and William Boyd, Lecturer in Education at Glasgow University) WEA branches were formed in Edinburgh in 1912, Aberdeen in 1913, Glasgow in 1916 (after earlier attempts in 1905–7) and Dundee and Ayrshire in 1917 (see Ministry of Reconstruction, 1919).

From 1913 and throughout the war years, fee-paying, one-year preparatory and two-year tutorial classes, primarily in the WEA subjects reckoned to enhance insight into the complexities of modern society – economics, history, philosophy, natural science and literature – were organised within the four university centres (St Andrews facilitating Dundee) and guaranteed by relevant school boards (Ministry of Reconstruction, 1919). Unfortunately, no records survive of the composition of the student body at this time, but strict insistence on long academic courses at university standard was bound to have had a limited appeal. Insofar as they attracted worker students, such courses could benefit only that tiny elite of adult participants who were already equipped with the necessary combination of confidence, intellectual ability, time, energy and discipline for this level of academic study. Clearly, at this stage, the WEA in Scotland still had a long way to go to open up liberal adult education to a wider constituency of workers. When a more flexible policy was agreed from the 1920s, which involved the introduction of courses of a less rigorous nature (provided both within and outside the universities), a considerable expansion of demand occurred.

In other respects, the WEA at this stage was developing a public campaigning role. In 1917–18, the provisional WEA Scottish Council, its labour movement affiliates and five branches organised large meetings on national educational reform and post-war reconstruction in the lead-up to the Education (Scotland) Bill of 1918. From wartime onwards, the WEA became concerned not only with prospects for adult education but also with exerting pressure for a fully-funded comprehensive education system from nursery to adult continuing education (WEA, 1919). Over the years, acting with its allies in the Educational Institute in Scotland and local authority education committees as well as progressive politicians and educationalists, the raising of the school leaving age from 14 to 16 became a major plank in WEA conference agendas and public platforms.

During the Second World War, the WEA in Scotland played the leading role within the campaigning Scottish Council for Educational Advance, again in anticipation of national legislation on education. A sustained programme of regional conferences, public meetings and press coverage during 1943–45 was organised from the WEA office in Glasgow. The other three national bodies participating in the campaign – the Scottish Trade Union Council, the Scottish section of the Co-operative Union and the Educational Institute of Scotland – ensured the involvement of trades councils, the teaching profession, and the Women's Co-op Guild organisations (WEA Scotland *Annual Reports* 1943–44; 1944–45).

Also during the Second World War, the WEA's public profile was heightened as a result of its concentrated efforts in promoting and providing classes, discussion and study groups on active citizenship, social policy and current affairs among workers at camps, civil defence workers and members of the armed forces. In Scotland, this took the form of publicly-funded special project work. Together with a record-breaking expansion of classes, including substantial trade union educational work, it is not fanciful to claim that the WEA's wartime contribution to education for citizenship, democratic values and social service helped prepare the climate of opinion for the 1945 Labour landslide (see WEA Scotland *Annual Reports* 1940–45).

While trade union support for and affiliation to the WEA was evident in its formative years, these connections were often limited and tenuous. Before 1918 the WEA had made no concerted moves to forge cohesive educational links with the trade union movement and to target its large membership. In 1919, however, the WEA and the newly-amalgamated Iron and Steel Trades Confederation (ISTC) formed the Workers' Educational Trade Union Committee (WETUC) scheme, which many other unions subsequently joined (Corfield, 1969). Under WETUC in Scotland members of subscribing trade unions could make use of existing WEA course programmes and request additional provision to cater for their special interests and needs.

The first salaried WEA tutor organiser post in Scotland was created in 1920, specifically to deliver this new partnership, initially with iron and steelworkers in west-central Scotland. During the 1920s industrial workers, other trade unionists and Labour Party activists helped to promote courses and form industrial branches and study groups in various mining and steel communities (Marwick, 1975).

At the same time, the influential, political – and politicised – class programme of the rival Labour College movement maintained a formidable challenge to the WEA's involvement in trade union and industrial work. Certainly during the 1917–20 period, at the height of the worker militancy associated with wartime unrest and Red Clydeside, the combined Plebs League and Scottish Labour College programme of classes in Marxist economics, industrial history and class struggle, held throughout central Scotland and led by the revolutionary socialist teacher John MacLean, entirely dwarfed the comparatively insignificant WEA academic programme (Duncan, 1992; Holford, 1988). By 1921, however, the tide of industrial and political militancy had subsided and control of the Labour College project was assumed by left reformists who, like the WEA, wanted to formalise permanent educational links with the trade union movement. In 1922, the National Council of Labour Colleges therefore set up a rival, parallel scheme to WETUC. Although it initially adhered to the rhetoric of Marxist ideology its classes and correspondence courses soon became little different from those of the WEA. A mix of social science, humanities subjects and enabling organisational skills were offered as a general service to the labour movement (McIlroy, 1990a).

Of particular interest in the debate concerning ideological and political hegemony in worker education is the thesis, recently reiterated by Fieldhouse (1996), that the state in early twentieth century Britain officially and financially backed the WEA as a potentially moderating influence on the emerging labour movement and consequently a sound political investment against extremism. Yet, as previously outlined, no such direct political and financial support was forthcoming for a struggling WEA in Scotland. If this thesis was correct, it would surely have been crucial, given the prevalence of militancy and the demonstrable attraction of Marxist-oriented political education in Scotland during 1917–20, for the state to boost and bankroll the WEA effort at this time.

It is undoubtedly the case that the WEA ethos was anti-Marxist, and the very openness of its organisation and work made it susceptible to the pressure and influence of moderate tendencies. When the battle for the hearts and minds of organised labour was especially sharp during this period of the class struggle, the capitalist state could always rely on the more subtle persuasions of certain university professors to guide participants in their WEA classes into non-subversive channels of thought. Davie (1986) cites the case of Kemp Smith, professor of philosophy at Edinburgh University who, as lecturer to WEA classes and WEA Edinburgh Branch President in the early 1920s, used his influence to dissuade worker students and members from the doctrines of Marxism and the rival claims of Labour College agitators. A major concern of Kemp Smith and others was to cultivate close links between the universities, the WEA and moderate elements in the Labour Party.

Reviewing the WETUC scheme, it is clear that considerable internal tension could arise over the direction of social purpose education for trade unionists and, in particular, the politicisation of trade union education. However, only one open split occurred, and this was provoked by exceptional circumstances. In January 1926, the largely white-collar, middle class Edinburgh branch seceded from the Association, alarmed by the national WEA initiative to merge with the National Council of Labour Colleges in a Trades Union Congress-led trade union education scheme. Although this proposed scheme was later aborted (Fieldhouse, 1981), a majority of the Edinburgh branch could not subscribe to its declared objective to equip workers for the task of 'securing social and industrial emancipation' and the implied surrender of WEA branch autonomy to a determined class politics identity.

Through WETUC in Scotland, until its absorption in the Trades Union Congress Education Scheme in 1964, thousands of trade unionists participated in varied programmes of liberal studies. These encompassed a wide range of core social subjects: economics, economic and labour history, social policy, politics, and international relations as well as literature and language. Transferable enabling skills were also important, such as public speaking and presentation and critical thinking for effective decision-making and negotiation with employers. Applied studies related to particular sectors of industry or workplaces were also available, especially as day and weekend schools. After the 1920s, these increasingly became the norm as the scheme grew and demand continued for issue-based shorter courses. Only the lean years during the inter-war period interrupted a steady growth of classes and schools which were located throughout Scotland, often bringing a fresh dimension to WEA branch life outside the urban areas. In 1947 alone, WETUC in Scotland organised 24 day schools and four weekend schools, and in 1959 the three Scottish districts organised no less than 36 weekend schools and several day and summer schools (WETUC, *Annual Reports*). Even after the scheme ended in 1964, and despite problems of reduced funding, the Scottish districts continued to contribute short course programmes for trade unionists – although, as discussed below, a new and contested Trades Union Congress-dominated scheme of shop steward training was by then beginning to replace the traditional wider focus of educational provision negotiated with the membership.

Identity crisis, 1945–1970

Historians of the WEA agree that it faced a crisis of identity and confusion of roles in the first part of the post-war period (eg see Jennings, 1979; Fieldhouse, 1977; 1996). In Scotland, the voluntary base of individual membership, branches and affiliates declined steadily from its peak in the 1940s, as did its outward campaigning profile. In the 1950s and 1960s, material improvements – including fuller employment, welfarism, mass culture, privatisation of leisure time and increased opportunities for further and higher education – have all been put forward as a complex of influences serving to undermine the appeal of serious-minded, social purpose, liberal education and of voluntary participation in the WEA. Apart from maintaining a healthy profile in trade union education, within the WEA in Scotland there were visible signs of a diffused idealism, a diminished sense of pioneering mission and, in its mainstream educational work, a corresponding inability to reach out to the more disadvantaged sections of the working class.

The problems of maintaining a separate public identity and social purpose dynamic were not entirely new. They had emerged noticeably in Glasgow and the west of Scotland during the 1930s when the rapid expansion of general adult education programmes organised jointly by the local authorities and the university threatened to marginalise the WEA. In one respect, it had become a victim of its own success as a pioneering catalyst for adult education. As a small voluntary movement confronted by a rapid growth of class programmes and student enrolments, the branches and meagre staff could not exert anything like the same influence as they had in the 1920s to win students into member-ship and activism. The large Glasgow branch – the jewel in the crown in WEA Scotland – reflected both the strengths and the weaknesses of the movement. In the 1930s it was a vibrant branch of 500 members, rising to 700 in the 1940s, with various activities for women's outreach, an unemployed workers' committee, several subject-based clubs, societies and study groups as well as its own magazine *Adult Student*. It embodied a social class mix and projected a respectable image of liberal culture and social concern (see WEA Glasgow Branch *Annual Reports*). However, by the 1960s, membership had fallen away and the programme reflected the dominant self-culture, extra-mural approach of a university which had begun to expand its own departmental programme.

The relative weight of university and local authority programmes is all too apparent in any annual report of Scottish WEA districts in the 1950s and 1960s. Only a small portion of the classes listed, especially in the west of Scotland, belonged to or could be attributed to direct WEA effort. Allowing for considerable social and political education components in work with trade unions, co-operatives and community organisations, the overall impression is, nevertheless, that of a diminishing WEA presence. In the late 1960s, severing the formal joint committee structure signalled the start of an honest reappraisal of the WEA's rationale and effectiveness in Scotland and, eventually, a recovery of its social purpose dynamic.

Renewed social purpose, 1970–1993

The final section of this chapter presents a necessarily brief overview of more recent WEA achievements (prior to the reconstitution of WEA Scotland in 1993) in terms of recovering its social purpose dynamic and reconnecting its work with the trade union and labour movement, the women's movement and single issue campaigns.

Reviewing the WEA record, the Alexander Committee (Scottish Education Department, 1975) recommended that the WEA renew its social commitment. The Committee recommended that it should concentrate on developing work with educationally and socially disadvantaged adults; reinforce its contribution to role education, as in citizenship and enabling work with other voluntary sector and local community organisations; develop its pioneering effort in pre-retirement and retirement education; and, finally, expand its distinctive contribution to trade union education. On all accounts, the evidence (see Gerver, 1985) suggests that the WEA acquitted itself well in fulfilling its commitment to the agenda set for it by the Alexander Committee, and to much more besides.

However, to meet the challenges posed in the mid-1970s, the WEA first had to revise its policies and ways of working, and to acquire fresh resources. New settlements were negotiated with most of the new regional authorities from 1975, and with Fife and Highland in the 1980s. The most significant breakthrough was in Strathclyde, where tutor organisers were appointed to each of the former education authority divisions, thus allowing the WEA to extend its programme and to reorient itself towards community-based social priority work. From the early 1980s, this work was closely incorporated into partnership agreements with Strathclyde Regional Council, the WEA adopting a service role in relation to the Region's Social Strategy and focusing on targeted outreach provision for women, the unemployed and community organisations within designated areas of multiple deprivation.

The emphasis on social priority work was not universally popular with the WEA membership, however. Concern was expressed about the apparent marginalisation of the more open liberal studies tradition and its replacement by a non-academic social service type of provision which integrated the WEA into the priorities of local government and threatened its autonomy as a voluntary association. Nevertheless, important developmental work was initiated. In the South-East District, for example, a New Directions Policy was agreed, opening the way for innovative small-scale initiatives in Freirian and human relations approaches to community action, work with unemployed people, and piloting writers workshops (see WEA South East District Scotland *Annual Reports*, 1978–79; Kirkwood and Griffiths, 1984; Kirkwood, 1990).

The WEA in Scotland has maintained an unbroken tradition, stretching back to 1920, in social purpose, trade union and worker education. In the 1970s and 1980s it participated in the new Trades Union Congress Education Scheme, but also initiated and developed member education programmes with several trade unions. WEA participation in this scheme provoked constructive internal debate. The thrust of the centralised and prescribed curriculum appeared to contradict traditional liberal and political workers education in favour of a restricted, functional, mainly skills-based and workplace-related focus. In a sustained political critique, for example, McIlroy (1990a; 1990b; 1995; 1996) has accused the Trades Union Congress of bowing to state-funded corporatism and the management of industrial relations as the ideological basis for its day release training programmes. He has also criticised the compliant role of the WEA in servicing the scheme.

Nevertheless, the offical WEA perspective on the scheme was also adopted in Scotland (Lochrie, 1981). Participation in Trades Union Congress courses was seen as part of an intended wider trade union education provision, and one means, among other more radical initiatives, of assisting organised labour. While some voluntary members and tutors had reservations about the restricted, training-oriented curriculum of shop steward and health and safety courses and the lack of control over course planning and recruitment, most welcomed a scheme which provided and resourced various intrinsically valuable training courses aimed at more effective collective bargaining and workplace action (see Henderson, 1981). As one of several Scottish-based tutor organisers deployed on the scheme until 1989 (when the SED removed the supplementary grant from such courses and it was decided to centre provision in particular colleges), I always found it possible, while fulfilling the course training remit, to find opportunities and space for more widely-based, critical and informed discussion of fundamental political and economic issues such as state power under capitalism, employer and trade union rights, and structural inequality and discrimination.

Important offshoots from working on the day release courses included the formation of a West of Scotland Hazards Group in the early 1980s and an unofficial Employment Rights Information Centre in Aberdeen which, in turn, led to a developmental WEA-led project for unemployed people. Moreover, the methods and expertise developed on these new courses were subsequently transferred to the other, growing sectors of enabling skills and awareness raising work with community groups. The activity-based, student-centred approach, retained a pro-active role for the tutor and was successfully adapted for community activist training in, for example, credit unions (Turner, 1993), urban aid projects and housing and tenants' associations.

Outside the Trades Union Congress Education Scheme, more overtly political and campaigning educational initiatives were eagerly sought and implemented with the trade union and labour movement during the 1980s as it was confronted by the Thatcherite onslaught on workers' democratic rights. For instance, issue-based day schools and short courses were frequently held on such subjects as alternative economic strategy, women and trade unionism, labour history, the politics of unemployment, and, memorably, with the major public sector unions on the significance of the Political Fund Ballot in face of the 1984 Trade Union Act. Linked to the peace movement in the mid-1980s, National Union of Public Employees (NUPE) Peace Studies packs were adapted for radical education and used to debate the politics of nuclear weapon deterrence, non-nuclear defence policy and employment conversion. These concerns, combined with the inspiring example of sustained non-violent direct action by the Greenham Common women, helped inform the WEA's episodic peace education work with trade unionists, old and new peace activists and interested members of political parties and groups.

More typical of the general WEA effort in the 1970s was pioneering work in women's trade union education and women's education in general (Aldred, 1981; Marshall, 1985). On the trade union front, women's induction courses and equal pay workshops led the way. In the 1980s there was also a rapid expansion of courses focusing on women and health and the politics of health. Here, as in the emerging partnership with NUPE to deliver return to learn courses, membership education, personal development and social purpose objectives were closely intertwined.

Women's education

The 1975 Alexander Report contained a deafening silence on the significance for adult education of the women's movement, the influence of feminism and the possibility of distinctive forms of women's education. It is true that educational work with young mothers was specifically mentioned in this respect, but this was essentially in terms of rectifying supposed deficiencies in women's domestic and coping roles. In stark contrast, the historic role of the WEA in pioneering pro-feminist women's education has to be emphasised. The appointment of several feminist educators to organising, teaching and management posts prompted an early and growing commitment to the development of women's education. When in the 1980s, the acronym 'WEA' was sometimes taken to mean 'women's educational association', this misconception did indeed reflect the visible prominence of women in the student body and the high profile of women's education in the overall WEA curriculum.

New, experimental, less formal outreach approaches aimed at bringing adult education into the lives of younger working class women, especially in deprived areas, were piloted successfully in WEA programmes in the 1970s (Beale, 1978; West, 1981; Marshall and Johnson, 1983) and further developed in the 1980s:

> The original aims of this work were quite consciously to do with empowering women: through increased knowledge and critical reflection women would be better placed to make more choices in their personal lives; through coming together to discuss their shared concerns and to make connection between their own lives and social, economic and political conditions they might become part of a movement for social as well as individual change. (WEA, 1989)

The practice in women's education tended to reject the softly, softly 'education by stealth' approach in favour of an explicit and openly negotiated dialogue, starting from and validating personal experience before engaging in more critical and sustained enquiry (see Barr, 1987; Marshall and Johnson, 1983). WEA initiatives emphasised the importance of group assertiveness, women's self-defence courses, women writers' workshops, away days, women's issues and second chance and return to learn courses. In some areas women's branches were formed. Giving priority to work with working class and unwaged women reflected a commitment to the practical 'really useful knowledge' and equal opportunities feminism which has typically informed recent WEA practice in women's education. Such a development could hardly have been foreseen prior to the impact of the women's movement on adult and worker education – and yet it is, arguably, the crowning achievement of the WEA in Scotland in recent years.

Also central to the WEA effort from the early 1980s – but on a lower scale of achievement than the promotion of women's education – was the pioneering development of grassroots writers' workshops, people's history workshops and a crop of associated community publications. Their combined thrust has contributed to the making of a more democratic culture in Scotland. Although such initiatives have not been consistently and overtly political and have yet to constitute a movement, for many participants they have acted as springboards for community activism, informal cultural politics and independent critical thought.

Conclusion

Throughout the twentieth century two dominant and connected concerns thread constantly through the work of the WEA in Scotland. These are, firstly, the aspirations and claims of the 'old' social movement of organised labour and the working class (however defined) for liberal and social purpose education and, secondly, the promotion of active citizenship in a democratic society. Moreover, while governments of right and left have emphasised individual and social responsibility as key features of citizenship, the role of the WEA and of popular educators, as ever, is to champion the exercise of democratic rights, civil liberties and egalitarianism. And if the WEA is to run true to its record of public campaigning for the 'right to learn', it must continue to stand firm for lifelong learning for all.

In the final analysis, attempts to market 'WEA, Scotland' as an effective, professionally-run, quality-assured body acceptable and attractive to funders have always to be balanced against the continuing need to reverse its ageing and declining voluntary base and to renew itself as a popular movement in its own right. To that end, 'keeping the workers in the WEA' will serve not only as an abiding badge of identity, it could also signify and uphold the mission of workers' education against the threat of postmodernist pick and mix tendencies and, in the emerging Scotland, be an important source of inspiration for rebuilding voluntarism.

References

Aldred, C (1981) *Women and Work*, London, Pan Books/WEA.

Armstrong, P (1988) 'The long search for the working cass: socialism and the education of adults, 1850–1930', in Lovett, T (ed), *Radical Approaches to Adult Education*, London, Routledge, pp 35–58.

Barr, J (1987) 'Keeping a low profile: adult education in Scotland', *Adult Education*, 39 (4), pp 329–334.

Beale, J (1978) 'Talking with women', *Scottish Journal of Adult Education*, 3 (2), pp 11–14.

Brown, G (1980) 'Independence and incorporation: the Labour College Movement and the Workers' Educational Association before the First World War' in Thompson, J (ed), *Adult Education for a Change*, London, Hutchinson, pp 109–25.

Corfield, A. J (1969) *Epoch in Workers' Education,* London, WEA.

Davie, G (1986) *The Crisis of the Democratic Intellect,* Edinburgh, Polygon.

Doyle, M (1986) 'Social purpose in adult education', *Adult Education,* 59 (2), pp 141–46.

Duncan, R (1992) 'Independent working class education and the formation of the Labour College Movement in Glasgow and the West of Scotland, 1915–1922' in Duncan, R and McIvor, A (eds), *Militant Workers: Labour and Class Conflict on the Clyde, 1900–1950,* Edinburgh, John Donald, pp 106–128.

Fieldhouse, R (1977) *The WEA: Aims and Achievements, 1903–1977,* New York, University of Syracuse.

Fieldhouse, R (1981) 'Voluntaryism and the state in adult education: the WEA and the 1925 TUC Education Scheme', *History of Education,* 10 (1), pp 45–63.

Fieldhouse, R (1996) 'The Workers' Educational Association' in Fieldhouse, R and Associates, *A History of Modern British Adult Education,* Leicester, NIACE, pp 166–198.

Gerver, E (ed) (1985) *Alexander: Ten Years On,* Edinburgh, Scottish Institute of Adult Education.

Henderson, S (1981) 'A strategy for Scottish trade union education' in Schuller, T (ed), *Is Knowledge Power? Problems and Practice in Trade Union Education,* Aberdeen, Aberdeen People's Press, pp 12–24.

Holford, J (1988) *Reshaping Labour: Organisation, Work and Politics in Edinburgh in the Great War and After,* London, Croom Helm.

Jennings, B (1979) *Knowledge is Power: A Short History of the WEA, 1903–1978,* Hull, University of Hull.

Kirkwood, C (1990) *Vulgar Eloquence,* Edinburgh, Polygon.

Kirkwood, C and Griffiths, S (1984) *Adult Education and the Unemployed,* Edinburgh, WEA.

Lewis, R (1993) *Leaders and Teachers: Adult Education and the Challenge of Labour in South Wales, 1906–1940,* Cardiff, University of Wales Press.

Lochrie, R (1981) 'The service from the WEA' in Schuller, T (ed) *Is Knowledge Power? Problems and Practice in Trade Union Education,* Aberdeen, Aberdeen People's Press, pp 90–98.

Lovett, T (ed) (1988) *Radical Approaches to Adult Education,* London, Routledge.

McIlroy, J (1990a) 'The demise of the National Council of Labour Colleges' in Simon, B (ed), *The Search for Enlightenment: The Working Class and Adult Education in the Twentieth Century,* Leicester, NIACE, pp 173–207.

McIlroy, J (1990b) 'Trade union education for a change' in Simon, B (ed), *The Search for Enlightenment: The Working Class and Adult Education in the Twentieth Century,* Leicester, NIACE, pp 244–275.

McIlroy, J (1995) 'The dying of the light? A radical look at trade union education' in Mayo, M and Thompson, J (eds), *Adult Learning, Critical Intelligence and Social Change,* Leicester, NIACE, pp 146–168.

McIlroy, J (1996) 'Independent working class education and trade union education and training' in Fieldhouse, R and Associates, *A History of Modern British Adult Education,* Leicester, NIACE, pp 264–289.

Marshall, M (1985) *Breaking our Silence,* London, WEA.

Marshall, M and Johnson, C (1983) 'New opportunities for women? Women's education in the north of Scotland', *Scottish Journal of Adult Education,* 6 (2), pp 14–22.

Marwick, W H (1975) 'Workers education in early twentieth century Scotland', *Scottish Labour History Society Journal,* 8, pp 34–38.

Mayo, M and Thompson, J (eds) (1995) *Adult Learning, Critical Intelligence and Social Change,* Leicester, NIACE.

Ministry of Reconstruction (1919) *Final Report of the Adult Education Committee*, Cmmd 321, London, HMSO.

Scottish Education Department (1975) *Adult Education: The Challenge of Change*, Edinburgh, HMSO.

Shearer, J G S (1976) 'Town and gown together: two hundred and fifty years of extra-mural teaching at the University of Glasgow' (reprint from *College Courant*), *Journal of the Glasgow University Graduates' Association*.

Simon, B (ed) (1990) *The Search for Enlightenment: The Working Class and Adult Education in the Twentieth Century*, Leicester, NIACE.

Turner, R (1993) 'Training for credit union volunteers: a WEA project', *Scottish Journal of Adult Education*, 1 (4), pp 14–24.

WEA (1919) *How to Get the Best out of the Education Act for Scotland 1918*, Glasgow, Scottish Council of the WEA.

WEA (1989) *Women's Education Past, Present and Future: A WEA Policy Statement*, London, WEA.

WEA Glasgow Branch *Annual Reports, 1916–1966* Glasgow, WEA.

WEA Scotland *Annual Reports, 1920–1947*, Glasgow, WEA.

WEA North of Scotland District *Annual Reports, 1947–1993* Aberdeen, WEA.

WEA South East Scotland District *Annual Reports, 1947–1993* Edinburgh, WEA.

WEA West of Scotland District *Annual Reports, 1947–1993* Glasgow, WEA.

West, A (1981) 'Using video with discussion groups', *Scottish Journal of Adult Education* 5 (2), pp 19–21.

WETUC *Annual Reports*, (1920–1964) London, WEA.

9 Muslims in Scotland: challenging Islamophobia

Elinor Kelly and Bashir Maan

If the new Scotland is to be genuinely democratic and inclusive, it must give practical recognition to religious belief as a basis for Scottish identity and citizenship. The case of Muslims in Scotland for religious autonomy, instruction and respect has been consistently denied, and systematically distorted by a confusion of 'religion' with 'religiosity'. This produces a groundless and demeaning form of Islamophobia, which is deeply rooted in Christian Europe's historic fear of the exotic yet essential 'other' and its own religious sectarianism rather than the realities of cultural pluralism in Scotland today. In the new Scotland, Scottish Muslims claim the right to an education which gives them equality and parity of esteem. This is no more and no less than a demand for justice. It requires recognition of the legitimacy of social movements based on the 'faith communities' of religious identity as well as 'secular political ideology'.

Introduction

This chapter has been written as an initial stage in dialogue and debate between a secular adult educator, Elinor Kelly, and a leading member of the Scottish Muslim community, Bashir Maan. Frequently, in the course of collaboration in research, we find ourselves pausing from the task in hand in order to discuss the latest manifestation of 'Islamophobia' in the media, in academic publications or policy papers. Each of us, independently, has noted with growing concern the transformation of the word 'Muslim' from a neutral term of description of a person's faith to a term of mistrust and abuse. Each of us has become aware that phobia about Islam has spread, even among friends and colleagues who share our commitment to human rights and civil liberties.

Muslims across Britain have organised an impressive infrastructure of mosques, *madrassahs* (mosque-based classes of religious instruction which run after school hours during the week and weekends), community centres and schools. But they are also calling for full recognition as a religious minority. It is anticipated that in 2001 the decennial Census will include 'religion' as a category for the first time in mainland Britain. Discussions are also now underway regarding the recognition of 'religious discrimination' within the Race Relations Act and Public Order Act. In January 1998, after many years of campaigning, two Muslim secondary schools in England were awarded state funding.

There is little doubt that, instead of subsiding into a monocultural, secular landscape, Muslims are holding firm to their religious identity and to a religious agenda for action. Indeed, religion is central to the self-definition not only of Muslims, but also of Christians, Hindus and Sikhs who have migrated from South Asia. On the one hand, religion among the indigenous population is declining year by year, to such an extent that one in three 'white' respondents in the most recent Policy Studies Institute survey stated that they had no religious affiliation. On the other, only two per cent of South Asians stated that they had no religious affiliation and their 'religious identification is so high that it varies little by factors such as age, gender and class' (Modood and Berthoud, 1997). We therefore have to ask, how we can support the rights of the South Asian minorities without taking their religion into account.

Progressive adult educators often claim to be in touch with progressive social movements and campaigns for minority rights. However, when faced with issues about religious rights, especially Muslim rights, there is considerable unease. Why is it that the undeniable achievements of Muslims in organising themselves, challenging conventional politics and radicalising young people have not been celebrated as indicators of an important contemporary social movement? Every one of the concessions now granted to Muslims in education – the provision of *halal* meat, the acceptance of modest codes of dress, the right to prayer rooms, the separation of girls and boys in sports and recreation, and, most recently, the right to state funding of denominational schools alongside other minority faiths – has been won through prolonged, persistent campaigns. Moreover, throughout their campaigns, Muslims have been subjected to intimidating levels of hostility and abuse which, for the most part, they have endured with dignity.

In drafting this paper, we searched for a word which could summarise the hesitations, doubts, misgivings and distrust that are manifested when it comes to matters of religion and faith. After much scouring of dictionaries, we arrived at the definition of 'religiosity' which summarises a key element in the challenge that we perceive. If observers or commentators feel that the religious sentiments of others are 'excessively, obtrusively or sentimentally religious' (*Websters New Collegiate Dictionary*, 1973), then the term 'religiosity' is appropriate. Muslims today are not respected for their *religion* but are denigrated for their *religiosity*. We feel that the socialist, secular and humanist traditions of adult education are biased towards the assumption of religiosity and against the legitimate claims of religious groups.

What better time to raise this issue than now when the massive vote in favour of the restoration of the Scottish Parliament has brought an invigorating sense that every issue should be studied afresh? In a thought-provoking article, Sean Damer recently wrote:

> The Scotland in which I want to live in the 21st century . . . would be
> outward-looking rather than introvert, open rather than closed,

internationalist rather than nationalist, welcoming rather than rejecting, inclusive rather than exclusive, tolerant rather than intolerant, a democratic country it would be a pleasure to visit wherever one came from. It is high time for all of us resident in Scotland to concentrate on thinking seriously about how to construct such a nation. (*Herald*, 11.11.97)

Muslim Scots want to be included in the construction of the new Scottish nation and this chapter is intended to be a contribution to that process. We have thought long and hard about the key obstacles which need to be overcome if Muslims are to be included. We decided that our first priority should be to challenge religiosity and monolithic views of Islam. Our second should be to challenge sectarianism and suggest alternative ways in which the religious aspirations of Scots of different faiths should be met. Muslim Scots are well aware that their calls for recognition are being entangled in the net of sectarianism. But, they ask, do we really want to move into the new Scotland with politicians and policy-makers so fearful of opening Pandora's Box that they would rather keep the status quo?

Closed and open views of Islam

In a liberal democracy, discussion and debate, disagreement and dissension on basic issues must thrive. Adherents of different world faiths disagree with each other on points of theology and religious practice; agnostics, atheists and secular humanists disagree with all religious believers when it comes to the fundamentals of faith. The basic principles of human rights and freedoms, enshrined in United Nations conventions, are a legitimate measure against which to judge the records of different regimes, whatever their supposed religious affiliation. Indeed, in every country of the world debates and arguments are taking place, and even the most autocratic and authoritarian of regimes have learnt that, while they can drive dissent underground, they will never succeed in eradicating it (Khan, 1996). In every country in the world there are also women's movements and democratic forces seeking to develop and sustain liberation (Mumtaz and Shaheed, 1987; Saadawi, 1980). Robust debate is one indicator of the democratic health of a nation, respect for the struggles of others in less privileged positions is another.

So why are Muslims so troubled about the way in which they are being viewed and the kind of criticisms that are being levelled against them in Britain today? In 1997 the Runnymede Trust, an independent research and policy agency dedicated to the development of a successful and equal multi-ethnic society, published the report of its Commission on British Muslims and Islamophobia. This summarised key distinctions to be made between 'closed' and 'open' views of Islam. 'Closed' views are developed from unfounded prejudice and hostility, in which phobic dread of Islam – Islamophobia – is the most distinctive characteristic. 'Open' views are based on respect which nevertheless allows legitimate disagreement and criticism.

Closed and open views of Islam

Distinctions	Closed views of Islam	Open views of Islam
1. Monolithic/diverse	Islam seen as a single monolithic bloc, static and unresponsive to new realities	Islam seen as diverse and progressive with internal differences, debates and development
2. Separate/interacting	Islam seen as separate and other – (a) not having any aims or values in common with other cultures (b) not affected by them (c) not influencing them	Islam seen as interdependent with other faiths and cultures – (a) having certain shared values and aims (b) affected by them (c) enriching them
3. Inferior/different	Islam seen as inferior to the West, barbaric, irrational, primitive, sexist	Islam seen as distinctively different, but not deficient and as equally worthy of respect
4. Enemy/partner	Islam seen as violent, aggressive, threatening, supportive of terrorism, engaged in 'a clash of civilisations'	Islam seen as an actual or potential partner in joint co-operative enterprises and in the solution of shared problems
5. Manipulative/sincere	Islam seen as a political ideology, used for political or military advantage	Islam seen as a genuine religious faith, practised sincerely by its adherents
6. Criticism of 'the West' rejected out of hand/considered	Criticisms made by Islam of 'the West' rejected out of hand	Criticisms of 'the West' and other cultures are considered and debated
7. Discrimination defended/criticised	Hostility towards Islam used to justify discriminatory practices towards Muslims and exclusion of Muslims from mainstream society	Debates and disagreements with Islam do not diminish efforts to combat discrimination and exclusion
8. Islamophobia seen as natural/problematic	Anti-Muslim hostility accepted as natural and 'normal'	Critical views of Islam are themselves subjected to critique, lest they be inaccurate and unfair

Source: Runnymede Trust, 1997

The eight distinctions made by the Runnymede Trust in the first column of the table amount to a form of intellectual checklist which can be used to assess the balance in any discussion about Muslims or Islam. Most newspaper articles, television and radio newscasts and documentaries fall clearly into column two (Closed views of Islam). So, disturbingly, do many pieces of academic writing. The writers, artists and media presenters whose work falls within the framework of column three (Open views of Islam) are few and far between. Little wonder that Muslims in Britain feel beleaguered. And, little wonder that adult educators are at a loss when it comes to engaging in healthy debate. An essential first step in raising awareness and in reorienting debate towards an approach in which communication can flow constructively and creatively is an examination of the roots of prejudice within our history.

Islamophobia: the spectre of fundamentalism

> In recent years a new word has gained currency. The word is 'Islamophobia'. . . . The word is not ideal but is recognisably similar to 'xenophobia' and 'europhobia' and is a useful shorthand way of referring to dread or hatred of Islam – and, therefore, to fear or dislike of all or most Muslims. Such dread and dislike have existed in Western countries and cultures for several centuries. In the last twenty years, however, the dislike has become more explicit, more extreme and more dangerous. (Runnymede Trust, 1997)

When the countries of Europe sought to regenerate after the devastations of the Second World War, they had no anticipation of the long-term consequences of calling for migrant workers from their former empires to fill gaps in the labour market. The basis on which they recruited from Africa, Asia and the Caribbean was immediate and urgent, with little thought of the ways in which the demographic profile of Europe would be altered, or the ways in which the relationship of their former colonies to their metropolises would be transformed. The people who were recruited were viewed variously as 'guest workers' or 'immigrants', mere numbers in a world-wide labour reservoir which should respond to the need for workers to fill the niches left vacant by the indigenous population which could not sustain the demand for the shiftworkers, shopkeepers and professionals who were needed if the European economies were to recover.

The possibility that the 'labour reservoir' would contain people proud of their heritage who would sustain close ties with their homelands while settling into their new homes, was not considered. Even less considered was the possibility that the experience of life in European countries would lead not to forms of 'assimilation' in which the migrants would merge into some form of monocultural landscape, but to the flourishing of ethnic identities and faiths that challenged the hegemony of secularism to which the Europeans had resorted in their search for an ethos which would allow them to turn away from the most recent past. The pain of the immediate xenophobic and anti-semitic past was assuaged for Europeans by forgetfulness rather than by searching reflection on the ways in which some of the societies in their 'civilised' world had colluded in genocide. The European climacteric of the Second World War is in many ways a barrier to understanding the continuities which underlie, in particular, the history of Gypsies, Jews and Muslims who have sustained world views which are radically at variance with prevailing assumptions. Today, Muslims carry a heavy burden because, throughout Europe, they are being demonised in ways which are reminiscent of the time of the Crusades (Armstrong, 1991; Said, 1978).

Muslims have a unique position in European history and culture. They have been 'indigenous' since the glorious days of Muslim rule in Spain. For example, Andalusia saw the burgeoning of a civilisation which aroused the admiration of medieval Europe (Armstrong, 1991; Brockelman, 1982). Arabic literature, scholarship, medicine and sciences were the foundation and inspiration of the European Renaissance.

> Michael Scot (1175–1235), the famous Scottish translator, mathematician and astrologer, studied at Toledo in Spain. He is reputed to have been born at Balwearie Castle and lived at Aikwood Tower, Fifeshire. He left Scotland in order to advance his learning. Being of deep intellect, he became proficient in Arabic and began translating Arabic works into Latin. During his stay in Spain he read and translated a number of books and treatises of famous Muslim philosophers, doctors and authors such as Abu Ali Sina (Avicenna), Al Ghazali, Ibn Rushed (Averroes). In 1217, he translated *Kitab Al Hal'a*, the astronomical works of the well-known Arab astronomer Al Butrugi. (Maan, 1997a)

But Muslims are also the 'essential other' – the only faith to have challenged Europe across the centuries. In the seventh century, the Muslim armies penetrated deep into the European heartland and the great civilisation of Islamic Spain was established, to last for centuries until Granada was conquered in 1492 (Armstrong, 1991). In the eighteenth and nineteenth centuries, the Europeans were trading and contending with the great state organisations of India, Turkey and the Near and Middle East (the Mogul, Ottoman, Safvid and Uzbek empires). Throughout their domination of great tracts of land in the Mediterranean, Africa, the Middle East and Asia, the Europeans failed to subjugate and eliminate the faith of the colonial peoples. At every level, from the intellectual to the visceral, fears of Islamic domination can be stirred by selective reference to the past.

Having failed to come to terms with the xenophobic past when programmes of genocide were launched against the Gypsies and the Jews who were, and remain, minorities indigenous within Europe, it is hardly surprising that Europeans are now failing to come to terms with the minority who challenge today both as indigenous and as essential other. Muslims have been demonised since the first of the Crusades was called by Pope Urban in 1095. There is a deep well of demoniac mythology on which to draw.

At the core of Islamophobia is a monolith – the assumption that all Muslims are the same and, if they are all the same, then they must support all actions, however wrong, which are undertaken in the name of Islam. Within this monolith there is no room for understanding the horror of Muslims who are subjected to barbaric excesses in various countries or sympathy for Muslim Scots who feel despair when they are associated, as Muslims, with terrorists and murderers.

> The treacherous massacre at Luxor must be condemned in no uncertain terms. I am a Muslim citizen of Britain . . . I feel hurt and I mourn the deaths of all the victims of this wanton tragedy . . . The damnable acts of violence perpetrated by the terrorists in Algeria and Egypt are generating more and more Islamophobia in the midst of the people because these criminals are being portrayed as Islamic fundamentalists by the Western media. It is high time that the media acted responsibly and stopped blaming Islam for the misdeeds of some depraved terrorists . . . In the light of the Quranic ordinances those who were involved in the outrage at Luxor and killed sixty innocent visitors were contravening the Islamic law. They were acting against the code of Islam. They have their own political agenda and they are abusing Islam to achieve their political aims. They cannot and should not be termed Islamic fundamentalists. They are terrorists . . . unbelievers. (Maan, 1997b)

The spectre of 'fundamentalism' so effectively obscures communication between Muslims and others that it is difficult to recall that the term was first adopted in the middle of the nineteenth century by a radical movement within American Protestantism and then, from 1919, by the World Christian Fundamentalist Association. It was not until 1981 that it was first applied in a polemical sense to Islam when Anthony Burgess published an article in the *Observer* in which he spoke of 'the phenomenon of the new, or rather very old, Islam, the dangerous fundamentalism revived by the ayatollahs', compared the *Qur'an* to *Mein Kampf* and concluded that there is 'more blood and stupidity than glamour in the theocracy of the Sons of the Prophet' (*Observer*, 27.09.81). The speed with which 'fundamentalism' was adopted by leading intellectuals and journalists as a term of abuse was extraordinary, as was the widespread nature of its adoption. On most topics, one would expect to find something of a distance in vocabulary between the tabloid press and the broadsheets, but not on this one – as the Runnymede Trust find in their regular monitoring of the press.

The depth to which this spectre has penetrated was brought home to us recently when a European Parliament paper was drawn to our attention. Written by Arie Oostlander, on behalf of the Committee on Civil Liberties and Internal Affairs, this report purports to deal with 'Fundamentalism and the challenge to the European legal order' (Oostlander, 1997). Three main rhetorical devices are used in the paper. First, there is a lack of clarity about its explicit focus, but fundamentalism is consistently characterised as intrinsically violent, as in references to 'violent forms of religious fundamentalism' and to 'violent fundamentalism in the European Union'. Second, its implicit focus emerges simply because there is only occasional reference to other forms of fundamentalism. The overwhelming focus is on Islam – of the seven pages of the statement, five are devoted exclusively to discussion of Islam. This focus is all the more threatening because it is not stated openly. Third, the text is so drenched in statements which are biased, unsubstantiated and even inflammatory, that one cannot extricate the constructive and positive content because it is systematically contaminated.

In a subsequent letter to European Members of Parliament, Bashir Maan made the following points:

> I am writing on behalf of the Scottish Muslim Community to express my deep concern . . . Put simply, we are concerned that if it stands as drafted, then it will contribute to Islamophobia and further alienate Muslims who are well aware that Governments are reluctant to grant Islam equal status with other religious traditions.
>
> The tone and content of the paper are such that we fear that Islamophobia may be inflamed in place of the centuries-old hostility to Jews, who were, until the nineteenth century pogroms and the twentieth century Holocaust, the largest of the religious minorities within Europe. Surely the governments of the new Europe of the Union should learn the lessons of the past and ensure that they do not create 'an enemy within' of the kind which this paper is propagating? (Maan, 1997b)

To anyone who has studied the chilling history of European anti-semitism and who can read statements about Muslims with a critical eye, the devices used in the Civil Liberties and Internal Affairs document are disturbingly familiar. Anti-semitism was entrenched in Nazi Germany by means of policy papers and administrative guidelines. They were drafted and revised by politicians and civil servants who knew how to cloak prejudice and bias in seemingly reasonable terminology. Such devices belong to what the Runnymede Trust has summarised as 'closed views of Islam' in which the monolith of Islam is alien, inferior, violent and aggressive, and regarded as a political ideology. If we remain locked within these 'closed views', then there can be no way forward for Muslims in Scotland. What we require is a move towards 'open views of Islam' in which we can perceive diversity and internal debate, interdependency with other faiths and potential partnership.

Diversities within Islam in Scotland

Looking at Scotland with an 'open' view, what do we find? How are Muslims responding to their position as the 'second faith' minority? What stage have Scottish Muslims reached in development of a religious infrastructure? What agenda do Muslims have in relation to education?

Bashir Maan's research indicates that the very first Muslims to come to Scotland were probably diplomats, traders and travellers from Spain and North Africa in medieval times – including 'Black Mores', one of whom is recorded to have been a drummer and choreographer in the court of James IV. Sir Walter Scott mentioned that six black trumpeters were attached to the Scottish Life Guards in 1679, and there were black musicians (Moors) in Scottish regiments in the eighteenth and nineteenth centuries. From the eighteenth century onwards, Muslim seamen and servants began to arrive in Scotland, subsequently including Muhammad Bakhsh and Abdul Karim who were royal servants and favourites of Queen Victoria. Early in the twentieth century, colonies of seamen (Lascars) became established in the ports of Glasgow, Leith and Dundee.

It was only after the First World War that settlements of Muslims began to develop as South Asian seamen turned to hawking and peddling and began to make a steadier living. By 1930 there were about 100 Muslims in Scotland, and by 1939 Muslims in Glasgow were estimated at 400. In 1934 the first branch of *Jamiat ul Muslimin* (the Muslim Association) was established in Glasgow and the Muslim community began to gather for Friday prayers in one house. They then rented a hall for feasts and festivals. In 1942 the *Jamiat* leased this hall for conversion into a temporary mosque, and in 1943 a tenement building was purchased and converted into a mosque and meeting place. In 1944 a burial plot was purchased in Sandymount Cemetery in Glasgow.

Following the end of the Second World War and the creation of the state of Pakistan, migration to Scotland increased markedly (Maan, 1992). As a result, in 1955 the Pakistani Social and Cultural Society was formed, and in 1956 weekend and evening classes were started for religious instruction and mother tongue teaching for children. In 1958 Glasgow Mortuary agreed to provide facilities for burial. Between 1958 and 1974 there were prolonged negotiations about the purchase of a plot of land and the design and construction of the mosque which now stands as a landmark beside the River Clyde.

Pakistanis are now the largest of the Muslim minorities in Scotland, and have taken pride in their ability to spearhead the establishment of the infrastructure of mosques (at the latest count, there were 30 across Scotland), burial facilities and *madrassahs* that is essential for any Muslim community living as a minority within a non-Muslim society. As Muslims, they are enjoined to obey the law of their adopted land, but in return, they require the conditions and facilities which will allow them to participate fully as citizens in the mainstream of life while practising their religion.

By 1997, when the Pakistani community commemorated the fiftieth anniversary of the founding of Pakistan, Muslims numbered about 40,000 throughout Scotland and around 20,000 in Greater Glasgow alone. The celebrations were led by the Scottish-Pakistani Association, founded in 1982, and included a formal dinner, a series of public lectures, a *mushaira* (poetry reading) and an impressive donation of £250,000 by a leading member of the community towards an educational foundation at the University of Strathclyde (*Scotsman*, 15.08.97).

There could not have been a clearer statement about the priority which senior members of the Scottish Pakistani community give to education. After all, they are Muslims, enjoined by the Prophet to remember that 'The pursuit of knowledge is incumbent upon every Muslim, male and female'. They are also Pakistanis who are acutely aware of the shockingly low level of literacy and poor state of education in their country of origin (Yusuf, 1997; Saeed, 1998). And they are Scots, as proud as any other Scottish citizen, of our national traditions of educational excellence. Pakistani Scots view education not only as a right, entitlement and need, but as a duty.

The movement for education rights

When Akram Khan-Cheema, a former inspector of schools and currently chair of the governing body of a Muslim school in Bradford, was asked his opinion about life in Britain, he answered: 'We have a wonderful opportunity in a country like Britain. We have freedom of expression to develop our own thinking without oppression, in spite of the Islamophobia. And we have the opportunity to mix with Muslims from many parts of the world in a multifarious Islamic cultural mix'. His words are echoed by Fozia Bora, one of the editors of *Q-News*, a weekly newspaper for young British Muslims: 'Britain is a good place to be . . . there is a tradition of religious and intellectual freedom. And tolerance. We were visited by a journalist from *Le Figaro*, the French newspaper, recently, who expressed surprise that we were allowed to have our own newspaper and say what we wanted' (*Independent*, 6.12.95). The name of *Q-News*, deliberately neutral in an attempt to overcome factionalism, was itself chosen as part of the assertion by a new generation that they are entering the mainstream of British society while maintaining their Muslim identity.

However, what British Muslims also agree is that their sense of well-being in Britain is being undermined by the reluctance of central and local government to grant them full rights in education as a religious minority. They welcome the provision on religious education in the National Curriculum because all Muslims should learn respect for other faiths, especially the Abrahamic faiths of Judaism and Christianity – the People of the Book. There are, however, problems of inaccurate teaching which need attention and should be put right through the local consultation processes prescribed in legislation. Muslims also welcome the measures which some schools are implementing in order to protect pupils from Islamophobic abuse. They wish that these measures were being taken by all schools, so that they could be more assured that their daughters and sons are safe.

What Muslims do not welcome is the fact that facilities for pupils to pray are few and far between, even during the holy month of Ramadhan. Nor do they welcome the fact that no state schools provide facilities for religious instruction. Muslim families who wish to ensure that their children pray regularly and receive religious instruction must rely on the network of *madrassahs*, but:

> The teachers are often untrained and not well qualified. The methods of their teaching are outdated and incomprehensible for the children born and growing up in this country. The teaching is done in their mother tongue that in most cases is not fully understood by the children who speak and are taught in English in the schools. (Maan, 1997b)

The *madrassahs* are supported by communities among whom there are disproportionate numbers of people impoverished as a result of industrial decline and unemployment. Quite apart from the weight of financial responsibility which these communities bear as they sustain their educational rights through voluntary effort, there is an enduring sense of injustice because the children are suffering through deprivation of play and leisure time and their parents are criticised by teachers for the burden they place on them.

Muslim families in Glasgow are caught between a rock and a hard place. They cannot solve the problem of religious instruction because only Catholics are allowed the facilities which they seek. In Scotland the Catholic sector is supported by state funding of denominational schools and teacher training. In 1994 the head of the Catholic Church in Scotland chaired the commission which produced the Catholic National Guidelines on Religious and Moral Education 5–14. Significantly, these guidelines

> are intended to assist teachers as they help Catholic pupils to develop a knowledge and understanding of their own faith and to support their faith formation . . . It is hoped that this document can also be used to benefit Catholic pupils unable to attend Roman Catholic schools and contribute to the wider field of religious and moral education. (Scottish Office Education Department and Scottish Catholic Education Commission, 1994)

In other words, Catholic families can choose to send their children to Catholic schools, and request teachers to teach the Catholic religious education curriculum in non-denominational schools. All other faiths represented in Scotland today (Buddhist, Hindu, Jewish, Sikh and Muslim) are confined to an approach which is summarised as follows:

> . . . Christianity has shaped the history and traditions of Scotland and continues to exert an influence on national life. Other major religions . . . are also represented. It would not be possible to develop a comprehensive knowledge and understanding of all these faiths within the school curriculum. However, it is important that while recognising the role of Christianity as the major religious tradition of this country, pupils should also be encouraged to develop understanding of and respect for people of other faiths and people who adopt a non-religious stance for living. (Scottish Office Education Department, 1992)

Schools are also required to provide for pupils to take part in religious observance not less than once a week in primary and once a month in secondary schools, in consultation with the school chaplain. Within denominational schools, the Scottish Office goes on to state that religious observance should:

> express, develop and deepen the faith of the individual, school and community, celebrate the faith that has been explored in the religious education programme, allow pupils to experience the community at worship, help pupils to confirm and deepen their own prayer life, sacramental life and commitment.

Within the non-denominational sector religious observance should:

> allow pupils to engage in a shared activity reflecting and expressing their spiritual needs and aspirations, and allow those who wish, to worship; celebrate important occasions in the life of the school and community; involve pupils in experiences which stimulate, challenge and extend their capacities for spiritual response to the world in which they live. (Scottish Office Education Department, 1992)

Schools are exhorted to respect the different beliefs of pupils, teachers and parents and to consult with the School Board and parents in determining the pattern and frequency of religious observance. However, the inequity between the Catholic sector, where religious observance is intended to deepen the faith of the pupils, and the non-denominational sector, where the emphasis is on expressing their spiritual needs and aspirations, is clear. The arrangements for religious observance for Catholics (both within and outwith denominational schools) are far closer to what many Muslim parents would hope to achieve as a seamless, integrated experience of religious education for their daughters and sons.

In Glasgow several attempts have been made to establish a Muslim school, most recently in 1989. Then, the local Muslims ran headlong into the issue of sectarianism:

Not so long ago there were really only two kinds of Glaswegian, the Catholic and the Protestant. Today there are Moslems, Sikhs, Hindus, Jews and Christians mixing together in a city which can truly be described as multi-racial.

Speaking as a product of a Protestant education, I find it sad that we continue to perpetuate the folly of having separate Catholic schools. What we need is all-denominational schools rather than non-denominational schools. However, such a step forward is too much for the Roman Catholic hierarchy to contemplate, for the moment at least . . .

Dr Malcolm Green, Strathclyde's convenor of education, expressed grave fears when told about the Asian plan for a breakaway school . . . at a time when people are moving closer together across the traditional religious divide, it is unfortunate that others are talking about further fragmentation. The creation of an all-black school is the exact opposite of what we want to see. (*Herald*, 13.02.89)

Here is the nub of the problem. If Muslims ask for state funding for a school, they are accused of 'further fragmentation'. If they ask for a facility which is already allowed to another religious minority (in this case Catholics), the west of Scotland sectarian problem is brought into the frame and held against them. If they claim their rights as a 'religious' minority, they are told that they are not Muslim, but Asian or black. If they insist on being respected as Muslims, they are suspected of being 'fundamentalists'. Such a situation is manifestly unjust.

In reflecting on this issue, Bashir Maan recalls his own schooldays in government schools in Punjab, where he studied alongside Christians, Hindus and Sikhs. There was no distinction made between pupils of the four faiths as they followed the set curriculum until the period which was set aside for religious instruction, when each denomination separated for lessons and devotions led by an approved religious leader. Why, he asks, cannot the same be done in Scotland? His position has not changed from the one reported in the local press in 1991:

Parents are to be asked to vote on an opt-out scheme that could create Scotland's first Moslem school . . . Bashir Maan, chairman of Strathclyde Community Relations Council, said: 'I don't like the idea, but the Government are to blame. They have not taken notice of parents' wishes and force all pupils to participate in a Christian system. If they catered for all different religions in school, the demand for denominational schools would disappear.' (*Daily Record*, 14.06.91)

Will the inequity between Catholics, Muslims and pupils of other faiths be resolved in the new Scotland? Will Muslims continue to be refused their rights in education for fear of sectarianism? Will provision for Muslims be grafted onto the existing denominational arrangements? Will the sectarian nettle be grasped and radical changes be made in statutory arrangements for school curriculum and support for supplementary schools? Will politicians acknowledge that one way to reduce denominationalism – and its dark shadow, sectarianism – would be to bring religious instruction into specific periods, thus permitting the secularising of the rest of the week?

Conclusion: religion or religiosity in the new Scotland?

> My Scotland has been given to me not just by my country but by many countries. Cultural identity is not something we hold like a passport; it is something we continue to discover by looking at ourselves through the eyes of other cultures. The world contains a fascinating babel of diversity. And the more we attempt to understand others without prejudice, the more we will be rewarded with an enhanced understanding of ourselves. (William McIlvanney, speaking at the opening of the 64th International Pen Congress, August 1997)

William McIlvanney was not necessarily thinking about the new faith communities in Scotland when he spoke about a 'fascinating babel of diversity', but his account of his Scotland is one which underscores the approach we have adopted in this chapter. Serious damage is being done to community relations by the prejudiced denial of the right of religious expression to Scottish Muslims. Even more damaging is the silence of those people who should be the natural allies of Muslims. Muslims are deeply concerned about the fact that their religion is not accepted as part of their 'ethnicity' and their political allies prefer to see them as 'black' or 'Asian'.

Allowing Muslims and other religious minorities respect, dignity and understanding does not require agreement with their beliefs or conformity to their principles. On the contrary, it opens up the possibility of dialogue and discovery. In countries such as Pakistan, popular educators and feminists are challenging the traditionalists while remaining Muslims and functioning within the cultural realities of Islam (Khan, 1996; Mumtaz and Shaheed, 1987). Why can we not acknowledge that their movements are as challenging as the secular movements that are more familiar in the West?

The overwhelming majority of Muslims in Scotland are utterly and resolutely opposed to the forces of totalitarianism, authoritarianism and even theocracy, which are as threatening to their livelihoods and freedom of thought as they are to any other people who seek to live in freedom and peace. As Robert Fisk has pointed out in his challenging discussion of the fearsome Christian, Jewish and Muslim extremists to be found in the Middle East:

> adherents of these faiths often seem more liberal, the further they are from their holiest cities of Jerusalem and Mecca. The English vicar, the liberal

rabbi in London, the Muslim sheikh in Birmingham are the folks we enjoy meeting. (*Independent*, 03.12.97)

'Fundamentalism' was a term first coined by conservative Christians of the Right who draw on literal interpretations of the teaching of Christ in order to develop an exclusive and intolerant world view. It is imperative that, in the immediate future, educators in the tradition of theologies of liberation and popular education put aside their studied neglect of the issue of faith and realise that alliance with Muslims is not only possible but essential. How else are we to come to terms with social movements which arise out of religious faith – rather than secular political ideology? All the signs are that in the new millennium we will experience an increasing diversity of religious movements and thus an even greater challenge to educators. Islam is a cultural reality in Scotland. Educational justice needs to be done, and be seen to be done, for Muslims and for other religious minorities in Scotland.

References

Armstrong, K (1991) *Muhammad: A Western Attempt to Understand Islam*, London, Gollancz.

Brockelman, C (ed) (1982) *History of the Islamic Peoples*, London, Routledge and Kegan Paul.

Khan, A H (1996) *Orangi Pilot Project: Reminiscences and Reflections*, Karachi, Oxford University Press.

Maan, B (1992), *The New Scots: The Story of Asians in Scotland*, Edinburgh, John Donald.

Maan, B (1997a) *Notes towards a History of Muslims in Scotland*, Unpublished.

Maan, B (1997b) *Open letter to European Members of Parliament*, Unpublished.

Modood, T and Berthoud, R (1997) *Ethnic Minorities in Britain: Diversity and Disadvantage*, London, Policy Studies Institute.

Mumtaz, K and Shaheed, S (1987) *Women of Pakistan: Two Steps Forward, One Step Back?*, Lahore, Vanguard Books.

Oostlander, A (1997) Draft report *Fundamentalism and the challenge to the European legal order*, Brussels, Committee on Civil Liberties and Internal Affairs, European Parliament.

Runnymede Trust (1997) *Islamophobia: A Challenge for Us All*, London, Runnymede Trust.

Saadawi, N (1980) *The Hidden Face of Eve: Women in the Arab World*, London, Zed Press.

Saeed, F (1998) *Literacy for Women's Empowerment: An Evaluation of the Present State of Education in Pakistan and Proposal for Future Development*, M. Phil dissertation, Faculty of Arts, University of Glasgow.

Said, E (1978) *Orientalism: Western Conceptions of the Orient*, New York, Pantheon Books.

Sarwar, G (1994) *British Muslims and Schools*, London, Muslim Educational Trust.

Scottish Office Education Department (1992) *Curriculum and Assessment in Scotland. National Guidelines: Religious and Moral Education, 5–14*, Edinburgh, HMSO.

Scottish Office Education Department and Scottish Catholic Education Commission (1994) *Religious Education, 5–14: Roman Catholic Schools*, Edinburgh, HMSO.

Websters New Collegiate Dictionary (1973), London, G & C Merriam Co.

Yusuf, K F (1997) *British influence on education in India and Pakistan*, Lecture given to Scottish Pakistani Association in Glasgow, Unpublished.

10 'A band of little comrades': Socialist Sunday Schools in Scotland

David Fisher

This is an account of the now largely hidden history of the Socialist Sunday School movement which endured in many parts of industrialised Scotland for over 50 years. Very much part of the 'old' socialist tradition, it sought to instruct children in the universalist and internationalist values of equality, justice and peace. They were taught systematically – if in a highly restricted way – to relate the personal to the political, combining self-discipline with a wider sense of political awareness and social responsibility. Socialism was cultural – a way of living – as much as political, a set of principles and institutions for organising public life. Conservative in its pedagogy and radical in many aspects of its curriculum, the Socialist Sunday School movement harboured deeply embedded contradictions. These served both to keep it alive and, eventually, to hasten its demise.

Socialism as a way of life

Every Sunday in Scotland for over 50 years, hundreds of children put on their best clothes and trooped to meetings where they sang hymns, listened to uplifting stories and learned how to live decent and worthwhile lives. Summer picnics, Christmas parties and musical soirées filled in their leisure time. They recited poems. They behaved.

Appearances can be deceptive. These were the children of the Socialist Sunday Schools, and in amongst the recitations and moral tales they were also learning lessons that might not have gone down so well with dominie or minister. They learned, for example, that the existing order of society was unjust and had to be overturned, that war was evil and should be resisted, that everyone, including children, should think for themselves.

The Socialist Sunday School movement began in the 1890s, in the west of Scotland. It was part of the same flowering of socialist activity that saw the emergence of independent labour politics and the first labour MPs. Its lifespan roughly coincided with that of the Independent Labour Party, from the 1890s to the immediate post-war period, though in Glasgow a few schools survived well into the 1960s.

The aim of the schools was simple: to teach socialist values to children. However, the movement was not evangelical. The point was not to convert unbelievers, but to make sure that socialist beliefs continued from one generation to another. For the founders of the movement, socialism was not just a system of thought, but *a way of life*. This meant it was not something that had to wait till the 'age of reason', when an adult could make a rational choice for or against socialism. If socialism encompassed the whole of life, it encompassed childhood also. The organisers of the Socialist Sunday Schools would have no more seen the point of restricting their beliefs and way of life to adults than Christians would.

The socialism they taught was ethical rather than scientific, humanistic rather than ideological. As the schools' magazine the *Young Socialist* put it in March 1901, the aim of socialists should be to 'build up the City of Love in our own hearts, and so, by and by, help to build it up in the world'. This was an intensely subjective socialism, confident in the worth and ability of the individual, certain too that history was going its way. The movement was born of an era when socialism was often experienced as conversion (see Yeo, 1977), and the schools were shot through with religious imagery and terminology. For example, just as the church had its Ten Commandments, so the schools had their Ten Precepts. These included: 1. 'Love your school fellows, who will be your fellow-workmen in life', 3. 'Make every day holy by good and useful deeds and kindly actions', and 7. 'Remember that the good things of the earth are produced by labour. Whoever enjoys them without working for them is stealing the bread of the workers'.

Revolution in due order

Children were encouraged to take an active part in the running of the school, to be more than just pupils. One of the children always acted as minute secretary, for example. Teachers sought to make lessons as lively and interesting as possible, and children were actively involved in lessons through mock elections and role-playing, for instance, to a degree that was perhaps unusual for the time. All the same, there was a set order to the classes, as regular in its way as sermons, notices and hymns in an ordinary church service. There was the roll call, the reading of the minutes and then the giving of 'items' by the children. Here they might talk about something they had read in the newspaper, or sing a song, or recite a poem.

Then there was the lesson. In many ways the Socialist Sunday Schools were like a church service, a coming together of the faithful to reaffirm their commitment, both to the cause and to each other. But the didactic element was not forgotten. Through stories, parables and lectures, the children were instructed in the elements of socialist thinking. The Minute Book of the Central Edinburgh School provides examples. A natural history lesson about how certain species of birds co-operate to ward off birds of prey teaches us that people can co-operate too (Minute Book, 9 March 1913). The story of how the gas in the gaslight gets there is the basis for an elaborate metaphor of socialism (gasworks were the 'great reservoir of socialism', the large pipes were the 'socialist orators' like Jaurés and Keir Hardie, and so on down to the 'young comrades' who were like 'gas burners, burning with a pure clean light' – Minute Book, 7 November 1915). Or on a more personal basis, the superintendent describes the homeless people he saw at a 'free breakfast' and how socialism would do away with such scenes.

And sometimes there was, simply, knowledge for its own sake:

> A very interesting lesson was given on 'The Bee' by Comrade Green who came provided with a microscope through which the children were able to see clearly the different parts of the bee which he also brought with him. (Minute Book, 26 May 1907)
>
> Miss Dalrymple gave us a very interesting lesson on the Romans and the Greeks; how they had slaves and how they bathed in the forenoon and talked in the afternoon. (Minute Book, 7 February 1915)

Practical politics was not forgotten. While they were at the schools the children would help however they could in the adult political activities going on around them. The schools were, after all, the children's wing of a wider movement, not just a way of keeping 'the weans' entertained for an afternoon. So the children would deliver leaflets at elections, carry the banner at parades and gatherings, and generally help with some of the fetching and carrying that goes with any political activity.

As the children got older, more opportunities for political involvement opened up: the Labour Party's League of Youth, the Young Communist League, the Independent Labour Party's Scottish Socialist Party Youth Movement – there was no shortage of 'universities' to move onto after graduating from the Socialist Sunday Schools. Indeed, many moved further, into lifelong activism of various kinds, official and unofficial. But there was no standard outcome. For some, the schools were part of a socialist background that encompassed family, work and leisure. For others, they were a stimulus towards forms of education and activism they might otherwise have missed. But for all those who attended, even if they later drifted away from the movement, it was a formative experience. The schools opened up new horizons for working class children whose lives might otherwise have been bounded by the worlds of work and home. For one Edinburgh pupil who later became hostile to the labour movement, his time in the Socialist Sunday School was nonetheless a treasured part of his childhood: 'it was a good education for me . . . it taught me that there was more in the world than just a few people in Edinburgh' (Interview).

Socialism begins at home

Clearly, the schools were part of a socialist movement which sought ways to challenge and overturn the existing order. The outside world, when it took notice of the schools at all, generally perceived them in this light – as a threat, and a breeding ground of subversion. And yet, it has to be said there is to our eyes today something almost disturbingly conventional about the Socialist Sunday Schools. The lessons were often of a kind that would not be out of place in the most traditional church Sunday school. For example, choosing almost at random from the Minute Book of the Central Edinburgh School gives us the following lesson headings: 'Truthfulness', 'Tidiness', 'Honesty is the Best Policy', 'The importance of saying "No"'.

And however much stress Socialist Sunday School teaching placed on independence of thought and action ('bow down to none', 'observe and think in order to discover the truth'), testimony from those who were involved in the schools makes it clear that socialism for children did not equate with doing whatever they liked. One former pupil commented that: 'We were told we were not entitled to pocket money unless we earned it, such as going messages, or helping mother with the housework, as socialism begins at home' (Interview).

'Socialism begins at home' could indeed serve as a kind of motto of the Socialist Sunday School movement. The *Socialist Sunday School Manual*, published in 1923, developed the point: 'We work from the known to the unknown and thus lay the foundations for future lessons. There is enough "Practical Socialism" in every decent family to provide a foundation for building up future notions in the child's mind of an "Ideal Society of Humanity"'. The manual suggests a series of lessons beginning with a portrayal of the solitary life, using the example of Robinson Crusoe, and goes on to advise: 'help the child to realise that he does not live like Robinson Crusoe. He lives with others. His father and mother take care of him, his brothers and sisters play with him. He lives in a little "Society"'.

At the conclusion of this series of lessons, the 'Big Society' (the nation) is compared with the 'Little Society' (the family) and comes off badly. The Little Family provides food for all its members, the Big Family only in cases of dire need. The Little Family provides work as a matter of right for its members, the Big Family does not. The manual draws out the pedagogical point:

> A child's definition of Socialism may be worked out here, eg the nation should be like a big family and provide all its members with these necessary things – life, food, work, education and the use of tools, lands and capital . . . Always keep in view that injustice between members of a family is an obstacle to love between members. Justice must therefore be the foundation if love is to be the spirit of the family.

The same thought was taken up by a *Young Socialist* editorial in 1917, using a domestic image that occurs frequently in Socialist Sunday School texts:

> Just as it would be vain to expect love and peace to reign round the family table if some were sumptuously fed and attended to, while the others were neglected, starved, or only the leavings contemptuously thrown to them –

so it is vain to expect the family of humanity to live in peace and social unity, while this is the prevailing method of our social existence.

The model of the family these lessons presupposed was a deeply conventional one: woman the homemaker, man the breadwinner, children following suit according to gender. Under the heading 'Division of Labour', the manual gives the following lesson outline:

Daddy goes out to work. Mother works about the house. Mary does the sewing. Dick splits the sticks etc. What is the advantage of this?

Later, under the heading 'Altruism':

For whom does Daddy work? and Mother? Elicit that all who work in the family do so for the benefit of all the members of the family, eg Daddy earns the money to buy things for the dinner, Mother cooks the dinner, Mary sets the table. All sit round the table and enjoy the dinner.

So was the Socialist Sunday School movement just a case of the skilled working class aspiring to bourgeois respectability? In the domestic sphere, the ideal of the Socialist Sunday Schools was clearly that of enlightened, bourgeois family life. We have already seen the strong religious and ethical colouring of much of their teaching. And ironically, for a movement so concerned with communal values, its greatest achievements may have been at the individual level. Ask a former Socialist Sunday School pupil what they think the schools achieved and the reply is unlikely to relate to changes made in the outside world – a reform achieved here, a campaign furthered there. Instead, the answer will be framed in terms of individual achievement, the building up of character, the broadening of the mind. As one former 'little comrade' remarked: 'If everyone lived up to the things they were taught at the Socialist Sunday School, they'd have turned out to have been good adults' (Interview).

Home Sweet Home and The Internationale

But Socialist Sunday Schools have to be set in the context of the socialism of their era. In general, this socialism was one whose opposition to the status quo never strayed far from the realm of politics pure and simple. Outside that realm, there were many aspects of cultural and social life which socialists happily embraced along with the bourgeoisie – an embrace that to an observer from our own era can sometimes seem naive. But for the moment, the notion of 'hegemony', of a power that extends beyond the world of politics into the world of culture, remained confined with Gramsci to an Italian prison. Cultural criticism from a socialist standpoint awaited the arrival of the post-war New Left. Meantime, when it came to culture, socialists and non-socialists drew from the same well. Both assumed familiarity with stock items of the Western canon – the Bible, the Greek and Roman myths, Shakespeare – as well as the Victorian 'standards' such as Tennyson, Longfellow and Dickens. It was the same with life in the workplace, ways of behaving, family relationships: socialist or not, you had to have rules.

> Get the children to give some of the regulations their mothers make, eg 'Put things back in their place'; 'Go to bed at 8 o'clock'. Who makes them? Who obeys them? What is the advantage of them? etc. Show that Social Life would be impossible without some such regulations, written or unwritten. (*Socialist Sunday School Manual*)

The problem with capitalism, from the point of view of this style of socialism, was twofold: it had a stranglehold on the good things in life and it managed them badly. But there was no dispute about what these good things were: culture, the arts, leisure, good health, job satisfaction. The kind of socialism that flourished around the turn of the century and to which the Socialist Sunday School movement belonged – the socialism of William Morris and Robert Blatchford – is often described as utopian. But the things it valued had nothing utopian about them. They were all in the here and now and they were at least as needed and valued by socialism as by capitalism. There was to be no throwing of *sabots* into the machinery, because the machinery was not an enemy, it just happened to be in the enemy's hands. And, anyway, to exercise skill in the service of that machinery was itself an accomplishment, a source of pride:

> We taught them [at the Socialist Sunday Schools] to work at their lessons at school and when they came to take on their job to be good at their job. If you're an apprentice in the shipyard, you should be the best apprentice, not because there's a prize but because you, as a young socialist, are required to be the best apprentice, because one day you will be required to build socialism and you will need to be a good worker. (Ireland, 1996)

Conclusion

It is doubtful if the founders of the Socialist Sunday School movement would have understood any characterisation of the schools as 'alternative'. Their aim was not to rethink the idea of education, but to extend it to the working class and to the socialist movement – making it, in the process, as humane, attractive and child-centred as possible. Their values were universalist. They drew on popular traditions and rituals as a source of strength, singing from a hymnbook that contained both *Home Sweet Home* and *The Internationale*. Their universalism was not straightforward, but was made up of contradictions: between rationality and ritual, between a call to revolution and a desire for order. It is possible that it was the very fact of harbouring these contradictions – of offering multiple satisfactions – that kept the movement alive for so long. And for the children, unconcerned with contradictions, it was at the very least a spot of colour on a dreich Scottish Sunday afternoon – and for some of them, at any rate, a route to political involvement and a stimulus to the mind.

References

Ireland, D (1996) 'Unity Halls', *The Herald* 24 February.
Yeo, S (1977) 'A new life: the religion of socialism in Britain, 1883–1896', *History Workshop* 4, pp 5–56.

Acknowledgements

My thanks are due to all the people I talked to in Edinburgh and Glasgow about their time in the Socialist Sunday Schools. The oral material was originally recorded as part of a project funded by the People's Story Museum, Edinburgh, with whose kind permission it appears here.

11 Defiant sisters: exploited workers

Sue Mansfield

The author of this chapter uses a case history of women workers in the Dundee jute industry to explore the distinction — and the connections — between the oppression of partriarchy and the exploitation of class. On the basis of this account, she argues that any attempt to recover the role of women in history for a popular education curriculum must confront problems of both epistemology and mythology. In particular, the complex relationship between gender and class needs to be analysed and understood. Feminist historians and educators should take urgent action to preserve the documentation and other material evidence of their own contemporary struggles if — as in the past — they are not to be written out of the historical record.

Introduction

Dundee has been described as 'the biggest village in Scotland', a curious way of describing a city with a population of approximately 165,000 (Government Statistical Service, 1992) but one which reflects something of the homogeneity of a city which historically had a small middle class and a working class which was heavily dependent on a single industry for employment. Jute, the first of the triumvirate of industries associated with Dundee (the others being jam and journalism) was the most important, not only economically but also culturally. By 1989, when I moved to Dundee to take up a teaching appointment, it had all but closed down. Nevertheless, it had left behind a strong oral tradition about defiant and spirited women workers who were the main wage earners whilst their male partners stayed at home as 'kettle bilers'. Both students and local community education workers frequently cited these women to me as inspirational role models for women today – an example of how Scottish women in general and Dundee women in particular were more emancipated than their contemporaries elsewhere. This folk history is very attractive, especially if one is looking to establish, as I was, an historical tradition of emancipatory action by women within social movements.

The case has already been well established elsewhere that history is a social construct (Carr, 1964; Grosholz, 1988) and that the gendered nature of most written histories has resulted in women being actively written out of history (eg Rowbotham, 1974; Lerner, 1979; Beddoe, 1987). I was in the process of applying the same analysis to the history of community-based adult education (Mansfield, 1992). My hypothesis was that the historical contribution of women had been discounted and that an alternative history could and should be written. Initially, I was selfishly dismayed at the apparent irrelevance of this hypothesis to the local situation. Here were women who, far from being written out of history, were in fact an integral part of the local self-identity. I consoled myself with the thought that these were women whose history I could build into on-going research on the historical development of popular community-based education in Scotland. I tried to convince myself that if the hypothesis was to be proved wrong in the Scottish context, then that would be something both to celebrate and incorporate into my teaching with predominantly mature women students.

My initial research, however, indicated that though the image is a very attractive one, it was also an overly romantic one which focused on the consequences but not the causes of the regendering of employment that occurred in nineteenth century Scotland. Both women and men took pride in the stories they had been told by their mothers and grandmothers of these early pioneers, whose role swapping prefigured what many of them were experiencing today. However, nobody seemed to be asking questions about why and how the situation had arisen, much less whether there were parallels to be drawn with the present. The recognition that contemporary employment patterns for women could not be divorced from the wider socio-economic context made me realise that the historical experience of women textile workers in Dundee is one that needed to be set against the background of the Scottish textile industry of the time as a whole.

Once I began to do this, I also began to view the oral accounts in a far less positive light. More worrying still for me was the thought that this process of romanticisation might still be at work today. For example, I began to wonder whether the actions of women during the 1984–85 Miners Strike would similarly enter the collective folk memory – and just what exactly would those memories consist of? Would they be about women on the picket lines or of women in the kitchens of the strike centres? Would they highlight the growth of sisterly solidarity and the collective political gains that were achieved, or would they focus on individualised empowerment and personal development? Would we mythologise the role of women in one of the last big industrial disputes of the twentieth century?

This paper, therefore, begins by examining ways in which we can conceptualise women's history based on the work of Lerner (1979) in order to offer a framework for applying a more rigorous approach to the way we interpret Dundee women's experiences from the historical record. As a result of reinterpreting their history, it moves on to the proposition that far from being proto-feminists or community activists, women workers and their families in the Dundee textile industry were caught up in the same processes that have changed employment patterns nationally in the latter half of the twentieth century. To continue to regard them as role models or to view their life experiences in a such a romantic light is to reinforce the processes and values that oppressed women workers rather than emancipated them in the first place. As such, the reconstructed history deserves a place within a critical feminist curriculum in its own right. The paper ends by suggesting how we can try to ensure that our own contemporary experiences are not only written into the historical record but also into a popular education curriculum.

Conceptualising women's history

Lerner (1979), in tracing the development of women's history as an academic field of study, identifies three ways of conceptualising women's history. She describes these as 'compensatory history', 'contribution history' and 'transitional history'. These should not be regarded as rigid, mutually exclusive categories because any given work of history will probably contain elements of all three, but this framework provides us with a useful way of identifying both the raw material we need and the ways it can be presented in order to construct empowering histories of women.

Compensatory history is the history of 'women worthies', the women of achievement who have been written out of the conventional histories because of their gender. This could be an important starting point, not least because Dundee had some notable women worthies such as Mary Lily Walker, who founded Grey Lodge in Dundee and was one of the pioneers of the settlement movement and of nursery and day care provision (Henry, 1992). Another might be Mary Slessor who, as an educator and missionary to the Calabar Coast of West Africa, had an impact far beyond Dundee (Henry, 1992). What these women have in common though is that their activities were developed as an extension of traditional female caring and domestic roles. They themselves might have stepped outside of such roles, but in the main they did not question them for other women – nor do most of those who recorded their activities. Frances Wright, on the other hand, holds far greater appeal if one is looking for a more feminist or 'empowered' role model. Born in Dundee in 1795, she came from a family with radical connections and not only rejected a conventional life for herself but actively campaigned against it being imposed on other women (Lane, 1972). As a public speaker she advocated equality for women, political rights for workers, free public education for everyone, birth control and equal treatment for illegitimate children (Spender, 1988).

These women all deserve to have their lives recorded and their achievements celebrated, but it is their very uniqueness which makes them unsuited to the purpose of helping us gain an insight into the lives of more ordinary, especially working class, women. Compensatory histories, focusing as they do on such exceptional women, are in the end as limited for our purposes as conventional histories with their focus on men. They share many of the same assumptions about who is worthy of a place in history and are, therefore, inadequate for the purpose of constructing critical histories that have a place in a radical curriculum.

Contribution history takes as its primary focus the movement or phenomenon under examination and describes the contribution that women made to it. This is the approach taken in most of the current historical treatments of community-based adult education (for example, Brookfield (1983) on Jane Addams or Vicinus (1985) on the settlement movement). It also has certain attractions in more specific areas of interest such as the jute industry because it presents the opportunity to examine the role of women like Mary Macarthur, who was instrumental to the trade unionisation of the industry in the twentieth century through the formation of the Jute and Flax Workers' Union (JFWU) in 1906 (Whatley *et al*, 1993). The JFWU replaced the earlier and largely ineffective Mill and Factory Operatives Union (MFOU), which had been founded by the Rev Henry Williamson (Walker, 1979), and it was a significant development in the improvement of working conditions in the industry. Another possibility would be to look at the work of Mary Muirhead Paterson from Glasgow who organised working girls' clubs and health education classes and was appointed the first woman factory inspector for Scotland and the north of England in 1893 (McFeely, 1988). She not only did much to improve working conditions throughout the textile industry but also established that women were just as able as men to take on the roles and responsibilities of the Inspectorate. Likewise, this approach would also enable us to examine the contributions made by Mary Brooksbank and Ellen Johnston (who was a powerloom weaver) – both better known today for their vernacular poetry about the injustices and inequalities that the poor experienced (Whatley *et al*, 1993).

Such accounts, however, tend to examine the role women played from what is still largely a male perspective. For example, it characterises the predominant approach to the part played by women in Chartism which focuses on the support they offered to the campaign for manhood suffrage (eg Epstein and Thompson, 1982) rather than the way in which they politicised their personal domestic and sexual worlds (eg Rowbotham, 1992). Lerner (1979) argues that any attempt to counteract this approach by focusing on women's oppression within the movement is not sufficient in itself. Thus, while it is important that a feminist critique of established histories is offered, it is not enough to rectify their omissions by reclaiming and incorporating the history of notable women into them and highlighting feminist activity within the movement or phenomenon as a whole.

Transitional history is the term that Lerner (1979) uses to describe what she sees as an on-going process, the first stage of which is to add new categories to those used by historians to organise their material such as sexuality, reproduction or female consciousness. She suggests that the second stage

> . . . may be to explore the possibility that what we call women's history may actually be the study of a separate women's culture. Such a culture

would include not only the separate occupations, status experiences and rituals of women but also their consciousness, which internalises patriarchal assumptions. In some cases, it would include the tensions created in the culture between the prescribed patriarchal assumptions and women's efforts to attain autonomy and emancipation. (Lerner, 1979)

I would suggest that it is this approach that offers us a way forward for reconstructing the history of women in the Dundee textile industry. This does depend, however, on our ability to detect their voice amongst the predominantly male ones of the existing histories, derived as they are from the minute books of the boards of directors, factory commissions, welfare societies and Dundee Yearbooks and Directories. Nevertheless, the attempt must be made because the telling of their story would encourage and enable women in comparable situations today to find their own voice.

Critiquing the folk history

Dundee has been justifiably characterised as a women's town. Not only were there, for example, nearly three women for every two men in the population between the ages of 20 and 45 by the turn of the century (Smout, 1990), but there were also proportionately more of them in paid employment than anywhere else in Scotland. In 1851 83 per cent of working women in Dundee were employed in the textile trade (Whatley *et al*, 1993) and by the 1860s manufacturing industry as a whole employed eight out of 10 women in Dundee (Scott, 1989). It is clear, therefore, that the workforce in the jute and flax mills and factories could not have been made up only of single women. In fact, just under 25 per cent of married women were employed as 'artisans, not housekeepers', with the figure for working widows being higher still (Whatley *et al*, 1993). This was quite different from the situation in Aberdeen, for example, where only three per cent of married women worked. This pattern of employment continued into the present century, the 1921 Census indicating that 24 per cent of married women in Dundee worked compared to 6 per cent in Glasgow and 5.6 per cent in Edinburgh (Smout, 1990). What this appears to indicate is that women in Dundee did not subscribe to the prevailing ideology about women's roles. Even by 1911, when the industry was beginning to suffer from increased foreign competition, 48.2 per cent of the working population was still employed in textiles and nearly seven out of 10 (69.2 per cent) workers in the industry were women (Watson, 1990).

An examination of how and why these patterns of employment had developed makes it clear, however, that they were replicated elsewhere in the Scottish textile trade. The breaking of the 1837 cotton strike, which included the leaders of the Glasgow cotton spinners union being sentenced to transportation in 1838 (Royle, 1989), resulted in the destruction of the militancy of the textile workers (Knox, 1992). One rapid consequence of this was that the employment of women workers increased because they were non-unionised and cheaper to employ than the previously male workforce and by 1839 69.9 per cent of the total workforce in the Scottish textile industry was female. The situation in Dundee was not, therefore, so different from elsewhere in Scotland as regards the male/female split in the workforce and, as 57 per cent of women in the national workforce were over 18 years of age, there was probably a significant number of married women employed in textiles nationally too (Knox, 1992).

Where Dundee did significantly differ from the rest of Scotland was in the level of pay that the women could expect. By the 1870s textile wages in Dundee were 20 per cent lower than those in Glasgow (Whatley *et al*, 1993). Weavers could earn more than spinners (and, unlike the Lancashire cotton trade, it does appear that women were not so heavily restricted to just the spinning trades), but both groups were heavily dependent on the overall economic health of the industry which was subject to periodic boom and slump conditions related to the prevailing political climate and the consequent effects on the price of raw jute and finished products. For example, during the Napoleonic wars the price of flax rose from £40 to a peak of £170 per ton in 1809 causing many mills and factories to close down, whereas the shortage of cotton during the American Civil War (1861–65) increased the market for flax and jute products and many firms extended their operations (Watson, 1990). The industry was, therefore, volatile and periods of relatively secure employment were just as likely to be followed by periods of privation as workers were laid off (Whatley *et al*, 1993). Yet despite low pay and insecurity, very few Dundee women took up employment in domestic service (7 per cent) compared to, for example, Edinburgh (where the figure was 44 per cent). This, however, probably has less to do with them choosing not to accept such work and much more to do with Dundee being an overwhelmingly working class city with a correspondingly smaller middle class to employ them (Scott, 1989). The evidence suggests that women were not working by choice in such an unpredictable industry in preference to domestic service but out of necessity because there was no alternative work available. Thus, the most likely explanation for the lower wages in Dundee is that employers realised they could depress wages without losing their workforce.

However, this does not on its own fully explain why it was that the women went out to work and the men stayed at home. One has to ask, also, whether the 'kettle bilers' were at home by choice – and even how many there actually were. It has already been demonstrated that men were outnumbered by women and it should also be noted that the 1901 census recorded that a third of all households were headed by women (Smout, 1990). It cannot be assumed that this implies a relatively high number of single parent households (as it would today) – only that the the major wage earner in those households was a woman.

One should therefore be cautious about what can be concluded from this with regard to how many men were at home whilst their wives were out earning. Likewise, it is just as important not to make assumptions based on present trends about what their role in the home was, especially in relation to family responsibilities. Most mills and factories provided half-time schools, thus enabling them to employ children as young as eight years old for up to eight hours per day (Watson, 1990), rising to 12 hours for 13-year-olds (to be followed by two hours schooling in the evening). The half-timers system, and the associated exemptions from the rules concerning minimum school leaving ages, was not fully abolished until 1936 (Smout, 1990) and even then some of the mill schools continued in operation, offering what amounted to a workplace creche. Child care, therefore, did not necessarily form part of the male 'kettle bilers' domestic role and, though there is some anecdotal evidence of them doing housework, one should not generalise. Certainly, it is difficult to find material that provides an insight into how these roles were negotiated and perceived by the people concerned. Without this it is difficult to construct a transitional history.

Nevertheless, the question why, if there was employment available in the textile industry, it was the women and the children rather than the men who took it up still remains, and trying to answer it does offer the possibility of constructing a more dialectical history than the oral tradition presents. One possible explanation is that both spinning and weaving were considered to be unskilled occupations in Dundee (Smout, 1990), unlike in the Lancashire cotton trade where weaving was regarded as a skilled trade, generally followed by men, whereas the unskilled spinning was largely done by women. The implication is that the traditional gender divide between skilled, male trades and unskilled, female labour was drawn differently in Dundee but that it continued to play an important role in who worked where. This supposition is strengthened when one considers the development of the regendered division of labour in the Scottish textile industries in the nineteenth century. The increasingly female workforce was not passive and accounts abound of spontaneous and localised strikes (Walker, 1979; Whatley et al, 1993), but it was unorganised. An effective trade union was not recreated until 1906 when the industry was already starting to decline. One is therefore led to the conclusion that employers paid wages that women and children were prepared to work for but that were unacceptable to a male workforce.

The Dundee textile industry and the role of women in it is an example of the fragmentation of the Scottish working class that followed from skilled tradesmen being able to bargain for and justify a 'family wage' which allowed their wives to remain in the home – in contrast to unskilled, unorganised workers who lacked such bargaining power. The issue, it seems, is also more likely to be one of patriarchy, with attendant notions about a man's worth and responsibilities, than of female emancipation, for the idea of the 'family wage' was widely supported by women as well as men within the unionised element of the skilled working class (Knox, 1992). Looking back, it is difficult for us to be sure that had well paid, socially acceptable work for men been available in Dundee, women textile workers would not have gladly exchanged the mill or factory for a domesticated role in the home. When the folk history is set against the recorded social history, the women in the Dundee textile industry come to seem less like positive, aspirational role models for women today and more like the precursors of Scottish working class women in the 1990s, who are now being increasingly forced into low-paid and/or part-time work in service industries for lack of alternative male employment.

Nevertheless, if the accepted folk history is a less than adequate account of the experiences of women in the Dundee textile industry, this does not mean that it should be discounted. Despite the fact that the industry has been in decline from the 1900s, it still clearly plays an important part in the self-identity of many Dundonians. Furthermore, it needs to be seized upon as an example of how mythologising our history can render invisible the lessons to be learnt from it, whereas reconstructing it helps us to understand the present. Women workers in the textile trade were spirited. The recorded pattern of spontaneous strikes (Walker, 1979; Whatley et al, 1993) indicates that they did deserve the title of 'defiant sisters', but even the briefest examination of their working conditions and the general economic context makes it clear that they were also a low paid and exploited workforce, one which has much in common with many female workers today. For example, 56.7 per cent of women workers in Scotland earn less than £220 per week compared to 26.3 per cent of men workers (Central Statistical Office, 1994) and this is almost certainly due to the fact that, whereas only 7.1 per cent of male employees work part-time, 42.8 per cent of female employees do (Government Statistical Service, 1996). It is parallels like these that should make them of interest to the popular education movement or to adult educators wishing to develop a radical curriculum. Similarly, rather than being distracted by romanticised accounts of role reversals, we should be more concerned with the patriarchal assumptions about what was and is defined as men's work and women's work.

Whose voice?

Current historical accounts of the Scottish popular education tradition appear to be dominated by a continuing male discourse. For example, Alexander (1994), in the context of a paper arguing for the continuing need for a democratic curriculum, states that Scotland has a strong tradition of independent working class education, but the historical overview he presents of the development of adult education within the Scottish labour movement makes no mention of women in this tradition. It is impossible to tell from this account whether women had any instrumental or even participative role in it – certainly only men are mentioned as having played key developmental roles. Similarly, Alexander and Martin (1995), in arguing that Scottish adult and community educators should look to 'their own indigenous histories, democratic traditions and communitarian values' instead of other discourses, are essentially offering evidence drawn from a tradition that once again appears to exclude women. Their own quotation of Fasheh (1992) is appropriately, if unintentionally, ironic:

> Cultural hegemony is characterised not only by what it includes but by what it excludes, renders marginal, deems inferior and makes invisible.

The notion of 'voice' as a critical consciousness arising from the dialectic of thought and action is central to critical pedagogies, especially that of Freire. It therefore might be assumed that there is less cause for concern with regard to current practice. In Scotland, however, this has tended to be interpreted in a restricted way, in that the voice to be found is assumed to be a working class voice, undifferentiated by gender or race (eg Kirkwood and Kirkwood, 1989; Kirkwood, 1990; Denwette *et al*, 1992). This derives in part from Freire's own writings, but such a narrow interpretation does not allow for the different life experiences of women which give rise to a different voice. To use King's terminology of the community of the oppressed and the community of the preferred (King, 1989), the community of the oppressed in this context is nearly always defined as the urban working class and the underlying assumption is that it speaks with a male voice. Feminist pedagogies, in contrast, would define men as the community of the preferred and are designed to enable women to find not just a voice but to also develop a critical language for that voice.

It is only after we have enabled this to happen that we will be able to move on to writing the third stage of transitional histories:

> . . . a history of the dialectic, the tension between the two cultures, male and female . . . their tensions and interactions being as much the subject of study as their differences (Lerner, 1979).

But in order to do this we need also to be prepared to redefine the parameters of the histories we are setting out to write, to redraw our conceptual boundaries so that women workers, especially feminists, can write their own histories. In these circumstances the distinction between the history of the group and the auto/biography of the individual is hard to maintain. I would suggest that few third-stage transitional histories of women have yet been written because so little auto/biographical evidence has been available to feminist historians. If one accepts the idea, referred to at the beginning of this paper, that all history is a social construct which is defined by the attitudes and values of those who record and analyse it – rather than those who live it – any attempt to write a transitional history of, for example, women in the jute industry is going to be problematic because the sources derive from within a set of 'prescribed patriarchal assumptions' (Lerner, 1979). For example, the best known history of the Dundee textile industry, *Juteopolis: Dundee and its Textile Workers* (Walker, 1979), relies heavily on archival documentary evidence. As a result, the source material inevitably suffers from being filtered through the minds of those who were responsible for recording and preserving the data and who were, in the main, men acting in an official capacity rather than the workers themselves. Nor should we assume that transcribed oral histories will offer us a more authentic source because they too are subject to decisions about what should or should not be included.

For the record

Does this mean that it is impossible to write transitional histories by reinterpreting documentary evidence from existing sources? I would argue that it is not impossible, but where it has been done, the writers have usually been able to draw on archival material written by and for women. For example, the women's suffrage movement lends itself very successfully to this approach (see Kent, 1987) because of the archives of books, newsletters, posters, photographs and newspaper cuttings that were assembled at the time by key activists and some of the suffrage societies. These were gathered together to form the core of the Fawcett Library which has continued to be the major archive of primary source material. Generally though, in the absence of alternative sources to those used by the existing histories, there are limits on how effectively contemporary material can be gathered in retrospect. The lesson seems to be that unless women originate and maintain their own sources, they cannot rely on others to do it for them. The scope for reclaiming the past is severely constrained, but those of us who are currently engaged in work with women can at least try and ensure that historians in the future will have appropriate contemporary source material available to them. Lerner (1979) saw one of the functions of her paper as being the encouragement of a new paradigm of history. One of the purposes of this is to encourage the collection and development of archival material so that future historians can construct our histories within that paradigm. Women have been written out of history in the past because they were constrained from writing themselves into the records of the time.

How then can we write ourselves into the record for the future? One way is certainly to ensure that formal records are kept – for example, minute books and annual reports of women's organisations. These are not, however, sufficient on their own without other material that often gets discarded because it is of a more ephemeral nature. For example, many embroidered banners from the suffrage struggle have found their way into museums, but what makes the Fawcett Library archive so valuable is the poster collection, the scrapbooks of newspaper clippings and placards from demonstrations. Will historians at the end of the twenty-first century be able to draw on similar comprehensive archives relating to the Greenham Common protests, women's activities in the

Miners Strike or the environmental movement? What, for example, has happened to all those pin-badges from the reborn women's movement of the 1970s?

Collections of first-hand accounts of women's experiences have always been another obvious way, as was realised by the Co-operative Women's Guild in the past (Llewellyn Davies, 1977). Anthologies, such as Henderson and Mackay's (1990) *Grit and Diamonds: Women in Scotland Making History 1980–1990*, contain accounts of events such as the Lee Jeans factory occupation by women workers in 1981 and the experiences of women from the Dysart Women's Strike Committee during the Miners Strike. The latter, in particular, is an example of a history of the dialectic referred to by Lerner (1979):

> The thing with men, I think, was that a lot of them were very happy to see the women involved, as long as the women were doing things the men's way and for the men's benefit. But as soon as we wanted to do things for ourselves and taking our own initiatives, they didnae like that very much. Maybe it was the way they were used to working, doing everything very strictly through procedures and that. If we did something without consulting them, they used to go absolutely mad. They didnae like us doing things without their permission. Plus a lot of men used to sit on their backsides all day pontificating while the women were trying to run a house . . . I know a lot of women whose husbands were never home during the strike. It was almost as if they had a 24-hour job. They were at the strike centre all day and there were meetings at night and you would actually see less of them than you did when they had a normal working day. And the woman had to do the house, she'd possibly be working herself part-time and maybe doing work in the centre, looking after their kids and maybe doing meetings theirselves . . . I'm not making a general statement because I know a lot of men did pull their weight and I know a lot of them changed their attitude during the strike. (quoted in Henderson and Mackay, 1990)

However, the generation of such accounts is not just for the benefit of future historians or to provide teaching material for some future curriculum. It can be the foundation for an emancipatory, feminist curriculum for today. Such a curriculum would take account of the idea that

> 'feminism' is not merely a 'perspective', a way of seeing; nor even this plus an epistemology, a way of knowing; it is also an ontology, or way of being in the world (Stanley, 1990).

Conclusion

A feminist curriculum is not just women-centred, for it arises not from gender or sex but from consciousness. The purpose of such a curriculum in giving voice to women's experience is not simply to record it but to enable critical examination of its social construction and to interrogate the interests and ideologies that inform the meanings that women place on their experiences (Giroux, 1989; Thompson, 1995). If women's current struggles are not to become part of a distorted folk memory which denies the reality of our experiences in exchange for an idealised vision of the past, it is vital that the process is one of critical reflection rather than mere reminiscence. According to Grosholz (1988), it is this very dialogue between events and the recorder of them, and the act of deliberation on the part of the writer, which make the event significant – rather than the event itself. A radical curriculum based on these principles not only enables the generation of auto/biographical material for archive purposes but also ensures that the very act of producing it furthers a radical agenda.

Women in the Dundee textile industry deserve to be remembered and celebrated, but in a way which recognises the exploitation they suffered, the role patriarchy played in their lives and the strength they displayed in living with privation. An uncritical acceptance of folk history does little to help us either understand women's experience or apply insights to be gained from it to contemporary contexts. Let us learn from their experience and write our own histories before they are lost.

References

Alexander, D (1994) 'The education of adults in Scotland: democracy and curriculum' *Studies in the Education of Adults*, 26 (1), pp 31–49.

Alexander, D and Martin, I (1995) 'Competence, curriculum and democracy' in Mayo, M and Thompson, J (eds), (1995) *Adult Learning, Critical Intelligence and Social Change*, Leicester, NIACE, pp 82–97.

Beddoe, D (1987) *Discovering Women's History: A Practical Manual*, London, Pandora.

Brookfield, S (1983) *Adult Learners, Adult Education and the Community*, Milton Keynes, Open University Press.

Carr, E M (1964) *What is History?*, Harmondsworth, Penguin.

Central Statistical Office (1994) *Regional Trends 29*, London, HMSO.

Denwette, B, Walker, M, and Tett, L (1992) 'Breaking down barriers: a local approach to adult basic education' in Hautecoeur J-P (ed), *ALPHA 92: Current Research in Literacy*, Hamburg, UNESCO Institute for Education.

Epstein, J and Thompson, D (eds) (1982) *The Chartist Experience: Studies in Working Class Radicalism and Culture, 1830–1860*, London, Macmillan.

Fasheh, M (1992) 'West Bank; learning to survive' in Poster, C and Zwimmer, J (eds), *Community Education in the Third World*, London, Routledge, pp 17–29.

Giroux, J B (1989) 'Feminist theory as pedagogical practice', *Contemporary Education*, 61 (1), pp 6–10.

Government Statistical Service (1992) *1991 Census, Tayside Region 1*, Edinburgh, HMSO.

Government Statistical Service (1996) *Regional Trends 31*, London, HMSO.

Grosholz, E (1988) 'Women, history and practical deliberation' in Gergen, M M (ed) *Feminist Thought and the Structure of Knowledge*, New York, New York University Press, pp 173–181.

Henderson, S and Mackay, A (eds) (1990) *Grit and Diamonds: Women in Scotland Making History, 1980–1990*, Edinburgh, Stramullion Ltd/Cauldron Collective.

Henry, B (1992) *Introduction to Community Education: A Reader*, Dundee, Northern College.

Kent, S K (1987) *Sex and Suffrage in Britain, 1860–1914*, Princeton, New Jersey, Princeton University Press.

King, M (1989) 'On transformation: from a conversation with Mel King' in *Harvard Educational Review*, 59 (4), pp 504–519.

Kirkwood, C (1990) *Vulgar Eloquence*, Edinburgh, Polygon.

Kirkwood, G and Kirkwood, C (1989) *Living Adult Education: Freire in Scotland*, Milton Keynes, Open University Press.

Knox, W (1992) 'Whatever happened to radical Scotland? The economic and social origins of the mid-Victorian consensus in Scotland' in Mason, R and McDougall, N (eds), *People and Power in Scotland: Essays in Honour of TC Smout*, Edinburgh, John Donald Publishers, pp 218–239.

Lane, M (1972) *Frances Wright and the 'Great Experiment'*, Manchester, Manchester University Press.

Lerner, G (1979) *The Majority Finds its Past: Placing Women in History*, Oxford, Oxford University Press.

Llewelyn Davies, M (1977) *Life as We Have Known It*, London, Virago.

Mansfield, S (1992) 'Histories of community education: a feminist critique' in Allen, G and Martin, I (eds) *Education and Community: The Politics of Practice*, London, Cassell, pp 9–16.

McFeely, M D (1988) *Lady Inspectors: The Campaign for a Better Workplace, 1893–1921*, Oxford, Blackwell.

Rowbotham, S (1974) *Hidden from History: 300 Years of Women's Oppression and the Fight Against It*, London, Pluto Press.

Rowbotham, S (1992) *Women in Movement: Feminism and Social Action*, London, Routledge.

Royle, E (1989) *Modern Britain: A Social History*, London, Edward Arnold.

Scott, A M (1989) *Discovering Dundee: The Story of a City*, Edinburgh, Mercat Press.

Smout, T C (1990) *A Century of the Scottish People*, London, Fontana Press.

Smout, T C and Wood, S (1990) *Scottish Voices, 1745–1960*, London, Collins.

Spender, D (1988) *Women of Ideas and What Men Have Done to Them*, London, Pandora.

Stanley, L (1990) *Feminist Praxis: Research, Theory and Epistemology in Feminist Sociology*, London, Routledge and Kegan Paul.

Thompson, J (1995) 'Feminism and women's education' in Mayo, M and Thompson, J (eds), (1995) *Adult Learning, Critical Intelligence and Social Change*, Leicester, NIACE, pp 124–137.

Vicinus, M (1985) *Independent Women: Work and Community for Single Women, 1850–1920*, London, Virago.

Walker, W M (1979) *Juteopolis: Dundee and its Textile Workers, 1885–1923*, Edinburgh, Scottish Academic Press.

Watson, M (1990) *Jute and Flax Mills in Dundee*, Tayport, Hutton Press.

Whatley, C, Swinfen, D B and Smith, A M (1993) *The Life and Times of Dundee*, Edinburgh, John Donald Publishers.

Section 3:

Social and cultural action

12 The disability movement and the struggle for inclusion

Margaret Petrie and Mae Shaw

The disability movement has proved itself to be a genuinely popular social move-ment: autonomous, counter-hegemonic, subversive and creative. The authors of this chapter argue that the struggle of disabled people for inclusion is, in essence, part of the wider struggle for a renewal of democracy. Their struggle is paradigmatic because it prefigures a new kind of politics in which civil society begins to reconstruct the state and the discourse of needs is transformed into a discourse of rights. The promise of this struggle is an enriched and inclusive understanding of what it means to be a citizen in a democratic society

Introduction

What is at stake in this dispute between old and new views of integration is nothing less than our view of both the nature of social reality and the role of politics in society. The old view sees integration as a humanitarian response to unintended consequences in our past history which can be changed by the development of paternalistic policies. The new view sug-gests that integration is not a thing that can be delivered by politicians, policy makers or educators, but a process of struggle that has to be joined. (Oliver, 1990)

. . . it is perhaps time we renamed that struggle inclusion. (Oliver, 1996)

This chapter starts from the view that inclusion itself is a problematic term which can serve to mask a range of ideological interests and policy imperatives. This makes it all the more important to be clear about what we mean. The struggle for inclusion is, first and foremost, a struggle against exclusion, against injustice. We therefore see inclusion as a project in cultural politics which fundamentally challenges not only underlying assumptions about the nature and significance of difference in our society but also traditional notions of citizenship which have systematically excluded certain voices.

We wish to argue that education for a more inclusive democracy has been inhibited by the discourses of 'special needs' and other such 'clauses of conditionality' (Slee, 1997) which carry an assumed authority, simultaneously privileging professional judgement and silencing discordant voices. It is our view that discordant voices are the lifeblood of democracy – democracy is a process as much as an outcome. One fundamental consequence of an inclusive participatory democracy must be the presence of different and sometimes conflicting interests. The role of politics in society must accommodate the dissenting as well as the consenting citizen. Education for democracy must therefore equip people to say no to those cultural and material conditions which arise from, or reproduce, inequalities.

What Roger Slee (1997) calls the 'distractive discursive noises of integration and latterly inclusion', which have dominated much policy and practice in recent years, have been detrimental to such a project because they have subsumed and thereby contained difference within a professional agenda which focuses on defective individual pathologies requiring special provision. This reduces whole groups of people to bundles of need – deficit individuals requiring help without anything to offer – objects rather than active subjects. In the end, the politics of 'special education' is profoundly anti-democratic because the process of inclusion is reduced to a set of technical challenges to the smooth running of society. As educators, we are often implicated in this discourse of deficiency. The disability movement, however, rejects the dominant discourse, the force of which, it argues, is disabling in itself. In challenging its framework of benevolent authoritarianism, the position of disabled people in society is instead located in broader political, social and cultural processes which inherently exclude the 'other'. In doing so, it is attempting to shift the discourse of disability from one of 'in-person' deficiency to one of discrimination and rights. It is our argument that it is precisely this collision of discourses which offers possibilities for a popular education agenda.

The reality of exclusion

Inclusion, as a political and cultural goal, requires a reconsideration of the structures of power as well as their social relations and mediation through the institutional values and practices of policy. In the context of disability, this means refocusing on the ways in which people with impairments are disabled through active social and political discrimination and the discourses which support it.

> What would our attitude be if we were to learn that a group of people, by virtue of being resident in a particular council estate, were routinely not even interviewed for paid work and were offered, instead, time in segregated day centres with no training for paid employment, were refused complex medical attention on the basis that 'it wouldn't make any difference because they have limited life expectancy or the quality of their life is so low anyway', were given such a limited choice of housing options that they had to live in hostels or share with people they had not chosen to live with, were actively discouraged from having sexual relationships in case they had children, were refused entry to local pubs, clubs, restaurants in case other customers objected, were not admitted to schools or colleges in

case they disrupted the education of children from other areas, were detained without due legal process and given drugs to prevent them behaving in unsocial ways, were ridiculed and spat at when they walked down the main street? And what would our attitude be if we were to learn that similar things happened to people from a particular minority ethnic group by virtue of their being black? The point is that we are more likely to join together in condemning these events when we choose to become aware of them. (Tait, 1997)

This account of the everyday experience of people with learning difficulties is shocking at a number of levels. First, we are outraged at a human level about such patently unfair treatment of a recognisable group of people. Second, the suggestion here is that this is neither accidental nor incidental but systematic and systemic – we are confronted with the consequences of the structures and relations which constitute the social order. Finally, and perhaps most unsettlingly, our faith in a democratic and caring society – and the discourses and practices which sustain it – is turned on its head. What is particularly disturbing, however, is that we do not question its authenticity or its veracity. We recognise what we thought of as 'caring' turned back on us, as it were, and remade as 'wounds'. And then there is the undisguised accusatory tone implicating not only those who make and implement policy, but also the wider community which has failed to see – or chosen not to! We can no longer say we didn't know. We are compelled to respond.

The capacity to turn things on their head and compel us to acknowledge an alternative reality is precisely what has characterised the disability movement, and the politicisation of disabled people has owed much to the transformation from victim to survivor. Characteristic, too, is the insistence that disabled people experience such extreme marginalisation as to render them almost invisible. As Colin Barnes argues:

> . . . there are few, including politicians and policy makers, who would not concede that disabled people experience a particularly pervasive form of social oppression or institutional discrimination . . . (quoted in Campbell and Oliver, 1996)

Whilst disability is not a unitary category – class, 'race', gender, sexuality and age all mediate the experience of being disabled – it nevertheless is a significant means of social differentiation: 'To be disabled *means* to be discriminated against and involves experiencing varying degrees of poverty, stereotyping, social isolation and restriction' (emphasis added) (Barton, 1996). These are not the necessary outcomes of impairment, but the consequences of social exclusion.

Although there is broad agreement within the disability movement about the idea that 'disability is something wrong with society', there are diverse explanations for the exclusion of disabled people. These have historical, material, cultural and social dimensions and reflect the different interests and voices which have been brought to bear on the debate. This vigorous debate – characteristic of the disability movement as disabled people strive to represent their own experience of disablement – is important to the broader political agenda in two fundamental ways. First, it reasserts the undeniable significance of 'lived difference'; second, it adds a new and vital dimension to the wider struggle for social justice based on the conviction that 'no one is truly free until we all are' (Thompson, 1997).

Theorising disability

In support of its claims and critiques, the disability movement has offered a range of theoretical perspectives which extend our understanding of social reality itself. Finkelstein (1993), for example, argues that the predominant factor contributing to the disablement of different groups is the extent to which people can participate in the creation of social wealth. The ability to produce to a great extent determines status in contemporary Western societies. The competitive nature of capitalism has also ensured that organised labour (largely male, white, non-disabled) has consistently colluded in this process of marginalisation by enhancing its position at the expense of other social groups and interests, including disabled people.

Oliver (1996) distinguishes between what he calls the 'personal tragedy' model and the 'political economy' model of disability. The former, which he claims has been dominant, suggests that disability is a tragic happening that occurs to unfortunate, isolated individuals on a random basis. This then results in compensatory policy responses or therapeutic interventions designed to help individuals come to terms with their personal 'tragedy'. Political economy, on the other hand, suggests that all phenomena (including social categories such as 'disability') reflect the economic and social forces of capitalism. The outcome of this is the structural dependence of disabled people arising from conditions in the labour market and the organisation of work in society. Disabled people's effective exclusion from the labour market ensures that they don't play a key role in the processes of production and that they are largely dependent on those who do. This, in turn, defines political and cultural responses to disabled people themselves.

This position is challenged, however, by some disabled feminists (eg see Morris, 1991) for whom it does not adequately recognise the differential experience of disabled people, particularly the impact of gender-based social and economic relations. For others, focusing on structures alone neglects significant psychologically-inclined explanations. Shakespeare (1994), for example, argues that a link needs to be developed between culture and material relations:

> The social model needs to be reconceptualised: people with impairment are disabled, not just by material discrimination, but also by prejudice. This

prejudice is not just interpersonal, it is also implicit in cultural representation, in language and socialisation.

These processes of cultural representation and objectification are not simply an outcome of material relations, but also the product of a deeply held fear because '. . . disabled people remind non-disabled people of their own vulnerability':

> Our disability frightens people. They don't want to think that this is something which could happen to them. So we become separated from common humanity, treated as fundamentally different and alien. Having put up clear barriers between us and them, non-disabled people further hide their fear and discomfort by turning us into objects of pity, comforting themselves by their own kindness and generosity. (Morris quoted in Shakespeare, 1994)

There is also another dimension, however, which has particular salience in and for the experience of disabled people: the danger of ignoring the daily realities of impairment. So, although the development of the social model has been a conceptual breakthrough with significant mobilising potential, it should be regarded more as a strategic focus than a truth claim. However, whilst advocating re-evaluation of the social model in light of experience, the disability movement is anxious to ensure that internal debates do not provide legitimation for a professionally-driven agenda. Spurious divisions within the disability movement can only too easily be used to undermine the social model and justify the reduction of commitment to social improvement whilst at the same time reinforcing the more efficient targeting of limited resources.

We would argue that, far from discrediting the social model, such debates prefigure the kind of open and critical culture which is essential in and for democratic social movements because: 'Parallel understandings are always present when people struggle to change their conditions' (Clegg, 1996). The important thing is that these parallel understandings are not presented as divisions in order to hijack the agenda for change. Social movements are often, in themselves, contradictory formations and it is partly in the collision of different positions and interests around common goals that action towards change is generated.

The focus for unity around the notion of the 'disabling society', however explained, has been crucial for the development of progressive politics both within and beyond the disability movement. The particular importance of this essentially counter-hegemonic notion for educational practice is that it establishes a particular kind of analysis. This acknowledges structural and structured inequality, enabling us to develop a critique of social policy which – despite the current rhetoric of inclusion – continues to define disabled people as a 'problem' to be solved by various forms of management and professional intervention.

Redefining disability: the making of a social movement

Social movements would be of very little significance if they did not call into question not only particular phenomena but a general representation of social life. (Touraine quoted in Campbell and Oliver, 1996)

In 1976 the Union of Physically Impaired Against Segregation produced a document entitled the Fundamental Principles of Disability which was to become a seminal paper in developing what is now commonly known as the social model of disability (see UPIAS, 1976). It argued that:

. . . it is society which disables physically impaired people . . . Thus we define impairment as lacking part or all of a limb, or having a defective limb, organ or mechanism of the body; and disability as the disadvantage or restriction of activity caused by a contemporary social organisation which takes little or no account of people who have physical impairments and thus excludes them from participation in the mainstream of social activities. Physical disability is therefore a particular form of social oppression. (Oliver, 1996)

UPIAS was also significant in representing what would become one of the fundamental tenets of the emergent Disabled People's Movement: the development of organisations run and controlled by disabled people. The British Council of Organisations of Disabled People (BCODP) was formed in 1981, International Year of Disabled People. During the 1980s this umbrella body for organisations of disabled people was to expand to include more than 100 organisations including seven in Scotland. Campbell and Oliver (1996) argue that the redefinition of disability has played a key role in this development:

This growth was not merely a numerical phenomenon, but also reflected the individual and collective empowerment of disabled people through the organisations they were creating. This can be seen in a number of ways. It can be seen in the challenge to the dominant social perceptions of disability through the development of a politics of personal identity. It can also be seen in the development and articulation of the social model of disability which, by focusing on disabling environments rather than individual impairments, freed up disabled people's hearts and minds by offering an alternative conceptualisation of the problem. Liberated, the direction of disabled people's personal energies turned outwards to building a force for changing society.

In recent years, disabled people have become much more visible and vocal in demanding civil and human rights. There is a growing body of literature by disabled academics challenging both traditional models of disability and hegemonic perceptions that it is only non-disabled 'experts' on medical conditions who hold legitimate knowledge about disability. There is also a growing arts culture both challenging the negative images of disability still peddled by the media and positively celebrating difference. The Direct Action Network, for example, has mounted highly visible campaigns, most notably against charity events which are seen to patronise, objectify or demean disabled people. In addition, the introduction of the Disability Discrimination Act (1996) by the then Conservative Government, though inadequate in its own terms, was in part an outcome of high profile campaigning for civil rights which forced discrimination against disabled people onto the political agenda. Subsequent action by articulate and well-organised disabled activists over continuing threats to disability benefits under New Labour, and the coverage this received in the media, further demonstrate the extent to which the disability movement is increasingly regarded as the legitimate voice of disabled people. Above all, what this movement has consistently argued and campaigned for is a fundamental shift from a discourse of needs to a discourse of rights. In the process they have effectively demonstrated how the emphasis on needs alone can reinforce the professional domination of welfare provision, resulting in a retreat from active to passive citizenship (Lister, 1997).

The illusion of inclusion

The Warnock Report (DES, 1978) conceptualised 'special educational needs' in terms of the interaction between the child and the environment, rather than simply deficiencies within the child. However, despite this significant conceptual development, in practice the predominant view of disability remains 'in-person' and individualised.

Furthermore, if we look not only at who gets special provision but also at how and why, it is clear that the process of classification not only reinforces unequal social relations but can also act as a form of surveillance and regulation. In this respect, it is interesting to note that research carried out in relation to 'race' and gender, for example, indicates that black working class boys are more likely than others to be diagnosed as requiring 'special' provision (see Daniels et al, 1995). The situation is now exacerbated by the way in which 'special' status has been stretched almost to bursting point in order to manage children or young people defined as having social, emotional and behavioural difficulties (SEBD), who are being increasingly excluded from school. This can clearly be seen to be linked to the introduction of market forces into the education system and the managerial culture it spawns: easily measurable performance indicators, and league tables of pupil, teacher and school performance. Those who are perceived to be undermining the marketability (and thus the competitive advantage) of schools by virtue of their deficiencies become regarded, therefore, as a threat to those who are forced to maintain these practices in the educational marketplace. Managing such conflicts of interest in a context of contracting resources has often resulted in regressive and divisive responses. For example, commenting on the increasing number of excluded pupils, Nigel de Gruchy (1997), general secretary of the National Association of Schoolmasters and Union of Women Teachers, states:

> I chiefly blame the ill-advised policy of indiscriminate inclusivity whereby youngsters with severe emotional and behavioural difficulties are placed in mainstream schools. Meanwhile more special schools are closed. There is a bitter irony in overemphasis on 'inclusion' leading to more 'exclusion'.

The point here is that neither the rhetoric of 'special' status nor of 'inclusion' in this context offers any real possibilities for change. For example, the discursive force of 'special needs' has been critical to the management of increasing tensions precisely because it obscures its own logic – it implies privilege whilst, in reality, it encourages and legitimises exclusion. At the same time, however, the rhetoric of inclusion can also result in exclusion because it disguises the realities of underfunded mainstream educational provision. Inclusion has, therefore, come to refer to the integration of 'deficit' individuals into the existing system, rather than a challenge to a competitive system which inherently excludes them. So, whilst there has been something of a discursive shift, it has simply obfuscated the reality of deepening inequality. There is indeed a double irony here for disabled people: they lose out both ways.

This draws attention to the ambivalence of the state for disabled people. This has traditionally been experienced in the ways in which it has provided services which are urgently needed by them, but has done so on terms which have both reinforced their dependence and justified inequality. Current plans to include disabled people in the New Deal strategy to tackle unemployment, for example, are underpinned by a rhetoric of reducing dependency and tackling social exclusion, but they still focus on individualised solutions – and, of course, they save money. Furthermore, the introduction of market mechanisms adds a particularly sinister motive to the process of defining the 'deserving' disabled. The discourse of social rights has, ironically, been very effectively manipulated, therefore, to justify cuts in social expenditure by 'rebranding' disabled people – it is difficult to sustain the image of 'tragic but brave' people while you cut their benefits and cast suspicion on their honesty. A bitter irony is that, whilst the regulation of disabled people has become a lucrative business for those awarded the contracts for determining their rights to benefit, for disabled people themselves this represents a further continuity in their surveillance – with the added danger of becoming victims of the new image, as evidenced by increasing reports of personal and physical abuse.

In the context of current policy, specificity can either legitimise inequality or obscure it from view as can be demonstrated in health, education, housing and welfare services, all of which are becoming ever more selective and targeted. The concept of difference, therefore, 'has become a substitute for more critical concepts such as privilege, conflict of interest, oppression and subordination' (Meekosha, 1993). What this indicates is that the anti-democratic politics of 'special' status have emerged not from the real needs of disabled people themselves but from politicians, policy makers, professionals and academics. The illusion of 'special needs' (particularly as it is framed in current policy) offers little to the development of a genuine participating democracy. In fact, forced to claim 'special rights', the status of disabled people as citizens with existing rights is largely negated. On this reading, as Meekosha and Dowse contend, the concept of the 'disabled citizen' is a contradiction in terms. Consequently, what we really need is:

> . . . a redefinition/renegotiation of the public that incorporates groups of disabled citizens granted social and welfare rights and benefits, but not classified as passive recipients . . . (Meekosha and Dowse, 1997)

Caring rhetoric: disabling reality

The construction of disability within contemporary policy discourse owes much to political and social debates which date back to the early twentieth century. These centred on concerns about 'moral degeneracy' and dominated much Victorian social reform. Converging developments in biological theory, which implied the screening out of degenerate tendencies through selective breeding, found expression in the eugenics movement whose support came largely from the new middle class, including the emergent welfare professions. Although it was numerically small, it had a disproportionate influence due to the strategic positions of some of its most prominent advocates. Eugenics found various forms of institutional expression in the early twentieth century, but perhaps its greatest impact was in the way it informed the development of social policy:

> [The eugenics movement] was probably more important in setting the context for policy-making than in influencing detailed policies themselves, but a wide spectrum of people, from far right to socialist left, worked until the 1930s and even beyond within a eugenics framework, or at least with a eugenics terminology. (Weeks, 1985)

We would argue that this framework, however residual, continues to justify custodial measures to contain those defined as menace, sterilisation of those who constitute a burden and surveillance of those who are deemed to be vulnerable and in need of 'protection'. So, whilst there would be widespread distaste for eugenicist ideas within contemporary welfare, it is nevertheless the case that welfare policy – tacitly framed around the construction of disabled people as dependent, deficient and 'other' – has institutionalised and legitimated a kind of apartheid, albeit humanely conceived and enacted.

In this context, the discourse of 'care' which has historically informed welfare policy can be seen, in part, as sustaining an effective form of social apartheid. This can perhaps most clearly be seen in the institutionalisation of the dichotomy between 'carer' and 'cared for'. This distinction – with its implicit dependence – has been an essential factor in sustaining this discourse and the practices it supports. For example, a continuity, which has survived both feminist critiques and community care legislation, is the way in which the 'us' and 'them' dichotomy is reinforced – families and *them*, women and *them*, the community and *them*. In this way, common ground is obscured to the detriment of all. This is exacerbated in the context of current community care legislation by the construction of informal 'carers' as service providers. For example, support for carers' organisations, which is included in the legislative framework, indicates the significance given to 'care' as essential labour. Guidance on implementing the legislation assumes that informal carers will provide unpaid help and that government will fulfil an enabling role in this process through 'support' which encourages carers to carry on such unpaid work. The economic necessity of caring labour is revealed in the following statistic: 'the value of [the unpaid work which carers do] saves the state between £15 and £24 billion per year' (Department of Health quoted in Morris, 1993). Support for carers is not, therefore, just a cheap alternative to the provision of domiciliary services; it is at the heart of community care legislation.

There are two outcomes of this focus on the needs of carers (seen to be coping with the consequences of individual impairments) which are relevant to our argument. First, there is no acknowledgement of the social and economic context in which those consequences are located; second, the dependence of those on the receiving end of such care is further reinforced. As Morris (1993) points out,

> . . . instead of identifying the way that an inadequate income and inadequate (or inappropriate) services create the need for unpaid assistance, the public representation of informal carers has tended to take the need for informal care for granted and addressed the interests of those who fulful the role thereby created.

However, the establishment of carers' organisations is another outcome of the ambivalence of policy. The restructuring of welfare and the ideological and economic imperatives from which it derives have, paradoxically, brought evidence of the organisation and conduct of care to public attention. This has created a space in which previously invisible groups have become visible and what were once very private experiences can be made political. This space has been peopled, therefore, by a range of new 'publics', established or legitimised in many cases by policy itself. It has also exposed both real and spurious conflicts between the interests of disabled people and informal carers. For example, the construction of 'carers and their dependants', which pervades policy developments, runs counter to the interests of the disability movement with its emphasis on the rights of disabled people to choose in relation to personal assistance. Furthermore, the insistence on 'user-involvement' in planning and development of services has often been dominated by carers as an interest group (Morris, 1993).

These contradictions and seeming conflicts of interest can offer a resource for an educational practice which seeks to expose the politics of 'care'. For example, disabled people have become service consumers who also have to be consulted (however tokenistically) about the planning, implementation and evaluation of services. One consequence of this rhetoric of inclusion is that organisations traditionally run by non–disabled people for disabled people are increasingly coming under pressure from funding bodies, including government, to have direct representation of disabled people within their management structures. Ironically, the ambiguity of a marketised model of 'participation' has offered a space in which previously excluded voices have begun to make their demands heard.

The current policy context has, therefore, provided the impetus for, and been a significant factor in, the emergence of a politics of care which raises fundamental questions about established notions of 'caring', the nature of independence and, ultimately, about what it means to be human. As the American political theorist Joan Tronto puts it, modern political theory locates care both 'above and below' politics (quoted in Sevenhuijsen, 1998) – either transcending 'real' politics by virtue of its personal nature or not important enough because it is hidden, gendered and private. Consequently, there is now an opportunity for 'care' to be considered as a political and ethical issue at the heart of democratic citizenship. Feminist debates emerging around the ethics of care, for example, consider the possibility of caring work as an essential life experience, lack of which renders people deficient in their ability to make judgements about competing needs – a pre-condition for democratic citizenship (eg see Sevenhuijsen, 1998). There must also be an opportunity for this debate to engage with disability politics which take issue with the concept of 'care as a burden' and the dependency it implies: the discourse of 'care' is often experienced as oppressive by disabled people who wish to emphasise interdependence.

Community care and the debates which converge around it have created new collective identities which have arisen from and are defined by their previous exclusion – for example, carers and disabled people. These identities have undoubtedly reflected different positions and interests, but conflict cannot be taken for granted anymore than can consensus because, as Segal (1991) points out, identities are not static:

> That which at one minute we may wish to embrace in defiance of shared oppression, we may, at the next, wish to discard as trapping us in traditional cultural discourses, institutions and practices.

Identities may shift precisely because, in the end, they are linked to exploitative practices and oppressive discourses. Morris (1993) reminds us that the enforced dependence of disabled people on relatives (particularly women) can be mutually inhibiting. A discourse and practice based on dependence cannot address the conflicts which inevitably arise as people try to change their reality. Consequently, an approach needs to be developed which acknowledges both differential experiences of dependency and common purpose, seeking to resolve conflicts creatively and in a way which does not advance the independence and choices of one group simply by reinforcing the dependency of the other.

From disabling discourse to a politics of inclusion

What we wish to highlight is the continuity of disabling discourses which have their roots in historical, economic, political and cultural contexts and processes. The significance of the social model of disability is that it reconceptualises the problem, exposing a history of discrimination and developing a discourse which emphasises human interdependence as the only way in which an inclusive citizenship can be imagined and enacted. Such a discourse offers us *all* the possibility of being more human. It is the collision of discourses – dependency and exclusion or interdependence and inclusion – which offers a unique opportunity to re-examine the ways in which socialisation processes have resulted in the subordination of disabled people. As a popular social movement, the disability movement therefore challenges all of us to turn ' . . . the failure of indoctrination into an educational opportunity' (Allen, 1992).

It has been argued that the disability movement, and particularly the development of the social model of disability, offers disabled people the tools to tackle their own oppression (Campbell and Oliver, 1996). But we would also argue that it forces a wider recognition of the historical, political and social consequences of a competitive economic framework which inherently excludes those who cannot compete on other people's terms. One outcome of this is that the management of the 'casualties' of such a system requires a discourse of deficiency, however conceived, in order simultaneously to obscure and justify the consequent inequalities of the social order. In contrast, disability politics fundamentally challenges the hegemony of personal handicap, offering instead a convincing critique of the existing social order and a vision of a more humane polity. In this sense, an acknowledgement of the historical context of disability forces us to confront the 'dangerous memories' (Giroux, 1992) of an enforced apartheid. This confrontation must not be avoided.

Inclusion, as a project in cultural politics, challenges traditional notions of citizenship which have often resulted in the stigmatisation and exclusion of 'difference'. In essence, it means that we have to develop a vision of 'democracy through difference' (Barton, 1996). Working towards inclusion reshapes human relationships on a basis of more equal participation. It seeks to eradicate barriers of exclusion and to redefine disabled people's experiences as 'valid, valued and valuable' (Herd, 1998). Citizenship, therefore, needs to be reformulated to reflect a diversity of experience. The language and imagery of citizenship have been imbued with a hegemonic norm which excludes disabled people. Active citizenship, for example, which is often reduced to voluntary efforts on behalf of the dependent 'other', offers nothing to an inclusive democracy because such charitable practices and discourses require the subordination of disabled people, ie as the 'recipients of charitable largesse who constitute a significant component of the group, "the cared for"'(Meekosha and Dowse, 1997). In contrast, a concept of citizenship which embraces disabled people enhances our common citizenship, just as a citizenship which excludes disabled people diminishes all of us. Indeed, as they go to argue, 'A citizenship that acknowledges people with disabilities is fundamental to a re-imagining of local, national and international collectivities'.

The social reality of 'lived difference' must therefore be welcomed as an enrichment of democracy, not a justification for injustice or inequality. The preoccupation with ideal types which characterises our cultural and political terrain actually excludes more people than it includes. The message that to be *not* white, *not* young, *not* rich, *not* physically perfect is to be inferior is hegemonic, despite the reality of most people's lives. The iconoclasm of the disability movement in this respect offers liberation beyond its immediate scope. There is something intensely liberating for all of us about the rejection of aspirations towards perfectibility, about the existential understanding that human beings are more than their physical form. This understanding is not only counter-hegemonic in cultural terms, it also challenges the very core of consumer capitalism which relies on the marketing and homogenising of image. The message of the disability movement, then, is essentially *popular* since it offers to liberate us all in and for a new and genuinely inclusive kind of citizenship based on what Raymond Williams calls the 'essential quality of being'.

However, an inclusive popular education agenda must also be prepared to be and to confront the unpopular, for there are entrenched popular prejudices to be countered in the struggle against the systematic exclusion of disabled people. Solidarity can only be the outcome of an active acknowledgement of the way in which the 'disabling society' has been sustained not only through structures and institutions but also the common sense assumptions and conventional wisdoms which inform our daily actions and exchanges. The disability movement, therefore, offers a distinctive resource for a popular education agenda which seeks to engage with cultural politics. The construction of an ethics of care can only proceed from an acknowledgement of the subordination of disabled people in the traditional discourse of care.

The reality of the exclusion of disabled people has too often been obscured by the perspectives of the non-disabled majority which have dominated the narratives of disability. Subjugated histories have to be excavated – an insight of both feminism and anti-racism:

> A significant feature of the oppression of disabled people is the way in which their voice has been totally excluded both from decisions affecting their own lives and from the wider political arena. (Barton, 1996)

A popular education agenda would aim to give voice to those who have been excluded – to redefine what constitutes 'the people' as a way of renegotiating the space between the personal and the political.

Perhaps because of the restrictions placed on the lives of many disabled people which have brought them into compromising relationships with (non-disabled) professionals of one kind or another and the ways in which the professional agenda has been so pervasive in their lives, the disability movement has been understandably wary of professional interests. As non-disabled people ourselves we have had to think carefully about the nature of our interventions as educators. The necessity to theorise and define the educational role in this context is clear. There is a need to clarify the terms of educational engagement with social movements which are struggling for change. Fundamental to the principles of the disability movement is the right of disabled people to speak for themselves and to organise for themselves. Within this framework, perhaps Foucault's warning to all who would be intellectuals goes also for those who would be professional or political allies:

> The role of the intellectual does not consist in telling others what they must do. What right would they have to do that? . . . The job of an intellectual does not consist in moulding the political will of others. It is a matter of performing analysis in his or her own fields, of interrogating anew the evidence and postulates, of shaking up habits, ways of acting and thinking, of dispelling commonplace beliefs, of taking a new measure of rules and institutions . . . it is a matter of participating in the formation of a political will . . . (quoted in Oliver, 1996)

Educational practice, in these terms, is based on solidarity and shared social purpose rather than the kind of paternalism or manipulation in which disabled people are treated as the objects of professional intervention. This requires a re-imagining of educational practice precisely because the policy context often establishes educational contact with disabled people on precisely these terms.

From practically zilch to inclusion

This is the title of a research report (Herd, 1998) published by Access Ability Lothian, a disability-led organisation. It encapsulates both the experience and the aspirations of the disability movement in Scotland today. But the struggle for inclusion must be a common struggle because the disabling society ultimately disables us all. Neither should its demise be seen as the responsibility of disabled people alone, anymore than the struggle against racism should be left to black people for, as Williams (1961) reminds us, 'in wasting individuals, by shutting them out from effective participation, it is damaging our true common process'. Our shared humanity is impoverished by the reality of exclusion. We are essentially social animals – interdependent and authenticated as human beings through our relationships with each other. A discourse of interdependence therefore needs to be developed which acknowledges not only 'lived difference' but also common purpose. This can only be realised, however, within a collectivist framework which addresses inequality. We need a new kind of politics which seeks to reject and replace traditional structures, institutions and processes that reinforce hegemonic norms. Seriously and systematically to include disabled people *in politics* as subjects rather than objects means 'democratising democracy' so that it gives expression to diverse, sometimes conflicting, voices.

> What distinguishes a radical perspective on democracy is not its expectation of future homogeneity and consensus, but its commitment to a politics of solidarity, and challenge, and change. (Phillips quoted in Barton, 1996)

The possibilities of reformulating the relationship between the state and civil society which democratic renewal in Scotland offers may provide an opportunity to ensure that new voices are heard, new knowledges generated and 'old' principles of egalitarianism and democracy given new life. This opportunity has to be grasped and made real. In the end, inclusion is not optional – because the alternative is exclusion. The disability movement has put inclusion firmly on the political agenda. But, in the words of Access Ability Lothian 'The most important question remains unanswered. We need to ask it together: What happens next?' (Herd, 1998)

References

Allen, G (1992) 'Active citizenship' in Allen G and Martin I (eds) *Education and Community: The Politics of Practice*, London, Cassell, pp 130–144.

Barton, L (1996) 'Citizenship and disabled people: a cause for concern' in Demaine, J and Entwistle, H (eds), *Beyond Communitarianism: Citizenship, Politics and Education*, Basingstoke, Macmillan, pp 179–192.

Campbell, J and Oliver, M (1996) *Disability Politics: Understanding our Past, Changing our Future*, London, Routledge.

Clegg, S (1996) 'From the women's movement to feminisms' in Barker, C and Kennedy, P (eds), *To Make Another World: Studies in Protest and Collective Action*, Aldershot, Avebury, pp 45–69.

Daniels, H, Hey, V, Leonard, D and Smith, M (1995) 'Gendered practice in special educational needs' in Dawtrey, L, Holland, J, and Hammer, M with Sheldon, S (eds), *Equality and Inequality in Education Policy,* Clevedon, Multilingual Matters Ltd/Open University, pp 204–218.

de Gruchy, N (1997) *Special Children*, November/December, p 3.

DES (1978) *Special Educational Needs* (Warnock Report), Cmnd 7212, London, HMSO.

Finkelstein, V (1993) 'The commonality of disability' in Swain, J, Finkelstein, V, French, S and Oliver, M (eds), *Disabling Barriers – Enabling Environments,* London, Sage, pp 11–16.

Giroux, H (1992) *Border Crossings: Cultural Workers and the Politics of Education*, New York, Routledge.

Herd, D (1998) *From Practically Zilch to Inclusion: One to One Tutor Support Services for Disabled Adults Seeking Access to 'Mainstream' Education,* Access Ability Lothian, Edinburgh.

Lister, R (1997) 'Citizenship: towards a feminist synthesis', *Feminist Review*, 57, pp 28–49.

Meekosha, H (1993) 'The bodies politic: equality, difference and community practice' in Butcher, H, Glen, A, Henderson, P and Smith, J (eds) *Community and Public Policy* London, Pluto Press/Community Development Foundation, pp 171–193.

Meekosha, H and Dowse, L (1997) 'Enabling citizenship: gender, disability and citizenship in Australia', *Feminist Review,* 57, pp 49–72.

Morris, J (1991) *Pride Against Prejudice: Transforming Attitudes to Disablity,* London, The Women's Press.

Morris, J (1993) *Independent Lives, Community Care and Disabled People,* Basingstoke, Macmillan.

Oliver, M (1990) *The Politics of Disablement,* Basingstoke, Macmillan and St Martin's Press.

Oliver, M (1996) *Understanding Disability: From Theory to Practice,* Basingstoke, Macmillan.

Segal, L (1991) 'Whose left? socialism, feminism and the future', *New Left Review,* 1 (5), pp 81–91.

Sevenhuijsen, S (1998) *Citizenship and the Ethics of Care: Feminist Considerations on Justice, Morality and Politics,* London, Routledge.

Shakespeare, T (1994) 'Cultural representation of disabled people: dustbins for disavowal?', *Disability & Society*, 9 (3), pp 283–299.

Slee, R (1997) 'Imported or important theory? Sociological interrogations of disablement and special education', *British Journal of Sociology of Education,* 18 (3), pp 49–71.

Tait, M (1997) *Curriculum for the Competent Community,* Unpublished.

Thompson, J (1997) *Words in Edgeways,* Leicester, NIACE.

UPIAS (1976) *Fundamental Principles of Disability,* London, Union of the Physically Impaired Against Segregation.

Weeks, J (1985) 'The population question in the early twentieth century' in Beechey, V and Donald, J (eds) *Subjectivity and Social Relations: A Reader,* Milton Keynes, Open University Press, pp 189–202.

Williams, R (1961) *The Long Revolution,* Harmondsworth, Pelican Books.

Acknowledgement

Thanks to Hazel MacFarlane, disability activist and development worker with Access Ability Lothian, for her comments.

13 'History, justice and the law': the struggle of the Assynt Crofters

Isobel MacPhail

The struggle of the Assynt Crofters was not only a material struggle for ownership of their land but also a cultural struggle for crofting as a way of life. The success of the campaign, in which the author of this chapter was directly involved, marked a historic turning point. By taking control of their own future, through collective action, the Assynt Crofters reasserted their cultural identity and recreated the struggles of the past in the context of the present. In doing so, they skilfully adapted the contemporary discourse of 'enterprise' to their cause and, in the process, systematically accommodated it to their purposes. In their victory, the Assynt Crofters won back both their land and their self-respect as agents of their own history.

We the crofters have resolved to band together to buy the estate, not for reasons motivated by political or romantic sentiment but because we believe that to give our crofting communities the best chance of surviving and prospering in the future, control of our resources – especially the land – will be our best chance. (Assynt Crofters' Trust)

The Assynt Crofters' Trust took control of the Assynt Estate in February 1993 after campaigning to raise the money to buy the land on the open market.

Imaginary geographies

Imaginary geographies are about the manner in which places, their people and their cultures are represented. Edward Said (1978) has shown how this works on a global scale between the 'East' and 'West': the West constructs beliefs that the east is mysterious, erotic, uncivilised and brutal in order to constitute its own identity as rational, civilised and decent. He suggests that the process of symbolic exclusion is achieved through a strategy of positional superiority whereby the 'high' is maintained in a myriad of possible relationships with the 'low', whilst always maintaining the upper hand. The same process can depict the relationship between England and Scotland: the latter is seen as parochial and backward whereas England is represented as cosmopolitan and advanced. Within a country, similar processes are also at work. The Gaidhealtachd (gaelic speaking areas) could be said to be in the same relationship within Scotland, cast in opposition to the lowlands. Since the fourteenth century the highland region has been seen as separate and culturally inferior. This has been the basis of a discourse of improvement or 'development', reinforced by the imagined 'wildness' of highland clans.

But why should characterisations of the highlands provide the central symbols in representations of Scotland as a whole? The Highlands and Islands are very much a place made in the minds of outsiders. The highlands today are imagined as an empty wilderness and crofting provides a remnant of the past on the doorstep of the present.

> The top includes that low symbolically, as a primary eroticised constituent of its own fantasy life . . . It is for this reason that what is socially peripheral is so frequently symbolically central. The low–Other is despised and denied at the level of political organisation and social being whilst it is instrumentally constitutive of the shared imaginary repertoires of the dominant culture. (Stallybrass and White, 1989)

The impact of this symbolic exclusion on political thought and policy and planning is enormous. And where does it leave the highlander's own idea of identity and opportunity? What are the psycho–cultural dimensions of such subordination?

Customary rights

Anthropologists and historians have charted Gaeltachd attitudes to land and identity (see Hunter, 1976). Historically, the land was seen as their land, no matter who held the title deeds. This idea of *duthchas* or customary rights, wrongfully usurped by a variety of landlords, has been expressed in a variety of forms. In mediaeval and early modern times, the *duthchas* was generally thought to have been established when a family had maintained effective occupation of township or joint farm for three generations. This gave the family an inalienable right to reside on the land. Crofters never accepted the idea of private ownership of land or the game on it. Nor did they give up their belief that they had a hereditary right to their holding. In conjunction with religious beliefs, these fundamentals from ancient Celtic law were central to the crofters of the 1880s in their agitation over land rights and landlords.

In whatever form, the system of beliefs and material practices of crofters has no place in the logic of contemporary capitalism. It is incompatible with the operation of private property and land as a commodity. Before the Crofting Act of 1886 such a culture had no foundation in law. While legislation brought security of tenure, rights of succession within the family and a right to fair rents, it did not return lands already cleared or 'taken' – the single most important demand of the crofters' movement at that time. The persistence of this attitude to land and society has been seen as another indication of the backwardness and lack of culture of the highland people. It is not a 'real' world view. Neither is the belief that land cleared of people has been wrongfully taken and should be returned to the people.

Until recently, the writing of history has dismissed this as romantic and sentimental nonsense – an irrational attitude. It is often said that highland com-munities lack self-confidence and that the clearances remain an emotional millstone round the neck of the highlander – standing in the way of progress and innovation. It is often overlooked that the weight of the past is inscribed on the present, not just in memory and imagination, but equally in the material circumstances of everyday life. When your own history is systematically denied, what becomes of your sense of self? In this century, voluntary migration has been a common strategy to evade economic and cultural marginalisation. There is also a public and a private life: one story for the locals, another for the rest. Behind closed doors there is still a fierce pride in what remains of this culture, but for decades many have ensured that their children are fluent English speakers. Gaelic might only mark them out and hold them back. The rise of the Gaelic media shows a turning of this tide – in attitude and cultural confidence, in the first instance.

Government agencies established to deal with 'the highland problem' provide records of various development solutions. The steady depopulation through out-migration faltered in the mid-1970s and population growth began. The pattern, however, is uneven and evidence from the Highland and Islands Development Board suggests that the sloth and indolence historically attributed to the Gaidhealtachd in its entirety is now perceived to have receded to lurk on the margin of the margins – in the north and west, the remaining strongholds of crofting and Gaelic culture: Said's spatialised 'low'.

The struggle of the Assynt Crofters

In 1992 the North Lochinver Estate in the parish of Assynt in north-west Sutherland came on the market. It was described by estate agents John Clegg & Co in their sales brochure as follows:

> One need only enter Assynt to see the great sphinx-like mass of Suilven, to sense the atmosphere of unreality, almost fantasy, which permeates even the character of the people who live there. Mountains such as Quinag, Canisp, Ben More, Assynt, Cul Beag, Stack Polly and Conival all have the immense power to impress and all serve to emphasise that man himself is perhaps the alien element in this landscape.

In the same year the Assynt Crofters mounted a campaign to buy the land they lived on and to bring it into community control. At that time, their estate was in the hands of the liquidators, having been bought by a Swedish property development company which subsequently went out of business. This resulted in the North Lochinver Estate being put on the market at an asking price of £473,000. The estate was to be sold in six lots, raising the possibility of not one but several absentee or disinterested landlords. Incensed by this situation and the fear of each crofter having to pay rent to several disparate landlords, the crofters in North Assynt met to discuss the issue. The result of these discussions was the establishment of the Assynt Crofters' Trust, formed with the intention of raising the necessary funds to bid for the whole estate themselves. In July 1992 they set about the task.

It would be easy in retrospect to see this as inevitable. It was not. Why should these people, in the face of the sale and fragmentation of the estate on which they were resident, have taken this step? Estates are sold and broken up all the time. The North Assynt Estate itself was created by sale and fragmentation in the 1980s, having formerly been part of the larger Assynt Estate held by the Vestey family. Why then should this fragment of estate inspire such a resolve as the Assynt Crofters demonstrated?

The Assynt Branch of the Scottish Crofters' Union (SCU) organised a public meeting for everyone in the area – union member or not – to discuss the sale. This was the Assynt Crofters' Trust in the making. There are two important points to note here. Without the Scottish Crofters' Union, there would be no Assynt Crofters' Trust because without previous experience of action and campaigning, the Assynt Crofters' Trust would never have been the success it so clearly is. The SCU did not create the Assynt Crofters' Trust, but it created the circumstances which made such a bold move first thinkable and then possible.

The SCU was established in 1985, replacing a number of local groups linked through the Federation of Crofters' Unions. Among other things, the SCU became the vehicle through which definitions of crofting and crofters were forever altered: no longer as failed farming, but as extensive, low-intensity land use; the social glue which ensures the survival of remote communities; a way of life with social, cultural and environmental value. The important point is that the SCU provided a voice and a platform for crofters, created by crofters, and the branch structure provided an arena for debate, discussion and policy formation never before available in the lifetime of those involved. It created energy, excitement and pride. The SCU was taken seriously. In Assynt, therefore, the union branch provided a respected and appropriate local organisation which offered a forum for everyone to discuss the sale of the estate. Union activists were tried and tested and had an awareness that they could make a difference – and that they were not alone. It was agreed that an attempt should be made to prevent the break-up of the estate. The earlier sale which had created the North Assynt Estate was now viewed as a break in trust by the landlord.

The campaign

The first significant step in the campaign was when members of the crofting community took the view that these circumstances were their business. The ownership of the issue was with the local people from the start. Past experience of other local initiatives created a predisposition for action. In particular, resistance to proposals for a national park in the area had shown that it is not enough simply to disagree with proposals. To be effective you have to say no, say why and then come up with a workable alternative for which you are prepared to take responsibility. A public meeting format was used for debate and decision making. The manner in which this was managed is significant. Every effort was made to ensure that the information and agenda were presented in accessible forms. Local expertise was used for this and additional expert advice brought in. At all stages, the aim was to enable the community as a whole to take positive and collective decisions. The experience of taking negative decisions – or continually rejecting the options presented – does not build momentum or resolve. It does not produce in the imagination a notion of a future worth striving for.

This approach requires considerable skill on the part of those leading the initial discussion – and subsequently the campaign. Some people cannot bear to sit through a meeting of any sort, while others thrive on it. Able leadership is crucial. The ability, clarity and conviction of Allan MacRae and Bill Ritchie, two of the leading campaigners, gave others confidence and inspiration. The practical implications of any course of action were quickly and professionally addressed. It was a process of creative thinking based strictly on the facts. Simply celebrating a position of powerless moral superiority would not have been transforming. A Steering Group of 12 crofters was elected. The experience of many of those involved in past efforts – for example, to build a community hall or run the Assynt Highland Games – provided a good grounding in getting organised and getting the job done. The will to prevent the break-up of the estate quickly translated into the decision to try to buy the land into community ownership. The proposal enjoyed the unanimous support of the public meeting to which it was presented.

A feasibility study was commissioned to assess the assets for sale and the commercial viability of a crofter-managed estate in North Assynt. The decision to pursue the option of community ownership was the result of unanimous agreement in principle that the crofters should form a company to buy the land. Every move was contingent on a continuous flow of information and a rapid assesement of events as they unfolded. The other necessary expert knowledge was legal advice. This was imported. A lawyer experienced in crofting law and estate management was crucial. Simon Fraser, a lawyer from Stornoway and himself a crofter who factored several estates in the course of his legal duties, joined the team. He was both committed to the project and had been part of the team which had carried out the feasibility study on community ownership of estates in Skye and Raasay in 1990. His experience was therefore both relevant and broad.

The legal structure of the company formed to buy the land was both a crucial element in the strength of the campaign and a future investment in maintaining the integrity of its aims. The legal structure adopted ensured that the crofters remained tenants and elected a Steering Group and subsequently a Board of Directors from amongst their number. Any crofting tenant or subtenant was eligible for membership. To raise the necessary funds every household on the estate – as distinct from every member of the Trust – would attempt to donate £1,000. It was assumed from the start that many, on low or fixed incomes, would be unable to raise this amount, if anything at all. Those who could afford it would try to contribute more to compensate for those unable to pledge money. This had no bearing on the rights of members, who had the same voting rights irrespective of ability to pay or the amount of land held. Non-crofters could not be members, but this did not exclude anyone from discussion or meetings. It was hoped in this way to raise £80,000. A number of public agencies would then be asked to match the monies raised by individual donation to allow a realistic bid to be made. To achieve this the crofters required two things: as much support as possible from the general public and the ability to convince quangos and other grant-giving bodies that this was a serious matter which merited their financial backing.

The credibility of the cause had to be established beyond all reasonable doubt. The creation of the Scottish Crofters' Union with its branch in Assynt had already gone some way to dealing with the matter of personal and com-munity credibility. Confidence is a quality often found to be lacking in crofting communities and, in the beginning, many in the community doubted whether buying the estate was either feasible or sensible. In any group there is inevitably a variety of attitudes. Some were uncomfortable with references to past wrongs from the time of the Clearances, feeling that such talk was old fashioned and made them look ridiculous. Others were unashamed in viewing any move towards community land ownership as 'taking back what was taken from us'. It was necessary to concentrate on what could be agreed upon. Many had to confront within themselves, and in other people, the popular conviction that crofters can never agree. Amongst the women, due to their involvement in other community activities, there was an early awareness that both the campaign – and later, if it came to it – the management of the estate would involve a lot of time and work. The feasibility study provided evidence that a crofting trust was economically viable. This, combined with ongoing legal advice, went a long way to breaking down the traditional mystique of estate ownership. It became increasingly clear that you didn't need an oak panelled office, a factor and a four-wheel drive vehicle full of labradors to run an estate. Much of the necessary knowledge was available locally.

The feasibility study was paid for by a grant from the Local Enterprise Company, Caithness & Sutherland Enterprise. The Chief Executive at the time, Andrew Thin, was impressed by the professionalism of the Steering Group in putting their case and understood quickly that any money spent would be an investment in the intangibles which move any community or local economy forward – an investment in vision, energy and 'enterprise', as defined at the local level. Other public bodies proved more difficult to convince. A strategy to achieve this as well as wider public support was needed.

For this, a public launch of the appeal was required. In July 1992 everyone in the community was invited to a public meeting in a local primary school. All those eligible for membership of the proposed Company were asked to bring £1 and a pen. Meetings thus far had been packed – standing room only, with people perched on every windowsill. This meeting was no exception. A press release had been sent out and the media were there in force. At the front of the room sat the Chairman, Vice-Chairman and Secretary of the Steering Group along with the lawyer. The meeting opened and the story so far was laid out for meeting and media alike. The team at the top table handed round an appeal document to all present. This A4 leaflet set out the aims and objectives of the proposed Company. The motion that 'you agree in principle that we should form a company to buy the land' was presented to the meeting and passed unanimously. One by one the crofters came forward to sign with their pens and pay their £1 membership to form the Assynt Crofters' Trust Limited. By the end of the evening, the Trust had 111 members.

The next day this moment was broadcast to the nation on the Six O'Clock News. What had been achieved? It established beyond all reasonable doubt that the Assynt Crofters' Trust was much more than one or two over-excited activists. It demonstrated that the Trust had an extremely high level of support within the community and had been formally and legally constituted on a democratic basis. The appeal document further established its professionalism and seriousness of intent. It began, 'We the people of Assynt, . . . ', a phrase with a powerful resonance for both local community and wider public alike. The document went on to outline the aims and objectives of the Assynt Crofters' Trust which included:

- to raise funds to buy the land
- to improve the social, educational, cultural and natural environment of the crofting communities in Assynt, Sutherland
- to help fund viable investment and secure property development for the crofting communities.

The appeal document talked of viable investment and the creation of an atmosphere of optimism and opportunity. The discourse thus created had strong resonances with the language and ideology of the Local Enterprise Company and Highlands and Islands Enterprise. The Assynt Crofters' Trust Limited presented itself as the very epitome of community enterprise. In so doing, the Trust gained credibility with those who held the purse strings. The campaign was therefore a strategy based on the use of enterprise discourse while clearly standing in opposition to the ideologies on which that discourse is based. It was not about free markets and the end of society, but rather the strength of community and culture: a subversion which remade meanings.

What had happened here? The public launch required the Assynt Crofters' Trust to represent themselves in the public arena. In doing this, the Assynt Crofters were aware of the sort of stereotypes they would encounter and they reinvented themselves. Any successful group stage-manages its entrance into the public domain. This is not about cynicism and marketing: it is about identity and representation in a transforming moment created by action. They did not deny the effect of the past on contemporary material circumstances. Indeed, they boldly declared that they had 'history, justice and the law' on their side. This appealed to the general public who donated generously to the fund. But they simultaneously perfected the art of living in their own times: the whole plan was played out by the field rules of the dominant culture. They sought to buy the land on the open market, set up a limited company and encouraged appropriate inward investment. They were crofters of the 1990s, businesslike and professional. They didn't ask anything for nothing – only support for their plan. James C Scott (1987) refers to this as 'talking up'. A subordinate group's challenge to the dominant ideology or its demands on democracy tend to be hidden. In seeking to achieve its aims, social interaction involves power-laden encounters. Forms of discourse are tailored accordingly. The Assynt Crofters' demand 'to take back the land' could be construed as the epitome of enterprise. But such apparent consensus in the public arena does not automatically negate dissent. The tactics of the less powerful should not be mistaken for the whole story. Scott's work focuses on examples from the developing world, but the usefulness of his approach is that it privileges issues of dignity and autonomy which are often seen as secondary to material exploitation. The evidence in Assynt was that it was this very issue of dignity and the legitimation in a public arena of certain values and historical readings which were at stake.

The public transcript involves 'talking up' – employing certain sanctioned discourses to gain access to the public arena and so to an audience and legitimacy. In parts of the world where dissent rarely finds public expression the public declaration of the hidden transcript, or the 'raw declaration' in Scott's terms, is a euphoric moment. In less extreme instances of subordination, he talks of 'cooked' rather than 'raw' declarations:

> Cooked declarations are more likely to be nuanced and elaborate because they arise under circumstances in which there is a good deal of off-stage freedom among subordinate groups, allowing them to share a rich and deep hidden transcript. In a sense the hidden transcript of such subordinate groups is already a product of mutual communication that already has a quasi-public existence. (Scott, 1987)

The general public warmed to the cause and the public agencies approached for funding would have looked as though they were failing to fulfil the logic of their own remit if they did not support the campaign. Donations and pledges from individuals flooded in and reached levels far beyond the community's early expectations. Caithness and Sutherland Enterprise, Highlands and Islands Enterprise, Highland Regional Council, Highland Prospect, Scottish National Heritage and the John Muir Trust all agreed to provide grants or loans. The Assynt Crofters' Trust was in a position to bid for their land. In the event of their bid being refused, they had a powerful fallback position. In June of the same year came the legal case of MacDonald versus Whitbread and what became known as the Whitbread ruling. This significantly challenged previous legal precedent in establishing that if a crofter bought from the land owner and transferred directly to a third party the land owner was not entitled to claim a 50 per cent development cut of the sale price. The Assynt Crofters' Trust pointed out therefore that should anyone outbid them and take ownership of their estate, the crofters would begin to buy all of their ground at 15 times the annual rent as decreed in the 1976 Crofting Reform Act and transfer this ground directly to a third party – the Assynt Crofters' Trust. If the publicity their campaign had created didn't scare off the opposition, then this surely would. It would make the estate worthless to any potential owner other than themselves. The crofters carefully prepared the legal groundwork for this fallback position and were in a position to proceed if necessary. Their seriousness in this strengthened their position despite the fact that in reality such a move is legally complex and extremely time consuming. It was nevertheless a powerful and well researched option which posed a real threat to any other potential buyer not dissuaded from purchase through support of the local cause or fear of unfriendly natives.

Without the groundswell of public support, due in large part to favourable media coverage, the Assynt Crofters' Trust would not have got far. The idea and the crofters themselves inspired people all across Scotland and beyond. Given the pressure of the media exposure, their professionalism and conviction were powerful. They literally spoke for themselves. Donations poured in to support the courage and determination of these people. There is no doubt that much of the support from individual members of the public was prompted by an awareness of the wrongs of the past, a wish to support the individual against the giants of international capital and the place of the crofter in the Scottish consciousness. Others were influenced by an interest in environmental issues and many were holiday makers familiar with the place and the people.

Rewriting the history books

By the autumn of 1992 the Assynt Crofters' Trust were in a position to make a bid for their land. Their confidence and determination had increased in those summer months, as had their unity of purpose. The early bids were rejected and times were tense. In the end, it took all the funds given or promised:

£300,000. On the afternoon of 8 December 1992 the news came through that the Assynt Crofters' Trust bid to buy their land had been successful. It spread rapidly around the area. A meeting was quickly arranged for that evening. In the dark of a December evening people drove from miles around to hear the announcement. The reporters, now familiar faces about the place, had also trekked through that dark, windy night.

And what was said? Did the campaign leaders stand up and celebrate the prospect of commercial viability in a new era of enterprise? Did they throw off the burden of crofting's blighted past? After thanking everyone present and all those across Scotland and beyond who had stood firm, this is what Allan MacRae, Chair of the Assynt Crofters' Trust, had to say:

> Well, ladies and gentlemen, it seems that we have won the land . . . and I think that's certainly a moment to savour. No doubt about that. And certainly, my immediate thoughts are to wish that some of our forebears could be here to share this moment with us. I must say, I don't think there's any doubt that in winning the land, the Assynt Crofters have struck an historic blow for people on the land right throughout the Highlands and Islands.

Bill Ritchie, Secretary and Vice-Chair of the Trust, added:

> I'd like, if I may, to quote from a book – it's called *Mightier than a Lord* by Ian Fraser Grigor. It's an account of the Land League struggle of the people after they were cleared off the land to get their land back. This is him writing after he's detailed the history: 'The 1886 Crofters Act represented a remarkable victory for the highland crofters. It was not the end, however, but a beginning. The greatest single demand of the crofters' movement – the land to the people – was not met. Nor has it yet been met.' Well, they can start re-writing the history books because we have our land!

It was a euphoric moment. What they had won was not just the land. What they had achieved was to bring the crofting community's understanding of what land is, and what their history meant into the centre of late twentieth century Scottish politics – and to legitimate those feelings, those views, that culture and that identity. They had brought the values and history of the periphery back to the centre. What they had won was dignity. As one crofter from north Sutherland put it, 'because of the Assynt Crofters' Trust, crofters no longer have heather behind their ears'. They had remade the identity of crofters – and touched the identity of Scotland itself in so doing. The social and cultural values of the Gaidhealtachd had acquired a 'real' contemporary status through this act. As a consequence, representations of Scotland which revolve around notions of things Highland lost some of their stigma.

The future is the hostage of our imaginations. While the Highlands and Islands have been central to the configuration of Scottish identity, contemporary issues relating to this place and the people living here have tended to be totally marginal. Since 1992 this has changed. We have seen the development of a lively and varied debate on land issues in the broadest sense. This debate has focused not just on the rights and access of those who live on rural land, but also on the rights, responsibilities and demands of those who live elsewhere. Other rural communities have sought the same road. Some have been successful in taking land into community ownership, some were unable to achieve this and others have rejected community ownership as an option.

References

Hunter, J (1976) *The Making of the Crofting Community*, Edinburgh, John Donald Publishers Limited.

Said, E (1978) *Orientalism*, London, Routledge and Kegan Paul.

Stallybrass, P and White, A (1989) *The Politics and Practice of Transgression,* London, Methuen.

Scott, J (1987) *Weapons of the Weak,* London, Yale University Press.

14 Not on the curriculum: the story of Scottish working class material culture

Elspeth King

The material culture of working class communities is a rich historical resource for a popular education curriculum. And yet it is either wilfully ignored or actively suppressed by most of the experts: both educators and many museum curators. One effect of this is that the real struggles and achievements of ordinary people are written out of the revisionist historical record – although, ironically, they continue to be re-enacted and celebrated in the culture of everyday life in many Scottish communities. It is essential that any genuinely popular education should reconnect with these hidden histories before they are merchandised as heritage or simply forgotten. The alternative is 'a slavery of intellect and a servility of attitude' which would be a betrayal of the historic struggle for freedom and dignity.

There seems to be very little credence given to the study of material culture in our schools, colleges and universities. There is not much interfacing between museum curators and educationalists because of this and one of the results is that those who could benefit most from museum work and ways of thinking obtain no benefit at all. The title of this paper comes from long experience as a museum curator of organising temporary exhibitions and being unable to attract the school audiences I had hoped for. More often than not, a temporary exhibitions' programme is harnessed to some commemorative anniversary or other which offers the opportunity for collecting and interpreting significant pieces in a museum display. Time after time, I have organised exhibitions only to learn that the schools were 'not doing it'.

This has included the sixtieth anniversary of the Representation of the People Act in 1978 when the subject was women's suffrage, an exhibition called 'Scotland Sober and Free' which commemorated 150 years of the temperance movement in 1979, an exhibition on the bicentenary of the Calton Weavers' Strike in 1987 and the centenary of the Scottish Labour Party and Celtic Football Club – both in 1988. 1990 was also a good year for anniversaries, being the 800th anniversary of the establishment of the Glasgow Fair and the 300th anniversary of the Battle of the Boyne. Schools in Glasgow found a difficulty in dealing with these subjects and letting their children out to see them. I was repeatedly told that it was 'not on the curriculum' or 'we don't do that kind of thing'.

Note: This is the edited text of a paper presented at the Third Edinburgh Biennial Adult Education Conference in February 1996.

Today, I am still meeting this problem. I have just been told by a teacher serving a number of primary schools in the Stirling Council area that it will be pointless sending out information on our William Wallace exhibition – a blockbuster organised to commemorate the 700th anniversary of the Battle of Stirling Bridge – as none of her classes are 'doing a Scottish subject' this year. I felt that even if I took the time to explain Wallace's legacy in inspiring other national liberators, including individuals like George Washington, Simon Bolivar, Giuseppi Garibaldi, Giuseppe Mazzini and Louis Kossuth and not to mention poets as far apart in time and space as William Wordsworth and Maya Angelou, the idea of the exhibition would still not have overcome her prejudices. When you find out what is actually on the curriculum, it tends to be something as anodyne and as meaningless as 'The Victorians' or that hoary old chestnut, 'The Desperate Journey'.

In every respect, the temperance movement, the Scottish Labour Party and the Celtic Football Club were Victorian phenomena, but not of the type which feature on the school curriculum. After the set lessons on 'The Victorians', it was always possible to get the children in to the temporary exhibition gallery to look at another aspect of 19th century cultural history and one with which the older members of their families could identify.

To those of us working in museums, it is evident that the objects which people keep, treasure and hand down are in no way related to mainstream history as taught in schools and universities. At university level, historical studies are often so empirical, so document-focused and centred on charters and written evidence that if you can't find a document of an event or phenomenon, it is judged to be of no significance and therefore not worth studying. However, even when the documentary evidence is plentiful but the phenomenon is judged a 'failure', like the temperance movement is perceived to be, the effect is the same.

I was struck by the sheer volume of material I was able to collect on temperance in 1979. This included pledge cards, badges, certificates, Band of Hope medals, the little white ribbons of the British Women's Temperance Association, the banner of the Scottish Prohibition Party and the magnificent banner of the Sons of Temperance, painted in 1902 with Kelvingrove Art Gallery in Glasgow on one side and the Good Shepherd on the other but found in four pieces by a refuse collector in the course of his duty. Scarcely a family in the west of Scotland could have been unaffected by the temperance movements, in one way or another. Yet there was only one unpublished, inaccessible PhD thesis on it at that time.

I should say that I am well aware of the use made of certain historical objects in schools, like gas masks and other Second World War memorabilia. The National Museums of Scotland have also made sterling efforts to make their collections available to children in rural schools, through photo CDs and multi-media essays, whereby you are able to look inside the Galloway mazer or turn the Hunterston Brooch round on the screen in front of you. However, the time when the material culture of the ordinary people of Scotland will be treated in this fashion is a long way off. With socialism widely perceived as having 'failed', it seems to me unlikely that any of the political movements which came under that umbrella – the Co-op, the Socialist Sunday Schools, the Unemployed Workers movements – will be studied much at any level, in the schools, colleges and universities.

During my years of working for Glasgow Museums, I felt that I had an uphill struggle to persuade certain sectors of the community that the artefacts from their working lives were worth keeping. Unlike in the Scandinavian countries, where there has been an academic framework for collecting such objects for at least a century and a half, there is no such practice within museum curatorship in urban Scotland. (Rural Scotland is slightly different – there seems to be an expectation that museums can and should collect obsolete agricultural equipment of all kinds.)

So, for example, in Glasgow, one of the great shipbuilding cities of the world and a major port with extensive docks and cargo terminals, there was, as late as 1988, not a single docker's hook in the museum collections including the vast collection of the Museum of Transport. A docker's hook is an unimpressive object, consisting of a wooden handle and a tough forged metal hook, but it was the indispensable tool of the dock labourer, vast armies of whom kept the cargoes moving and the docks turning. They were the poorest and worst off among the labouring classes, dependent upon casual and seasonal work and they were among the last to be unionised. Without a hook or hooks, the dock labourer did not work and time and again when collecting oral evidence, I learned that the hooks were frequently in the pawnshops, the pawnbroker operating in the knowledge that the docker would somehow find the means to redeem the pawn. An appeal brought in about half a dozen of them, together with a flood of stories from retired dock labourers about the practices and conditions at the docks. Having them on display stimulated even more. It is amazing how everyday objects, seen again after an absence of years or decades, can be keys to unlocking memory which can be the means of producing histories which would otherwise be lost.

The object in the museum often has an immediacy and a message which can cut through the obfuscation of the academic thesis. I have heard and read, for example, a number of comfortable, revisionist papers on the Scottish mining industry in the eighteenth century, in which economic data are assembled to prove that the serfdom of the Scottish colliers was a mere myth, that the colliers, being thirled to the workplace of the coal owner, had – and I quote – 'steady work, secure jobs for their children and a roof over their heads', unlike the self-employed weavers who were at the mercy of the boom and slump of trade. Indeed, apologists for the slave trade in the tobacco and cotton plantations of North America have taken this line for decades.

There is no body of evidence extant from the Scottish colliers who endured this slavery to challenge such revisionism. However, there is one item in the collection of the National Museums of Scotland which for me speaks volumes and it is a brass collar from the neck of one of the miners who managed to escape and dump his shackles in the River Forth. The inscription reads 'Alexr. Steurt, found guilty of death for theft at Perth, the 5th December 1701 and gifted by the Justiciars as a perpetual servant to Sir Jo. Areskin of Alva'.

I think such objects can offer a corrective to the revisionist and I find it a cause for concern when they are patently and consistently ignored. There is, for example, a very active organisation in the mining villages of the Falkirk area called the Sir William Wallace Grand Lodge of Free Colliers of Falkirk. To see this group on the march is like taking a step back into the nineteenth century. The organisation takes to the streets on the first Saturday of August every year and embarks on a 10 mile walk through the villages of Redding, Shieldhill, Westquarter and Brightons, ending up at Wallacestone. Although the Sir William Wallace Lodge of Free Colliers were formally constituted in 1863, the practice of marching and demonstrating at the Wallacestone goes back two centuries, to the time when in the late eighteenth century, the colliers technically obtained their freedom from serfdom.

In 1997 many of us celebrated the 700th anniversary of William Wallace's great victory at the Battle of Stirling Bridge. In 1797 it must have seemed much more immediate to the colliers who compared their new found freedom to the freedom won by William Wallace. When Burns, in 'Scots Wha Hae', writes:

> By oppressions woes and pains
> By your sons in servile chains
> We will drain our dearest veins
> But we shall be free.
> Lay the proud usurpers low
> Tyrants fall in every foe
> Liberty's in every blow
> Let us do or die

the tyrants like Sir John Erskine, rather than Edward I, were probably uppermost in his mind. It was also safer to identify with the liberty won by Wallace, rather than the liberty of the French Revolution – but that was only to a certain degree. Colonel William Fullerton, who issued a celebratory commemorative token in 1797, with Wallace on one side and 'Scotia Rediviva' on the other, was censured by the London Parliament, of which he was a member, for issuing coinage which was too close to that of a coin of the realm.

The colliers closely identified their cause with that of Wallace. In 1810, the first Wallace monument of modern times was erected when the ancient Wallace Stone at Wallacestone was replaced by a 10-foot high inscribed stone pillar, proclaiming the importance of Wallace and freedom in an area of a free people. Later on in the century, some Falkirk masons went south and brought back part of a parapet from London Bridge, because Wallace's head had been displayed there and this piece of stonework is still, like a trophy, deposited at Wallacestone.

Few people outside of the Falkirk area seem to know about the Free Colliers' annual march and I would like to recommend it to you as one of the spectacles of Scotland, as venerable as Lanark's Lanimer Day, as regular as Kirkcaldy's Links Market and as much of a non-pc procession as the Hawick Common Riding. The Sir William Wallace Lodge of Free Colliers appear in morning dress, wearing top hats, blue sashes and white gloves and because they march in pairs with their little fingers interlinked they are known as the 'Pinkie Men'. Every year they bid for the honour of carrying one of the three or four large flags during the 10 mile march, and the money collected goes to charity. The flags depict Sir William Wallace on one side, modelled on the portrait made famous by the Eleventh Earl of Buchan, and on the reverse side are paintings of the brethren wearing formal dress and doing good works for the less fortunate. These images are of a kind once very common and in every respect – from the Victorian iconography on the banners to the landau at the rear which carries the aged members – this organisation is very much a nineteenth century brotherly society. All of the participants are ex-colliers, or from a family of colliers and one of the tasks of the march is to lay a saltire wreath in memory of the 40 men who lost their lives in the Redding Pit Disaster of 1923. The march lasts several hours, with frequent refreshment stops along the way, all the people of the villages turning out to see it, and the penultimate stop is the Wallace Stone, where the speeches are delivered, before moving on to the Wallace Arms to celebrate again.

The Sir William Wallace Free Colliers of Falkirk were once part of a nationwide organisation, dedicated to improving the lives of the members, but now only the Falkirk colliers remain. I have heard the organisation witheringly dismissed as a bunch of bigoted masons with an anti-Catholic bias, and it is very true that when people are oppressed, they will take shelter in secret societies' masonic practices. If the labour market is flooded with cheap labour, which happens to be Irish and Catholic, as a means of keeping wages down, it is again true that such organisations will be anti-Irish and anti-Catholic. It's very difficult to know. I've looked long and hard for an academic study which would explain or interpret the organisation, but there has been nothing.

I think it is a wonderful achievement when this type of working class organisation can survive against all the odds. All too often, in the aftermath of the disappearance of an industry, especially in a one-industry place, you get the collapse of all social cohesion and identity within the community. This is compounded when the product of the industry is destroyed or taken elsewhere, but it is the very stuff of the story of the de-industrialisation of Scotland over the last 30 years.

I would like to mention by way of example the turkey red dyeing industry, which was in its time a world leader. It was introduced into Scotland by George MacIntosh in 1785, when he brought in the Frenchman, Papillion, to set up what were known as the 'secret works' in Glasgow. The process involved discharge dyeing, which in its time produced a colour fastness with bright reds, yellows and greens and a potential for very intricate pattern work. The industry expanded and was for a time in the 1830s on a greenfield site in Barrowfield. The need for more land and a clean water supply and the attempt to shake off the unionised labour saw this dye works and many similar ones relocate in the Vale of Leven to make use of the Loch Lomond water. A combination of employers' interests got together to maintain their edge in overseas markets. This led to the establishment of the United Turkey Red Company of the Vale of Leven. Until the demise of the company in 1960, it was a main employer in the west of Scotland.

One of the reasons for its demise was the demand for new patterns every season, dictated by the Indian market. This meant that overheads were high, with the need to employ large numbers of designers and pattern cutters. However, the work had great beauty. The production of bale labels was an art form in its own right, with the subjects being Indian legends like Ganesha and Krishna, drawn up in India but colour printed in Glasgow, with the firm's name round the edges. In the art-hungry Rajesthan area, when the cloth bales arrived, the labels, which were a maximum of about 6 × 4 inches, were stripped off, squared up and turned into huge wall murals, complete with copied text round the margins. These were fast disappearing in the 1970s and are probably now gone. A recorder working for the poorly funded Indian National Trust did what he could.

The United Turkey Red Company, part of a contracting cotton industry, was subject to a take-over bid by a bigger Manchester company, and closed down. Thousands of pattern books for both textiles and labels were destroyed. A few found their way into the Royal Scottish Museum and there are some in the Glasgow University Business Archives. Glasgow Museums declined to collect anything, for the transport and technology staff were too busy creating the new Museum of Transport. One man employed in clearing the works, who later came to work as an attendant for Glasgow Museums, described how he took lorry loads of pattern books to the municipal dump to have them ploughed into the ground by bulldozers. From the point of view of material culture, the whole operation was a disaster.

In the 1970s and 1980s, I was forever on the lookout for fragments of turkey red material to represent this once great industry. Luckily, in 1988 I acquired a collection of almost 100 original pattern designs, hand painted on paper by a woman who was one of the casualties in 1960. The work was intricate, fresh and beautiful and I felt that, at last, I could do some justice to the industry and its workers in the museum displays.

Regretably, Glasgow Museums was moving into its corporate identity mode. This collection was seized on as a basis for new merchandising, including silk ties at £25 a time, gift tags, wrapping paper and note books. A tiny fragment of a pattern was used as part of the logo on the museum's letter heading and the attendant staff wear the ties and scarves based on the patterns. This is fine, except that there is no explanation, not even in the misleading title 'Glasgow Red' which these products carry.

Thus a rich and interesting history has been ignored and robbed of its meaning and the material trivialised. Worse still, whilst the collection was passing between administrators, business managers, corporate identity experts, designers and printers, some 27 of the 100 pieces went missing and have never been recovered. This is what happens when collections are regarded as expendable. Thus, the Mennons printing press which printed the *Glasgow Advertiser* in 1783, is now on its way back to its former owners, the *Glasgow Herald*, who gifted it in 1983. With it, the newspapers illustrating the struggle for the freedom of the press – the *Herald to the Trades Advocate*, the *Trades Advocate*, the *Liberator* (the only known copy outside the British Museum), the *Greenwich News Clout*, printed on cotton, and the late lamented *Scottish Daily News*, have also vanished. There has been much talk of sending the Glasgow trade union banners collection to the Manchester Museum of Labour History, which has developed a specialist conservation unit.

The People's Palace collection in Glasgow once had the potential to inform and to change lives. Now the political and the cutting edge is not only to be blunted but is to be excised and the content reduced to a mash of lumpen tabloidese, catering for the lowest common denominator and serving up information on subjects such as the bevy, the steamie, the dancing, at a level to which not even the *Sunday Post* would stoop. With curators being instructed to write labels for none-too-literate 12-year-olds, there will be no intellectual challenge in these displays. Had working class material culture ever been part of the curriculum, this could never have happened. If no care is taken, our children will be chained in a slavery of the intellect and a servility of attitude which not even the original free colliers could have anticipated.

I think there is a great potential for those interested in popular adult education to turn to the study of material culture and become involved in the work of museums, both for the cultural enrichment which it can bring and for the sake of the very future of Scotland's museums.

15 Representing women: the tactics of gender in Scotland

Alice Brown

One of the key issues in the campaign for a Scottish Parliament was gender equality. This chapter gives an acount of the strategy and tactics adopted by a broadly-based and pluralist movement of women activists across Scotland to change the state and to extend democracy in this most obvious and fundamental way. The new parliament represents a unique opportunity to achieve equal representation as well as women-friendly procedures and practices. Much has been achieved but the struggle for political reform is far from over. On a wider note, the politics of this struggle may, indeed, be indicative of the emergence of a 'third wave feminism'.

Introduction

The constitutional question in Scotland has opened up real opportunities to advance the representation of women. The belief that women must be proactive in shaping a new political institution has been instrumental in mobilising large numbers of female politicians, party activists and women's groups in Scotland to campaign for gender equality and women friendly practices in the Scottish Parliament. Women activists in Scotland have exerted and maintained political pressure on the political parties to promote the policy of equal representation of women and men in the first elections for the new parliament in Scotland. This continuing advocacy has ensured that the issue of gender equality has remained on the political agenda over the long, uneven and eventful campaign for constitutional reform in the 1980s and 1990s. Developments have been both positive and negative: on the positive side, there is an acknowledgement that women's political representation is a salient political issue; but on the negative side, there is continuing political resistance and potential challenges to the introduction of mechanisms for achieving this (see Brown, 1996, 1998).

This chapter examines the way in which the tactics of gender have been employed to keep the issue of women's representation high on the political agenda in Scotland, both in the run-up to the 1997 general election and in the referendum campaign which followed. It charts the strategies used by women political activists, the way in which they have operated both inside and outside the political parties, and assesses the success of their campaigns. Finally, it asks whether such mobilisation of women can be categorised as part of what has been described by some as a third wave of feminism.

Note: This chapter is largely based upon material used in Brown, A (1998) 'Representing women: The tactics of gender' in *Parliamentary Affairs*, Special edition, July, 1998.

What have women done?

The role of women in Scottish politics, their campaign for gender equality in a Scottish parliament, and their participation in the Scottish Constitutional Convention and the Scottish Civic Assembly have been charted elsewhere (Brown, 1996). New women's organisations, such as Engender, have been established and new networks and coalitions forged between women both inside and outside the political parties. Much of the campaign has been brought together by the Scottish Women's Co-ordination Group, which has published information and campaign leaflets on women and politics, organised seminars and conferences on the topic, invited women from other countries to share their experiences and strategies for change with women in Scotland, organised questionnaire surveys of political candidates for local, Westminster and European elections, lobbied politicians and others in decision-making positions, and held press conferences publicising the key objective to achieve gender balance, or 50:50 representation, in Scotland's first parliament since 1707. A major achievement of the Co-ordination Group was their success in brokering an agreement between the representatives of the Scottish Labour Party and the Scottish Liberal Democrats in which both parties accepted the principle of gender balance and gave a commitment to field an equal number of male and female candidates in winnable seats at the first elections for the new parliament. This Electoral Contract was subsequently endorsed by the Scottish Constitutional Convention and included in their final report published in November 1995 (see Brown, 1995; Scottish Constitutional Convention, 1995).

The steps towards equal representation in a Scottish parliament

It is worth recording the involvement women have had in the long process and campaign for change (see Engender, 1997):

- *Step 1: Campaign for a Scottish Assembly (Parliament) – CSA/CSP*
  The CSA was established following the failure of the Scotland Bill in the 1970s. It aimed to keep the issue of home rule on the political agenda and to work towards creating a wide consensus for constitutional change. The organisation changed its name to the Campaign for a Scottish Parliament in the 1980s reflecting the shift of policy to establish a parliament in Scotland with tax varying powers.
- *Step 2: The Claim of Right 1988*
  Following the 1987 General Election in which the Conservative party was re-elected for a third period of office with only 10 MPs from the 72 Scottish constituencies, the CSA published the document *A Claim of Right for Scotland* in July 1988. The document proposed the establishment of a

Scottish Constitutional Convention (SCC) as a forum for discussing and planning the future government of Scotland.

- *Step 3: The Scottish Constitutional Convention 1989*
  The SCC was established in 1989 with representatives from the Scottish Labour Party, the Scottish Liberal Democrats, the Green party and the Communist party (now Democratic Left) together with members from a broad range of organisations that make up Scottish civil society – trade unions, churches, business community, voluntary sector, local authorities and other interest groups. Women's groups were also represented in the Convention which held its first meeting in March 1989 and unanimously acknowledged the sovereign right of the Scottish people to determine their own form of government. Committees were formed to examine detailed constitutional questions including the Women's Issues Group chaired by Maria Fyfe, MP.
- *Step 4: A Woman's Claim of Right 1989*
  A Woman's Claim of Right Group was formed in recognition of the need to make a specific claim for women and partially in response to the fact that the Convention had only 10 per cent female representation. It, and other women's groups, made a submission to the Convention's Women's Issues Group. The group no longer exists, but the campaign for gender equality has continued to flourish.
- *Step 5: 50:50*
  The Convention's first report *Towards Scotland's Parliament*, published in 1990, put forward the view that the Scottish Parliament would provide the opportunity for a new start and that positive action would be taken to 'allow women to play their full and equal part in the political process'. Although women involved were agreed that steps had to be taken to improve the participation and selection of women, no consensus existed at that time between activists on the best method of achieving gender equality. Some women, particularly those in the Scottish Liberal Democrats and the Scottish National Party (SNP), believed that electoral reform itself would improve the representation of women, whilst others argued for positive action in the form of quotas. What was, in some ways, the most radical option – the 50:50 scheme (one man and one woman to represent each parliamentary constituency, thereby achieving equal representation at a stroke) – was proposed first by the Scottish Trade Union Congress (STUC) Women's Committee. This policy was subsequently adopted by the Labour Party in Scotland at its conference in March 1991 and later endorsed by the STUC itself at its congress in April of the same year.
- *Step 6: 1992 General Election*
  The return of the Conservative government to power in 1992 (this time with 11 MPs from 72) meant that a Scottish Parliament was not established following the election. However, the pressure and demand for change

continued and women's groups and women within the parties, trade unions and local government continued their campaign.

- *Step 7: Campaign Groups Post-1992*
  A number of campaign groups were formed following the 1992 General Election and women in Scotland also continued to work for change. Engender itself was formed and launched in 1992 and an umbrella group, the Women's Co-ordination Group, was also established in the same year to co-ordinate the campaign for equal representation within a future Scottish Parliament. The aim of 50:50 representation was re-stated.

- *Step 8: Scottish Constitutional Commission 1994*
  The Scottish Constitutional Convention established a Commission which reported in 1994 and recommended:
  - parliament of 112 (72 constituency and 40 additional members)
  - AMS (Additional Member System: whereby some members are directly elected on a constituency basis, and additional members are elected from regional 'top-up' lists to ensure the overall result more closely reflects the share of votes cast for each party) electoral system
  - 40 per cent voluntary target for women's representation.

- *Step 9: Electoral Agreement 1995*
  Women activists in Scotland responded to the Commission's report, and were critical of the voluntary target of 40 per cent for women's representation and the small size of the parliament. The Women's Co-ordination Group brought women together from the main parties in the Convention (Labour and Liberal Democrats) to see if they could agree a scheme that was acceptable to both sides. They were successful in getting their respective party conferences to endorse an Electoral Contract to ensure gender equality in the first Scottish Parliament.

- *Step 10: Scottish Constitutional Convention's Report 1995*
  The final Report of the Convention, *Scotland's Parliament, Scotland's Right* (Scottish Constitutional Convention, 1995), was published on St Andrew's Day (30 November) and contained proposals for a parliament with:
  - 129 Scottish MPs (73 constituency and 56 from the additional list)
  - AMS electoral system.
  - The Electoral Agreement/Contract on women's representation was also included in this document, having been signed separately by the party leaders and also by Rhona Brankin from the Scottish Labour Party and Marilyn McLaren from the Scottish Liberal Democrats.

There have been significant political developments since the publication of the Convention's Report in 1995 including the controversy that followed the Labour Party's announcement in 1996 that it would hold a referendum on constitutional change if elected (see Brown, 1997). In this climate the debate on gender balance was somewhat overshadowed. However, the Scottish

Women's Co-ordination Group, together with other women's organisations, played their part in keeping the issue on the political agenda during the election campaign itself, in spite of the media's preoccupation with the views of male politicians. For example, they produced material to be used by women throughout Scotland setting out the case for a parliament with equal representation of men and women and provided suggested questions to be asked of candidates standing for election. Joni Lovenduski (1997) notes the contrast to previous elections, namely 'the active intervention of feminist advocacy organisations determined to raise the profile of women in the election' (120 women were elected as MPs at the 1997 general election – 102 Labour, 13 Conservatives, 3 Liberal Democrats and 2 SNP – a representation rate of 18.2 per cent. The Scottish figures are: 9 labour, 1 Liberal Democrat and 2 SNP – a 16.6 per cent representation rate). The advocacy of women in Scotland was further galvanised by the substantial increase in the number of women MPs elected to the House of Commons and by the new Labour government's plans for constitutional reform. The government kept its pre-election promise to make constitutional change a key aspect of its programme, publishing a White Paper on Devolution in July and announcing its intention to hold the two-question referendum in Scotland on 11 September 1997. Voters were to be asked whether they agreed or did not agree that there should be a Scottish Parliament and whether they agreed or did not agree that such a parliament should have power to vary tax (Scottish Office, 1997a).

Immediately following the election, the Scottish Women's Co-ordination Group organised a conference inviting the new Minister for Women's Issues, Henry McLeish (also Minister for Devolution and Home Affairs at the Scottish Office), to give the keynote address. The Minister re-affirmed his party's commitment to achieving a gender balance in the elections for the Scottish Parliament, his intention to promote the representation of women in public life and his desire to create a woman-friendly parliament. The principle of gender balance was endorsed by the representatives from the other political parties, the Scottish Liberal Democrats and the SNP, who were also represented at the conference. Bronagh Hinds from the Women's Coalition in Northern Ireland talked about the way in which women there had worked together to achieve their objectives.

The women activists in Scotland went on to play their part in the broad-based campaign for a 'Yes'/'Yes' vote organised by Scotland Forward. Again, they used the opportunity for a cross-party event, holding a press conference at which Rosemary McKenna, MP (Labour), Roseanna Cunningham, MP (SNP) and Marilyn McLaren (Liberal Democrats) re-affirmed their own parties' support for constitutional change and for equal representation in Scotland's parliament. The Conservative Party, who were still arguing against the establishment of a parliament in Scotland, were not represented at the press conference.

The referendum, held on 11 September 1997, produced a substantial endorsement of the government's proposals, with 74.3 per cent of those participating agreeing with the proposition that a Scottish Parliament should be established and 63.5 per cent supporting the view that the parliament should have the power to vary taxation by up to 3 pence in the pound. Following the success of the referendum, the government published a Scotland Bill in December 1997. As the government's specific proposals for a Scottish Parliament began to emerge, women political activists turned their attention to aspects of the legislation, including the standing orders and procedures and provisions for equal opportunities in the new parliament. The argument was made that, while it was crucial to have a parliament that more fairly represented men and women in terms of those holding political office, it was also vital that the views of other women should be represented in the structures, operation and appointments of the parliament.

Successes and setbacks

We have outlined the way in which women have used different strategies to intervene and stake their claim for equality. It is now necessary to assess how successful they have been in their campaign. As is evident in the following discussion, there are both positive and negative outcomes to report.

First, there are a number of positive developments. The government's White Paper on devolution endorses the Scottish Constitutional Convention's proposals for a parliament with 129 MPs elected on a version of the Additional Member System. The government also state that they are 'keen to see people with standing in their communities and who represent the widest possible range of interests in Scotland putting themselves forward for election. In particular, the government attach great importance to equal opportunities for all – including women, members of ethnic minorities and disabled people'. The government urges 'all political parties offering candidates for election to the Scottish Parliament to have this in mind in their internal candidate selection process' (Scottish Office, 1997a).

The new Minister for Women's Issues, Henry McLeish, appointed a small group of women advisers to brief him on the issues of key concern to women and proposals for change. The Women's Advisory Group (WAG) first met in the autumn of 1997 (one commentator has dubbed it the New Advisory Group (NAG)!). One outcome of this development was the setting up of a new consultative process with women and women's organisations in Scotland. The Scottish Office published the consultative document *Reaching Women in Scotland* in October 1997 in which it invited views on proposals for taking forward measures to ensure that the parliament is woman friendly and to establish a Scottish Women's Consultative Forum to provide a direct channel to government for women in Scotland. It is intended that the forum would consist of representatives from women's organisations and that they should participate in networks with the government in order to develop ideas and proposals on woman-friendly policies (see Scottish Office, 1997b).

There are mixed fortunes for women in terms of the continued resolve, or otherwise, by three of the main political parties in Scotland to devise mechanisms to maximise the participation of women as members of the new parliament. Joni Lovenduski and Pippa Norris (1993) have noted that the policies adopted by political parties to redress gender imbalance normally vary across ideological lines, with more left-orientated parties favouring positive action. Brown and Galligan (1993) have classified the response of political parties to pressure from women activists into three broad categories: adherence to the 'status quo' with no specific policies targeted at women; 'promotional strategies' to encourage more women to participate through training and other measures; or 'active intervention' such as the use of quotas or the legal system to effect change.

Prior to March 1998, the Conservative Party was alone amongst the four main parties in Scotland in adhering to the status quo. All of the other political parties had adopted both promotional strategies or mechanisms for active intervention. In doing so, the Scottish Labour Party and the Scottish Liberal Democrats were honouring the electoral agreement reached between them and endorsed by the Scottish Constitutional Convention in 1995. Although the SNP were not members of the Convention, they nevertheless stated their support for a mechanism to deliver a more equal balance of representation between men and women. In considering the AMS electoral system to be used and their potential support in the elections, the parties have agreed appropriate policies to meet their commitment to gender balance. As it will gain most of its seats on the constituency side of the elections, the Scottish Labour Party has twinned constituencies so that both men and women can compete for a pair of parliamentary seats. The man with the highest votes will be selected to represent the party in one seat and the woman with the highest number of votes will be selected for the other. Any disparity between the overall number of men and women selected and elected in the constituencies will be redressed through allocation of additional seats on the top-up list.

The Scottish Liberal Democrats had proposed to put forward two men and two women in the selection process in each constituency in the first past-the-post side of the elections. They had intended to use the additional seats and a zipping mechanism – whereby equal numbers of male and female candidates would be listed alternately – to achieve gender balance if this is not met in the constituency seats. However, the campaign for gender equality received a setback when Scottish Liberal Democrats voted to abandon these plans at their Scottish party conference in March 1998, stating their concern at being vulnerable to legal challenge. The SNP have encouraged women to put themselves forward for selection for constituency seats and also intend to use zipping in the top-up list should there be an imbalance in the number of men and women elected.

The selection processes have begun in all parties, with the first elections to be held in May 1999.

There have been further setbacks and disappointments for women activists. The government decided that equality legislation should continue to be a reserved power at Westminster and that the Equal Opportunities Commission should not be included as a cross-border political body with responsibility for both reserved and devolved matters. This decision was met with some disappointment, although it should be stressed that the Scottish Parliament will have responsibility for ensuring the operation of equal opportunities in all its areas of competence, including education, economic development, environment, health, housing, local government, social work and transport.

The second area of disappointment surrounded the government's decision not to include a clause in the Scotland Bill exempting the selection processes of the political parties for the first elections for the Scottish Parliament from the provisions of the Sex Discrimination Act.

This clause was sought by women activists in order that the political parties should not be inhibited from introducing selection procedures to maximise women's representation. The Labour MP, Maria Fyfe, took up these issues with the support of other MPs from her own party and from the Liberal Democrats and SNP. Her proposed amendments to the Scotland Bill, which were formulated to help protect the political parties from legal challenge, were unsuccessful. The issue had become more politically contentious with the leaked Cabinet committee minute in which the Lord Chancellor, Lord Irvine, was reported to have said that the advice from the legal officers was that such an exemption would not protect the parties from a challenge under domestic law and even with the requested amendment, a legal challenge could be made under the European Equal Treatment Directive. In setting out the issue and the proposal from Donald Dewar, the Secretary of State for Scotland, that the Sex Discrimination Act should be amended for the first elections to the Scottish Parliament, Lord Irvine stated: 'Donald described the recent history of the issue in Scotland and the particular pressure which had led him to make his proposal'. He went on to add that 'It was particularly awkward that Donald's proposal was limited to the first elections to the Scottish Parliament, because this would allow it to be presented as an artificial and expedient response to a particular political problem' (*Guardian*, 3.3.98). While the Lord Chancellor did acknowledge the existence of political pressure, his last remark particularly upset women campaigners in Scotland as it appeared to disregard the United Nations Committee on the Elimination of Discrimination against Women (CEDAW) Convention which encourages the use of temporary special measures to give effect to Article 7, which sets out the right to participate in the formulation of government policy, to hold public office and to participate in non-governmental public and political organisations. Noreen Burrows has also argued that, far from inhibiting Donald Dewar's attempts to achieve parity in the new Scottish Parliament, European law and the forthcoming Amsterdam Treaty would support him (*Guardian*, 4.3.98). Whether a legal challenge will be made to the procedures adopted by the different parties remains to be seen.

Overcoming divisions: 'third wave' feminism?

Although women political activists in Scotland have not achieved everything they wanted in terms of gender balance and equality in the plans for the Scottish Parliament, it is widely acknowledged that, without the presence of women and the constant pressure from a cross-section of women throughout the process, the advances that have been gained would not have been so extensive. At every stage in the long campaign for constitutional reform women, with the support of some men, have intervened in the process to make their specific claims. It can be argued that in the wider campaigns to redress the so-called democratic deficit in Scotland and promote the case for greater democratic participation, women were successful in gendering much of the debate. They used the language of democracy, participation and representation to stake a claim on behalf of women. Commenting on the debates within the Scottish Constitutional Convention, Yvonne Strachan, a leading member of the Scottish Women's Co-ordination Group, states that:

> Their [the men's] agenda was different, and we had to keep raising the issue. Although some men on the Electoral Reform Group were supportive and sympathetic to our demands, we doubt whether they would have pursued the issue. We were the ones who had to argue the case again and again.

The tactics employed by women activists to promote the representation of women were varied. They did not adopt more traditional forms of 'protest' such as signing petitions or engaging in public demonstrations. Instead, they worked hard to develop a strong network of women and to build a consensus on the key aim of improving the representation of women in political office and in the operation of the new Scottish Parliament. They were successful in bringing together women of different political persuasions, both political party women and non-party women, women in the trade unions, women in the voluntary sector, women in the churches, women in business and the professions, and women in different communities throughout Scotland. Attendance at the many events organised by the Scottish Women's Co-ordination Group demonstrated that this activity could not be dismissed as the indulgence of a few white, middle-class feminists. A second tactic was to produce materials accessible to different constituencies of women to be used in promoting their case for equality. They kept up political pressure on politicians by distributing questionnaires during local, general and European elections seeking the views of candidates on equality issues, by lobbying politicians behind the scenes, and by sharing their knowledge and expertise and providing key data and evidence for MPs sympathetic to the objective of achieving gender balance. The fact that women across the party divide were united in this campaign, helped put pressure on individual parties to implement their specific proposals for achieving equality of representation. In this way, the representation of women has become one of the issues on which the parties will be judged in the first elections to the Scottish Parliament. Should the political parties fail to field and support a significant number of women candidates in the elections, then the possibility of the creation of a women's party or a women's coalition cannot be ruled out. Women from the Women's Coalition in Northern Ireland have participated in several events organised by the Scottish Women's Co-ordination Group to share their experiences of participating in the political process.

Finally, it is necessary to consider what, if anything, this political activity tells us about the women's movement in Britain. Some commentators have put forward the view that the women's movement has experienced something of a setback in the 1990s or is less easily identified than in the past (see Byrne, 1996). Such a judgement does, of course, rest on how one defines the women's movement and the way in which one measures its impact. Descriptions and analyses of what has been described as the first wave and second wave of feminism exist in numerous sources. In an attempt to understand contemporary conditions, some feminists have developed the proposition that we may be in a third wave of feminism. The contention is that in the wake of recent economic, social and political turmoil, feminism has been provided with fertile territory for radical alternatives and the political space to build alliances and coalitions of interest between women in order to effect change. Attention is drawn to the increased demands for women's rights, empowerment of women through women's groups, challenging institutions in which women work, highlighting the democratic deficit in representation experienced by women, and proposals to change citizenship culture. To quote from the originators of this idea:

> Women in positions of power or within formal political structures are increasingly linking up with women in the wider community to form a powerful movement for women. The third wave is pluralist. It aims to work creatively with difference while forging a common agenda. It has the beginnings of a strategy and a historic opportunity to re-shape a social, economic and political future which is literally up for grabs. The third wave of feminism has the potential to connect women's practical strengths with feminist ideas in ways which are truly transformative for democracy world-wide.

[Note: *The Third Wave of Feminism* was the intended title of a book edited by Helena Kennedy, Caroline Ellis, Yasmin Ali and Christine Jackson in

1995. The idea for the book developed from a conference on women's representation held in London. In the event, the book was not published.]

If they are correct in their interpretation, then it could be argued that the women's movement is beginning to overcome some of the past divisions between women and the divisions between theory and practice and is currently working towards a stronger movement as a result. The concept of the 'new suffragettes' in particular accords with the increased focus on representation in government, a focus which is not confined to Scotland nor to the UK but should be interpreted as part of a wider movement influenced by developments at United Nations and European Union levels (see Brown, 1998).

Conclusion

It is difficult to predict what would have happened if women in Scotland had not decided that equal representation was such an important issue for them to take up. After all, during the constitutional debate in the 1970s, there is little evidence of women mobilising as women and across the political party divide on equality matters. Since the 1970s a number of factors have contributed to the politicisation of the demand for gender balance in the Scottish Parliament. International and European developments, changing political conditions in the UK, and the operation of women's agency in Scotland have combined to add pressure to the claims for equality and an equal role for women in decision-making arenas.

The protest made by women has not taken the form of mass demonstrations. Nevertheless, the tactics employed to ensure that equal representation became a salient political issue have been varied. It has been argued in this chapter that these tactics have also been effective. Although women political activists have not achieved all their aspirations, they have made significant advances. The establishment of a new political institution in Scotland has provided a specific and real political opportunity for women to achieve much greater parity with men in terms of their representation in political office and in terms of the representation of their interests in the workings, appointments and policies of the new parliament. Women activists have decided that this is a window of opportunity that could not be missed. They have been successful in bridging the ideological and political party divisions between them and in bringing together a wide range of women from different backgrounds and with different perspectives. After the elections for the parliament are held in May 1999 we will be able to assess more accurately the outcome of their endeavours. Whether or not we can classify this period in the development of the women's movement as a new third wave will also require time before a firm conclusion can be reached.

Acknowledgement

Thanks to Fiona Mackay for revising and editing the material for this publication.

References

Brown, A (1995) 'The Scotswoman's Parliament', *Parliamentary Brief*, 49 (1), pp 8–9.

Brown, A (1996) 'Women and politics in Scotland', *Parliamentary Affairs*, 49 (1), pp 26–40.

Brown, A (1997) 'Scotland: paving the way for devolution?', *Parliamentary Affairs*, 50 (4) pp 658–671.

Brown, A (1998) 'Representing women: the tactics of gender', *Parliamentary Affairs*, 51 (special edition) July.

Brown, A and Galligan, Y (1993) 'Changing the political agenda for women in the Republic of Ireland and in Scotland', *West European Politics*, 16 (2), pp 165–189.

Byrne, P (1996) 'The politics of the women's movement', *Parliamentary Affairs*, 49 (1), pp 50–70.

Engender (1997) *Gender Audit,* Edinburgh.

Lovenduski, J (1997) 'Gender politics: a breakthrough for women?', *Parliamentary Affairs*, 50 (4) pp 708–719.

Lovenduski, J and Norris, P (1993) *Gender and Party Politics*, London, Sage.

Scottish Constitutional Convention (1995) *Scotland's Parliament, Scotland's Right*, Edinburgh, CoSLA.

Scottish Office (1997a) *Scotland's Parliament*, Cmnd. 3658, Edinburgh, HMSO.

Scottish Office (1997b) *Reaching Women in Scotland*, Edinburgh, HMSO.

16 Liberation theology in Scottish community empowerment

Alastair McIntosh

This chapter argues the case for a distinctively Scottish liberation theology. This is needed as urgently in many parts of Scotland today as it is among the exploited and oppressed peoples of Latin America and Africa. It is first necessary, however, to 'decolonise the soul' by distinguishing spirituality from hegemonic forms of institutionalised religion. In addition, historical analysis is required to expose the active collusion in Scotland's history between authoritarian religion and the growth of capitalist exploitation and expropriation. Reference is made to the successful campaign to return the Island of Eigg to community ownership in order to illustrate how a recovered and redeemed spirituality can, in the author's view, be part of the dynamic of empowerment in Scottish communities.

Betwixt tome and tawse

Over the past seven years my work in such areas as land reform, environmental protection and urban renewal has richly drawn on spiritual understandings of community empowerment for authentic human development. Bringing spirituality into popular education requires a little justification before proceeding to elaboration. In this paper I want to discuss some of the theory behind it and conclude with a practical example from the Isle of Eigg. My focus here is on Christian theology, mainly because the history and construction of Scottish communities, like the wider Western world, has been primarily Christian. However, I would not want this to detract from the importance of understanding other spiritualities, including shared understanding between established non-Christian faiths and newly recovered nature religions. These, however, go mostly beyond the scope of this chapter.

Because spirituality and religion overlap so much, many people confuse them. That is unfortunate because a lot of us in Scotland have suffered bad experiences of 'religion'. The very word can turn on the cringe factor. Too easily it brings to mind the fearsome school 'dominie' whose instruction was through tawse-armed domination as whole chapters of the Book of Daniel and chunks of the 1647 Westminster Shorter Catechism got belted into our memories. Most Scottish teachers were not like this, but enough were to taint the milk of youthful spiritual awareness. The spiritual abuse of children is like any other form of child abuse: it leaves traces, neurotic symptoms, which replicate themselves long after the original traumatic event has passed. These can pass on down the generations. Such traces must be recognised and healed if we are to become capable of understanding authentic human and community development as being, at its fullest and most empowering, spiritual development.

In *The Final Cut*, their album about the Falklands and nuclear war, Pink Floyd graphically capture the mindset that cauterises the soul. They show how this creates a violated heart, surging with blocked emotion and impervious to its own capacity further to perpetuate violation of community. This is part of what psychotherapist Alice Miller calls 'soul murder'. In books like *For Your Own Good: The Origins of Violence in Child Rearing* (1983), she persuasively argues that much of British and Germanic culture has been emotionally crippled by a punitive 'poisonous pedagogy' that denies children their basic need for unconditional love. Where this has been perpetrated under the guise of 'religious instruction', it is important that we recognise it to have been a travesty of the teachings of Jesus, whose primary purpose was to communicate the 'good news' of cosmic unconditional love. The crippled croakings of the 'cold and religious' are, instead, a diluted successor of Old Testament passages that allow women's hands to be cut off in punishment, boys to be stoned to death for crimes like gluttony, genocide against one's enemies, and the sexual violation of women captured after battle and taken as 'booty' (see the Bible, *Deuteronomy* 20–25, *Numbers* 31 and *Judges* 21).

Too often Scottish Christianity has failed to distance itself from such 'Satanic verses' in the Bible. I believe this failing to be due to the degree to which organised religion in our nation (and elsewhere) retained, until very recently, a highly un-Christian condemnatory cutting edge. This had its origin in the use of religion for political control. Yet spiritual life does not have to be like that. We can find resplendent alternatives demonstrated, for instance, in the triple unit of community, nature and God that distinguishes Celtic spirituality. These derive from parts of Scotland – the far West – which remained substantially beyond the pale of that politicised spiritual manipulation which, elsewhere, inverted the cross to fashion a sword.

The birth of capitalism: spiritual and community strangulation

Political manipulation of the soul in Scotland has its roots in the extension of state control throughout the realm during the seventeenth century. Commencing with James VI and (especially in the Highlands) his 1609 Statutes of Iona, measures were introduced which advanced the Protestant religion, cultural and linguistic Anglicisation, and capitalism – particularly the transformation of clan chiefs into lairds or private landlords who then treated the land not as the birthright of the extended clan family but as personal property to be rented and traded as a commodity. As in colonies around the world, evangelisation hand-in-hand with education was at the heart of this misappropriation that Paulo Freire calls 'cultural invasion'. Thus it was that in the Education Act of 1616, King James ordained that:

> . . . the true [Protestant] religion be advanced and established in all parts of this kingdom, and that all his Majesty's subjects, especially the youth, be exercised and trained up in civility, godliness, knowledge and learning, that the vulgar English tongue be universally planted, and the Irish [Gaelic] language, which is one of the chief and principal causes of the continuance of barbarity and incivility among the inhabitants of the Isles and the Highlands, may be abolished and removed . . . [thus] in every parish . . . a school shall be established. (Meek, 1996)

James himself was a victim of early parental deprivation and abuse perpetrated by cruel uncles who brought him up after Elizabeth had executed his mother, Mary Queen of Scots. His policies for the Scottish Highlands and Ulster, as well as those he championed for inquisiting and burning 'witches', betray an understanding that to control the souls of individuals is to control the body politic of their communities.

The Swiss-based French theologian John Calvin (1509–64) unwittingly provided the perfect framework for religion to be twisted into underwriting the legitimacy of the newly emerging capitalism. First, Calvin provided an 'accommodation' that allowed for money to be loaned at interest, in contrast with the teachings of the medieval Catholic church; second, he asserted the doctrine of double-predestination. Today's Swiss banking industry stands as an enduring testimony to the consequences of the first. Those of the second are more subtle and complex. One of the Protestant reformer's great insights was that 'justification', the means of salvation, is by faith and not by such works as the buying of indulgences. However, his followers understood 'heaven' and 'hell' in caricatured, black and white ways, shaped by the fire and brimstone metaphor of the Book of Revelation. They grasped, in only too small a way, the significance of Christ's teaching on forgiveness. Their God was more as understood by Moses and Job than that of Jesus: he was transcendent, jealous, harshly 'loving' and otherworldly – a projection, perhaps, of the 'cold and religious' patriarchs themselves. They saw 'Him' in the absence of God's feminine face as revealed, for example, in *Proverbs* 8, where Sophia warns against the heresy of forgetting God's woman-wisdom nature by saying of Herself, 'Whoever finds me finds life . . . but those who miss me injure themselves; all who hate me love death'.

Calvinism thus dealt in the 'double death' of both this world and Hell. 'Double predestination' would demarcate the 'chosen people' of the 'elect' from the 'damned' in a manner whereby it was pre-ordained who would go to

Heaven and who to Hell. Yes, justification is by faith – but, in Calvinism, that faith is God given. Thus Calvin surmised: 'our salvation flows from God's free mercy . . . freely offered to some while others are barred from access to it. Eternal life is foreordained for some, and eternal damnation for others' (McGrath, 1995). Although modern Calvinists would say that Calvin's thought can be understood in more complex and subtle ways, the popular effect on the Scottish psyche was to damage its noble objective of giving spiritual authority to the individual (as distinct from priests and bishops) and make for a religion that preys on fear, uncertainty and a self-righteous obsession with being 'worthy'. As such, perfect conditions were created for breeding an authoritarianism of latter day Pharisees.

How did this spur the development of capitalism, both in Scotland and much of Protestant Europe? Sociologists like Max Weber have controversially suggested that such Reformation theologies created a 'Protestant work ethic'. Those who prospered and had power believed that their success was the sign of being blessed by God. St Paul, after all, true to the conservative that he was, had stated that the 'powers that be' are there by the grace of God (*Romans* 13). To be in such manifest receipt of divine grace as to be prosperous and powerful therefore implied a good chance of being amongst the 'elect'. Conversely, those who suffered were perhaps the wretched of the Earth – their human worth hopelessly undermined by sin.

Such theology is 'victim blaming' on a cosmic scale. The effect was to usurp the very life force of the poor and conform them to the creeds and greeds of the emerging modern capitalist economy. Under the 1712 Patronage Act, landlords gained the power to appoint clergy in the established church. Sycophantic Church of Scotland ministers could thereby be selected to persuade the people that their sufferings were due to their sin. This undercut resistance to the Highland Clearances and their earlier Lowland and Borders equivalent. The political consequences played straight into the hip pockets of the powers that be. A testimony to this hypothesis is scratched on the church windows of Glen Calvie. In 1845, 92 people, who had been evicted from their land, waited in the church yard for an emigrant ship to take them to America. The minister had given no succour. Scored into the church windows, some left their names, with a tragic little self-blaming inscription: 'The people of Glen Calvie, the sinful generation'.

Many clergy resisted the attempts of the lords temporal to control the Lordship spiritual, especially those who in the 1843 'Disruption' broke away to create the Free Church. But the Free Church's need to assert narrowly strict scriptural legitimacy exposed it to the in-built psychological tendency for revolution to breed conservatism. Thus, the Rev Prof Donald MacLeod, a leading twentieth century Calvinist reformer in that church, says of Highland Presbyterianism: 'I confess that it instilled a spirit of resignation which went far beyond Christian humility. I confess its guilty silence. Like the German

Christians under the Nazis, the clergy of the Highlands failed to open their mouths for the dumb. That is a guilt which I feel deeply.' (*Scotsman*, 24.05.95)

The Scottish Presbyterian churches of the eighteenth and nineteenth centuries, then, often portrayed this world as being deeply 'fallen'. The femininity of God, expressed through such figures as St Bride of the Isles, 'foster mother of Christ', paled to such insignificance that today, for instance, only a tiny handful of people on the Isle of Harris know that their island was once the heart of the parish of Kilbride, the church of Bride, and that the old Gaelic name for the Hebrides is *Innis Bhrighde*, the Isles of Bride. The consequence of having a rich tradition of spirituality suppressed in this way was to replace the excesses of an institutionally corrupt pre-Reformation Catholicism with a spiritual vacuum which, though in theory democratic and free, was open to abuse for the political colonisation of the soul of the people. An immanent ancient spirituality of *reverence* in this world was therefore damaged by a transcendent and life-displacing obsession with whether or not one would be 'saved in the next'. The church of a Jesus, who was tempted by the fruits of landlordism and insisted instead on justice for the poor and for the Earth (*Luke* 4), became enmeshed in institutional 'fall'. Only today are parts of it undergoing redemption.

Nowhere are the ambiguities of these aspects of the Scottish psyche captured with more influential and contemporary global relevance than in the thought of the Kirkcaldy born economist, Adam Smith, who is now claimed by both the political centre and the right. The 'invisible hand' of the market is Smith's secularised version of providence. Smith believed that self-interest both depended upon and would be to the benefit of the community. However, that community can be seen to have been, firstly, the *secular elect* of the ruling privileged class. The proof of this is in his 1776 masterwork *The Wealth of Nations* in which Smith was enthusiastic to justify slavery if it more efficiently served to concentrate wealth into the hands of the rich (see Smith, 1986).

Spirituality: the bedrock of community

Recognition of the need to decolonise the soul has led to fine work by people who found that soul was both all they possessed and everything they possessed when struggling for and with racial equality, women's rights, youth, the poor, ecology, housing, disability issues and in the peace movement.' (see Shields, 1991; Peavey, 1986; Macy, 1983; Hope *et al*, 1984). Behind many community activists is a strong, if silent, spirituality.

What, then, is spirituality? Whereas theology is concerned with the study of matters relating to God and religion is about the institutional expression of this, the word 'spirituality' has much less specific meanings that may not involve postulating 'God' at all. Some writers, like Paul Tillich, use 'spirituality' to mean our utmost or ultimate concerns. Others, like Walter Wink (1992), see the spiritual as being the interior reality of outward forms such as persons, institutions and nations. For Wink, a spiritually engaged activism entails working to redeem the good but fallen nature of power in the world. This calls for a three-fold process of 'naming the powers' to find words with which to get a grip on them, 'unmasking the powers' to reveal how they oppress, then 'engaging the powers' to liberate their redeemed potential.

Here I shall use the word 'spirituality' to mean that which pertains to th nature, meaning and consequent articulation of our lives. Underlying this is inter connectedness. It is about the expression of life abundant in all its meanings. It becoming alive to the aliveness of life. It is the opposite of that inner death tha comes from self-strangulating selfishness and preoccupation with things morbid It affirms a very here-and-now 'Heaven' and refutes the mindsets and behaviour that lead to a living 'Hell' – both being eternal in the present moment.

I often use the back of my hand as a metaphor for spiritual awareness. Normally we are only aware of ourselves as separate entities, like the nails on each finger. But as we enter into that wrestling-match engagement with love in the company of others – including all the 'bastards' of everyday encounters! – we move down the fingers and the psycho-spiritual distance between us reduces. Ultimately, the perspective of God consciousness is the view from the main body of the hand looking upwards. We can then see that each finger, each life, is part of the whole. We are, as *John* 15 has it, all branches on the vine of life; 'members one of another' in the Body of Christ, as *Romans* 12:5 says. To be syncretistic, we are all parts of the 'Body of Islam' expressions of the 'Buddha nature', offspring of the Goddess, or, as the Hindus say, *Tat tvam asi* ('That thou art'), meaning that individual soul (*Atman*) is ultimately at one with universal soul (*Brahman*).

Spirituality, then, is about what we most profoundly *are* together; it is about that deep poetic upwelling that our nation's bards have always understood and which is, quite simply, a matter of being and becoming ourselves. 'Justification' is by faith in the underlying goodness – redeemability – of what we have been fashioned to be by a God-cum-Goddess in whose image we are *both* male and female (*Genesis* 1:27). The doctrine of original sin can thus be seen to liberate, because it allows acceptance of the truth, as Gandhi put it, that 'all life entails violence' – and it invites a presumption of forgiveness, which is to say, deep *acceptance* of self and others *as we are*. But such a recognition of original sin must be counterpointed by an understanding of original blessing – a recognition that, as Gandhi also understood, we can minimise the violence that we personally exert in life. This is achieved by trusting one another to come into the empowerment of the goodness that also rests within us. Such letting go of various uptightnesses, our hang-ups and neurotic obsessions, frees the energy previously consumed by inner demons and demonisations. At the level of society, it transforms the cesspool of 'shit' from something that stinks into a rich compost that grows community.

This happens by a community starting, quite simply, to face reality and stop living the idolatry of its own or others' lies. To become more spiritual is to get more real; to recognise and abandon, progressively, the onion layers of inauthentic living wrapped round us by dysfunctional childrearing, education for regimentation, industrial workplace behaviour modification, TV and advertising mores, and so on. Spiritual teachers capable of bridging East and West, like Kahlil Gibran and Anthony de Mello, point out that spirituality is simply about *presence*. It is about becoming fully aware of the 'sacrament of the present moment' as we walk, breathe and eat the fruits of nature's providence – sharing our human nature in community with others and with that community of the Earth by which we comprise a human ecology (see de Mello, 1994). It is about an economics of considering the lilies (*Matthew* 7:28), which is to say, trusting to the possibility of creating a pattern of community inter-relationships – social and ecological justice – that can connect us with a providential sense of grace and blessedness. This implies much more than any abstract, heady obedience to commandments on tablets of stone. We are divinely interconnected, like islands appearing above the sea. This makes mutual reverence the foundation rock of community, and love the mortar that builds upon it.

Liberation theology and the spirituality of community development

To place the spiritual at the centre of a concern, motivation and methodology for 'community development', 'sustainable development', 'third-world development', 'economic development', 'child development', or any other kind of 'development', may at first seem audacious. But perhaps it is not so when we look at what 'development' actually means.

'Development' is an abused word which, in our society, has come to be virtually synonymous with capitalist economic growth. However, the etymology derives from *de* (to undo) and the Old French *voloper* (to envelop, as in our word 'envelope'). To *develop* is therefore 'to unfold, to unroll, to unfurl'. The biological application, as in 'foetal development', accurately captures correct usage. Here the foetus develops in right relationship with its environment of the womb and the wider world that the parents move in. We can also see from this that *too little* development implies stunted growth – a condition of the poor; development in the *wrong place* means deformity – inequitable wealth distribution; and development *without limits* is a cancer that extracts life from the rest of the body or the planet.

Properly used, then, 'development' means 'a gradual unfolding; a fuller working out of the details of anything; growth from within'. Community development should therefore be about enabling a community to become more fully itself. Development ought, therefore, to be spirituality expressed socially.

Because spirituality is about becoming ourselves, I argue that the recovery of spirituality is central to authentic community development. From time to time there have been forerunners of this in history. These include the radical politics of the Diggers, Levellers, Ranters and early Quakers in seventeenth century England (Hill, 1994) as well as the Scottish Highland nineteenth century land reformers who achieved the 1886 Crofting Act (Hunter, 1976). The discovery that God had been misrepresented, and the 'good news' that 'he' is actually on the side of the poor lend legitimacy to aspirations for social and ecological justice. From legitimacy comes claim of right and, thus, the first step towards empowerment. In this respect, the liberation theology that I am about to describe has directly influenced people and processes leading to the re-establishment of our Scottish Parliament (see Mackie, 1995). It is a methodology of no small consequence.

Most modern liberation theology traces its roots to the post-Vatican II theology of Latin American priests who worked amongst the landless and urban poor, like Gustavo Gutierrez. Gutierrez was himself partly inspired by the educational work of the late Paulo Freire. Freire worked for part of his career with the World Council of Churches and, personally, I would see his work as expressing a theology of liberation in secular language (see Freire, 1972). Freire uses the word 'conscientisation' as a socially engaged expression of what, in spiritual reflection, is called 'presence'. Conscientisation is the process of becoming aware of the circumstances that cause oppression. This invites action, which is then further reflected upon. The continuous process of action and reflection is known as 'praxis'. Conscientisation therefore entails the sense of both consciousness (the *presence* that is reflective awareness) and conscience (the *presence* that spurs to action).

To subvert and transform attack by the often powerful 'cold and religious', it is useful to describe liberation theology from an impeccably scriptural perspective. To minimise any cringe factor I shall keep this down to as few textual references as possible. I also wish to reassert that most of what is said here is not exclusive to Christianity: it can be universally inclusive, as was Jesus' intention. Gutierrez (1974) defines 'to liberate' as 'to give life'.' Jesus said we should be living not just any old life, but life abundant (*John* 10:10). This is not some transcendent pie-in-the-sky-when-you-die promise of deferred gratification, but a very practical concern. It starts with such outward necessities as having 'daily bread' (*Matthew* 6:11) in a this-worldly immanent realm of God that is 'all around' or 'within' (*Luke* 17:21), and from there it develops an inner life of living from more than just 'bread alone' (*Matthew* 4:4). But the sequence is important: before preaching, Jesus liked to see that the people were fed (*Mark* 8).

In launching his ministry in the synagogue at Nazareth, Jesus placed primary emphasis on social and ecological justice (*Luke* 4:18–19). He did this by taking a reading from *Isaiah* 61, thereby linking Old Testament prophesy to his mission. Consistent with the insight that 'God is love' (I *John* 4:8) and concerned not with self-interested tribalism but with the 'healing of the nations' (*Revelation* 22:2), Jesus' reading is intriguingly selective. I find it telling that he proclaims good news for the poor, liberty to captives, healing of the blind, freedom for the oppressed and, rather pleasingly in the King James version, succour for the broken hearted: but he misses out what Isaiah also said about enjoying the wealth of the nations and having the 'sons of the alien' placed in subservient service (*Isaiah* 61:5–6). That is, he omits the un-right-on bits, choosing instead to highlight what liberationists call 'God's preferential option for the poor' (as in *Luke* 6 and *Amos* 5).

The ecological, land rights and economic dimensions of Jesus' ministry, are incorporated where he concludes his *Luke* 4 'mission statement' by proclaiming, in verse 19, something translatable as the 'acceptable year of the Lord'. This refers to the 'Jubilee' cycle of seven and fifty years of *Leviticus* 25, which makes provision for the periodic returning of the land to a state of nature, redistributing the land so that it is not owned in perpetuity by anyone except God, and the cancellation of debts.

Liberation theology, in addition, understands God as being revealed through history. Not only does this free us from narrowly tribal constructs of God as expressed in barbaric parts of the Bible, it also affirms the importance of people understanding their place in human history. From this it derives a special concern to 'contextualise' biblical material in contemporary people's everyday lives. Thus, for example, the twentieth century 'Mothers of the Disappeared,' whose children were killed by the Argentinean junta, have been identified with the women who were powerless to do anything but bring their powerful presences to Jesus' cross. In such witness, brutal power lies named and unmasked – and so ready for later engagement.

The Isle of Eigg Trust: a case study in liberation

In my own community empowerment work I have applied aspects of liberation theology using a triple approach that I call Re-membering, Re-visioning and Re-claiming. I have used it, I think to modest effect, in urban contexts like Glasgow and in opposing the proposed superquarry on the Isle of Harris. Here I shall briefly use reform of the Scottish feudal land tenure system as an example.

In 1991 I was asked by a Scoraig crofter, Tom Forsyth, to become one of the founding trustees of the Isle of Eigg Trust. A process was started which, in 1997, led to the people of Eigg successfully bringing their land into community ownership after seven generations of landlordism. There are many reasons why Eigg succeeded, most of which had little to do with our influence. But what I think was very important initially was the emphasis we laid on Re-membering history. This was done in speeches, publications and through the wider mass media. We often integrated theological references to enhance legitimacy, encourage reflection and aid discernment. For instance, on 25 October 1991 I gave an address on Eigg which resulted in a 73 per cent vote of confidence in our work being given in secret ballot by the community. At that time many did not feel free openly to air their support from fear of their laird. This speech (McIntosh, 1992) was widely circulated and it contains the phrase: 'Can we, as in the words communicated by Moses, "proclaim the liberation of all the inhabitants of the land . . . a jubilee for you; each of you will return to his ancestral home. Land must not be sold in perpetuity, for the land belongs to me" (*Leviticus* 25)?' In other words, I was trying, as has been done in Africa and Latin America, to create resonance with a deeper historical religious theme by linking the history of Eigg with that of the Exodus. The relevance of this puzzled many, but was poignant to some – especially the influential elderly.

Opening out history has the effect of freeing up blocked cultural energy. The effect is what I sometimes call cultural psychotherapy. Just as a traumatised individual can be helped on by remembering the original trauma, so a traumatised community can start to understand its dysfunctions if it can understand what made it the way it is. This was demonstrated brilliantly on Eigg one day when, charged with being an irresponsible community by their laird, a woman replied: 'We have never had the chance to show that we can be responsible'.

But Re-membering, rebuilding the 'member' or body of a community, generates only anger, disappointment and frustration unless there is also a vision around which it can galvanise. What made Eigg happen at the end of the day was not so much opposition to the laird and his antics – like his attempting to evict 12 per cent of the island's population for no obvious reason – as Re-visioning. That vision was one of community: community with one another, with place or nature, and – for a few residents – with God. It was a Celtic spiritual vision and one that, as far as non-native incomers were concerned, saw belongingness redefined in accordance with the old Gaelic proverb that 'the bonds of milk'(ie nurture and fostership) are stronger than the bonds of blood (ie genetic lineage). When Keith Schellenberg, the laird, tried to whip up racist sentiment, virtually every indigenous household signed an open letter to say how much they resented such divisive tactics. The status of 'belonging' to a place thereby became less a matter of where a person was from as of how willing they were to cherish and be cherished by that place and its peoples.

The vision of a regenerated human ecology on Eigg went deeper than the mere grassroots – which is so often about TV culture, beer and spectator sport. It went right to the taproots of cultural values and spiritual belief. This showed, for instance, in young people starting to learn from their elders Gaelic place name meanings. It showed in women's empowerment and interest in old legends about the 'big women' and 'holy women' of Eigg. And I remember, to take a rather pious example, being present as a small group of island women prayed in their church, not for the success of the Isle of Eigg Trust as such, but for the 'right thing' to happen. That is, they put their faith in a process that was higher than any merely 'political' aspirations.

The fact that Eigg did finally 'happen' was a Re-claiming. Re-claiming involves the hard work of consensus building, managing the media, fundraising, politicking, recognising and reconciling conflict, and all the elements it takes to learn anew how to become fully a community. Many of the people doing this were not in the least overtly 'religious', yet I do believe there was a strong spirituality present as ordinary people developed extraordinary capabilities.

There are many who might think that the only theology involved was when three clergy from differing denominations jointly blessed the 12 June takeover celebrations at the second of the newly erected standing stones on Eigg. Others might say that the most inspired piece of 'ministry' was when the Scottish Office minister, Brian Wilson, stood in a marquee erected on the former laird's tennis court and declared 'game, set and match to the people of Eigg'. And still others might quip that the most valuable spirit on Eigg came out of the barrel of Talisker gifted from Skye. There is, of course, spirit and there is Spirit. In ways deeper than I can tell in a short piece like this, I believe that both were at work here – and I would certainly be recommending the Talisker too!

References

de Mello, A (1994) *Sadhana: A Way to God*, India, Gujarat Sahitya Prakashh.
Freire, P (1972) *Pedogogy of the Oppressed*, Harmondsworth, Penguin.
Gutierrez, G (1974) *A Theology of Liberation*, London, SCM.
Hill, C (1994) *The English Bible and the Seventeenth Century Revolution*, Harmondsworth, Penguin.
Hope, A, Timmel, S and Hodzi, C (1984) *Training for Transformation: A Handbook for Community Workers*, Zimbabwe, Mambo Press.
Hunter, J (1976) *The Making of the Crofting Community*, Edinburgh, John Donald.
Mackie, S G (1995) 'Liberation theology for Scotland?', *Theology in Scotland*, 2 (1), pp 35–43.
Macy, J J (1983) *Despair and Personal Power in the Nuclear Age*, Philadelphia, New Society.
McGrath, A E (1995) *The Christian Theology Reader*, Oxford, Blackwell.
McIntosh, A (1992) 'A collector's item or community ownership? the Isle of Eigg debate', *Edinburgh Review*, 88, pp 158–162.
Meek, D E (1996) *The Scottish Highlands: The Churches and Gaelic Culture*, Geneva, World Council of Churches.
Miller, A (1983) *For Your Own Good: The Roots of Violence in Child Rearing*, London, Virago.
Peavey, F (1986) *Heart Politics*, Philadelphia, New Society.
Shields, K (1991) *In the Tiger's Mouth: An Empowerment Guide for Social Action*, Australia, Millennium Books.
Smith, A (1986) *The Wealth of Nations*, Harmondsworth, Penguin.
Wink, W (1992) *Engaging the Powers: Discernment and Resistance in a World of Domination*, USA, Fortress Press.

17 Workers as citizens: trade union education in the new Scotland

Mick McGrath

Trade unions have traditionally had a deeply ambivalent relationship with the state, and in recent years they have been subjected to legislative control which, combined with changes in the economy, has systematically weakened them and reduced their membership. During this period the focus of trade union education has been on a narrow instrumentalism which concentrates on workers as economic units of production rather than focusing on their role as citizens in the wider society. Nevertheless, it is important to remember that trade unions remain one of the largest and most important voluntary membership bodies in civil society. This chapter argues that the trade union movement has, potentially, a key role to play in the process of democratic renewal and education for active and committed citizenship in Scotland. For this potential to be realised, however, it is essential that the shackles of instrumentalism are loosened and a broader curriculum is constructed with the aim of encouraging trade unionists to contribute to the struggle for both greater material equality and wider social justice.

Introduction

> There is a need to rethink and broaden the notion of lifelong learning. Not only must it adapt to changes in the nature of work, but it must also constitute a continuous process of forming whole human beings – their knowledge and aptitudes, as well as their critical faculty and ability to act. (Jacques Delors quoted in Fryer, 1997)

Both in the run-up to the General Election of 1997 and thereafter, the present government has declared for 'education, education, education' and in the field of adult education a strategy for lifelong learning is beginning, albeit somewhat falteringly, to emerge. Robert Reich warns of the consequences of failing to engage education in response to global economic and political transformation:

> Each nation's primary political task will be to cope with the centrifugal forces of the global economy which tear up the ties binding citizens together – bestowing even greater wealth on the most skilled and insightful, while consigning the less skilled to a declining standard of living. (Reich, 1991)

If lifelong learning is to play a part in 'the continuous process of forming whole human beings' rather than adding to 'the centrifugal forces which tear up the ties binding citizens together' then the education of adults will require to change dramatically. The relationship of the state to civil society will also need to alter if lifelong learning is to assist in engaging the energy and commitment of people to build the new Scotland. By virtue of their location within civil society and the nature of their commitment to education, trade unions could make a significant contribution to this process, provided certain strengths are built upon and weaknesses addressed. In order to do so, trade union education needs to recognise that its members are key agents within civil society.

It is not suggested that an antidote to the social fragmentation we daily witness can be found simply in a redefinition and realignment of adult education and its relationship to social forces aimed at the creation of positive change. It is contended, however, that in the new Scotland, with a parliament of its own, there exists the opportunity for bold experimentation in the way we view the process of lifelong learning and its potential contribution to material enhancement and the transformation of social relations. In order that this can be achieved, the concept of lifelong learning must provide a context for discussion and debate about the nature of the relationship between people and those processes conditioning and determining their life chances.

Because political parties and issue-based pressure groups tend to have agendas focused on attaining results in relatively short timescales, a refashioned vision of lifelong learning is required reflecting longer-term means and ends. It is the argument of this chapter that such a social transformation depends on the promotion of a robust and constructively critical civil society – not solely to forestall the fragmentation of which Reich speaks, but also because this is the necessary precondition of the struggle to attain a humane polity. In this respect, the new Scottish state could become the prime enabling agency, with the underlying drive for social justice residing in civil society (the development of which should be a key aim of adult education). This chapter attempts to argue this case in terms of the contribution which trade union education can make to the process.

Workers as citizens: enriching trade union education

Trade union membership at the start of the Conservative government's first period of office in 1979 stood at between 12 and 13 million, representing approximately one in every two workers in the UK. About one in three workers is now in membership (TUC, 1998). Despite this decline, trade unions organise 6.7 million workers in the UK, and in Scotland 659,000 workers belong to unions affiliated to the Scottish Trades Union Congress (STUC, 1997). As such, the trade union movement represents the largest single voluntary membership body of any organisation in both the UK and, importantly, the new Scotland.

Those concerned with the effective functioning of the Scottish Parliament, particularly those for whom the promotion of participative and popular democratic forms are important, should be able to look to trade union education in Scotland for active support. Yet much remains to be done – and undone – if the trade union movement in Scotland is to be harnessed to such a project. Along with the provision made by individual unions and the STUC, the vast majority of workplace representatives accessing trade union education do so on 10-day courses provided by the Trades Union Congress (TUC). This mainstream provision, comprising Stage One and Stage Two courses for workplace and health and safety representatives, and augmented by a range of short, issue-based courses, is mainly provided through public educational provision. Administered from London through a TUC Regional Education Officer in Glasgow, this educational provision has many strengths – principally its learner-centred focus and its resilience throughout a prolonged and difficult period for trade unionists and their organisations. Its central and debilitating weakness, however, resides in its failure to promote the notion of workers as citizens capable of using their organisations in pursuit of social and political, as distinct from economistic and instrumental, purposes – a deficiency attributable, at least in part, to the constraints of the public funding mechanism. This paucity of vision is deeply embedded in the curriculum currently offered to trade union workplace representatives attending TUC mainstream provision. However, through a process of realignment and refocusing, involving a rediscovery of the traditional uses of its educational provision, trade unionism could make a contribution of major significance.

The initial and most important contribution to the debate on the nature and purpose of trade union education in general, and of TUC provision in particular, was that of John McIlroy (McIlroy 1990a; 1990b; Holford, 1994). McIlroy's views are still of considerable relevance in terms of his critique of the instrumentalism and narrowly skills-based focus of TUC provision. Despite this, throughout what proved to be long years of Conservative rule, TUC and STUC provision as well as that of individual unions responded to each and every attack on working people and their organisations using, in particular, issue-based short courses as a key strategy of resistance.

While challenging the distribution of rewards in society, the very existence of trade unions depends on the continuation of the wage labour system. This helps to explain the curricular constraints imposed by funding arrangements whereby the state, through its educational agencies, retains control of what can and cannot be discussed. And discussion of the ideological agenda driving Conservative government policy in respect of trade unions, the economy and much else besides, was definitely 'off limits' in TUC courses. Yet, it should be noted that the system of funding and control of TUC provision had been established by the 1974–1979 Labour administration. From the outset of public funding of trade union education, the opportunity for the investigation of such issues as the relationship of ideology to policy and projects intimately affecting the lives of working people came to be marginalised through the mechanisms of state control. Now, some 20 years after the debate was originally stimulated by McIlroy and others, the dominance of an instrumentalist curriculum is such that the National/Scottish Vocational Qualifications (S/NVQ) model is not only firmly in place as the basis of employee education and training but it has also been enthusiastically embraced by the TUC as the model for workplace and full-time officer training.

Writing about the S/NVQ model of employee education and training, John Field typifies the position of those hostile to this approach, seeing in it:

> an attempt to use the vocational qualifications system to focus training solely on those tasks which have direct relevance to employment . . . combined with the suggestion that NVQs are intended to reinforce the subordination of labour power by ensuring that the reproduction of labour is controlled in such a manner as systematically to encourage the acquisition of parcellized elements of labour and nothing else (Field, 1993)

I have argued elsewhere that the National Management Standards to which the S/NVQs are intimately related are open to precisely the same critique (McGrath, 1998). Undeniably, much of the impetus for the adoption of the vocational qualifications model by the TUC and individual trade unions came from the rightful demand of trade union representatives for accreditation of the learning process. But I would contend that the vocational qualifications model, as it is currently constructed, is inappropriate for trade unionists who, while they require certain skills in order to fulfil their day-to-day functions, are not, in this context comparable to 'employees'. The motivation for their involvement in trade unions is the voluntary principle – as opposed to their motivation as workers which is the necessity to engage in wage labour.

Trade union representatives are at the very heart of their organisations. As such, they may be conceived of as, in Gramsci's phrase, 'organic intellectuals' providing organisation, leadership and, above all, understanding for others of the issues affecting the lives of working people and their communities. Gramsci's stress on the necessity to effect a mental transformation on the part of workers, involving persuasion, culture and mass participation as a necessary precondition for progressive change, could comprise a central aim of lifelong learning in the twenty-first century (see Buci-Glucksmann, 1980). In this respect, it is important to recognise that trade union representatives, while fulfilling their organisational role, are also citizens with the full range of obligations and duties, rights and entitlements attaching to that status. And since the fundamental aim of trade unionism is to secure justice in the sphere of employment, an educational model predicated on the creation of 'a world class workforce, competing in the global economy' that is constructed on a fundamentally skills-based and particularistic curriculum just will not do. It is all very well for individuals to be equipped with a 'tool box of transferable skills' in the interests of 'economic efficiency', but trade unionists and their organisations require a broader vision of their role within civil society if they are to contribute to the growth of a fully democratic Scotland. The instrumentalist nature of the inherited TUC educational model is just too narrow and restrictive if the Scottish trade union movement is to contribute to the project of building a new and dynamic civil society in Scotland.

Yet, despite the instrumentalism enforced by the current funding regime, there is much in trade union education which is inherently progressive and it is upon this tradition that the contribution of trade unionism must be based. Its learner-centred approach continues to be a positive and enabling methodology well suited to the project of contributing to the growth and power of civil society. For the vast majority of workplace representatives taking day-release provision, the activity is seldom if ever a hobby in the way that some (no less legitimate) aspects of conventional adult education provision can be. Nor, except in a tiny minority of cases, is attendance viewed as a path to career progression, although the acquisition of knowledge and skills is often transferable in relation to work as well as broader engagement in the life of the community. The vast majority of trade union lay officials want to be better at the job of representing their members. In this respect, a skills-based, utilitarian curriculum may be a necessary but it is certainly not a sufficient condition for what Delors terms the 'continuous process of forming whole human beings'. Many participants bring to their course of study a wealth of experience of life, trade unionism and the labour process which are indispensable resources for critical and creative learning. It is therefore important to consider the contribution trade unionism could make in securing a just society in the new Scotland.

Fostering critical autonomy for active citizenship

The promise of education in all its forms has traditionally been highly prized by trade unionists and those in the wider labour movement. Thus, the left and other progressive social forces have seen education as making a vital contribution to the development of a confident and self-aware working class capable of taking a leading role in the process of progressive social change. The importance attached to education by Scottish working class people was evident in the travelling libraries of the Lanarkshire miners and John McLean's lectures on Marxism which regularly drew audiences of hundreds in the early years of the century. The emphasis on social purpose education, which attempted to develop education and learning grounded in a broadly-based, inclusive and critical curriculum, has been important to various left political groupings in this and the last century. What was of crucial importance about this was its criticality of approach coupled with investigation of those factors determining or conditioning the material and emotional well-being of working people. The rediscovery of this tradition in trade union education is essential. In the new Scotland, the opportunity exists to refashion the relationship between the state and civil society so that working people are nurtured and enabled in their status as citizens.

Through lifelong learning, workers as citizens could be encouraged to see their primary role as the promotion of the just society. For this to become a reality, we require what David Held terms 'double democratisation', ie a process which defends

> the liberal principle that the separation of the state and civil society must be a permanent feature of any democratic political order and, on the other hand, the Marxist notion that this order must be one in which the power to make decisions is no longer subject to private appropriation (Held, 1991)

Central to such a project, according to Held, is the specification of 'certain socio-economic conditions for the possibility of effective democratic participation'. This might entail a degree of control over the deployment of private capital so that decisions taken in the economic sphere affecting the lives of citizens are measured against the promotion of the common good. While such a programme might well take many years to achieve in respect of private capital, a start could be made in the public sector. In this respect, what is required is a progressive alternative to the privatisation model whereby the Scottish Parliament divests itself of power and control through a process of ceding decision making to people in communities.

If the state is to relinquish elements of its considerable power, the dangers of private appropriation can be obviated by ensuring that organisations within civil society are robust and strong enough to cope with such a challenge. Lifelong learning which equipped people to take control of their own circumstances could make a powerful contribution to such a process of democratisation. If this applied to the trade union movement too, the curriculum accessed by workplace representatives could also be extended to members – as some unions have done. The dominant ideology of capitalism (understood here as a 'common sense' set of values and attitudes) and the economic power to control processes of investment and disinvestment must be reassessed in the context of the overriding aim of securing the just society.

If senior secondary school students can study theories of class and power, income distribution and wealth, surely this kind of curriculum should also be accessible to workplace representatives on mainstream provision if they are to develop into citizens capable of contributing to securing the just society? It is true that trade unionists, like anyone else, can attend courses of study dealing with such topics, but the fact that they are proscribed in their curriculum as workplace representatives is a telling indicator of how the state views such learning. Yet the omission from the curriculum of trade union education of such subjects is, in fact, a testament to the latent power of their organisations.

Adults or school students studying, for example, the distribution of wealth in society might or might not be moved to interrogate their learning critically and act on it. However, the context in which they learn encourages an individualised and atomistic response. The context of learning for trade unionists is very different. If they investigated explanatory models relating, for instance, to the private ownership of productive resources and the distribution of wealth within different societies, they would be in a far stronger position to act collectively on their experience and understanding. The result might well be uncomfortable for business, the state and trade unions themselves. And yet a society in which trade unionists tackled such issues could be one in which public discourse and debate on resource allocation added to the enrichment of the commonweal – especially if the explicit aim of progressive social forces was a commitment to investigating and constructing the contours of the just society through the process of lifelong learning.

This is not to argue for a trade union studies curriculum which covers everything in general and nothing in particular. Clearly choices have to be made about what is relevant and appropriate. While the current trend is towards social partnership and dialogue between employers and their employees, the fact is that trade unions are a formal expression of a fundamental conflict of interest between capital and labour. The location of trade unions within civil society therefore demands a curriculum which extends beyond the narrow confines of the workplace to encompass, for example, the relationship of paid to unpaid labour, and to questions of contribution and entitlement. It must also extend beyond making trade unionists better negotiators or representatives, important though these aspects of their work undoubtedly are. Critically, therefore, there needs to be a recognition that the contribution which trade unionists could make to the advancement of progressive values in their role as citizens is potentially immense. The structural position of trade unions and their traditions of endurance in the face of hostile forces, along with their power to resist and mobilise, comprise a potential not found in any other form of organised adult education for the working class.

The STUC with its progressive tradition of engaging a wide range of organisations in collaboration – the churches, employers, voluntary groups, Trades Councils and local authorities – in the interests of the Scottish economy and the Scottish people is uniquely well placed to take a leading role in redefining the relationship of the new Scottish state to civil society. While it is unclear whether the STUC will take over TUC mainstream provision following establishment of the Scottish Parliament, it is certainly well placed to make a significant contribution through the education of trade unionists to the growth of a vibrant democracy in Scotland of the kind proposed in Held's notion of 'double democratisation'.

This is particularly true given the massive changes in the labour market since the mid-1970s, resulting in the shrinkage of core economic activity characterised by full-time, permanent employment and the expansion of low paid, insecure contract working. Add to this the decline of Scotland's traditional industrial base, then the need for a broad-based curriculum permitting investigation of the relationship between economic change and social change becomes clear. Trade union education thus has a dual role in helping not only to improve the material well being of working people but also to create the conditions whereby they can play an increasing role in achieving a more just society. In order that such aims be secured, however, trade union education has to rediscover a traditional axiom of the left that political democracy must be accompanied by a recognition of the need for economic democracy. As David Marquand (*Guardian*, 16.7.97) argues, 'Good citizens debate, argue and question: they don't simply accept what is handed to them. And they cannot switch off their citizenship when they go to work.' It is therefore time to restate the case for industrial democracy as a necessary corollary to the extension of political democracy.

Social justice and the enabling curriculum

A revival of trade union education could help to ensure that the fundamental questions raised by Alasdair McIntyre are placed at the heart of the curriculum of lifelong learning. McIntyre (1987), starting from the Aristotelian view that justice is the first virtue of political life, argues that:

> since virtue is now generally understood as a disposition or sentiment which will produce in us obedience to certain rules, agreement on what the relevant rules are to be is always a prerequisite for agreement on the nature and content of a particular virtue. But this prior agreement on rules is . . . something which our individualistic culture is unable to secure.

There is scarcely a society in the world which has the kind of moral consensus which McIntyre seeks, but the fact that a community based on an assumption of the virtues of individualism is incapable of gaining such agreement should lead us to cherish and encourage that which is mutual and reciprocal in the life of our communities and nation. If it is from such conditions that agreement on rules – disposing us to act in certain ways and not in others – emerge, we might well look to those organisations and groupings within civil society which are based on reciprocity, mutuality and the voluntary principle. The STUC in Scotland and its affiliated unions, as social formations predicated on collective endeavour in search of justice in economic relations, could begin, through a bold commitment to lifelong learning, to approach the question of what virtues we should work to extend in the civic life of the new Scotland. For this to happen, we need a debate involving all interested parties within civil society who view voluntary engagement in education as one way of changing our society for the better. The trade union movement has a crucial role to play in such a debate.

A Scottish state which facilitates the growth of education for citizenship within civil society and negotiates the scope for an enabling rather than instrumentalist curriculum could do much to help build a new kind of democracy in Scotland and assuage fears that a parliament in Edinburgh will simply replicate the more negative features of the British state. Through provision for more active and critical forms of participation in communities and groups, the growth of an informed citizenship – in contrast to the 'report a benefit cheat' model of the last government – may yet be secured. This would also provide the conditions for agreement on rules for the just functioning of a new social order in Scotland. Trade union education could play a major part in such a project, but only if the restrictions of a dull instrumentalism are rejected and discarded. We might take, as a guide to the kind of education to which all people should be entitled, the statement of the UNESCO Commission on Education for the Twenty First Century that it 'be based on the four pillars of learning to live together, learning to know, learning to do and learning to be' (Fryer, 1997).

Conclusion

In this chapter I have argued for the principle of justice as the end towards which an advanced polity should develop and that the best guarantee of this is the vitality of voluntary organisations within civil society. Trade unionism has much to contribute by virtue of both its fundamental collectivity and its distinctive educational approach grounded on the concrete experience of participants. But this will only be possible if the debilitating constraints of an overwhelmingly instrumentalist curriculum are replaced by a commitment to the promotion of the role of the worker as citizen in the just society. For this to become a reality, the new Scottish Parliament should adopt a co-ordinating and monitoring role to encourage the enlargement and empowerment of those organisations within civil society concerned with citizenship. Lifelong learning is seen as the principal means of promoting an educated and active citizenship capable of playing a greater role in shaping their own future in a just society. In this respect, the relationship of the state to civil society and the power inherent in the deployment of private capital require fundamental rethinking. Trade union education has a significant and distinctive contribution to make to this process of lifelong learning for democratic citizenship in the new Scotland.

References

Buci-Glucksmann, C (1980) *Gramsci and the State*, London, Lawrence and Wishart.

Field, J (1993) 'Developments in vocational qualifications: emerging implications for industrial relations', *The Industrial Tutor*, 5 (7), Spring, p 6.

Fryer, R H (1997) *Learning for the Twenty-First Century*, First report of the National Advisory Group for Continuing Education and Lifelong Learning, London, Department of Education and Employment.

Held, D (1991) 'Between state and civil society: Citizenship' in Andrews, G (ed) *Citizenship*, London, Lawrence and Wishart, pp 24–40.

Holford, J (1994), *Trade Union Education in Britain*, Nottingham, Department of Adult Education, University of Nottingham.

McGrath, M J (1998) 'Management education' in Halliday, J (ed) *Values in Further Education*, Stoke on Trent, Trentham Books.

McIlroy, J (1990a) 'The triumph of technical training?' in Simon, B (ed) *The Search for Enlightenment: The Working Class and Adult Education in the Twentieth Century*, London, Lawrence and Wishart, pp 208–243.

McIlroy, J (1990b) 'Trade union education for a change' in Simon, B (ed) *The Search for Enlightenment: The Working Class and Adult Education in the Twentieth Century*, London, Lawrence and Wishart, pp 244–275.

McIntyre, A (1987) *After Virtue: A Study in Moral Theory*, London, Duckworth.

Reich, R (1991) *The Work of Nations*, London, Simon and Schuster.

TUC (Trades Union Congress) (1998) *Directory*, London, TUC.

STUC (Scottish Trades Union Congress) (1997) *Congress Programme*, Glasgow, Scottish Trades Union Congress.

18 Building a pedagogy of hope: the experience of the Adult Learning Project

Vernon Galloway

This is an account of the work of the Adult Learning Project (ALP) in Edinburgh. ALP is a unique attempt to translate the philosophy and pedagogy of Paulo Freire to the context of a Scottish inner city area. The interest in issues of culture and identity has particular relevance and resonance at a time of democratic renewal in Scotland. The author uses the Gramscian distinction between 'organic' and 'conjunctural' change to show how the combination of community-based adult education and cultural action that characterises ALP's work offers a 'pedagogy of hope' for the reconstruction of political and civic culture in Scotland today.

Introduction

The Adult Learning Project (ALP) is an adult education organisation working in Gorgie/Dalry, an inner city area of Edinburgh. From 1979 to 1984 the project was funded through the Scottish Office Urban Aid Programme and it subsequently became part of the City of Edinburgh Council's Department of Community Education. Since its inception, ALP's work has been influenced by the principles and practice of Paulo Freire, with a commitment to politicise the curriculum, construct learning programmes grounded in the struggle for cultural equality, develop the use of dialogical learning methods, and build an authentic relationship between learning and cultural action. These four principles have helped the project to develop 'a pedagogy of hope' (Freire, 1996) which encourages participants to look beyond the limitations of their current condition and imagine a different kind of world which they themselves will then set out to build in their own lives.

This chapter argues that hope is built through a critical engagement with history which allows us to see how the struggles of the past are alive in the present day. I will suggest that the use of Antonio Gramsci's distinction between 'organic' and 'conjunctural' change applies to the historical development of political and cultural autonomy movements in Scotland. I then go on to propose that popular educators should seize the historical opportunity of the present conjuncture in order to engage a wider and more diverse group of people in building a new democracy in Scotland. In the latter part of the chapter I make specific reference to some of the experiences of ALP as a popular education organisation trying to apply the ideas of Paulo Freire in the contemporary Scottish context.

Sustaining vision throughout a visionless period has only been possible because of our on-going dialogue with the work of Paulo Freire which has driven our daily practice and kept our eye on a wider horizon of big ideas. His penultimate work, *A Pedagogy of Hope* (Freire, 1996), is the story of a life spent in the struggle for hope in the face of the pragmatism and sometimes the active repression of what is often called the 'real world'. Throughout his life, Freire tried to convince educators that education is not about the bland acceptance and reproduction of the status quo but rather that it is a chance to change and transform it. His passing has simply strengthened our own resolve not only to continue his work, but to build it anew in Scotland.

Scotland: a journey of hope

When Antonio Gramsci considered the failure of the revolutionary left in Italy, his reflections were imbued with the need to develop an historical view of change in which the forces for it could be analysed in two forms: the 'organic' and the 'conjunctural' (Forgacs, 1988). For Gramsci, the historical demand of subaltern groups for equality and justice evolves over extended periods of time. This constitutes the process of organic change – or slow, cumulative change. This kind of evolutionary change is the necessary precondition in order to capitalise on the inevitable, if only occasional, 'crisis of authority' that occurs when dominant groups fail to recognise or adjust to a breakdown in political consent. At such times, new forms of consensus built upon previously unimagined alliances of interests can combine to form an irresistible force for change. These periods of crisis he identified as times of 'conjunctural' change. In Gramsci's own words:

> When a historical period comes to be studied, the great importance of this distinction [between organic and conjunctural change] becomes clear. A crisis occurs sometimes lasting for decades. This exceptional duration means that incurable structural contradictions have revealed themselves (reached maturity), and that, despite this, the political forces which are struggling to conserve and defend the existing structure itself are making every effort to cure them and, within certain limits, to overcome them. These incessant and persistent efforts form the terrain of the 'conjunctural' and it is upon this terrain that the forces of opposition organise. (quoted in Forgacs, 1988)

In the historical struggle for political autonomy in Scotland we can clearly see this combined process of organic and conjunctural change at work. There is not the space here for a full account of the organic demand for greater political autonomy in Scotland, nor to describe in detail the conjunctural periods in which the hegemony of Westminster has been decisively weakened and this demand for autonomy has broken through to new ground. For the sake of my argument here, I simply offer an abbreviated version of this historical process.

Ever since the dawn of organised popular politics in Scotland – and, some would argue, before it – the case for increased political autonomy has featured as a central demand of both revolutionary and reforming forces (see Marr, 1992). From the anti-Union uprisings of the so-called 'mob' in 1707 through the radical clamour for democratic reform in the early nineteenth century to the formation of the labour movement in the late nineteenth century, it can be argued that the demand for home rule was a constant plank of popular politics. The theme was picked up by the organised labour movement in the early to middle part of the twentieth century again and this, combined with the emergence of early nationalist politics, secured its place at the heart of Scottish political debate. Three centuries of this political debate have been punctuated by periods of conjunctural crisis, during which the idea of Britain as a homogeneous political entity has been placed in question. The period following the First World War was just such a period. Roderick Watson writes:

> After the First World War, Scottish identity was recast from a complex crucible of historical, economic and class forces . . . the imperial adventure of Great Britain Incorporated was coming to a close, and returning servicemen, disemployed workers, intellectuals and a disaffected middle class began to be moved by Liberal and nationalist leanings towards Home Rule, the call of international socialism, ILP republican separatism, and various manifestations of neo-jacobite patriotism. Scottish national and cultural identity was at issue again with an urgency that had not been seen since 1707. (Watson, 1993)

But, arguably, few of these conjunctural periods have been as decisive as the last 20 years, during which the crisis of authority of the British state has culminated in the first significant fissure in British politics since the establishment of the independent Irish state in the earlier part of this century. Conservative governments from 1979 to 1997, with their policies of state centralisation, economic neo-liberalism and social individualism proved unpalatable to a wide cross-section of Scottish society. As McCrone (1992) puts it, 'Scots had a nation of their own, and the vision of recreating bourgeois England was out of kilter not only with Scottish material interests, but with its alternative sense of national identity'. This opposition to the policies of Westminster found expression in widespread popular resistance to the Poll Tax, water privatisation, the imposition of School Boards and local government re-organisation. But the consensus was not simply oppositional. The proposition that Scotland should have its own democratically elected parliament was a unifying demand which transcended the opposition to one-off policy changes and offered a wider focus for imagining a politics beyond that of permanent opposition.

An independent civic politics emerged beyond the reach of formal parliamentary politics with the formation of institutions like the Constitutional Convention and constitutional campaigning groups such as Scotland United, Common Cause, Democracy for Scotland and, latterly, the Scottish Civic Assembly. All of these are characterised by their engagement of a wide group of disparate interests and organisations, some of which had previously refused to work together, and their alliance encouraged many who had never had any direct involvement in political life to get involved for the first time.

However, this political and civic consensus as well as the breakdown in consent which it signalled were not built out of the simple politics of opposition to a supposed common enemy. Crucial to the development of this period of conjuncture was an intellectual and artistic project which mirrored and reinforced the more obvious signs of political change. It would be disingenuous to call this a movement or 'school' because its contributors worked mainly as individuals or in particular groupings, but their combined efforts presented an alternative view of cultures in Scotland and they opened up the intellectual space for new definitions of cultural identities. While the struggle for political identity may have been for the 'people's heads', the struggle for cultural identity was for 'people's hearts'.

In the early part of this century, when Hugh McDiarmid and his contemporaries like Lewis Grassic Gibbon and Edwin Muir wrote their classic works, they were offering an alternative version of Scottish reality. This stood in stark contrast to the couthy representations of life that had been portrayed by what came to be known as the 'kailyard' writers of the time. The latter, with their themes of 'domesticity, rusticity, humour, humility, modesty, decency, piety and poverty' (Shepherd cited in McCrone, 1992), painted a picture of Scottish society which was built on the construction of a rural idyll in which the peasants were cared for by patronising and paternalistic figures like the minister, the doctor and the laird. McDiarmid and the others pointed to the essential irrelevance of all this for the mass of urban Scots, but they also recognised its patronising sub-text of inferiorisation and dependency.

Some 40 years later this theme of realism and reconstruction was picked up by another generation characterised by Tom Nairn. He and his contemporaries railed against the 'tartan monster' representations of a romanticised Scotland as caricatured in the 'shortbread and whisky' images which had become synonymous with the international and, more importantly, local image of Scottish identity. In his view, these demeaning and often degraded images of Scotland had left Scots with an inferior sense of their own identity which was of no use in the real world. Nairn was joined by others like the Grigors and Colin McArthur in tearing down these 'tartan myths' and exposing their inferiorising effects which, they argued, carved a dangerous chasm between people's intellectual and emotional views of themselves.

Gramsci recognised the actively educational nature of the dominant culture and argued that people's consent to be ruled was a learned set of attitudes and behaviours. In describing 'every relationship of hegemony as an educational relationship', he recognised the role of knowledge transmission in ensuring popular consent and proposed two complementary processes of creating alternative knowledges. The first, which he called 'anti-hegemonic' knowledge, would resist the process of constructing consent by proposing oppositional ideas and practices. The second, which he called 'counter-hegemonic knowledge', would build new knowledges that imagine life beyond the current condition.

The anti-kailyard and anti-tartanry movement of the early to middle years of this century can be characterised in Gramscian terms as an anti-hegemonic project. It forced Scots to look at themselves and the representations which were both visited upon them and which they, in turn, internalised. The last 20 years have seen the continuation of this process in the form of a counter-hegemonic project in Scotland which has built upon the critique and deconstruction of iconoclasts like Nairn but has also moved beyond this to a process of active reconstruction, ie building counter-hegemonic knowledge. This struggle to construct new Scottish identities free of the homogenised and inferior images of the past has been joined by a wide variety of cultural actors and creators. In almost every field of cultural endeavour in Scotland, new voices have emerged to present new versions of Scottish experience, unfettered by the tartan mythology of the past. Working class writers, female visual artists, black musicians and gay directors have all presented their own particular versions of Scottishness.

> These ways of expressing Scottish culture are inclusive rather than exclusive, building on erstwhile alternative ways of being 'Scottish' – Lowland, Highland, Protestant and Catholic, male and female, black and white. This involves borrowing and adapting what is available. (McCrone, 1992)

McCrone points to the shift in the struggle for knowledge away from a singular preoccupation with national identity to the more pluralist project of cultural identities. In this process, decolonisation is not simply a question of reclaiming ethnicity but also involves an active rejection of all the forms of inferiorisation to be found in stereotypical, common sense thinking about, for instance, class, gender, religious beliefs and sexuality. This deconstruction and reconstruction has, in effect, turned the idea of Scottishness into a 'site of struggle' (Giroux, 1992) in which attempts have been made to pose more positive, realistic and inclusive representations of life in Scotland today.

My argument is, therefore, that the historical opportunity of the present conjuncture in Scotland offers a creative space to those committed to a 'pedagogy of hope'. In this space, hope need not be bound by the strictures of pragmatism. It is into this space that the Adult Learning Project has directed its efforts, attempting to build a curriculum of cultural reflection and action which seeks to respond to the spirit of the times.

In what follows I attempt to outline how ALP seeks to engage people in this process of collective learning and cultural action at a time of conjunctural change and to show how the principles and practice of Paulo Freire remain central to our task of creating new realities based on a pedagogy of hope. I want to look at the four key ideas of Freire which were identified at the beginning of the chapter: the politicisation of the curriculum; the construction of learning programmes around issues of culture and identity; the development of dialogical approaches to teaching and learning; and the move from learning into cultural action. Having outlined these ideas briefly, I will try to illustrate their application in ALP's practice before going on to consider their relevance to the current conjuncture.

Politicising the curriculum

For Paulo Freire the transmission of knowledge is essentially a transaction in power. In his own words, 'education is politics' (Freire and Shor, 1987). He stands firmly opposed to the proclaimed neutrality of traditional educators who deny the political nature of knowledge as a creation of human culture. It is the task of the educator to expose the constructions of power inherent in every form of established knowledge. For Freire, therefore, the politicisation of knowledge is at the heart of the whole approach of the radical educator and the epistemology of any given subject presents an opportunity to explore the nature and purpose of its construction.

Since 1990 ALP has been engaged in the building of a broad curriculum of cultural studies based on the findings of a Freirean-type co-investigation carried out in the local area in 1989 (see Kirkwood, 1991; Kirkwood and Kirkwood, 1989). This identified a range of learning challenges covering a wide variety of subjects such as politics, ethnicity and culture, gender, history, religion, language, writing, traditional music, and land and the environment. All of these have since become potential arenas for the politicisation of knowledge in which established discourses can be challenged and new knowledges created.

The study of history has been central to the ALP curriculum and perhaps best illustrates how knowledge can be constructed in order to support the hegemony of dominant political interests. Beveridge and Turnbull (1989) demonstrate the process very clearly when they point out the role of mainstream historical writing in creating and sustaining a discourse of inferiority in relation to the history of pre- and post-Union Scotland. They argue that Scotland before the Union is often portrayed as a dark, uncivilised and backward place as opposed to the reasonable, enlightened and advanced place it was to become after the union of parliaments:

The constant use of the metaphor of darkness and light, gloom and enlightenment to contrast pre- and post-Union Scotland underlines the crudity of such representations. Fantastic as they may be, however, these myths have acquired, thanks to endless repetition, the status of indubitable truth, and so are rarely subjected to critical analysis. (Beveridge and Turnbull, 1989)

This view of established historical discourse is often quoted at the beginning of ALP history programmes to demonstrate that such representations of history reflect and reinforce a political agenda and are thus contestable. It allows us to discuss why history is presented in particular ways and whose ends this serves. Following this, students are encouraged to see themselves as historians who can interpret history in their own terms, applying their own political interests and building alternative versions of the past which reflect their aspirations for the future.

By asking students to consider Beveridge and Turnbull's critique of established historical writing, we are not attempting to replace one version of the past with another. Rather we are trying to pluralise the idea of knowledge and to encourage students to become more active and sceptical readers of knowledge, whatever its source. Indeed, their own critiques may also be criticised for textual selectiveness or nationalistic undertones. The point is to help students see alternatives to established knowledge and conventional wisdom, and to develop their own critical and creative instincts. This process of politicisation is not based on the proposition of a single alternative knowledge but rather of many potential knowledges, which we may all have a role in creating.

The politicisation of the educational process is thus begun through the deconstruction and pluralisation of knowledge. This constitutes what could be seen as the preliminary anti-hegemonic phase of learning. It is important that, in the intellectual space which the current conjuncture offers, the task of creating this kind of new knowledge is not left solely to individual intellectuals or artists – as so often in the past. The democratisation of the process of creating critical knowledges should become a more popular project, engaging groups hitherto disenfranchised by mainstream educational approaches which fail to problematise knowledge and develop people's critical awareness.

Building a more critical relationship to knowledge is a creative and hopeful process which proposes the possibility of change by placing the certainty of received knowledge in question. This work prepares the ground for another phase of learning in which the role of knowledge in shaping our everyday lives is addressed and the theme of reconstruction, based on the creation of new realities, becomes central to the learning process.

Building a relevant curriculum

Freire's work was founded on the notion of making learning relevant to the learner in such a way that the cognitive act of learning was equally balanced by the impact this knowledge would have on the learner's life. His critique of established forms of learning asserted that learning had become abstracted from life and fulfilled a purely utilitarian or institutional function. It has been our attempt in all ALP programmes to develop a real link between the cognitive and affective domains of learning – a process that Brandes and Ginnis (1986) describe as 'confluence', ie making the connection between knowing and feeling. In order to create a basis for counter-hegemony in the act of knowing, we must begin by understanding how knowledge is at work in our daily lives, shaping our thoughts and actions. As an example of this, in ALP's politics courses we study the origins of democratic thinking and examine the different development of the same basic political ideas in different historical contexts. We consider the various ways that these ideas have been applied in the organisation of political structures and we explore the contemporary political ideologies which are at work in the world around us. The process of challenging established discourses is activated and our politics students, just like our history students, are encouraged to identify the vested interests inherent in their construction. The next step is to consider how this knowledge is at work in our daily lives. How is this relevant to us? The principles of democracy are not only relevant to political structures but permeate the whole of our lives. In the democracy courses we therefore consider the state of democratic relations in our workplaces and our families. We look at the representations of political ideology in the newspapers we read or in the television programmes we watch, and we describe how we hear those ideologies expressed in the common sense views of people around us.

This search for relevance often forms a structured part of the ALP curriculum, taking the form of a programme of investigation in which the students are asked to actively seek out the subject in the midst of daily life. Back in the classroom, the examples they return with become the subject of discussion and analysis and are fully integrated into the curriculum. These investigations can take a number of forms, depending on the subject under consideration. To give some examples: in Scots and Gaelic language programmes the participants are asked to search for examples of the language in use in their daily lives; in history courses students look for echoes of the past in the present day which show how history may be repeating itself; and students of ethnic and cultural studies may be asked to look out for instances of racism in daily life and in institutional settings.

The process of exploring the power relationships present in everyday life is described by Foucault in terms of the 'knowledge/power' nexus (Usher and Edwards, 1994). In linking knowledge and power in this way, Foucault asserts that knowledge is inextricably bound into the practice of power. Knowledge becomes the inherent expression of power learned through the countless experiences of our daily lives in which we have been taught to conform to the dominant norms of society. Foucault argues that these learned values become integrated into our consciousness as internal policemen, mediating our behaviour and reinforcing dominant norms by means of a system of checks and balances which have been taught and internalised through rewards and punishments. This process is subtle and insidious. In the present conjuncture in Scotland, for example, it is particularly important to build personal resources within people to resist knowledges which serve to pacify or manipulate them – such as, for instance, the persistent efforts by a conservative establishment since the Referendum on devolution to de-radicalise the debate about the Scottish Parliament.

Coming to terms with the idea that we are all the sum of what we know, and that some of the things that we know are designed to ensure our compliance with things as they are, is an important step. But it is not enough. The struggle to resist what Freire (1972) calls 'cultural invasion' is not complete in simply comprehending how invasion occurs. Resistance to cultural invasion depends on learning new ways of understanding and new skills. This requires a dialogical partnership between learners and teachers.

Dialogical teaching and learning

Freire's critique of mainstream education is not restricted to its content but is also concerned with process and methodology. In its reliance on what he describes as the 'banking' model of education, traditional didactic teaching depoliticises and objecifies the subject to the degree where knowledge is a mere commodity which passes through the student like money through a bank – but without necessarily leaving any interest! (see Freire, 1972). The use of monologue as virtually the only teaching method replicates the power structures at large in the world beyond the classroom. In its place, Freire proposes a partnership between teacher and student which engages both in a common endeavour to learn. This dialogical form of learning emphasises the plurality of knowledges and the dual role of teacher and student in a common search for contextual and cultural relevance.

In describing the dialogical relationship, Freire stresses the need for the teacher to approach the educational encounter in a spirit of empathy. It is important, however, to note that he does not use the word 'dialogue' to describe a patronising and spurious search for equality between teacher and student, but rather to describe the nature of the relationship between two partners who understand each other's roles and adopt a position of mutual trust. Dialogical teaching does not attempt to negate the unequal distribution of power inherent in the teacher-student relationship, but it does make this explicit so that it can become an integral part of the learning experience itself.

In ALP we try to apply the principles of dialogical learning across all of our programmes – with varying degrees of success. It has been our experience that most people take some time to adjust to this new kind of relationship. At first, the empathetic approach of the tutor is often greeted with suspicion – sometimes open hostility. People's previous encounters with teachers are, more often than not, based on their school experience and they are very familiar with monologue as the way in which 'serious' learning is conducted. In ALP we have had some quite painful and counter-productive experiences in introducing more radical dialogical methods at too early a stage. The result has been to alienate potential students who have either complained about the 'informality' or 'frivolity' of the approach or have simply left, never to return. Our practice has been tempered by these salutary experiences and we now adopt a more gradual approach to the introduction of dialogical methods. New courses therefore tend to begin with the tutor taking a fairly didactic approach. However, even in these early stages, students are introduced in small ways to the idea of participation and, over the period of a typical 10-week course, they are gradually pulled more actively into the learning/teaching process.

This gradual engagement is achieved through the progressive introduction of dialogical structures and methods by the tutor. Dialogue is often confused with informality or lack of structure, but nothing could be further from the truth (eg see Kirkwood, 1991). Dialogical teaching demands just as much, if not more, structure and preparation on the part of the educator. A typical dialogical lesson plan involves the tutor in the design of an opening section in which the initial views of the students about the subject are expressed, the planning of a teaching session about the subject itself which is delivered by the tutor, the design of a structured conversation in which the tutor uses a four-stage analysis of the subject which incorporates the initial views of the students and the generative themes that are at the core of the course, and, finally, a summary and review section in which the students can talk about what they have learnt and what they would like to do as a result.

Moreover, learning in dialogue is not just about the personal relationship between teacher and student. It is also about broader social, educational and cultural relationships with other students in the group. Working with others in dialogue demands these new ways of being and new forms of behaviour. These must be learned. Skills like active listening, paraphrasing, critical thinking and personal expression are essential for building new ways of relating to others, and they need to be taught as an integral part of subject-based courses.

The combination of transparent teaching methodology and dialogical relationship building is the key to democratising the culture of the classroom and turning it into a setting where real transformations can occur. It should become a place where people can experiment with knowledge and with each other, where creative responses to the challenges of the world outside may be imagined and tested. Thus the dialogical classroom becomes the practice ground of freedom. Paula Allman (1988) talks about the dialogical learning relationship as preparing people for change: 'the preparation hinges upon offering people a glimpse or an abbreviated experience of what it could mean to know, to learn, to be and to relate differently'. As these 'abbreviated experiences' multiply and students' familiarity with the approach grows, they become less dependent on the tutor and more autonomous in their learning. The ultimate step towards critical autonomy is the move from the lessons learned in the classroom to their application in the world outside it. It is crucial that the educator begins the journey with this final stage in mind so that the process of preparing people for independence is set in motion from the start.

This building towards autonomy has been attempted across all areas of ALP's work. A good illustration of it comes from our traditional Scottish music programme. Folk music comes from an oral tradition in which music was learned in a social setting without codified rules. Through a historical process of cultural invasion, this music was codified, inferiorised, militarised and commodified. Eventually it was completely removed from its original social context and segregated in closed clubs and societies which played only privately for their own members or in preparation for the annual round of competitions and prizes. The ALP traditional music programme has set out from the beginning to cultivate the skills of oral learning in order to relocate this kind of music in its original and authentic social setting. Students are taught how to learn by ear and memorise tunes composed both by the tutor and by each other. This oral learning technique then allows them to meet other musicians in informal settings and to learn and teach new tunes. Preparing students for autonomous action in this way is a core educational aim of the dialogical teaching approach, which ensures that the students are constantly faced with the challenge of applying their newly gained knowledge and skills in the wider cultural context.

Developing cultural action

When the progressive educationist, John Anderson, wrote about educational reforms in Scotland in the 1950s he argued against what he called the 'practicalists' who saw only utilitarian purposes for education (cited in Beveridge and Turnbull, 1989). In contrast, he advocated educational approaches which would help people explore knowledge, to see how it is created and how it shapes our cultural development. For Anderson, therefore, the aim of education was to help people discover a way of life – rather than enlisting them into a way of life that had already been chosen for them.

While Anderson was arguing against a narrowly utilitarian view of Scottish higher education, there is clearly relevance in his position for popular educators. Freire also saw radical education as a discipline that becomes a way of life, a constant process of reflection and action which forms a critical *praxis*. The combined process of neutralising knowledge and mystifying pedagogy serves to instrumentalise education and limit its purpose to an almost exclusively economic function. Freire, like Anderson, saw the need for education to help people find their 'ontological and historical vocation' as human beings (Freire, 1972) – not simply their economic vocation as workers.

The relationship between reflection and action has been central to the work of ALP. The cultural application of learning is present across the whole of the curriculum and a wide range of both individual and collective action has resulted from courses of study. At a recent review of the project's work a document listing the action outcomes of ALP groups was produced. These included:

- History groups had written and performed dramatic productions celebrating the lives and struggles of radical movements and individuals from Scotland's past, and demonstrated against the demolition of historic working class housing and the setting of charges for historic sites. These students are now in the process of forming a local history action group, and are organising a project called 'The Stair' which will bring to life a hundred years of tenement living in the local area.

- Democracy groups had helped to raise awareness of and had campaigned around issues like VAT on fuel, water privatisation, political autonomy, local school closures and traffic congestion. They are currently helping to structure an alliance of local community organisations and are actively working with the Scottish Civic Assembly.

- Music groups, who have built the largest programme of traditional music teaching in Scotland, had established a range of new pub-based music and song sessions, organised a series of mass learning and performance events like 'The Youth Gaitherin' and an annual international fiddle concert. They are now forming a traditional street band to join pageants and demonstrations.

- Land groups had publicised the need for land reform in Scotland, campaigned against the Criminal Justice Bill, supported several community-based land ownership campaigns, and are now actively experimenting with urban permaculture methods in the city of Edinburgh.

This is only a selection of the types of collective action undertaken by ALP in the past eight years. Of course, the actions of individuals in taking more control of their own lives are of equal importance. To list these here would be impossible, but it is worth noting that a participative research project organised by ALP four years ago found individual students acting decisively for change as a direct result of their studies in their personal relationships and families, workplaces, political parties, local organisations and educational institutions.

It is certainly true that some of our work has taken us into what might be considered dangerous areas of activity for a project which receives substantial funding from the local authority. In this respect, what may be of particular significance about ALP, as an organisation, is the fact that it is staffed by full-time employees of the local authority who have no direct management responsibility for the work of the project. This is vested in an association of ALP members, largely project activists and students, and allows the organisation and the individuals who constitute it to act with a high degree of autonomy without compromising the educational role (or the conditions of service!) of the staff. ALP invests considerable trust and autonomy in its constituent groups and encourages their alliance with wider external social movements and political groupings. Its students have thus been actively involved in many forms of social and political action, ranging from the Anti-Poll Tax Union and anti-roads protests to the women's movement and opposition to school closures. This kind of social, political and cultural action is undertaken not in the name of ALP but of its students and the groups which they themselves have created or joined.

I would argue that creating a permanent dialogue between reflection and action in this way should be central to the task of building a new democratic culture in Scotland today. Popular groups will need to create parallel agendas of consciousness raising and cultural action so that their programmes are continuously developing. In this respect, it must be emphasised that this kind of permanent dialogue is not a euphemism for indecision or weak mindedness. On the contrary, it is the dynamic of a society mature enough to open its mind to the possibility of new solutions and wise enough to confront the contradictions that will inevitably arise in this process.

Conclusion: sustaining the spirit of conjuncture

For we hae faith in Scotland's hidden powers,
The present's theirs, but aa the past and future's ours.
(Hugh McDiarmid)

The process of building a new democratic future for Scotland needs to be imbued with hope. The conjunctural moment presents the opportunity to build a vision based on the aspirations of all the peoples of Scotland – not just the usual suspects! In order to ensure this, we must look beyond the inauguration of the new parliament to sustain the spirit of conjuncture. The legislature itself will not be a 'popular' body. It will therefore be up to those who remain outside it to demand its responsiveness to the popular agendas that are at large in the country. And as Paterson (1997) argues, 'the moment it is established, we will have to be permanently sceptical about its every act'. This spirit of committed scepticism is not the spirit of detached cynicism which came to characterise Scottish public opinion about the Westminster Parliament. What we need is a positive, constructive and hopeful scepticism – one in which the spirit of dialogue is always present. However, we cannot simply assume that this will emerge – it will have to be built through a programme of popular education based on a pedagogy of hope which actively engages people in their own development as critical and autonomous citizens.

The hope generated in this moment should not treat the election of the Scottish Parliament as the completion of the historical task of building democracy in Scotland. The present conjuncture should simply be seen as the beginning of a movement to assert the rights of the Scottish people who, until now, have been denied their voice.

References

Allman, P (1988) 'Gramsci, Freire and Illich: their contribution to education for socialism' in Lovett, T (ed) *Radical Approaches to Adult Education*, London, Routledge, pp 85–113.

Beveridge, C and Turnbull, R (1989) *The Eclipse of Scottish Culture*, Edinburgh, Polygon.

Brandes, D and Ginnis, P (1986) *A Guide to Student-centred Learning,* Oxford, Blackwell.

Forgacs, D (1988) *A Gramsci Reader,* London, Lawrence and Wishart.

Freire, P (1972) *Pedagogy of the Oppressed*, London, Penguin.

Freire, P (1996) *Pedagogy of Hope: Reliving Pedagogy of the Oppressed*, New York, Continuum.

Freire, P and Shor, I (1987) *A Pedagogy for Liberation*, London, Macmillan.

Giroux, H (1992) *Border Crossings*, London, Routledge.

Kirkwood, G (1991) 'Fallacy: the community educator should be a non-directive facilitator' in O'Hagan, B (ed) *Fallacies in Community Education: The Charnwood Papers*, Ticknall, Education Now, pp 40–55.

Kirkwood, G and Kirkwood, C (1989) *Living Adult Education: Freire in Scotland*, Milton Keynes, Open University Press.

Marr, A (1992) *The Battle for Scotland*, London, Penguin.

McCrone, D (1992) *Understanding Scotland: The Sociology of a Stateless Nation*, London, Routledge.

Paterson, L (1997) 'Scotland and democracy', *Concept* 7 (3), pp 4–6.

Usher, R and Edwards, R (1994) *Post-Modernism and Education*, London, Routledge.

Watson, R (1993) 'Dialectics of "voice" and "place": literature in Scots and English from 1700' in Scott, P H (ed) *Scotland: A Concise Cultural History*, Edinburgh, Mainstream, p 115.

19 Cultivating knowledge: education, the environment and conflict

Eurig Scandrett

This chapter examines the problems and possibilities of transforming environmental education into popular education. In order to do this, it is necessary to locate environmental issues within the wider context of international capitalism and the social relations of production, and systematically to make the connections between the local and the global. Popular environmental education, as distinct from green consumerism, is rooted in people's struggles for health, security and socially useful production. It must derive from a coherent theory of knowledge which can be systematised as curriculum. Case material is used to show why environmentalists must become more serious about education and educators must become more serious about the environment.

Environmental education: an apple pie concept?

'Environmental education for adults is an apple pie concept. Everyone is in favour of it' (Field, 1991). Environmentalism is certainly everywhere, from the greening of multinationals to working class community action on local housing and play areas, from professional and scientific environmental management to what Pepper (1993) has called the 'preservationist and not-in-my-back-yard environmentalism of the bourgeois'. Agenda 21, the programme for sustainable development agreed at the United Nations Conference on Environment and Development (UNCED) – or 'Earth Summit' – in 1992 has been signed by some 150 states including the UK (Quarrie, 1992). All the political parties represented in Scotland have adopted a green hue and given rhetorical support to environmental education. The Scottish Office report *Learning for Life: A National Strategy for Environmental Education in Scotland* (Secretary of State for Scotland, 1993) put environmental education very much into the mainstream. Environmental education may be an apple pie concept, but is it a case of having your apple pie and eating it?

There is such a wide range of activities which can come under the category 'environmental' that it becomes difficult to make sense of it: from planting trees to giving energy advice, fungal forays to painting murals, formal qualifications in practical conservation to competitions for the 'environment queen', wildlife gardens to campaigning against the Criminal Justice Act. The focus of this chapter, however, is on the potential for environmental education as popular education, using case material from a working class housing scheme in north Edinburgh and examples of grassroots community and lay trade union action.

It will be argued that the knowledge content, or curriculum, of environmental education determines its liberating potential in so far as it reveals, or conceals, the economic relations in which knowledge is created. Knowledge, moreover, is part of a wider culture (see Williams, 1973) which includes values, meanings and social practices, and it is a site of struggle between classes and social groups. Environmentalism as a cultural practice is at the centre of this struggle – in which education plays a key role.

The Pilton Environment Group

The Pilton Environment Group emerged from the Pilton Health Project, a community organisation in a peripheral housing estate in north Edinburgh. Greater Pilton covers a number of areas dominated by public sector housing, much of it in poor condition, as well as an industrial estate. There was a great deal of local concern about an intermittent smell which seemed to be coming from the foreshore adjacent to the nearby Granton industrial area. Not only was the smell unpleasant, there were also concerns about the effect it was having on health – from breathing difficulties and lethargy to low birth weight babies. Investigation led the group to the Lothian Chemical Company Ltd, a solvent recycling business with a small non-unionised workforce, situated in the industrial area beside the foreshore (ENDS, 1994).

The story of the 'Granton Smell' is complex. The company is involved in the production of formaldehyde and the recovery of organic solvents. Wastes from this process were being dumped in a soakaway pit and were seeping into the foreshore. Anaerobic, sulphur reducing bacteria were then thriving on the organic wastes and producing hydrogen sulphide gas which has a 'rotten egg' smell. Hydrogen sulphide is toxic both from inhaling high doses (such as those measured at Granton) and from long-term low level exposure. Formaldehyde and other toxic organic solvents have also been identified in liquid emissions from Lothian Chemicals. The complexity of the problem is increased by the fact that the company is sited on land contaminated by former factories, which are inevitably blamed for the pollution and could certainly exacerbate the effect. A leaked Council report noted the presence of pockets of methane gas near the factory which might pose an explosion risk.

The Pilton Environment Group launched a campaign against the company. A wide range of regulatory bodies concerned were contacted and lobbied: the local authority Environmental Health Department, Her Majesty's Industrial Pollution Inspectorate, the Forth River Purification Board, the Health and Safety Executive, and even Scottish Natural Heritage (since a Site of Special Scientific Interest exists on the foreshore). Information was obtained from Friends of the Earth (Scotland) and the Lothian Trade Union & Community Resource Centre. The group conducted local surveys, handed out leaflets and displayed posters, got into the local and national media, made a video and held public demonstrations. Alliances were made with local fishing clubs, GPs, businesses, politicians and the trade union at the nearby GEC Ferranti works. Ultimately, Edinburgh City Council started legal action against the company which led to an out of court settlement with an assurance from the company that it would clean up the foreshore.

The campaign as popular education

During the campaign the group sought a more formal series of adult education sessions on environmental issues. The purpose was for members to learn some of the skills they required for the campaign and to set the problem in a wider context. Following negotiation, the course covered environmental regulation, planning, access to information, Agenda 21 and the economics of the environment. It also led up to ideas for a 'People's Plan' for the whole locality, including the industrial area.

The work of the group highlighted the lack of control which local people had over their environment, and local industry in particular. A further development was the launch by the local authority of a Granton Master Plan, a proposal to upgrade the industrial area, which was published for consultation. The plan was promoted as a means of attracting inward investment and providing jobs in an area with high unemployment.

The group responded with their newly gained knowledge of Agenda 21 and environmental economics. They demanded controls on companies moving into the area so that any new jobs were made available to local people and provided good wages and conditions, that increased traffic on already busy roads through the scheme be avoided and, crucially, further industrial development would not cause pollution which threatened the health of the community. They argued that the area was a prime site for labour intensive, environmentally positive industry if the right conditions and incentives were applied. In view of this, it is worth noting that the local authority's Granton Master Plan excluded popular accountability and was eventually dropped.

The experience of the Pilton Environment Group raises a number of theoretical issues about the role of education in social action which have implications for the providers of environmental education. The origins of the campaign were in a conflict situation in which a group of local people demanded the kind of knowledge they required to tackle an urgent environmental problem. The educational component was responsive to and integrated within the local campaign that followed. Local Agenda 21 and local authority consultation procedures were revealed to be inadequate because they ignored peoples' alienation from production at the root of the conflict, which was exposed by the subsequent combination of knowledge and action.

A great deal of social action is concerned with community participation in local government affairs. However, Lowe and Goyder (1983) comment on how an emphasis on participation in local government planning can serve to divert attention away from the responsibilities of central government which 'has been able to distance itself from environmental pressure'. In the context of the legacy of the increasingly centralised and deregulating Thatcher-Major governments, this is perhaps the 'hidden Agenda 21'. Local authorities in Scotland have lost powers of regulation relating to transport, housing, planning, service provision and resource redistribution, and many basic utilities and regulatory authorities have been privatised, quangotised or weakened at the hands of central government.

The social construction of knowledge and the relations of production

In a study of the curriculum in lifelong education, Griffin (1983) asks to what extent the curriculum reflects a transformation of the social construction of knowledge in the prevailing relations of production. Certainly the Pilton case exposed the relations of production and, in particular, the alienation of local people living in a working class peripheral housing estate from the economic decisions which directly affected them.

Knowledge is never neutral. It is always constructed within the context of the social relations of production and institutions which shape the kind of questions that can be asked, the knowledge which is produced, who has access to it, and the value, social status or economic power attributed to that knowledge, its producers and owners. Moreover, the social relations in which knowledge is constructed, and which are embedded in it, contain divisions and conflicts which have their origins in access to resources and economic production. This is not to be deterministic, but rather to assert that the complexities of unequal access to power, hegemony and the capacity for resistance all come into play in understanding the generation and distribution of knowledge.

Ettore Gelpi (1979) argues from this perspective that education should reflect this social construction of knowledge, and the conflicts of interest implicit within it. This position is seen by Griffin as historically related to the nineteenth century popular education movement for 'really useful knowledge', which was rooted in the experience of working class people and their struggle for liberation. If knowledge is constructed in the social relations of production, then a curriculum based on really useful knowledge arises out of the knowledge demands of marginalised groups in conflict situations (such as the Pilton Environment Group) and should reveal the structural sources of exploitation and oppression.

Another group, which drew on scientific knowledge in its struggle, discovered that even the most apparently objective knowledge exists within social conditions which are never neutral. Cambuslang, Carmylie and Rutherglen Against Pollution (CCRAP) were involved in a campaign around contaminated land discovered beside a local authority housing estate. The group supported a research project into the public health effects of this on local residents. This revealed no measurable effects which could be attributed to the contamination. The result of this finding was damaging to their campaign, and exposed the relationship between scientific knowledge and political struggle. Science is often assumed to be neutral, but its conventions and the knowledge it produces are shaped by social relations and the conflicts within them.

Doubt is an important factor in scientific research, and the reductionist testing of a hypothesis is designed to demonstrate that the results display a particular effect in response to a particular variable. However, a local health survey can rarely demonstrate – and can certainly never prove – that ill health is or is not the direct result of contamination or pollution. In this case, the question asked by the residents was 'Can any of the ill health effects caused by contamination be identified in a survey?', whereas the researcher's question was 'Can any ill health effects observed in this community be directly attributable to this contamination within conventions of scientific reliability?' This, of course, has wider implications. Scientific knowledge is often important in environmental campaigns, and is usually assumed to be neutral. In fact, scientific knowledge represents the social consensus of its producers and the dominant culture.

Local accountability and alliances

The Pilton Environment Group's challenge to the economy took the form of a demand for direct local accountability of industries settling in the Granton industrial area. There is a range of legitimate interests affected by economic development, including workers, suppliers and consumers as well as the natural environment. Devine (1988) proposes a system of social ownership at the level of the enterprise which involves economic decisions arising out of a negotiation between the representatives of the legitimate interests affected by that enterprise's activities, and in particular the four categories of workers' interests, community interests, user/supplier interests and general (ie global, national environmental) interests. As a form of institutionalised social accounting, this is a model which can be worked towards in community environmental action. It also provides a link with other social movements, such as global environmental campaigns and workers' struggles. In particular, because of their centrality to production, workers have a crucial role to play. Trade union action on the environment is, therefore, a significant area for the development of popular education.

Schnaiberg (1980) argues that trade union action is decisive in challenging the 'treadmill of production and consumption' which maintains an economic system of exploitation of the environment through constantly increasing use of resources and waste production. However, until recently trade union education on environmental issues has been negligible (Scandrett, 1990). One of the paradoxes of trade union action on environmental issues is that, although many traditional arenas for union activism relate directly to environmental concerns, they suffer from being separated out as categories for collective bargaining. This reduces them to issues in which interests are shared with those of capital accumulation – in particular, wage bargaining and job preservation, often 'paid for' by increases in productivity. There is, however, a strand within the trade union movement which has linked socially useful production with industrial democracy and environmental sustainability. The best known example is, of course, the Lucas Alternative Plan in the 1970s. More recently, trade unions at the heavily defence-dependent engineering company GEC Marconi Avionics used the threat of redundancies from the 'peace dividend' to put diversification for peaceful and environmental aims onto the collective bargaining agenda (Goudie, 1994).

An example of lay activists responding to environmental issues through popular education is the Work and Environment Project which developed from an EU-funded exchange of shop stewards between the Lothian area around Edinburgh and Tuscany in Italy. A group of local trade unionists collaborated with counterparts in similar industries in Tuscany and researched environmental and trade union issues in Italy and Scotland. The Lothian group continued as a network of trade unionists with an active interest in environmental issues. The approach which they took was to focus on health and safety issues in the workplace, using risk assessment and control methods. This then provided a lever into risk assessment of the same substances, materials and processes outside the workplace, both before reaching it and after leaving it (as product or waste).

The local trade unionists regarded education for union representatives and members as a high priority and worked to produce and deliver a course to other local activists and trades councils. The curriculum followed the same approach of risk assessment in and beyond the workplace and covered environmental policies, access to information and working with local environmental and community groups. It also introduced issues of product diversification and workplace democracy and their role in sustainable development.

The importance of the Work and Environment Project in theoretical terms is considerable. The knowledge content of the curriculum started from a conflict of interests between health and profit in the broader context of public expenditure cuts. This conflict in the relations of production underpinned the exploration of wider issues of environmental protection and sustainable development. The links with other groups' interests opened up the potential for alliance building and the place of these activities in the broader processes of social and political change, including the democratisation of the economy. It also set the discussion of environmental issues in class terms and the complex interactions of alliances between different interests. By focusing on health and safety, the identification of the interests of workers with the health of the environment was clearly established, and the conflict of these with the interests of unrestrained capital accumulation and consumerism was clearly demonstrated.

The growth of environmentalism within contemporary capitalism

The current growth of environmentalism is occurring in the wider context of the globalisation of capital. Some writers suggest that environmentalism is 'ideologically above' economic changes. Paehlke (1989), for example, claims it has a status equivalent to the major ideological movements of post-Enlightenment Europe, liberalism and socialism. Lowe and Rudig (1986), on the other hand, suggest that 'green politics has a peculiar inclusiveness and exclusiveness. It can accommodate other radical movements while resisting assimilation into their ideological agendas'. Here it is argued that, as with other cultural forms, environmenatalism is embedded in the socio-economic relations from which it is derived and that its position within the structure of class interests is crucial.

The origins of the modern environmental movement in scientific knowledge, romanticism and ideologies of duty identify it with what Raymond Williams describes as the 'professional class' (Williams, 1989) – those who rely on selling intellectual labour or, as Berger (1987) describes them, the knowledge class. By far the majority of the environmental movement's support is still drawn from this class (Lowe and Goyder, 1983) and environmental non-governmental organisations (NGOs) often represent its distinctive interests (O'Leary, 1996). Historically, modern environmentalism originated in scientific culture and has spread into other areas of culture through the classic process of incorporation through compromise with the interests of different classes. It has thus been more or less successfully co-opted by the dominant culture which itself reflects the interests of the most powerful groups – in particular, the global capitalist class. The incorporation of environmentalism by global capitalism is a historic compromise which has perhaps reduced some of the worst excesses of environmental devastation whilst ensuring the continued hegemony of capital. The discourse of 'sustainable development' therefore contains a compromise between the demands of the poor nations for the alleviation of poverty and those of the rich nations for multilateral environmental crisis management without threatening the system which creates both poverty and environmental destruction.

Sklair (1994) explores the implications of this process of incorporation. He describes consumerism as the 'culture-ideology' of transnational capitalism. This resists counter-cultural challenges, and ensures that:

> Those cultural practices that cannot be incorporated into the culture-ideology of consumerism become oppositional counter-hegemonic forces, to be rendered safe by marginalisation, and if that fails, destroyed physically.

This is a crucial point given the central place 'green consumerism' has taken in environmental discourse, including education – so much so that social action on the environment is often seen as synonymous with promoting green consumerism. The appeal to individual consumer action is seductive and serves as a form of 'merely useful knowledge' which reifies the underlying relations between production, consumption and the environment. As Schnaiberg (1980) argues, relying on consumer action alone to transform industry, without addressing direct action towards the means of production, is like the tail trying to wag the dog. It reinforces consumerist ideology and cannot challenge the 'treadmill of production and consumption' which underpins our economy and fuels the global environmental crisis.

Taylor (1994) notes the problems of culture in the professional provision of environmental education for working class adults. The popular education programmes of the Pilton Environment Group and the Work and Environment Project, on the other hand, demonstrate the potential for the assimilation and incorporation of environmental culture by working class cultures in a counter-hegemonic process. An aim of popular environmental education must therefore be the identification of the fundamental interests of the environment with the interests of the working class and other marginalised groups so that they 'transcend the corporate limits of the purely economic class, and can and must become the interests of other subordinate groups too' (Gramsci, 1971).

There are further implications for the class alignment of environmentalism. Yearley (1994) argues that the professional class

> is in an ironical position of hostility to the productive forces which have brought it into being. Without economic surplus this class would wither away. Thus, the very class in which environmentalism finds its most active and eloquent support has material interests antagonistic to a deep greening of society.

However, in an increasingly marketised public service sector important elements of the professional class are rapidly becoming proletarianised and now have more interest in building alliances with working class communities. Moreover, Gorz (1993) argues that material interests should be seen in terms not only of waged labour but also production outwith the formal sector of the economy as well as qualitative measures such as more leisure time. He goes on to suggest that 'in complex industrial societies it is possible to obtain an eco-compatible restructuring of production and consumption simply by giving workers the right to limit their effort voluntarily' (Gorz, 1993). A 'non-class of non-workers' is emerging: people drawn from various classes who reject the work ethic and lead much of their lives outside the formal economy (Gorz, 1982). The growth of the anti-roads movement may provide evidence for this. Opposition to the M77 motorway in Lanarkshire, for example, created an alliance between local communities and environmental activists which resulted in a Solidarity Centre in Glasgow for support and training in direct action on environmental and social justice issues.

Conclusion: towards a popular environmental education

In contrast to the popular education initiatives described here, some of the documents and resource materials produced for use in environmental education are not particularly helpful in responding to popular struggles. Among the best of these are materials published by the Scottish Environmental Education Council (see SEEC, 1985; 1987), but they consistently fail to identify and challenge the social construction of knowledge in the organisation of production (Scandrett, 1990; 1992). A similar criticism can be levelled against the Scottish Office report *Learning for Life: A National Strategy for Environmental Education in Scotland* (Secretary of State for Scotland, 1993). This document sees environmental education in terms of promoting 'environmental citizenship', understood as individual responsibility for caring for the environment. As Taylor (1994) notes:

> Education for environmental care appears to be more of a form of training so that people are directed towards using existing forms of environmental participation. There appears to be a danger of it reinforcing certain hegemonic values that may contribute to society's 'blame culture'.

The Green Community Chest compiled by Scottish Natural Heritage is a collection of educational materials for use in a variety of contexts with adults or children. Again, a strong focus on decontextualised individual action obscures rather than exposes the fundamental conflicts of interest that are involved and thus reinforces the uncritical acceptance of the current relations of production. This lack of political analysis is accurately reflected in the World Wildlife Fund for Nature's *Kiss it Better or Kiss it Goodbye* which is included in the Green Consumer Chest:

> History shows that environmental concern spreads from the scientific community through pressure groups to the consumer and then to local and central government. Therefore, your concern is vital in spurring the government into action. When governments join together to tackle the waste problem great advances will be made. (WWF, 1995)

Popular education, in contrast, starts in the struggles of groups which expose fundamental conflicts of interest in the existing relations of production and reproduction. The responsibility of committed environmental educators is to respond to the learning needs of these groups, help to expose the conflicts of interest that are inherent in all environmental issues, and seek to explore the potential for transformation towards a greener and more democratic society. The mainstream discourse of environmental education, dominated by the themes of 'awareness raising' and 'environmental citizenship', is part of the incorporation of environmental culture into the existing unequal and unsustainable economic relations of global capitalism. Green consumerism, in particular, encapsulates this hegemonic process, and popular education has a crucial role in challenging it by identifying its connections with the treadmill of production and consumption.

Popular environmental education often occurs outside the formal structures of adult education provision and it is important for us to respond to it where it is happening. Examples have been given from local communities and workplaces, but the increasing range of environmental voluntary organisations is where such education can also take place (see Martin, 1988; Field, 1993). In addition, there is evidence of growing interest in democratising the economy through the social accountability of industry and struggles are occurring over the transformation of work itself. Fundamentally, however, it is the knowledge that can contribute to the transformation of the economy and the social relations of production which remains the fundamental precondition for the development of environmental education as a genuinely popular form of education.

References

Berger, P (1987) *The Capitalist Revolution*, Aldershot, Wildwood House.

Devine, P (1988) *Democracy and Economic Planning: The Political Economy of a Self-governing Society*, Cambridge, Blackwell.

ENDS (Environmental Data Services) (1994) 'Polluting solvent recycler to get notice to quit', *ENDS Report*, 235, pp 13–14.

Field, J (1991) 'An environment for living', *Adults Learning*, 3 (2), pp 42–44.

Field, J (1993) 'Environmental education and training: reflections on a survey', *Adult Education and Development*, 40, pp 105–115.

Gelpi, E (1979) *A Future for Lifelong Education* (Manchester Monographs 13), Manchester, Department of Adult Education, University of Manchester.

Gorz, A (1982) *Farewell to the Working Class*, London, Pluto Press.

Gorz, A (1993) 'Political ecology: expertocracy versus self-limitation', *New Left Review*, 202, pp 55–67.

Goudie, I (1994) *Initiatives from Industry 1: Defence Diversification,* Edinburgh, SENSE.

Gramsci, A (1971) *Selections from the Prison Notebooks*, London, Lawrence and Wishart.

Griffin, C (1983) *Curriculum Theory in Adult and Lifelong Education*, London, Croom Helm.

Lowe, P and Goyder, J (1983) *Environmental Groups in Politics*, London, Allen and Unwin.

Lowe, P and Rudig, W (1986) 'Political ecology and the social sciences: the state of the art', *British Journal of Political Science*, 16, pp 513–550.

Martin, B (1988) 'Education and the environmental movement' in Lovett T (ed) *Radical Approaches to Adult Education*, London, Routledge, pp 202–223.

O'Leary, T (1996) '"Nae fur the likes of us": poverty, Agenda 21 and Scotland's environmental non-governmental organisations', *Scottish Affairs*, 16, pp 62–80.

Paehlke, R (1989) *Environmentalism and the Future of Progressive Politics*, New Haven and London, Yale University Press.

Pepper, D (1993) *Eco-socialism: From Deep Ecology to Social Justice*, London, Routledge.

Quarrie, J (ed) (1992) *Agenda 21: Earth Summit' 92*, London, Regency Press.

Scandrett, E (1990) *Environmental Curricula in Workers' Education*, Department of Education, University of Edinburgh, Unpublished MSc dissertation.

Scandrett, E (1992) 'Environmental education and ideology: the role of workers' education', *Concept*, 2 (2), pp 22–24.

Schnaiberg, A (1980) *The Environment: From Surplus to Scarcity*, Oxford, Oxford University Press.

Secretary of State for Scotland (1993) *Learning for Life: A National Strategy for Environmental Education in Scotland*, Edinburgh, Scottish Office.

SEEC (Scottish Environmental Education Council) (1985) *Learning for Living: Environmental Education in Scotland*, Stirling, SEEC, University of Stirling.

SEEC (Scottish Environmental Education Council) (1987) *Curriculum Guidelines for Environmental Education in Scotland*, Stirling, SEEC, University of Stirling.

Sklair, L (1994) 'Global sociology and global environmental change' in Redclift, M and Benton, T (eds) *Social Theory and the Global Environment*, London, Routledge, pp 205–227.

Taylor, M (1994) *Environmental Education and Working Class Adult Education: For 'Liberation' or 'Domestication'?*, Edinburgh, Moray House Institute of Education, published BA dissertation.

Williams, R (1973) 'Base and superstructure in Marxist cultural theory', *New Left Review*, 82, pp 3–16.

Williams, R (1989) *Resources of Hope*, London, Verso.

WWF (World Wildlife Fund for Nature) (1995) *Kiss it Better or Kiss it Goodbye*, London, WWF.

Yearley, S (1994) 'Social movements and environmental change' in Reclift M and Benton T (eds), *Social Theory and the Global Environment*, London, Routledge, pp 150–169.

Section 4:

Struggles in practice

20 Making connections: learning through struggle

Helen Martin and Cathy McCormack

This is an account, based on an interview with the editors, of the experience of two community activists who live in the Easterhouse area of Glasgow. In it they describe how they became involved in a local campaign about health and housing conditions and the ways in which this forced them to politicise their personal experience. In this process of struggle, fuelled by anger, they systematically transformed their 'personal troubles' into 'public issues', making the connections not only between poverty, ill health and environmental issues but also between other communities fighting for justice at both national and international levels. Implicit in this account is the leading role of women in collective forms of self-education and social action. One outcome of learning through this kind of struggle is their determination to support other local activists and campaigners by creating a Popular Democracy and Education Resource Centre in Glasgow.

Can you tell us a bit about yourselves and what made you become activists in your community?

Helen Martin

I've lived in the same street in Easthall, one of the 15 sub-areas of Greater Easterhouse in Glasgow, for 34 years. My mum was always active in the Residents' Association. When I married I moved from number eight to number nine in the same street. That is when I began to understand a lot more about the struggle my mum had been involved with. She was in the dampness campaign long before me. It wasn't just her problem – other people had the same sort of problems too. My first step into the community hall was to run a girls' club. After that I got involved in the Residents' Association and eventually became chairperson for five years.

At the age of six my son Scott was diagnosed as being asthmatic. As a mother you become totally paranoid that you've created a problem and that there is nothing you can do about it. I felt powerless. I was being continually blamed for creating the child's health problem because I wasn't doing the things I was supposed to do at home – like stop smoking or keeping my flat warm. Financial constraints didn't allow me to feed my electric meter any more than £25 a week, which was only heating the living room. Being in the community hall and listening to other women talking about how their kids were suffering similar problems, I realised that it couldn't just be our fault – there must be a different reason – and I became active in the dampness group. It was a very powerful experience. None of us were members of any political organisation. Our motivation was that we were mothers and our children were suffering.

Easthall was rewired in 1987 and many of the 976 flats had to get new electric meters. The folk had been forced into becoming criminals because they had jammed meters to stop them running all the time – not through choice, but through necessity. My husband worked full-time and I worked part-time cleaning in the school and we found it a struggle to feed the meter. It was much worse for the unemployed, single parents and the elderly who spent more time in their homes. The Association did door-to-door surveys to find out about other people's experience of the dampness problem and were horrified to discover the extent of fuel poverty. The poorest families in the community were paying £35 a week deducted from their welfare benefits by the DHSS and paid direct to the fuel companies. Some families had hundreds of pounds of fuel debt. This was in the 1980s! The cost of trying to heat these flats became more than the cost of renting them. So you can see how many families had to make real choices – feeding the children or feeding the fuel meters. Or stuffing the meters and risk being criminalised.

Cathy McCormack

I was born in Cranhill, the first sub-area of Greater Easterhouse, in 1952. My family were moved there during the massive slum clearance of the inner city – ironically, to address Glasgow's appalling health record. My mother said that when we moved from a single apartment in the Gorbals to a four bedroom flat in Cranhill, with an inside toilet and kitchen, our lives were transformed. But it was short-lived. Of course, the weans were excited with all the space, but the flats didn't have any sound insulation and soon the neighbour above started to bang down on his floor and the neighbour below started to bang up on his ceiling. Then in the winter we were shocked at how cold the rooms became and we had to pile coats on the bed to try and stay warm during the night. My mother called the flats pneumonia houses.

When I was two years old, I was in hospital with chronic bronchitis and my mother was always laid up in bed with pleurisy. When the Clean Air Act came into force to try and clear up the smog, families like mine were encouraged to change from a coal fire to a gas fire. This exacerbated the dampness epidemic. In their effort to clean up outdoor pollution, they polluted our homes with fungal spores. I slept in the room above the back close which was the coldest one and had chronic dampness problems. Before leaving school at 15 I had been a patient in almost every hospital in Glasgow.

I never related my health problems to my living conditions until I got married and moved to Easthall and had children of my own. The bedrooms were so damp that when we stripped off the wall paper the pattern was imprinted on the bare wall. When they were born, my children were bouncing with health, but once in our cold damp flat the doctor became a regular visitor. That is when my own nightmare began and my life became a constant struggle for survival between my family and the fungus family. In the winter the fungus spreads just like a fire, destroying everything that it comes in contact with. I always remember my own daughter saying when she was only a few years old, 'Mummy, see if the dampness is doing that to our furniture and my toys, what is it doing to us?'.

Although my children were breast-fed, they always had thrush and my health visitor had never heard of this before. It was then that my own personal fight with Glasgow District Council really started. At that particular time, the health problems associated with damp houses weren't really seen as the issue. The real issue was who was to blame for the dampness.

In 1982 my health visitor gave me a letter to say that the dampness was affecting the health of my children. At that time you could get medical points to get a house somewhere else. The problem was that my landlord kept blaming me for causing the dampness: I was boiling too many kettles, drying clothes on the pulley, breathing too deeply, not heating the house well enough, not opening my window and so on. I knew that if I couldn't do all the things that normal families do without causing dampness, then there must be something wrong with the house, and not the family that lived in it.

Unfortunately, none of the educated people in the Housing Department would listen to the common sense of people like me. I became so depressed that I pleaded with my doctor to give me a prescription for a warm dry home. It occurred to me that my doctor was also a public servant employed to treat the symptoms of our health problem because all he could offer me was a prescription for anti-depressants. I refused his medicine and joined my community's fight for justice instead. Easthall Residents' Association came into being in 1973 to address a number of issues concerning the community, and I joined in 1982.

Tell us about your experience of campaigning

Helen Martin

In the beginning, people were afraid or ashamed to admit they had a damp house because of the stigma and blame attached. Then in 1984, at our annual general meeting, angry tenants demanded that finding a long-term solution to damp housing should become our number one priority. As a result, the anti-dampness task force came into being. We did another door to door survey and found that 76 per cent of the tenants were affected by dampness. The survey also revealed the extent of the health problems and exposed the asthma epidemic and the common dependency of young children on inhalers. We were no longer speaking just as members of an Association but as the collective voice for the community.

Cathy McCormack

Our struggle was very difficult because we knew we would have to produce the evidence to prove that it was not poor people to blame for the dampness. In fact the cost of heating added to people's poverty. We were very fortunate in that the Technical Services Agency had just been established. They were a user-controlled community technical aid centre and the architects were independent of the City Council. They were really a godsend. We enlisted their help to explain to us the real cause of the housing problems. They carried out an in-depth survey of our flats and issued us with a long, detailed technical report which confirmed our suspicions. They also taught us the technical language so that we could translate it into a language in tune with our own common sense. This exercise was a powerful tool in our campaign. It meant that the experts of our landlord could no longer try and bamboozle us with their technical arguments. We could also explain the technical problems to tenants in a language which they could understand.

In simple terms, the flats were never designed for our climate. They never had insulation to keep either the heat in or the cold out. As soon as the tenants turned on the heat, it went straight out through the windows and walls. Because the internal walls of the flats were always cold, any moisture generated through boiling kettles condensed and they became the ideal breeding ground for fungus. We also enlisted the help of the Glasgow School of Building and Technology to see if they could estimate how much it would cost to heat our flats to avoid the risk of condensation dampness. A number of flats were wired up to test the rate of heat loss and the temperature inside and outside. We were horrified to find that some of the flats like mine were colder inside. Most of the flats tested were so cold that families, especially the young and old, were at risk from hypothermia. Because the flats didn't have central heating, people would have to spend up to £50 a week to heat them to the recommended healthy temperature level. They were able to estimate that in Easthall alone, the poorest families were spending up to £1 million between them each year heating the sky above Glasgow.

A health report revealed once again that Glasgow had an appalling health record and one of the highest premature death rates in Western Europe, and it was nominated heart disease capital of the world. This came as no surprise to us whatsoever. What did surprise us was that the blame was put on our diet and general lifestyle. There was no mention of living conditions or poverty, and we felt there was a conspiracy to cover up the cause of health problems.

Glasgow District Council, the Scottish Office, Greater Glasgow Health Board and central Government invested millions of pounds in their 'let's go out jogging, stop smoking and eat brown bread' health promotion campaigns.

Our own experience taught us that it was not keep-fit exercises that we needed but homes that were fit to live in and incomes that prevented us from having to choose between dying from hypothermia or malnutrition. We were also convinced that unless we could get the politicians and so-called medical experts to start exercising their minds, then people in communities like ours would continue to die before their time and our children damaged before they even got a chance to live. In our own ignorance, all we thought we had to do was to educate these people and the public. Our Association established its very own health task force.

We targeted other angry mothers who were concerned about their children's health. The first thing we did was to sit round the table and have a brainstorm. We wrote down all the health problems which we felt were linked to our living conditions – and the list was endless. At the top of our list was asthma, heart disease and cancer. Our next step was to find out what kind of evidence was already available to back up our own common sense. At that time, there was a local Adult Education Centre and we asked them to lend us a worker to show us how to go about doing health research.

Because of our involvement with the Technical Services Agency, we were invited to a conference on damp houses and that is when we first met Sonja Hunt, a Senior Health Researcher. I told Sonja about our group and handed her our list of health problems which we felt were linked to living conditions. I nearly fell off my chair when Sonja said, 'Cathy, you are right'. The problem is that there has been so much propaganda aimed at individualising health problems that it will take a long, painstaking process of re-accumulating evidence before the health problems that communities like mine experience are regarded as major public health issues.

At the conference I asked Sonja to mention the health problems that our group had identified and she said, 'Why don't you tell the conference yourself?' That was my first real nerve wracking experience of being a public speaker. That was in 1987. Sonja spoke about the housing and health research that both she and her colleague Claudia Martin had been doing with tenants in damp housing in Edinburgh. The research proved that a much bigger focus was needed and we became involved.

It was one of the biggest research projects into housing and health ever carried out in Britain – it involved Glasgow, Edinburgh and London. Two other communities in Glasgow agreed to take part. It involved the Technical Services Agency doing a technical analysis of the houses and Strathclyde University Microbiology Department taking air spore counts and samples of mould. The aim was to identify all the different moulds and try to establish which moulds were attributable to the symptoms that people were suffering from. We leafleted everybody in Easthall asking for their co-operation. We needed families with children under 16 and were delighted when 250 families agreed to respond.

The most common moulds in our houses were *penicillium notatum*, *cladosporium herbarum* and *aspergillus*. That is when I first made the link between the yeast mould and the thrush that plagued my children when they were babies. So it was worse than we had anticipated because it not only confirmed the things that we already knew, it also confirmed things that we hadn't even thought about – like how fungus affects you, how you breathe in the spores, how the spores formed mucous membranes in your lungs, and all that.

Helen Martin

The research was funded by grants from Glasgow and Edinburgh District Councils and the London Research Centre, but it was agreed with the professionals that the tenants would get the first copy of the final report so that we could decide what to do with it regardless of what the funders thought. When the summary results came out, the Scottish Office tried to prevent the researchers from making it public. The tenants' groups in Glasgow were determined when the final report was ready that the whole world would know about the results and that this research wasn't going to gather dust in the bowels of the House of Commons. Easthall had already made a lot of allies in the Scottish media. This time we were ready to take on the whole of the British media.

Cathy McCormack

The researchers worked on getting it published in the *British Medical Journal* so that the findings could become known and the tenants arranged a national press conference in the House of Commons to coincide with its publication. That was the 24th of June 1989. Donald Dewar, who is now the Scottish Secretary, agreed to chair the press conference and the tenants and researchers had to brief him and the other Labour MPs that wanted to sit at the top table before we faced the press. We managed to get the results covered by all the national newspapers, television and radio stations, and it was the focus of both a Scottish and national television documentary.

As a result, Donald Dewar told the tenant representatives that this report would be brought up at the next meeting of the Scottish Grand Committee, and Opposition parties used the research as a tool to fight the Tory Government's housing policy.

Can you tell us about the Heatfest campaign?

Helen Martin

While all the health activity was going on, Easthall was also involved in another initiative – the Heatfest Housing Project. The Technical Services Agency had strong links with the Scottish Solar Energy Group and together we organised a three-day ideas competition in Easthall to try and find a long-term solution to cold damp houses. We invited all the academics and tenants and students at different universities and colleges with an interest in housing and health. We got the tenants in Easthall to let the folk who took part live in their damp houses. The social committee group organised all the meals and fun times. This resulted in seven possible solutions.

The professional panel and the local dampness group spent three months, independently of each other, analysing the entries and, interestingly enough, we both picked the same winner. A recall conference was held and the £1,000 prize money was awarded to the tenants' group that had worked with the professionals on the winning solution. Somebody from Dublin University said, 'Why don't you submit an application to the European Commission for a passive solar energy demonstration project?' The more we thought about it, the more we realised that this could actually happen. We worked seven days a week trying to fill in the application form, which had to be written in French too. It was shocking – the hours that we spent! Relationships were breaking down and everything. How we got through four or five years of that intensity is unbelievable.

Up to that point, people regarded housing, health and the environment as separate issues. What the Easthall thing did was it allowed people to make connections. It was key for us. We wanted to know how much it was costing to treat people with the illnesses associated with damp houses because at that particular time I felt that we were living in a climate where people didn't matter any more. In 1996 it was estimated that it cost the NHS £10,000 million per year.

Helen Martin

Our solar housing energy project was costed at £1.3 million, and the European Commission granted us £400,000. We still needed the moral and financial support from the City Council to give us the other £950,000. They kept telling us that if they gave us the money, then other communities in Glasgow would lose out. So we called their bluff. There were a quarter of a million people in Glasgow and an estimated 10 million nationwide living in damp houses, so we organised a conference to try and enlist the support of other tenants' organisations. They were as desperate as us for a solution, so they in turn put pressure on their elected council representatives to give us the money.

Unfortunately, the council had other priorities in mind. After all, they were about to host the 1990 European City of Culture, an award which the tenants in Glasgow felt they richly deserved. So in 1989 we decided we would capitalise on this and write a play about our 'years of culture' – the sort that grows on the walls. The motive was to try and shame the powers that be in Glasgow and keep the results of the health research on the boil. At first the idea was to perform a play, video it and send it round other communities. But other communities didn't want a video. They wanted us to come and perform. So Easthall had to establish a theatre company and we all became actors. It was wonderful.

Cathy McCormack

It was a bloody terrible experience for me. I didn't mind helping to write, but I hated having to act as well. I was one of the funguses. We enlisted the help of a professional writer to work with local people who then became active in the writing and acting. It took a year to plan, write and raise the thousands of pounds needed to travel round the other communities. There were so many requests that we had to do another tour.

The idea was to write a comedy about the problem that people could enjoy and see themselves in. We designed programmes for the play and published the results of the health survey on that instead – the play was called 'Dampbusters'. The main characters were Aspergillus and Penicillium, the two funguses who came to life and couldn't believe their luck that humans had built these houses which they were thriving on whilst the people were dying. It was a challenge not just to the politicians but the people who live in damp houses because it was based on the real family of a woman who would not admit she had dampness. Her sister comes back from Australia – she has been away for 10 years – and she can't believe people still accept living in these conditions.

Helen Martin

We had housing officials in the play and we called them their real names, but the Director of Architecture decided he was going to stay in a flat in Easthall for a year. We sent him an invite to the play and, where possible, he made his officers attend 'Dampbusters'. The kids in the play were the councillors who were shouting and bawling and screaming at one another – just like weans would do. It was really powerful stuff.

Eventually, we got the money from the Council and the Solar Housing Project was completed in the summer of 1992. The heating bills were reduced to around £5 per week. The families who live there are a lot happier and healthier and can now grow fruit instead of mushrooms and other fungi.

What did you learn from these experiences?

Cathy McCormack

Easthall became a learning school for other tenant and professional oganisations, students and academics – not just from Britain but from Europe and the Third World. The people who came were very inspired and impressed. The only people who were not happy were our landlords, Glasgow District Council.

The 36 solar houses were a great success for the families who lived in them. But the success of the Residents' Association inadvertently brought about the downfall of the rest of the community. We exposed the true nature of the ruling Labour Party in Glasgow which is only now being revealed at a national level. Rather than embrace the energy and aspirations of our community, they regarded us as some kind of threat and did everything in their power to keep closed every door we tried to open.

It became obvious to us that they were terrified of people like us – not because we had any political power, but because uneducated people like us had become experts in understanding what we were talking about. When we talked, people listened. We hadn't been brainwashed by other people's political ideologies, but were talking straight from the heart. Easthall Residents' Association will be 25 years old in 1998 and we are in the process of our next popular education exercise: writing a book about the good, bad and ugly story of our community's struggle for survival.

Helen Martin

The struggle took over our lives, but it really opened up our minds. The majority of people in the community are so busy trying to win the wars in their own homes, busy trying to survive, that it prevents them from seeing what is outside their door and seeing that their neighbours are suffering the same. I think it is deliberate that everything has been individualised. What the tenants' organisation tried to do was to blow that open and say, 'Hold on a wee minute, we're all in this together!'

Cathy McCormack

Before I became involved in the struggle I was very naive and politically ignorant. I used to think what my ma used to say was true, that working class people should always vote for the Labour Party as they were the party that served their best interests. My experience of living in a city like Glasgow, which has always been controlled by Labour, has taught me something very different.

I used to associate oppression with something bad that happened to poor people in Third World countries. Frankie Vaughan made Easterhouse famous for its gang warfare, but a much deeper violence has been done to the hearts, minds and spirits of the people who live here. The people in Easterhouse, like other working class communities in Glasgow, have been used as fodder to service the well-being of the middle class. Our struggle is not all that different from the townships in South Africa. Michael Docherty, another activist, always said that social and economic oppression is far more efficient than racial oppression and it looks more innocent when your oppressors are the same colour.

People like me and Helen celebrated the end of apartheid in South Africa, but we will never understand the minds of our civic leaders who gave Nelson

Mandela the freedom of the city – a freedom denied our people in their very own townships. I refuse to believe that they were oblivious to their own social and economic aparthied. Our experience, however, has taught us that it is the oppressed who are oblivious, in the same way that we used to be. Why else would they keep voting them into power? Our struggle took a big chunk out of our lives and I feel dead fucking angry about that. History always repeats itself, and we want to try and help people make the connections.

We have been learning from our counterparts in Third World countries who have come to visit our community. They are the real experts and have taught us a lot about popular education and liberation theology. That is why we have been struggling to establish PODER (Popular Democracy and Education Resource Centre). We don't want to tell people what to think, we just want to provide the space and the tools that will support groups involved in their struggle for justice to think for themselves – instead of the way that people like me and Helen now understand we were programmed to think by our formal education and the media.

Only through understanding their past and their present, only through understanding and analysing their reality can people choose their future. Nelson Mandela ended his autobiography *The Long Walk to Freedom* with the same conclusion as Paulo Freire: the oppressed will never be free until their oppressors are liberated. On reflection, I realise that is exactly what we tried to do. Through analysing my community's struggle, I have come to the conclusion that for the first time in history the survival of the rich is dependent on the liberation of the poor. Poverty is not only costing us our lives, it is costing us all the earth!

21 Neighbourhood as classroom: reflections of an activist

John Dickie

In this chapter a community activist looks back on two campaigns waged in an inner city area of Edinburgh in the early 1990s, one as part of the national struggle againt the Poll Tax and the other a local battle to prevent the closure of a primary school. Drawing on interviews he conducted with local activists after the event, he recognises that, whilst much transferable learning was gained, a more systematic approach to the underlying educational aspects of campaigning could have consolidated the collective learning process more effectively. The possibilities for both politicising everyday life and linking the local with the global make neighbourhoods a key site in struggling for democratic renewal and learning for active citizenship.

I've seen a woman who could hardly walk, standing barring the door to sheriff officers. That, to me, is a political lesson.

I live in the Broughton area of Edinburgh in which there are three active residents' associations. In the last few years two single-issue action groups waged very intensive campaigns – one against the Poll Tax (see Dickie, 1992) and the other to resist closure of the local primary school (see Dickie, 1996). Taken together, this adds up to considerable experience of social action within one inner city neighbourhood. What was learnt from this – and what *could* have been learnt? How could individual learning have been shared more effectively by drawing together all the different experiences and making more systematic connections to the benefit of the local community as a whole? Any sharing of experience between action groups can be valuable, of course, but what I want to suggest is that there could be a special kind of learning potential in experiences that have all been gained within the context of one particular neighbourhood. I want to explore this idea by focusing on the local Anti-Poll Tax group and the parents' campaign to resist the proposal to close London Street Primary School.

The neighbourhood context

The Broughton/Inverleith Anti-Poll Tax group took its name from the regional electoral ward (comprised of two district electoral wards) but, in fact, it never drew hard and fast geographical boundaries round its field of action. Most of its work took place within the Broughton area as did the London Street parents' campaign, ie in the immediate neighbourhood of the school itself.

At the time of the 1991 Census, Broughton Ward had a resident population of 6,146 with a minority ethnic population more than twice the Edinburgh average (5.5 per cent compared to 2.3 per cent). 70.9 per cent of housing was owner-occupied, 19.6 per cent privately rented and only 3.2 per cent local authority (83.9 per cent of accommodation being in flats or tenements). Walking down Broughton Street, the impression is one of prosperity in the many restaurants, pubs, antique shops and so on. However, the Census tells us that in 1991, eight per cent of households suffered from overcrowding (compared to six per cent for Edinburgh as a whole) and 10.5 per cent of those of 'economically active' age were unemployed – more recent figures compiled by the District Council showed Broughton amongst the top dozen or so wards (out of 62) in terms of unemployment. Also, there is the contrast between the transient part of the population, on the one hand, and second and third generation families on the other. An informal local survey revealed that individuals with local residence of 20, 30 or even 40 years were not exceptional. Broughton seems to have a 'dual personality': it is a city centre service area and yet at the same time a local community with its own distinctive identity and history.

The survey involved interviewing 50 local residents in autumn 1993. Although this was not in any way a scientific sample, the responses did give some idea of how local people viewed their area. When asked if they liked living there, the overwhelming response was 'yes'. They liked the convenience of living in such a central area with 'the city on your doorstep' and yet with the feel of a residential area: plenty of gardens, parks and open areas – 'space'! There were complaints too, of course, with traffic coming out way ahead of all the others – sheer volume, speed, noise, wear and tear on houses, pollution and parking problems. Many made favourable comments about the friendliness of their fellow locals and the good social mix: 'mixed people and cultures', 'not too snobby and not too desperate', 'a balanced feel about the place'. But there were differing opinions about how strong community feeling was in Broughton. Some felt it was just about right: 'quiet, friendly in an unoppressive way'. Others felt it was not as strong as it had once been. Some of the younger families who had moved in were not so outgoing and chatty; the sense of community had not gone, but it had weakened as a result of social changes such as women going out to work.

Campaigning: the local experience

The Anti-Poll Tax struggle and the campaign against the closure of the local primary school were both fought out within this neighbourhood context, but the original impetus to action came about quite differently. In the case of the Poll Tax, people throughout Scotland – and later the UK as a whole – were reacting against the perceived injustice of central government policy. In the case of the school, parents and others were responding to an immediate threat to a very local resource. However, while there were national Anti-Poll Tax campaigns and demonstrations, the nature of the struggle, with its emphasis on non-payment and therefore the need for mutual support, meant that a key role developed for a network of local resistance groups, of which ours was one. For parents with children at the local primary school, on the other hand, pursuing a local issue soon led them to engage with wider issues – funding for education, perceptions of the place of schools in their communities and the vexed question of what constitutes a 'viable' school, the potential divisiveness of denominational schools and (through their experience of the 'consultation' process) the nature of local government and its accountability.

Organisationally, the Broughton/Inverleith Anti-Poll Tax Group arose from a meeting in neighbouring Stockbridge to discuss launching a local campaign against the new tax. It emerged that many of the people attending came from Broughton and Inverleith and so it was decided to set up a separate group. I only became involved after this was up and running. I had read about the proposed new tax, heard that a group was meeting in the local secondary school and went along. At that point, I simply felt something had to be done – not necessarily non-payment. In the years that followed, having become firmly committed to non-payment, I sometimes had to remind myself that this tactic had not seemed self-evidently right to me from the outset – a necessary reminder when considering other people's positions!

Throughout 1988 and into the spring of 1989, our group was active in informing local residents about the implications of the Poll Tax and encouraging disruption of registration for it. When the tax came into force in April 1989, and until it was eventually abolished four years later, the group gave advice and support to all those refusing to pay. For much of that period, we met weekly – organising public meetings, producing leaflets and distributing them door-to-door, putting up posters, joining other groups in demonstrations and turning out to resist sheriff officers' attempts to carry out poindings (the listing of personal belongings for compulsory sale as a means of recovering debts). Frequent newsletters were sent out to a mailing list of supporters and a phone tree was developed to facilitate speedy communication when necessary. The Broughton/Inverleith group often worked with other Anti-Poll Tax groups and was a member of the Lothian Anti-Poll Tax Federation, but members also valued their independence and the fact that they were first and foremost a *local* group. I had previously been active in the local branch of a national political party and in the local work of a development education agency, but this was a new level of commitment for me – to both cause and people (people who lived within walking distance of my home). A late starter, eventually I became the main local contact on Poll Tax matters and helped provide continuity from one meeting to the next.

In June 1991 – in the midst of the Anti-Poll Tax struggle – Lothian Region's Education Department proposed the reorganisation of primary education in East-Central Edinburgh. This involved one denominational and two non-denominational primary schools in our area. A 'consultation paper' outlined four options, two of which would mean the closure of London Street Primary School. For the next 18 months, parents united in determined resistance to this proposal. This involved them in drafting detailed arguments against the Regional Council's case and suggesting alternatives to closure, mobilising support throughout the local community, seeking maximum media coverage, lobbying councillors, eventually applying to the Scottish Office to 'opt out' under central government legislation for self-governing schools – and, when all else failed, taking the Regional Council to court. A year and a half of very concentrated experience of social action! I was only marginally involved in all of this. My own sons had long since completed their primary education and Poll Tax matters demanded a lot of my time. But I had taken an interest in London Street Primary School in years gone by (at a time when male parent involvement was not so usual!) and served on the local secondary school council, which had itself success-fully fought off a closure proposal.

After both the struggles were over, I interviewed some of the most active participants in order to establish, for everyone involved, what had been learnt from the two campaigns.

Activists learning through the experience of struggle

Those involved in both the Anti-Poll Tax and the London Street Primary School campaigns were certainly aware of learning:

> If something else happens that requires that kind of response, people have learnt a lot of skills – communication and organisational skills . . . Once the Poll Tax has gone, people should go back to base and then come out again next time – better equipped.

And from the London Street campaign:

> It's like all these things; you learn, and if I was ever in a situation like that again I'd obviously suggest we did things differently.

One parent pointed to lessons learnt about *the way the political system works*, resulting in 'an alertness amongst the community that they can spot something like this happening again and be more vigilant towards it'. In the Anti-Poll Tax group, members were aware of developing knowledge about the political system too. The question kept coming up: 'Just who is it that our local councillors represent – us or their party?'

Several Anti-Poll Tax campaigners mentioned the new understanding they had gained of other people in their neighbourhood:

I've met a lot of people and it's really opened my eyes. I really like knowing other people in the area, people of different ages and different backgrounds.

Sometimes knowledge came too late. For example, after the campaign over London Street Primary School had been lost:

> There's so many avenues I found afterwards. I have found where we could have got the information to challenge the statistics. There's so many things we could have found out if I had realised how much information we could have got . . . that we just assumed we wouldn't get.

Perceptions of society were sharpened:

> I go about Edinburgh . . . and I look at the tenements, and they're all living on top of each other . . . Then you go to the outskirts. The people with money who're paying the same Poll Tax as these people in tenements, they've got a big house – that's what really sickened me.

An Anti-Poll Tax campaigner gained a very positive perception of the mood locally: 'What it adds up to for me is a feeling that people want more power and they want collective power – collective *local* power'. However, faced with defeat and closure of their school, some London Street parents formed negative perceptions of how the system works as well as the prospects of influencing it: 'If it had been voting that counted, we would have won. But they paid no attention. They had already decided what they would do'.

> I was politically naive. I believed in the justice of things and if you proved things, if you made a case, then the case would have to be answered. I now realise that corruption, deals and 'I'll pat your back if you'll pat mine' – this all goes on. It makes you feel that only if it fits would you ever win a cause – if it fits for them to grant you it.

Others reached conclusions about *the nature of local social action*, without necessarily feeling pessimistic about it: 'As things evolved, I think people saw that there wasnae any negotiating to be done, that it was a trial of strength'. For one activist the Anti-Poll Tax campaign focused her perception of a previous experience:

> I like the local thing – the sort of local autonomy of the group. I never felt that somebody else was pulling the strings. I think with things like the Miners Strike, you could often feel political things going on, that you were sort of being left to deal with, whereas here, it was like we were the main actors, we weren't doing it on anyone else's behalf.

Another said:

> The movement proved that the grassroots can be self-organised, outside the traditional and conventional ways.

Communication and organisational skills were gained through working alongside more experienced activists and, in turn, becoming more experienced:

> He understood how to deal with the Press. He could call a news conference. He knew how to get the story out, how to get them to come.
> Probably I would structure a campaign committee a lot better so that there were clear channels of decision making. There was a tendency for people to go away, have a chat and say 'this is the latest strategy'. I don't think it was democratic enough. People were put off by the way meetings were run too.

Organising out in the wider community, one activist came to recognise the importance of using meetings as a means of keeping other activists up to date – and reinforcing their determination:

> You felt strengthened because, unless you're going to a group like that, you begin to see the other side and have a lot of pressure put on you – it's a lot harder to hold your stance.

Another activist found that, because he kept up to date by attending meetings, others resisting the poll tax used him as 'a sounding board for their worries'. And another stressed the importance of skilful use of the telephone tree to rally support:

> . . . to know what should be done now and also knowing there would be support if it did get to that situation, that you would have people rallying round to stop the sheriff officers.

However, some of the London Street parents wished they had developed more skill in conciliation and alliance building:

> We did try to communicate with the St Mary's parents. We did try to have some sort of discussion with them, but it never materialised. I think we could have been more conciliatory.
> We should have said 'Look, we don't like the separate education for Catholics, but in this instance, let's forget about that and see if we can work out a strategy for maintaining the status quo'.

Activists adopted various attitudes towards *the possibility of future social action* as a result of their experiences. The general view was that the London Street struggle had strengthened the potential for future involvement in local issues:

> . . . but this time round with marked reservations, because I would feel beaten almost before I started.
> I think I would probably be more likely to get involved now . . . if there was something I felt strongly about – so it wouldn't happen again.

Others drew clear lessons from the Poll Tax battle:

> If it's not right, get out in the street and tell them, the politicians, that it's not right and we're not going to pay – or whatever it'll be.

And attitudes towards particular approaches to social action were formed:

> I'm all in favour of direct action on such issues – pensioners getting on buses and demanding their rights, for example . . . Before the Poll Tax, that would never have occurred to me whereas now, that's the first thing I think of.

Many activists found *a strengthened belief in themselves*, in their ability to get together with others in their community and achieve something:

> There are people – who previously would never have said anything – circulating a petition at Broughton Primary asking for more multicultural allowances to be in the menu.

And from members of the Anti-Poll Tax group:

> But for all of us, we would have the tax on the statute book until forever. That's a great example – that if enough people get together and feel strongly enough about something, then things can be changed from the bottom upwards.
> You realise that politics is not an elitist thing, that you can get involved . . . and it gives people confidence to go on and do other things.
> What I've learnt is that if you're the meekest, quietest, most vulnerable person in the world, you're actually more powerful in a way – as long as you're resolved to do something.

Building on the experience

Individual activists felt they had gained new knowledge and understanding about how the political system works, about sources of information and expert assistance, about their own local community and the people living in it. Perceptions sharpened, or altered – of politics, society, social action and the prospects of ordinary people bringing about change. Skills were learnt – in communication, group organisation, maintaining support systems in the local community. The need for skills in conciliation and alliance building was understood – if not fully realised! Activists' experience affected their attitudes – towards getting involved again and towards particular kinds of action. And many found a strengthened belief in their own capabilities.

Local Anti-Poll Tax campaigners were concerned, as a group, that the story should not end when the campaign ended. Shortly after the government announced in 1991 that the tax would be abolished (although not for another two years), a meeting was devoted to evaluating the campaign, deciding what to do in the immediate future and considering the question: 'When the Poll

Tax has gone – then what?' There was implicit agreement that the learning gained should be carried forward in some way, but this became submerged in discussion about whether there should be continuity of organisation (over which opinion was divided).

Months later, the urge to somehow carry forward the Poll Tax experience led to a small group meeting to discuss how we could influence the course of events. But when we moved into considering the general political situation – national and international – we lost the local focus and the experiment was short-lived. Despite further discussion, there never was a clear-cut decision as to whether the group should continue to exist and take up new issues. When the Poll Tax was abolished the group went into suspended animation, with the phone tree continuing to operate a while longer and then just a phone contact for non-payers needing support or advice. Longer-term continuity did emerge, however, in the form of a community newspaper planned by eight members of the Anti-Poll Tax group.

The first issue of the *Broughton Spurtle* was published in February 1994, clearly stating that it had been inspired by the success of the Anti-Poll Tax campaign, the struggle for London Street Primary School and the achievements of local residents' associations. The purpose of the paper was to act as a catalyst for local action; and for community learning – for example, making connections between local experience and 'the news', and cross-fertilisation between issues. However, whilst there have been occasional references to past local experience in relation to the present, as yet there has been no sustained discussion of knowledge and skills gained from it.

Realising the potential for collective learning

The learning by individuals recorded here emerged from simply asking ten Anti-Poll Tax activists and ten primary school parents if they had learnt anything from being involved in these campaigns. Although there was very limited opportunity for discussion with the interviewer, substantial learning was acknowledged and put on record. Could more have been made of it? Could more still be made of it?

With hindsight, I wish our Anti-Poll Tax group had organised more systematic discussion of what we had learnt from the experience – arguing over different conclusions reached and asking more searching questions (in spite of the fact that we had won!). A similar exercise might have been more difficult for the London Street parents – and yet perhaps it would have been even more valuable. After the disappointment of losing the battle and the trauma of the school closing – with the children being transferred to another school down the road – sitting down for a group discussion of the experience might not have been an immediately appealing idea! But what must have been a discouraging experience for some of the parent activists might have revealed more positive aspects through discussion. They lost the school, but there were undoubtedly real achievements along the way.

The learning process could have been developed further by bringing together members of the two groups. Apart from enlarging the pool of specific knowledge and skills gained, comparing outcomes would surely have led to comparing the circumstances in which the two struggles were fought and the implications of this for different kinds of social action. The neighbourhood context was common to both so it should have been possible to discuss its relevance with some shared understanding. Furthermore, the substantial minority ethnic population was important in the London Street Primary battle – the successful multicultural nature of the school being a main plank of the parents' case for keeping it open. What other implications might this aspect of the social mix have for social action?

A positive feature of the national Anti-Poll Tax movement was the alliance between those whose welfare was seriously threatened by the new tax and those who could pay without hardship but refused to pay on principle. This was reflected in Broughton. However, the combination of prosperity and unemployment indicated by the local statistics means that adopting an over-cosy concept of 'community' might be misleading. For example, what local conflicts of interest might be relevant to planning community action? And what about communication in this kind of neighbourhood, with its combina-tion of transient population and established families, and the lack of 'a central point to focus the community' perceived by some locals?

Then, again, what about the possibilities of cross-fertilising the learning of those single-issue groups with the rather different experience of local residents' associations? They all shared the same local context but discussion of differ-ences might turn out to be as productive as any similarities. The process could be a continuous one, assisting new local action groups as they emerged. For example, in 1995 a Broughton Traffic Action Group was formed – a single-issue group with leanings towards direct action. But local residents' associations have already engaged the local authority on traffic issues, so surely there must be something to learn from their experience.

Although it is important that community action itself springs from autonomous local groups, maybe there is a role for a professional worker in facilitating and developing the learning process. The starting point is local people's awareness that they have got the raw materials for learning – their own experiences; and a shared context in their neighbourhood. From this, they can work out their own curriculum: learning objectives, organisation of learning experiences, methods and evaluation. Their big advantage is that the most vital component for learning is already there – direct experience! Professionals could possibly serve as a source of information and raise questions which those more directly involved in the action may have missed – but local activists should keep firm control of the agenda.

Individuals have already learnt a great deal through their own experience. They can increase that learning by pooling it with that gained by others in the neighbourhood. This continuing process would be further strengthened if, at each stage, something of what has been learned is recorded – on paper, cassette or video – so that when community action is considered necessary again, activists are able to draw on this account of the neighbourhood as classroom. As further experience accumulates, it should be recorded so that it can be passed on. This is something more than lessons learnt by individuals; it is learning that becomes part of the local community's collective memory.

References

Dickie, J (ed) (1992) *Cause to be Proud: A Local Group's Struggle against the Poll Tax*, Edinburgh, Gecko Press.
Dickie, J (ed) (1996) *Save our School: The Struggle for London Street Primary*, Edinburgh, Gecko Press.

22 Past matters: memories and histories

Lorraine Dick

The author refers to practical examples from her own work in community-based and outreach education to show how marginalised and, all too often, silenced groups can be encouraged to see themselves as part of history. Unlike most documented histories, oral history allows the voices of silenced communities to be heard. She presents brief accounts of two pieces of work in which she was directly involved: a local social history project and a major exhibition on the Peoples of Edinburgh. Case material of this kind demonstrates the importance of enabling participants to develop a high degree of confidence and competence about both what they learn and how they learn. The relationship between methodology, content and purpose is critical to the success of such work. Only then are such groups in a position to show how their past matters.

Reminiscence work: an educational critique

We live in an 'ageing society'. The great social achievement of this century has added 25 years to life expectancy in the Western world. This is reflected in the number of day care centres and residential developments for older people we see in our communities. In social work and nursing the emphasis of work with the elderly is on 'quality of life' and 'care'.

As Mangan (1991) argues, 'If reminiscence takes place for no other reason, it is enough if it is done to provide a link between carers and cared for'. The term 'reminiscence group' is immediately recognised and accepted as a legitimate 'activity' for older people, and it is often welcomed as an alternative to carpet bowls or bingo for the 50+ age group. However, while reminiscence groups for independent and active older people are a common feature of informal education programmes, we have to ask what kind of objectives they reflect: therapeutic or educational? My own experience suggests that a lack of clear educational objectives leads to reminscence work being too closely linked to geriatric care rather than active educational engagement and development.

Being based on 'the group', reminiscence work provides a setting for some obvious benefits: for example, group solidarity, emotional support and a sense of belonging. Benefits of this kind are seen by some as the major aim of the activity: amongst 'the reasons why members valued the group, "tea and chat" was top of the list' (Abel, 1990). However, such social benefits, though valid in themselves, are not enough if this kind of work is to claim to be educational.

'Reminiscence for the sake of reminiscing' is all very well as a recreational and therapeutic exercise. The problem is that within an educational setting, such a reductionist celebration of experience may actually encourage a 'culture of silence'. It can even work in a reactionary way, presenting a sanitised past of apparently wholesome communities, which we have somehow lost through our own folly. This is a view of history without struggle, and it sends an oppressive message to young people facing their own struggles as well as to older people whose struggles and achievements are thus denied. In the end, it can amount to what Lynne Segal (1991) describes as a 'wilful and deliberate forgetting'. Programmes called 'A walk down memory lane' or 'The good old days' are in great abundance. If there is a place for this kind of thing within educational practice, it is surely only as a way of getting people involved – a starting point or 'hook'.

When personal reminiscence is accepted uncritically, all too often the 'we were poor but we were happy' syndrome takes over – and takes us no further than an uncritical celebration of cosy nostalgia. Dwelling on the past can also encourage a sense of loss – even a feeling of being besieged by a threatening outside world in a 'Crimewatch' kind of way! In this sense, it is far from empowering.

Developing a more critical approach

Critical reminiscence workers need to be aware of the tension between a search for something worth remembering and the manufactured history of 'heritage' which is all too often presented as a wholesome 'Hovis'-type view of the past free from strife, poverty and hunger. In addition, much reminiscence work – particularly, perhaps, in Scotland – seems to promote the idea of a uniform and uni-dimensional culture. There are strengths and weaknesses in this. On the one hand, it can help to create a sense of collective cultural identity; on the other, the problem is who and what are left out of the picture.

If we accept that to move the focus beyond personal reminiscence is the beginning of the educational process, then the central task of the worker must be more than a simple affirmation of participants' personal experience. What is required is that this experience is examined critically within a structured process of learning.

In attempting to develop this kind of approach, it is worth acknowledging the value of the process Richard Johnson (1988) calls 'rehistoricising' – looking at history from our own position in society in a way which contributes to our understanding of our own interests in the present and informs our choices about future action. This kind of 'rehistoricising' allows us to listen to the narratives of 'ordinary people', and so to challenge the dominant view of what counts as history. This, in turn, helps to suggest 'the social and political contexts in which pedagogical activity can function as part of a strategy of resistance and transformation . . . [working] for a public culture around issues that emerge out of daily life' (Giroux, 1989).

In this way, historical understanding is brought to bear on our everyday lives. Different historical perspectives are used to engage people in a critical and challenging form of learning as the official version of history is examined and questioned by those who have been written out of it.

The importance of 'rehistoricising' has been widely recognised within the development of the social movements. Indeed, over the past 20 years a key role of social movements has been to promote alternative voices, which recognise the significance of collective as well as individual experience – the collective voice, in particular, of those who have been excluded historically, culturally and structurally. What this kind of approach reveals is a multiplicity of standpoints contained within the idea of cultural identity: 'narratives of difference that recognise their own partiality and present the unrepresentable, those submerged and dangerous memories' (Giroux, 1992). Those who have been silenced – women, black people, gays and lesbians, disabled people – all these previously marginalised and muted voices are now demanding to be heard.

Different voices: voices of difference

If people are to be encouraged and assisted to recognise, develop and document their own history and culture, it is essential that the use of alternative source material is introduced into the educational process. The creation of 'learning products' such as exhibitions, tape-slide shows and publications not only benefits the participants – often by introducing a structure and rigour into their learning – but also stimulates the development of other potential study groups. From my own experience, I would emphasise the importance of producing high quality learning products which give significance and dignity to the lives and efforts of the participants. This also provides the opportunity to use high-tech tools like video and photography, desk-top publishing and computer graphics to tell their own story.

I would also stress, in particular, the importance and usefulness of photography and photographs as a resource for this kind of work. This is a highly accessible medium, and most people have their own collection of photographs or at least access to them. Moreover, searching for additional photographic material is a way into using libraries and other established archives. Visual culture also provides another level of communication, crossing language barriers and offering an alternative way of communicating for those with hearing impairments. In short, photographs can give us another 'way of seeing'.

Two examples from my recent work illustrate the ways in which we can encourage and enable people to remember, tell their own stories and engage in a wider debate.

The Pilton Social History Project was initiated by local community education workers who were assisting and supporting residents to organise themselves into tenants' associations and housing action groups. At the time, work on housing issues began to be focused on the Housing (Scotland) Act 1988. The project was launched to help community activists and other local people understand the implications of this legislation which would, in effect, open up the rented council housing sector to private landlord control. It soon became clear that people did not know much about the history of private rented housing or the reasons for the development of public housing in the first place. The educational process began by identifying this gap in their knowledge.

One outcome of the project was an exhibition called 'Hame Sweet Hame? Memories of 70 Years of Scottish Housing'. The residents who compiled the exhibition were mostly in the 65+ age group and had previously been involved in a one-hour a week reminiscence session at the local community centre. The exhibition provided participants with an opportunity to 'rehistoricise' their own housing experience, using it as a key resource for learning. It also encouraged them to 'locate' their memories critically with the help of TV, video and library resources, using discussion and debate to stimulate questioning and analysis.

Involvement in picture research in the Edinburgh Room of the Central Library saw the participants poring through photographic surveys of areas of Edinburgh designated for slum clearance in the 1920s. They were, in effect, looking at their own history and seeing themselves in history, having been moved out of these designated areas and rehoused in Pilton. This kind of picture research served two purposes: it stimulated critical discussion and provided an opportunity to select images for the exhibition. The educational process was designed to validate the group as holders of relevant knowledge and experience, so reversing the normal relationship between teacher and student, expert and lay person, giver and receiver.

The second example contrasts with this 'bottom-up' approach. The 'Peoples of Edinburgh – Our Multicultural City' was a museums-based outreach project (see Clark *et al*, 1996). It began in 1995 and led to a major exhibition at the City Art Centre in Edinburgh which ran from October 1996 to January 1997. The project was initiated by the local branch of the Workers' Educational Association and the Museums Section of the City of Edinburgh Council's Recreation Department. Unlike the Pilton project, it could be seen as a 'top-down' process in the sense that the exhibition and its theme were decided upon and scheduled as part of the Edinburgh City Art Centre's ongoing official programme of events and exhibitions. Nevertheless, there was a commitment from the outset to develop appropriate ways of involving and working with Edinburgh's minority ethnic communities. This offered opportunities for reminiscence work techniques to be used in the outreach and consultation process which preceded the exhibition.

Although the exhibition deadline and other pressures placed constraints on the educational process, the methodology employed did allow each local minority ethnic community to have quite a lot of control over the selection of exhibits, and consequently over how it would be represented in this very public and high profile event. The groundwork for the exhibition emphasised outreach strategies, working with minority groups and people not usually 'visible' in the conventional, public image of the city of Edinburgh.

The turnout at the exhibition launch was very encouraging. What is more, this level of interest and support continued throughout the period of the exhibition. Getting people in is always the first problem – but they came to this! The exhibition was a great success, as was recognised when it subsequently received a National Museums Council award.

The main point to emphasise is that the exhibition and the publications which accompanied it focused on the culture, identity and experience of 'ordinary' people – not the great and the good. In doing so, it avoided the pitfalls of portraying people as victims or problems and provided an opportunity to give what are often marginalised and silenced groups public recognition and their own voice.

Conclusion

These two examples reflect different contexts and purposes, of course. In both cases, however, the groups' sense of self-esteem and significance (both individually and collectively) developed not just from the work on the respective exhibitions but also from their participation in the critical and creative educational process which led up to them and by the fact that they were deliberately included in crucially important decisions and discussions. People's own experience was validated and systematically used to inform and resource educational work and cultural action in the wider community.

As was recognised at the start of this account, therapeutic reminiscence work has its place, but we should be sceptical about the educational value of something that is seen simply as a 'user friendly' activity for elderly people. Reclaiming the historic sense of struggle is vital if we are to understand how the past permeates people's perceptions of themselves and their world now, and how this can have an impact on their sense of themselves not only in the present but also in the future. Without this sense of their own significance and agency, people are left as victims, the passive onlookers of history – rather than critical, reflective and active citizens.

Much of community-based adult education work is conducted with people who are marginalised or excluded in some way. It is also true that the people we work with are all too often compartmentalised into exclusive and excluding categories defined in terms of their own characteristic 'needs': young people want 'fun', entertainment and activity; the elderly want nostalgia, bingo and lunch clubs. The kind of work I have described is potentially a way of breaking down such stereotypes and building links between people of different age groups, cultures and communities. What matters is that people see themselves in history, combining their own knowledge with expert knowledge, and that they work together on a common, collective project. Only then can people really begin to construct their own accounts of how and why the past matters.

References

Abel, J (1990) 'Oral history at an Urban Studies Centre', *Streetwise*, 3, p 29.

Clark, H, Dick, L, and Fraser, B (eds) (1996) *Peoples of Edinburgh: Our Multicultural City*, Edinburgh, City of Edinburgh Council.

Giroux, H (1989) *Schooling for Democracy: Critical Pedagogy in the Modern Age,* University of Minnesota, Routledge.

Giroux, H A (1992) *Border Crossings: Cultural Workers and the Politics of Education,* London, Routledge.

Johnson, R (1988) 'Really useful knowledge, 1790–1850: Memories for education in the 1980s' in Lovett T (ed) *Radical Approaches to Adult Education,* London, Routledge, pp 3–34.

Mangan, P (1991) 'As time goes by', *Reminiscence*, 1, p 5.

Segal, L (1991) 'Whose Left? socialism, feminism and the future', *New Left Review*, 15, pp 81–91.

23 Making racism visible: an agenda for an anti-racist Scotland

Rowena Arshad

If the new Scotland is to be genuinely democratic and inclusive, it must confront the reality of racism and develop a comprehensive and proactive strategy of anti-racist policy and practice. Despite clear and increasing evidence of racism in Scotland, there is still a tendency for official responses to be 'colour-blind' and for popular responses to be based on a complacent, if deeply ambivalent, mythology. Issues of gender equality have received considerable attention in the run-up to the Scottish Parliament. Issues of racial justice, on the other hand, have been systematically ignored. In this sense, racism in Scotland remains invisible. Nevertheless, this chapter argues that the present conjuncture in Scotland presents a unique opportunity to put this right and therefore concludes by proposing an agenda for an anti-racist popular education for the new Scotland.

Racism in Scotland: a living reality

Between January and November 1997 the Commission for Racial Equality (CRE) in Scotland received 328 reports of racial discrimination. During the same period, Scotland's six local Racial Equality Councils received complaints taking the total figure of reported racial incidents in Scotland to at least 1,000 (Commission for Racial Equality, 1997). The CRE is quick to warn that these statistics represent the tip of the iceberg, but they are nevertheless a significant indication that black people in Scotland experience racism. Moreover, this claim has been consistently supported by recent media coverage.

Police statistics also indicate a steady rise in the number of officially recorded racial incidents in Scotland. At an anti–racist rally in Glasgow in March 1998, following the death of a 15 year old Muslim boy, politicians agreed publicly that racially motivated abuse and attacks were on the increase in Scotland. The records of police forces in Scotland of racial incidents show a steady rise in recent years. To some extent, this is evidence of increased confidence to report incidents. On the other hand, it also reflects the reality of everyday racism experienced by Scotland's black population. Moreover, Lothian and Borders Police estimate that only one in twenty victims ever makes a complaint, and significant under-reporting is a fact widely accepted by both the police and anti-racist campaigners. The rise in xenophobia and anti-English feeling also contributes to the sense that racial prejudice and discrimination are intensifying in Scotland. Recent reports in newspapers of anti-English abuse and attacks demonstrate that the sentiments of extremist groups like

Settler Watch and Scottish Watch are gaining appeal. Recognising the growing problem, the government has proposed a new law under the Crime and Disorder Bill to tighten up legislation on racial harassment. This will permit heavier sentences for crimes proven to have racist motives and prevent racial factors from being dropped as aspects of a case during the process of trial or sentencing.

Despite all this evidence, however, education workers talk about the difficulties of persuading colleagues and community members, particularly those in predominantly 'white' areas, to acknowledge the realities of racism. The 'no problem here' attitude is still pervasive in Scotland. Consequently, efforts by professional groups, trade unions, local authorities and political parties to place the issue of racism on the agenda still face an uphill struggle. Where there is an acknowledgment of racism, it tends to be based on a recognition of overt racism, leaving its more subtle and insidious forms little understood or analysed. The reaction of politicians, educationists and the general public to racism has been to denounce it as an aberration from the 'Scottish way of life', which is apparently left-of-centre and non-racist (eg see McCrone, 1994).

So why, given all the statistics and recorded evidence, is racism not a live issue in Scotland today? Why is it still invisible? Why does it remain on the margins of public and popular discourse?

Racism by omission

The lack of attention given to race-related issues by the Scottish Office Education and Industry Department (SOEID) has been one of the primary reasons for this silence and failure to act. SOEID attitudes oscillate between an avoidance of discussion of the problem of racism and tokenistic gestures characterised by piecemeal short-term funding of racial equality initiatives within the voluntary sector. Official concern about racism has been *ad hoc* and superficial, without any real understanding of specific factors such as bicultural and bilingual status, the actual experience of racism or the social impact of policies on different racial and ethnic groups. The SOEID expects issues of race, gender and other types of equality to permeate all aspects of its work.

There are also striking inconsistencies in policy. For example, a Minister for Women's Affairs has recently been appointed, partly in order to make the Scottish Parliament as 'woman-friendly' as possible, and the establishment of a Scottish Women's Consultative Forum to provide a direct channel for women into politics has been proposed. In January 1998 the Scottish Office appointed a Women's Issues Research Consultant with a central role in developing consultation and communication mechanisms. The lobbying for the legitimisation of women's issues as part of mainstream Scottish politics seems therefore to have achieved some significant successes. On the other hand, this does not extend to issues of race and ethnicity, except for the recent appointment of an Advisory Committee on Travelling People in Scotland. Of the 97 listed non-departmental public bodies on the Scottish Office website, not one relates specifically to racial equality or to black people. The presence of black people in policy formulation and implementation in key political and civic bodies in Scotland remains conspicuous by its absence.

Scottish Office Factsheet 15 on ethnic minorities (Scottish Office Information Service, 1998) states that Scotland has proportionately fewer people from ethnic minorities than elsewhere in the UK. For example, compared to a figure of 5.5 per cent for the UK as a whole, ethnic minorities only account for 1.3 per cent of the Scottish population. According to the 1991 census, there are about 62,600 people in Scotland who classify themselves as belonging to non-white ethnic groups. Racial Equality Councils, however, claim that the census statistics are highly inaccurate and that in reality the number of black people (including people of mixed-parentage) in Scotland is likely to be double this figure. This is, nevertheless, a relatively small number and, combined with an absence of a coherent black network, it has resulted in limited lobbying power – unlike the case of women. One outcome of this is that race equality issues have been marginalised, or only included as an afterthought. What is more, the Scottish Office continues to deny funding for research on the impact of racism in education, health and housing. Given the dearth of research on race equality issues, the probable gap between the official line that 'all is well here' and the practical reality of everyday life for black people in Scotland is all the more difficult to gauge.

Part of the reason for official neglect in the past has certainly been the relatively small number of black people in Scotland. However, this alone does not seem to prevent other lobbying groups from making an impact. For example, a small group such as the Scottish Landowners' Federation can apparently be highly influential and lobby central and local government to considerable effect. The assumption by politicians and policy makers that black organisations and groups are not likely to be politically influential has led to the marginalisation of racism as an aspect of Scottish political, economic or public discourse.

The absence of political pressure has also led to a lack of Scottish Office commitment to ethnic monitoring. Since 1989 ethnicity, religion and identification of mother tongue language have been sub-categories in the annual school census, but in February 1997 the Statistics Office advised that these categories be omitted on the grounds of poor returns in previous years. Under the section on teacher monitoring, information on gender, age and religion continues to be collected, but the ethnicity of the Scottish teaching force remains unknown. The Scottish Office intends to reappraise the situation in 2001 when the next national census will be conducted, but in the meantime no attempts are being made to improve data collection and the dissemination of information on race and ethnicity.

This 'colour-blind' approach from politicians and policy makers leads some black activists to doubt that the agenda in the new Scotland will be any more concerned about racial justice than it ever was in the past. Indeed, the decision to keep equality issues at Westminster leads many to suspect that race equality will simply be left off this agenda altogether. Black activists therefore argue that devolution is unlikely to make a great difference to black people in Scotland. Rather, they foresee the prospect of minorities fighting to ensure that race issues are not treated simply as 'add-ons' to other policies.

The problem of popular culture: is 'a man a man for a' that'?

To address racism in Scotland without addressing anti-English attitudes, xenophobia and sectarianism would be to address racism outwith current Scottish cultural and political realities. Popular culture in Scotland, particularly since the Referendum on the Scottish Parliament, is a tangled web of confused and contradictory emotions around issues of national identity. In this context, anti-racist strategies need urgently to grapple with the interconnections between the politics of nationalism, identity and race. The point is that Scotland, perceiving itself a nation and a people subjugated by successive Westminster governments, has difficulty in also seeing itself as a potential oppressor. It is easier to live with the comfortable notion that 'racism is not a problem here'.

Popular beliefs in Scottish egalitarianism must be contextualised within a social identity informed by two dominant histories: a history of subjugation to dominant Anglo-British values and a history laced with distinctively Scottish myths, legends and traditions. Some of the latter include a widespread belief that most Scots have a basic affinity to socialism (Red Clydeside and so on) and also that they place a particularly high value on thrift, hard work and enterprise. What is more, being an oppressed people themselves, Scots have apparently learnt to be tolerant and accepting of others.

In my own anti-discrimination work in Scotland, I am often told that Scots are more concerned about whether someone is English than their skin colour. For years, I have attempted to discuss the difference between, on the one hand, wider concepts of racism in which ideas or beliefs become systematised into a philosophy of 'race' superiority and part of the way in which a society is organised and, on the other, anti-English feeling which takes the form of xenophobia and a dislike of foreigners which is sometimes linked to active racial discrimination. It is necessary to explore this anti-English phenomenon if popular education is to be effective in addressing racism or to incorporate a serious commitment to racial equality.

Lindsay (1997) examines the links between national identity and stereotypes in contemporary Scotland. She conducted a study in which 220 members of the public wrote down identity characteristics they associated with English and Scottish people. A strong pattern of stereotyping emerged about the Scots who saw themselves as fairly comfortable and positive about their identity as friendly, warm, down-to-earth, patriotic and humorous people. There were negative aspects to the Scottish self-image (eg it was tinged with low self-esteem), but these characteristics were not the dominant ones. In contrast, the main elements in the predominant Scots' stereotype of the English included being arrogant, reserved, racist, xenophobic, Tory, individualistic and materialistic. While Lindsay herself would be the first to express caution about the scientific validity of her research, it would be foolhardy to ignore the issues it raises for any attempt to popularise a discourse of anti-racism in Scotland.

Dunlop (1993) argues that the absence of race equality issues in Scottish politics has enabled racism and racial discrimination to become clouded in generalised discussions of nationalism and class politics. On the other hand, it has also been suggested that racism has never been as central to Scottish politics or nationalism as it has been in England. On this view, English nationalism is rooted in notions of empire-building and colonialism which are particularly dependent on a construct of 'race' that encapsulates racism: '. . . racism is the lining of the cloak of nationalism which surrounds and helps define the boundaries of England as an imagined community' (Miles, 1993).

I would argue that Scotland's political and nationalist histories are rooted in a more cultural context. Although the Scots were prominent in British colonial history, which has played an important part in the reproduction of racism and racist stereotyping, in Scotland its articulation with racism has been of a less hostile nature. This is not to deny that forms of racism have become systematised in Scottish institutional practice or the Scottish psyche, but rather to argue that they are not a cornerstone of Scottish politics or nationalism. This is precisely why the struggle for racial justice in Scotland remains so marginal and vulnerable. Lack of acknowledgment of the problem has left the more subtle manifestations of racism denied or simply ignored.

Any anti-racist popular education would seek to draw out these important points and relate them to issues of class, gender, nationalism and cultural identity. Racism dehumanises people. If it is to be understood and challenged, there must be forums and spaces for those who experience it to engage in direct and down-to-earth dialogue with those who are not familiar with it. We need to stop describing ourselves as 'patriotic' while simultaneously describing exactly the same sentiments in other people as 'insular' and 'xenophobic'. A consequence of this is that any popular anti-racist education in Scotland must confront the almost non-reflective consumption of the romantic Scottish stereotypes and myths such as the kailyard, Highland tartanalia and the heroic militarism propagated in recent Hollywood blockbusters like Braveheart and Rob Roy (see Edensor, 1997). This is where we need to start the process of revealing both the distinctions and connections between political and cultural forms of nationalism – and their racist overtones.

Anti-racism, not multiculturalism

Much educational work to achieve racial justice in Scotland has been conducted within a multicultural framework – an altogether apolitical approach with little analysis of dominant values and hegemonic processes. Educationists have utilised multicultural education mainly as a way of viewing differences between people as positive additions which enhance the cultural diversity of Scotland (see Arshad, 1996). This approach has by and large failed to galvanise 'friendships' into an active forum which would allow broader issues (such as law, policy, customs and the economy which promote racism at a cultural, institutional and structural level) to be analysed, addressed and acted on. Consequently, the capitalist and patriarchal systems, with their roots in colonialism and empire, remain relatively unchallenged.

In addition, there continue to be misconceptions by both policy makers and practitioners that racism is caused by fear and ignorance. Racism is no aberration of history, but the fact that it is one of the most consistent features of advanced capitalist societies is little taught – much less understood. Moreover, to equate 'ethnic sensitivity' with 'anti-racism' is to confuse the meaning of the terms. Anti-racist struggle needs to move beyond a concern with cultural difference in order to expose the real inequalities between different ethnic groups. This, of course, is objectionable to power holders because it exposes the material consequences of discriminatory economic and social policies.

Anti-racist education would also have to recognise that both black and white communities have their own views and boundaries as regards racism. There are black and white people who deny the existence of racism, believing deeply in the concept of meritocracy. There are those who support only a multicultural approach of tolerance and harmony and others who argue that racism is a political issue requiring political action and intervention and that racial harmony is no indicator of racial justice. Anti-racist programmes must also acknowledge that there has been little discussion of the kind of consciousness-raising education that is required among 'oppressed' groups about their own feelings, attitudes and experience. Black communities are as diverse as white communities and each person will have particular prejudices, aspirations and priorities. A proactive anti-racist agenda would therefore seek to engage both black and white communities in becoming aware of racism and identifying ways of actively challenging racist structures and behaviours.

Beyond additive strategies

Meekosha (1993) argues that, if we are to cross boundaries, we need to move beyond 'additive' strategies and reassess concepts of universalism, collective provision, multiculturalism and responsible citizenship. She warns that a strategy that satisfies only the needs of specific identity groups is a double-edged sword.

Such a strategy might achieve results for particular groups, but it allows mainstream provision to abdicate any wider sense of responsibility. A more jointly owned anti-racist strategy is required. Popular education which responds to community issues in a spontaneous way alone is also unlikely to be effective in challenging racial injustice. Indeed, anti-racist education should always be proactive. Shukra (1997) argues that all too often those advocating anti-discriminatory practice do so by responding spontaneously to new social movements. This response is often perceived as sufficient evidence of a desire to be anti-discriminatory. The fact that the structures that discriminate remain intact appears to be overlooked. For example, she cites the trade union movement as a change agent which publicly supports anti-oppressive practice whilst doing very little to create real change within union structures and practices in order to ensure a more equal distribution of power among members. It is never easy to create links or to learn to 'own' each other's issues or to develop solidarity from a sense of difference. And yet coalition and alliance building has to be the way forward if we are not to remain an exotic but ineffective myriad of voices and movements, old or new.

At present, due largely to financial cuts and policy fragmentation, different minority groups are beginning to come together to work collaboratively and speak with a united voice. There is a growing realisation that minority voices stand a better chance of being heard if they speak together. It is essential, however, that such partnerships are not just marriages of convenience but that they represent genuine opportunities for those involved to educate each other about how inequality and discrimination impact on them.

Strategic bridge building is not common in Scotland. We tend to opt for single-issue strategies and, when criticised for being exclusive, we adopt 'additive' approaches. Anti-racist education must therefore identify the imperatives for crossing boundaries. Why should a white community be concerned about the racism experienced by black people? Why should people who suffer no racism open themselves up to potential abuse by adopting anti-racist causes? There is an urgent need to convince majority communities of the benefits of anti-racism – as well as the psychological and societal costs of racism. Notions of our common humanity must play a prominent part in any such discussion. Failure to challenge racism legitimises discrimination against particular sections of society and this can, in turn, lead to discrimination against other vulnerable groups.

Consciousness-raising for educators

Many of the boundaries we work within are self-imposed. My work with students and practitioners highlights widespread resistance to placing the issue of racism on the agenda. This is in part due to workers' insecurity about their ability to challenge racism, coupled with anxiety about the types of anti-racist action required. Workers' values and their contact with people who suffer racism play an important part in their willingness to address racism in both theory and practice. They require systematic support both to boost their confidence and to develop their competence to tackle controversial issues in settings in which they may be lone voices and to challenge oppressive practices which are often rationalised in terms of culture and religion.

Research has shown that school children are well aware of racism and racial issues (see Wright, 1992; Burgess-Macey, 1992), but the children themselves also comment on the lack of space for discussion of them in day-to-day classwork. Children feel that their teachers seek to protect them from the ugly aspects of racism, which many already experience in the playground and within their communities. When children hear words like 'pakies', 'darkies' or 'chinks', or see grafitti or hear their parents talk, they need to make sense of what is happening around them.

It has beens suggested that the 'Achilles heel' of Scottish educationists is their unwillingness to engage in political debate. Anti-racism has acquired the stigma of being 'political' in this sense. To be political is to declare a position, thereby conveying a stance of non-neutrality. Neutrality is seen as the hallmark of professionalism. Anti-racism is therefore perceived as unattractive – even dangerous. Multiculturalism, on the other hand, is seductive precisely because it provides the illusion of respecting diversity without accepting the need to recognise or confront the reality of everyday racism.

Silenced voices

One of the most powerful ways to become sensitised to racism is to hear about it from those who experience it. Actively utilising these experiences to educate and awaken the critical consciousness of people is itself the beginning of a process of social change. And yet the voices of Scottish black men, women and children have been strangely silent. Perhaps this is because when they do speak, the authenticity of their voices is called into question. Voices that speak of racism, discrimination and unhappiness are either ignored because they tell stories no one wishes to hear or they are heard with pity. Only examples of overt racism seem to generate real interest. Stories of the racism which is subtle, grinding and destructive do not have the same impact. Anti-racist practice therefore needs to develop a maturity that is prepared to listen, understand and act.

There is little written about what it means to experience racism within a Scottish context. Is being black in Scotland different from being black in England? If so, what are the differences? Black people living in the Highlands talk about isolation and a curious feeling of being visible yet invisible. Others describe their frustrations about their experiences of racism being trivialised as over-reaction on their part. Real dialogue needs to move beyond descriptions of black peoples' life-styles, and attempt to produce explanations and develop theoretical frameworks that account for racism and its effects. It would seek to demonstrate that racism dehumanises and devalues not just its 'victims' but also its perpetrators. This is part of the new counter-hegemony that popular education for racial justice in Scotland must seek to establish.

Being Scottish: towards a definition for the Millennium

The time is ripe for issues of racism and racial discrimination to be taken seriously. On 11 September 1997 the 'settled will of the Scottish people' was expressed in a resounding call for a Scottish Parliament. Think tanks have mushroomed to discuss what form this should take and are actively searching for ways of ensuring that the new Scotland will be 'inclusive', 'open' and 'modern'. There are signs of positive change.

In 1997, after Labour's overwhelming victory in the General Election, the Secretary of State for Scotland signed the CRE's Leadership Challenge, thus committing the Scottish Office and his ministerial team to confront racial discrimination. He also confirmed that he wished the CRE to play an important role in the new Scotland. This is encouraging to those of us who have campaigned long and hard to place anti-racism on the political and civic agendas in Scotland. In addition, many anti-racist practitioners and campaigners recognise that, with proportional representation (including the 'additional member' system), some black candidates stand a realistic chance of being selected and elected. There is therefore a general expectation that the new Scottish Parliament will be more sympathetic to a proactive recognition and challenging of racism and racial discrimination.

Most people in Scotland wish to avoid the kind of national pride that is associated with racial intolerance. They look instead to a national identity that will liberate the Scottish people so that they can shape their own destiny. In this respect, it is important to note that the Scottish National Party leadership has gone to great lengths to say that 'whoever lives in Scotland and feels Scottish' will be regarded as Scottish. Inclusion is apparently the mantra of the new Scotland. Perhaps now more than ever before, there are real opportunities to enable meaningful dialogue to take place about racial justice in Scotland. Would a key task for popular education be to contribute to the shaping of a new sense of what it means to be a Scot? Could it help to build a new understanding of citizenship in a multiracial Scotland? What, then, might a charter for an anti-racist popular education in the new Scotland look like? In my judgement, such a charter would have to:

1) Make racism visible and recognise it to be a daily reality for black communities in Scotland.

2) Develop a critical understanding of the processes of racism within the contemporary Scottish context.
3) Actively confront and counter the reality of personal, cultural, institutional and structural racism.
4) Make the connections between racism and other forms of inequality.
5) Create conceptual and practical space for the systematic development of both anti-racist analysis and anti-racist practice.
6) Understand the difference between 'ethnically-sensitive' practice (which includes multicultural education) and anti-racist practice, ie actions and strategies to challenge racism.
7) Include those who experience racism in the process of shaping future action against it.
8) Engage in consciousness-raising in both black and white communities about racism, as well as other forms of inequality, injustice and discrimination.

An anti-racist popular education needs to lead black/minority ethnic communities beyond the raw sense of oppression towards a consideration of possibilities of living and working in the new Scotland. It must also make members of the white, majority community willing to address their responsibility as citizens to understand racism and counteract it and, most importantly, to incorporate in policy and practice the voices of those suffering the effects of racism. Such an anti-racist education must speak the language of rights (not needs), of lifechances (not lifestyles), of dismantling structures (not merely reforming them). The words of Sivanandan (1995), Director of the Institute of Race Relations, are pertinent to the task we face in the new Scotland when he urges us to:

> . . . organise not for culture but against racism, against fascism, against the erosion of civil liberties, against injustice and inequality – against racism *qua* racism – instead of particularising the racisms. We are organising not for the Bangladeshis in the East End of London but against racism . . .

Above all, popular education for racial justice in the new Scotland must begin from the experience and the aspirations of those who have been on the receiving end of racism.

References

Arshad, R (1996) 'Anti-racist community work: a radical approach' in Cooke, I and Shaw, M (eds) *Radical Community Work: Perspectives from Practice in Scotland,* Edinburgh, Moray House Publications, pp 151–168.
Burgess-Macey, C (1992) 'Tackling racism and sexism in the primary classrooms' in Gill, D, Mayor, B and Blair, M (eds) *Racism and Education: Structures and Strategies,* London, Sage Publications, pp 269–283.
Commission for Racial Equality (1997) *Connections* No 4, London, CRE, pp 8–9.

Dunlop, A (1993) 'Anti-racist politics in Scotland', *Scottish Affairs*, 3, Edinburgh, Unit for the Study of Government in Scotland, University of Edinburgh, pp 89–100.

Edensor, T (1997) ' Reading Braveheart: representing and contesting Scottish identity', *Scottish Affairs* 21, Edinburgh, Unit for the Study of Government in Scotland, University of Edinburgh, pp 135–158.

Lindsay, I (1997) 'The uses and abuses of national stereotypes', *Scottish Affairs*, 20, Edinburgh, Unit for the Study of Government in Scotland, University of Edinburgh, pp 133– 148.

Meekosha, H (1993) 'The bodies politic: equality, difference and community practice' in Butcher, H, Glen, A, Henderson, P and Smith, J (eds) *Community and Public Policy,* London, Pluto Press, pp 171–194.

Miles, R (1993) *Racism after 'Race Relations',* London, Routledge.

McCrone, D (1994) 'Who do we think we are?, *Scottish Affairs* 6, Edinburgh, Unit for the Study of Government in Scotland, University of Edinburgh, pp 1–4.

Scottish Office Information Service (1998) Internet at "www.scotland.gov.uk". See Recruitment: Women's Issues Research Consultant.

Shukra, K (1997) 'The death of a black political movement', *Community Development Journal,* 32 (3), pp 233–243.

Sivanandan, A (1995) 'Building unity', *Campaign Against Racism and Fascism* No. 24 , London, CARF Publications, pp 10–12.

Wright, C (1992) 'Early education: multiracial primary school classrooms' in Gill, D, Mayor, B and Blair, M (eds) *Racism and Education: Structures and Strategies,* London, Sage Publications, pp 5–41.

24 Instrumental objectives and liberal values: squaring the circle

Margaret Beveridge

This chapter is based on the author's experience as a WEA tutor, teaching a Scotvec module in the 'transferable skill' of Communication to a group of unemployed adult students. In it she suggests that the apparent contradiction between the instrumental objectives of competence and the liberal values of discussion and critical enquiry may be more imagined than real. Funding regimes increasingly demand the former, but the critical and creative autonomy of the educator can also promote the latter. In the contemporary Scottish context the curriculum of cultural studies presents peculiarly rich opportunities for squaring this particular circle.

Introduction

As Richard Johnson observes in his discussion of the roots of radical education, we have been living through 'a period of deep educational reaction', with an increasing emphasis on skills and training informed by a view of education for the majority which is heavily instrumental – 'merely useful knowledge' as opposed to 'really useful knowledge' (Johnson, 1988). In such times, independent, democratic organisations such as the Workers' Educational Association (WEA) have had to struggle to find ways to survive without compromising their fundamental purposes. The WEA, like other adult and community education organisations, depends on public funding. Of necessity, this requires accommodation to the interests of funding bodies. Accredited competence is now an integral part of this, and attainment must be verifiable and recorded. It is a view of the purpose of learning that is at odds with the traditional philosophy of the WEA with its general emphasis on the discussion-based tutorial group and, in particular, the Socratic method of enquiry. Despite this, however, in the scramble to attract increasingly elusive funding, the organisation has felt forced to offer vocational qualifications.

There are major issues here regarding the difference between education and training and whether the learning process can be adequately represented by a series of boxes to tick. At the same time, however, casually employed, part-time tutors like myself (and many others working in community-based adult education) must, at least in the short-term, find ways to engage as creatively as possible with the limitations of the present situation. In this chapter I would like to suggest two things: first, vocational qualifications can be offered without interfering too much with what we, as adult educators, may consider to be the 'real' educational aims of our work; second, there may actually be *positive* aspects to offering this kind of qualification – at least for our students.

Developing a critical curriculum

The dilemma for WEA tutors is to produce curricula which can offer students the type of education of which the Association is justifiably proud in the face of the narrowly conceived vocationalism and skills-based requirements of the present funding regime. This was the challenge taken up by the Lothian WEA in 1995 in a course targeting unemployed people and offering, as part of the provision, a Scotvec module in Communication. The course took place on a Friday and the day was divided into three sessions: Media Studies, Scottish Studies and Creative Writing. The idea was to build on the innovations of Colin Kirkwood and Sally Griffiths (1984) who developed a similar course in the 1980s. Our aims were in many ways similar, particularly in the attempt to combine critical understanding and practical skills in a course for unemployed people.

Students were recruited in a variety of ways: through the usual WEA channels – mailing members, leaflets in libraries and community centres, direct contact with job centres and benefits offices, and by liaising with other adult education agencies. This produced a diverse group of people joining the course for a variety of purposes. Most were attracted by the suggested course content, but several, at an early stage, expressed a specific interest in gaining a vocational qualification. One Middle-Eastern woman was hoping both to improve her English in order to study nursing and to find out more about her new country. Another woman was an expert in local history, but needed to improve her reading and writing skills to take a qualification in reflexology. Another was hoping to gain entry to Newbattle Abbey College (Scotland's only adult residential college), and then to university. The combination of Scottish issues and creative writing attracted two men with literary interests and aspirations. Another man, who was the main carer for elderly parents, had to fit his own career and educational goals around this. Two older women were only now 'finding time for themselves'. The promise of a creche also drew a few mothers with young children. This formed the core group of around 10 students, all of whom attended regularly and eight of whom formally registered for the module. In general, these were all people who, although perceiving themselves as 'unemployed', had a variety of aims, commitments and interests which they were keen to explore and share.

Whilst each session was offered by a different tutor who negotiated content separately with students, they were thematically linked. The priority was the development of a curriculum that would allow students to work through issues and relate them to their own situations. Central to this was the aim of encouraging people to develop a critical view of the world and their own position in it. The emphasis throughout was on the skills of textual analysis and the creation of meaning. Media Studies familiarised students with sophisticated techniques of critical reading: identifying preferred readings; reading oppositionally; identifying and examining representations and stereotypes; looking for exclusions; being aware of the ideologies and assumptions which inform texts and locating these within a context of ownership and control. The Scottish Studies input was an attempt to take the same skills of critical analysis and apply them to a wider social context. This was both an opening out from media studies to cultural analysis and a focusing in on the contemporary situation in Scotland – on us as Scots and any other identities we might have. Central to the curriculum that was negotiated with the group were their own experiences: as unemployed people, as single parents, as males or females, as Scottish (or not), as politically powerless, as displaced, or isolated, or homeless – as people with things to offer. These experiences were located in the curriculum in relation to three specific considerations: education, work and gender roles, identity, and the ideological construction of 'Scotland'. Each of these 'ways of seeing' was traced historically and politically, using a variety of resources. In this way, art and literature, which students had also identified as areas of interest, were not studied in isolation but seen as part of a wider social context, a way of examining attitudes past and present. Such an approach is not new. A major influence was Raymond Williams, himself a WEA tutor, who argued that by relating 'history to art and literature, including contemporary culture', learning becomes 'part of the process of social change itself' (Williams, 1989).

Accreditation: finding the spaces

Whilst there were opportunities to complete learning outcomes in all three sessions, the bulk of the assessment took place within the work on Scottish Studies. This was partly because I was the tutor most familiar with the Scotvec system and most at ease with the assessment procedures. The general aim, however, was to ensure that communication skills were not assessed in isolation, abstracted from their social, political or ideological context. My own previous experience of developing and delivering National Certificate modules, both in secondary schools and in various community-based adult education projects in and around Edinburgh, suggested that they need neither be narrowly vocational nor inhibit student choice or curriculum development. A module descriptor's emphasis on 'performance criteria' and 'learning outcomes' leaves a great deal of scope as far as content is concerned. This offers possibilities for purposeful educational engagement within the constraints of vocationalism.

The Communication module was chosen for two reasons. First, 'communication' is generally acknowledged to be a 'core skill' in vocational education parlance, ie a skill which enhances performance and efficiency in a variety of work-related situations. As such, it meets the requirements of funding bodies. Second, the module has four learning outcomes, covering reading, writing, listening and talking – skills (particularly writing and spelling) which adult returners often feel they lack. This proved true in initial interviews and curriculum negotiation, just as it had in the original work of Kirkwood and Griffiths (1984). Whilst Creative Writing specifically allowed students to write and tell their own stories, in all three sessions there were opportunities for people to create their own narratives in other ways (spoken, visual, using radio and video) both individually and as a group. This was a deliberate attempt to move students away from the focus on written skills as the only indicator of literacy in our society. Given this critical agenda, it seemed to me that a Communication module which specifically required students to examine and comment on the motivation behind the construction of texts and which required written responses in only one of four outcomes could be employed quite creatively. Rather unusually also, the module can be delivered at different levels (one to four) allowing a flexibility and route of progression not generally associated with vocational qualifications. I focused mainly on level three, quite commonly used with adults in community-based projects. Outcomes require students to: 'demonstrate an understanding of accessible written communication; produce well structured written communication; demonstrate an understanding of accessible spoken communication; deliver and participate in sustained spoken communication'. It is at a level which makes intellectual demands of students, but within contexts which should be fairly familiar to them.

One criticism of skills of this kind is that they are 'add-on'; they do not significantly change a person, are not really part of an educational process. This is reflected in the Scotvec module descriptors which are not about content but about what students have to do, as measured by 'performance criteria'. However, this creates a gap between intention and outcome which educators can exploit. Examination of the performance criteria for reading and listening, which focused on purpose, audience, stance and techniques used to achieve a specified purpose, suggested that they could be used to develop similar skills of critical analysis as students were learning in media studies. For example, as education and assessment were important issues for many students, an early activity was the examination of school league tables. Whilst the text as it stood was considered fairly straightforward and accessible, strategies were explored for extracting and examining specific information. Selecting local schools and plotting information on graphs served to emphasise inequalities in results. Locating the schools geographically added to the store of information. The aim here was to show how information can be distorted or obscured in texts which are apparently accessible by learning to read 'between' the lines! Looking at the sociology behind this raised questions of class and education's role in reproducing social inequality. This was then put in a specifically Scottish context by examining the 'lad o' pairts' myth which celebrates the allegedly egalitarian nature of Scottish education whereby no-one of ability, regardless of status, is denied educational opportunity. This can leave students for whom this has not been the case – many adult returners, for example – with a profound sense of personal failure.

There are, of course, parallels here with the present trend in vocational education in which, once again, failure tends to be individualised and personalised. These connections were made and examined. This did not solve the problem, but the course became something of a collaboration between students and tutors to bend the vocational element to their own ends. In the same way, the criteria for writing and talking are, from the student's point of view, about learning to take control. These criteria require students, for example, to adopt conventions appropriate to 'the writer's' or 'speaker's' (ie the student's) purpose and audience. This is about using skills as tools – not as an end in themselves. A study of the language of the module descriptor is itself useful because jargon can readily be identified and its purpose examined. Value-laden terms such as 'accessible', 'appropriate', 'coherent', 'justified' and 'evaluation' raise questions of power and control which can be addressed – in such a way, for example, that if the purpose of monitoring procedures is to suggest that students are culpable (ie personally responsible for their own unemployment), this can be countered and subverted.

Having identified issues such as class or gender, we were able to trace them historically, examining the role of the past in creating present conditions and looking for exclusions. Recently republished female writers of the eighteenth, nineteenth and early twentieth century, such as Susan Ferrier and Catherine Carswell, proved an excellent source of information about one group whose history has been suppressed within Scottish culture. The development of Scottish male stereotypes such as 'the hard man' were examined through texts such as William McIlvanney's stories and television programmes like Rab C Nesbitt. The use of texts as triggers or codifications in this way allowed students and tutors a way into an issue that was less confrontational and less threatening than relying solely on personal experience or anecdote.

Whilst there are similarities here with Freire's methods, there was no suggestion that these texts, when decoded, would reveal 'reality'. Students were already aware, from media studies, that a message could be read in a variety of ways and that there was no one, definitive reading. Any representation of reality is selective and exclusive. Much of the writing and art we examined, for example, was male-dominated with outdated ideas of workplace and gender. The concept of 'working class' was tied up with nostalgic ideas of a poor but happy, close-knit, supportive 'community' – as in the comedy of Billy Connolly. On the other hand, newer writers such as Irvine Welsh presented depictions of worklessness and survival which some of the students found difficult to accept. It became obvious that we all, to a certain extent, create our own reality and reject anything which does not fit into this construct. An important part of the learning process is to explore and challenge these boundaries. I used, for example, as a reading assignment, a piece from the *Big Issue* written by a member of Glasgow's Asian community which attacked the Western way of life. Her portrayal of an isolating, unsupportive society was completely at odds with the concept of community which many working class Scots adhere to. For students, the communication skill involved was in understanding and evaluating the argument. The educational process would be focused on the reasons for accepting or rejecting it.

Students explored their own responses further by, for example, reviewing contemporary literature, preparing reports on exhibitions and compiling media reviews. All of them were encouraged to present work in this way whether or not they were covering the 'outcomes' in reading, writing, listening and talking required by the module. For students who had identified writing skills as an area for development this was a more structured exercise than a piece of creative writing. For those aiming to progress to further education it provided useful practice in structuring arguments. Most importantly, what was demonstrated was that authoritative texts which inform our own opinions are created by individuals with specific agendas and preconceptions. Trips out emphasised this point. We visited places or exhibitions students might not otherwise have considered. There was a constant challenging of students' self-imposed or culturally determined boundaries. Edinburgh University's School of Scottish Studies, for example, with research projects on Gaelic place names, traditional ballads and folk tales, was creating a very different Scotland to that experienced by most students. Typically, I prepared information packs beforehand with questions structured to help explore specific issues identified by students. On a visit to the National Portrait Gallery, therefore, questions led students through displays chronologically focusing on issues of power (who was famous in seventeenth century Scotland? why?) and gender (why and how were women painted in the past? when did individual women achieve power or fame in their own right?). The information gleaned was useful not just to focus discussion, but could be used to prepare reports, verbal or written, which would fulfil the performance criteria for the communication module. In this way, study skills such as summary, note-taking, listening for specific information and report writing become an integral part of the course, enabling students to organise and consolidate their learning in a way that discussion alone could not. The limitations of such a strategy are obvious – to control the questions is to control the discourse. Students were not unaware of this and, as the course progressed, they began to formulate their own questions, creating their own narratives of inquiry.

Dilemmas and decisions

It would be disingenuous to suggest that there was no conflict between the intellectual independence promoted by the tutorial group and the demands of the module, which meant the tutor must decide when a student had reached a certain level of 'competence'. Yet by ensuring that assessment is something that students opt into they may still retain some control. In fact, here the 'add-on' nature of skills can actually be an asset. It is possible for students to acknowledge and utilise the professional expertise (skills?) of the tutor without conceding their own right to think and act critically, particularly if the purpose of much of the teaching has been to encourage them to do just that. Indeed, this has traditionally been fostered by the Socratic method employed in WEA tutorial groups. Williams, arguing the case for literary and cultural studies in the early sixties, saw no problem with the fact that the tutor had specialist knowledge that students did not possess:

> Of course the tutor knows his discipline better and wants to help the students to learn it, but he may not know how his discipline looks to people outside it, may not know the gaps between academic thinking and actual experience among many people; he may not know when, in the pressure of experience, a new discipline has to be created. (Williams, in McIlroy and Westwood, 1993)

The point is that students also have knowledge that the tutor does not possess. It would have been unlikely in any case that one tutor would have been expert in all the areas of Scottish culture which students wished to explore. I certainly was not. Students were encouraged to make presentations based on their own diverse areas of interest or expertise. These included, for example, local history, homelessness, Scottish ballads, single parenthood and childhood memories. In some cases, these were also assessed as communication learning outcomes. For students, this can be seen as a formal recognition of the significance of their own knowledge and experience as well as their skills.

If we see learning itself as part of a continuous process, rather than just an outcome, then the purpose of most assessment is diagnostic, and it becomes part of the educational experience itself for both students and tutor. And if the correct performance criteria have been identified, these should help lead students through a learning experience. For example, questions on a Scottish news programme were structured in such a way that students who had initially identified its purpose as simply to convey information were likely to reconsider this on the strength of their answers. Focus on the appearance, voice and function of the newsreader, the order and subject matter of news stories, the images chosen and the ideology behind such choices all suggested that this was more than a simple representation of a given reality. Gradually such textual support can be reduced so that students are left with a set of core questions, taken directly from the performance criteria, which can be applied to any text.

Furthermore, this type of externally imposed assessment may require education to be accountable, and it helps to demystify the assessment process for students who have been labelled 'failures' in the past without knowing why. This can be seen either as students being rendered 'responsible for their own surveillance' (Shaw and Crowther, 1995) or beginning to take control of their own learning. Probably both are true. Even summative assessment leaves space for remediation. We can all learn from our mistakes.

Tutors are certainly accountable, but I did not consider myself 'deskilled' by these procedures – another criticism of such instrumental approaches. Instead, I found the production of materials, which were integrated into the course as a whole and which enhanced the students' learning whilst improving their communication skills, a task of some intellectual rigour and, as such, both educational and satisfying. For the educator there is little that is *ad hoc* about such an approach, which requires a great deal more preparation than the acquisition of a few generic group work techniques. The non-directive approach adopted by many supposedly radical educators has been rightly criticised as a misinterpretation of Freire's work (Kirkwood, 1991), but it is still an attractive one for educators striving to be democratic and fearful of reproducing the school experience. It is for the same reason that many are suspicious of qualifications, but by rejecting assessment they could be denying students something which is, in fact, very important to them. Of the eight students who had registered for the module, six completed all the outcomes. The two who did not, continued to attend but, on being offered places on the courses of their choice (at Newbattle Abbey College and Second Chance to Learn), they felt that they did not need the module. For several, this was the first 'academic' qualification they had been awarded. Whilst some saw it as a first step into more formal education or employment, at least two women in their fifties or sixties had no such vocational goals. They had regarded it as a personal challenge and were delighted by their success.

The module was externally verified by a Scotvec moderator who was impressed by the range and scope of the topics covered and the assignments offered. On the other hand, the funding body for this work as, specifically, a 'course for unemployed people' was less impressed. Inspectors were quite specific about who qualified as 'unemployed' and suggested that the course was not attracting this 'target group'. People with long-term educational goals, married women with children, women over a certain age, and people with other commitments which limited their availability for work, were apparently not eligible. A course 'for unemployed people' is not the same as a 'training for work course' and the title had been carefully chosen, but funding specifications, unsurprisingly, were tied to the benefits system. There are real problems, however, in denying people, mainly women in this instance, even the status of being unemployed, when, as the group had discovered, in this society, class and identity are closely linked to work roles. For me, there are issues here for 'workers' education' – issues of gender and exclusion, for example, which are more pressing than any perceived liberal/vocational divide.

Conclusion: overcoming false dichotomies

Malcolm Tight (1996) points out that the terms 'liberal' and 'vocational' are 'imprecise, emotional and ideological', and warns of the dangers of dichotomising in this way: 'Liberal and vocational become defined in terms of each other, or, rather, in terms of distorted and partial perceptions of each other.'

At worst, 'merely useful knowledge' is, after all, not useless. Even at a purely instrumental level, the Communication module offered skills which students had wished to acquire or improve. Even adhering to the notion of 'transferable skills', central to the vocational discourse, it is quite logical that students could take the skills and techniques of textual analysis they had acquired and apply them to texts and situations in their own lives. A course in 'Communication', covering 'learning outcomes' in reading, writing, listening and talking need not simply be a course in functional literacy:

> The value of writing, speaking and listening should not be seen as access to 'refined culture' or to 'life skills' for our allotted (by whom?) places in the paid and unpaid labour market, but as a crucial means to gain power and control of our entire lives. (Apple, 1993)

The point of the course had been to show that liberal values and instrumental objectives could happily co-exist. Students were able to improve their communication skills in reading, writing, listening and talking and gain a recognised qualification whilst at the same time be involved in the sort of democratic educational process which the WEA has always seen as its goal. Despite this, however, it seemed to me that there was some element of collusion here. As adult educators, we were aware that to offer a course expressly 'for unemployed people' might seem to students to imply a personal culpability for their situation which the course was aiming to redress. And yet, in attempting to exclude this kind of message from the hidden curriculum, we could be accused of buying into accreditation and credentialism to foster an equally dubious form of individualistic opportunism and 'enterprise'. Perhaps whilst we must continue to operate within the current policy context, such compromises are the best that we can do.

References

Apple, M W (1993) *Official Knowledge: Democratic Education in a Conservative Age*, London, Routledge.

Johnson, R (1988) 'Really useful knowledge, 1790–1850: memories for education in the 1980s' in Lovett, T (ed) *Radical Approaches to Adult Education*, London, Routledge, pp 3–34.

Kirkwood, C and Griffiths, S (eds) (1984) *Adult Education and the Unemployed*, Edinburgh, WEA.

Kirkwood, G (1991) 'Fallacy: the community educator should be a non-directive facilitator' in O'Hagan, B (ed), *The Charnwood Papers: Fallacies in Community Education*, Ticknall, Education Now, pp 40–55.

McIlroy, J and Westwood, S (1993) *Border Country: Raymond Williams in Adult Education*, Leicester, NIACE pp 222–225.

Shaw, M and Crowther, J (1995) 'Beyond subversion' in Mayo, M and Thompson, J (eds), *Adult Learning, Critical Intelligence and Social Change*, Leicester, NIACE, pp 204–218.

Tight, M (1996) *Key Concepts in Adult Education and Training*, London, Routledge.

Williams, R (1989) *What I Came to Say*, London, Hutchinson.

25 Equal opportunities: back to basics

Jane Meagher

Equal opportunities work tends to be concerned with the politics of identity and difference rather than the politics of class. This creates real dilemmas and contradictions for the practitioner who has a serious commitment to working for social justice and equality of outcome. In this chapter, the author reviews her own experience of the confusions and delusions that arise in equal opportunities work when the distinction between exploitation and oppression is not understood or addressed. Political correctness is no substitute for hard headed analysis.

Whatever happened to class?

The struggle to make sense of, and do something about, the urgent and often contradictory demands of new social movements, whilst at the same time holding on to a fundamental belief in class analysis, has presented enormous challenges to me as both community education worker and feminist. Equal opportunities is the local authority policy context in which, over the last 18 years, I have tried – or been forced – to work out some of the dilemmas and challenges implicit in this. The ragbag of policies, legislation and local initiatives that jostle uncomfortably together under the banner of equal opportunities create a space for groups to challenge orthodoxy and stake out their own territory. Each emerging or nascent movement seems to claim anew our attention, energy and commitment, frequently challenging the traditional way of doing things – and sometimes asserting its primacy over other issues and interests in the scramble to secure scant resources from ever diminishing budgets. Nevertheless, in my time as a community education worker I have been surprised at the erosion amongst my colleagues of the language of class and the demise of class analysis as a way of informing practice. Perhaps we have been quietly putting away these notions, knowing that such talk would find no favour with our political masters or even believing that society has truly changed, making such old ideas irrelevant in the 'new' order. At the same time, there has been an upsurge in women's groups, multiculturalism and anti-racism, gay and lesbian rights and, most recently, the disability movement and its demands for inclusion.

In attempting to address the legitimate demands of these groups and individuals, is it still appropriate and relevant to assert an analysis that takes class into account? And – in some ways more of a challenge – how do we work with groups and individuals whose sense of identity is so strongly located in, say, gender or disability or sexuality that class no longer feels significant? Similarly, as workers employed, arguably, to manage dissent and disaffection, how do we approach the complexity and diversity of lived experience that crosses and recrosses the neat, discrete categories created by well meaning but clumsy equal opportunties policies and their funding requirements? And all this in a context where many would argue that class no longer exists or is an outmoded 'meta-narrative', irrelevant in a postmodern society that is pluralist and meritocratic.

The elisions and evasions of equal opportunities

Many of these struggles were crystallised in the equal opportunities group I belonged to in an inner city secondary school where I was employed for 10 years as a community education worker. In spite of its title, the group had started life with a specific remit for the development of multicultural education. From the early days, there were some who were content to continue in this vein but there were also others who wished to push the institution into a more critical awareness of its own role in perpetuating the very inequalities that the group was attempting to ameliorate, moving from a multicultural perspective to place other sources of inequality – in particular sexism – alongside racism. The question of class, ironically in the context of a largely working class school, was not explicitly referred to, although it was clearly a major issue as far as educational attainment was concerned.

In 1988, as part of a regular programme of annual lectures on the theme of equality, the group invited Gus John to speak on Anti-Racist Education and Democracy. Gus John had been a member of the MacDonald Enquiry which was set up to look into the circumstances surrounding the racist murder by a white school boy of a black school boy in Burnage, Manchester in 1987. The suppressed report was leaked to a local newspaper which quoted its conclusions word for word. The report was dynamite, coming as it did at the height of Thatcherism and incorporating a class analysis at the centre of its findings. It was, the report noted, strange that 'the practice of the Community Education Department at Burnage appears to have ignored the notion of "community" as necessarily embracing the white community and multiculturalism as including the culture of the whole working class. This we find regrettable' (*Manchester Evening News* 25.4.88).

There were clear parallels with our own situation in Edinburgh, as well as some significant differences. The challenge was to do something about the problem, but first of all there were many contradictions and tensions to be made explicit. Interestingly, Gus John indicated that Manchester City Council had originally intended to include 'class' in their equal opportunities statement, but eventually decided not to because they feared it would lead them into areas that were too controversial. This fear resonated with our own experience. Class was a risky subject, even in Scottish community education circles where it was part of our stated aim to equip people to address and challenge poverty, marginalisation and disadvantage. Any explicit attempts to consider class were resisted on the grounds that the whole notion rests on a structural conflict of interests. This way of thinking was, apparently, outmoded and inappropriate in a post-industrial era in which traditional working class occupations and the sense of identity and solidarity that goes with them had all but disappeared. Home ownership and increased affluence, it was argued, had led to a fragmentation of the working class, leaving a residual 'underclass' of chronically unemployed people with little or no stake in 'civilised' society. However, the evidence (eg Goldthorpe and Marshall, 1992) does not support this view: class remains a strong source of collective identity and there is little sign of a move away from a 'closed' class society towards a more 'open' and meritocratic one. Furthermore, writers like Sivanandan (1989), whilst acknowledging that we are living in what he calls 'a time of displacement', argue that little has fundamentally changed and that capitalism is merely in the process of global regrouping, creating deep divisions between the 'underdeveloped' and the (over)developed countries of the world.

Here, then, are two challenges for community-based popular education. First, we must resist the erosion of the language of class and consequently the removal of the reality of class from critical scrutiny. How are we to problematise the debate over inequality if we uncritically screen out of our thinking the idea that poverty and injustice are not merely pathological or accidental but rather the direct consequence of structural divisions and inequalities in our society? Second, how do we, in practical terms, operate within what Rattansi (1992) calls the 'complex intertwining' of race, gender, disability and sexuality with class in a way that acknowledges lived experience whilst avoiding the trap of creating a hierarchy of oppression – all the while working within a local authority culture that seeks to contain dissent?

I don't claim to know the answers to these questions in any final sense, but I do understand from my own work some of the consequences of ignoring them. An illustration of this comes from a workshop I was running with a group of white boys as part of an equal opportunities day which aimed to raise awareness of racism and sexism with the intention of combating them. In the course of the session, there was a sudden eruption of angry racism and sexism from the boys. They were clearly furious and resentful – obviously in no state to empathise with the experience of their black or female peers or to consider their own racism or sexism, let alone contemplate mending their ways. These boys were mainly working class and what I had failed to take into account and acknowledge was their own 'lived experience' of class as a fundamental source of inequality and exploitation. It seems to me now that a better starting point would have been to work with the group to begin to identify and express their own sense of alienation before attempting to make connections with any of the other forms of oppression they or their peers experienced and/or perpetrated.

Over the 20 years I have been practising, community education work has become increasingly concerned with the issues and challenges presented by the new social movements – feminism, the black and anti-racist movements, disabled rights campaigns, gay and lesbian rights, older people and the environmental movement. In responding to these legitimate challenges, there is a tendency among workers to treat people as if they should or could fit into neatly defined and discrete categories such as 'ethnic minorities', 'women', 'disabled' or 'disadvantaged' – ignoring the fact that their everyday, lived experience does not fit neatly into the convenient funding or policy categories we create for them. Moreover, there is a real danger than an uncritical acceptance of such 'category politics' encourages the postmodernist emphasis on diversity and difference at the expense of a class analysis as a way of explaining a system that creates and sustains deep inequalities within our society. And all of this in the face of incontrovertible evidence that, over these last two decades, there has been a systematic intensification of class-based inequalities: increasing social and economic polarisation; the disempowerment of the trade unions; deterioration in pay and conditions of women newly drawn into the labour market; new immigration controls; benefit reductions for single parents. In this context, it is easy to see how category politics of this kind can be used to legitimate a trend in policy that moves away from the provision of good, accessible, universal services towards one that develops selective services for specific groups – and is cheaper for increasingly cash-starved local government to provide. And, of course, we have to remember that the targeting of services remains at the heart of New Labour's commitment to 'modernise' welfare.

I have located my own struggle within the context of local authority equal opportunities policy because that is where the issues crystallise for me. I have come to feel that in some respects equal opportunities is actually a way of avoiding the fundamental problem of inequality and relegating all the other issues to the sidelines where they can be safely managed. It is still the case that the needs of minority ethnic groups are dealt with separately under equal opportunities policies in Scotland – so that Urdu, for instance, is not treated as a modern language in most schools but is taught after school hours and under less than ideal conditions. What is more, the emphasis on equal opportunities may be a convenient excuse for ignoring class. Manchester cannot be the only authority to find that trying to alleviate the effects of class-based inequality was simply too profound a challenge because it strikes at the very foundations of our society. It is far easier to seek comfort in parcelling out bits of equality of opportunity – not of outcome – to groups who can safely be accommodated in mainstream provision. Ignoring class makes this process of accommodation easier because it stifles dissent whilst allowing the articulate, middle class and acceptable faces of ethnicity, gender, sexuality or disability to negotiate their demands within a framework which filters out class.

Furthermore, we need to ask whether class can be taken as merely one difference among many others or whether there is something about class that is fundamentally different, that sets it aside from other equal opportunities issues. If class is primarily about structured economic inequality, where material life chances are linked with cultural differences, it is clearly inappropriate simply to subsume it within a discourse of difference. This is not necessarily to argue that a class analysis alone is enough, nor to belittle the demands or achievements of the new social movements. It is, however, to recognise that class analysis provides an historical explanation for a structure of inequality that is too deep rooted to be eliminated by equal opportunities initiatives. Raising the issue of women's right to equal treatment in the job market appears to be acceptable, and it is unquestionably desirable. Raising the spectre of class, on the other hand, seems to be simply too threatening – certainly at the level of policy making and often at the level of practice. Class analysis exposes the liberal values of tolerance and respect for difference that underpin much equal opportunities work as irrelevant and patronising. To celebrate difference on this basis is nonsensical.

Putting class back on the agenda

The reality of everyday practice is that we must look for spaces to engage in debate and find ways of developing our work around issues of social justice and equality in difficult circumstances. We must seek and find allies where we can, and this may of necessity be in equal opportunities work. But my experience is that to ignore class as a mediating factor and as a potential basis of solidarity is damaging and dangerous. This is not to suggest that we can ignore the problems, contradictions and tensions of an explicitly class-based practice, but it is to argue that we should set out to confront them in a more open and honest way.

References

Goldthorpe, J H and Marshall, G (1992) 'The promising future of class analysis: a response to recent critiques', *Sociology*, 26 (3), pp 381–400.

Rattansi, A (1992) 'Changing the subject' in Donald, J and Rattansi A (eds) *Race, Culture and Difference*, London, Sage, pp 11–49.

Sivanandan, A (1989) 'The hokum of New Times', *Race and Class*, 31 (3), pp 1–31.

List of contributors

Rowena Arshad is Lecturer in Equity and Rights at Moray House Institute of Education, University of Edinburgh and Director of the Centre for Education for Racial Equality in Scotland (CERES). A community activist in race equality and black civil rights issues, she was a member of the Scotland Forward executive, campaigning for a Scottish Parliament. An active trade unionist, she has recently taken up the first black woman's seat on the STUC General Council. She has published widely in the area of race and gender in education.

Jean Barr co-ordinates postgraduate courses in adult and continuing education at the University of Glasgow's Department of Adult and Continuing Education. She has worked in adult education since 1982, as District Secretary of the West of Scotland District of the WEA and then at the universities of Warwick and Stirling. She is the author (with Lynda Birke) of *Talking Science: Gender, Race and Knowledge* (1998) and is currently working on a book for NIACE called *Transforming Knowledge: Women, Adult Education and Really Useful Knowledge*.

Margaret Beveridge is an adult educator in a variety of community-based projects in and around Edinburgh. A former English teacher, her main areas of interest are communication, media and cultural studies and creative writing. She has worked extensively with adult returners in the WEA, Second Chance to Learn and The People's College.

Alice Brown is Professor of Politics at the University of Edinburgh. She writes and researches in the areas of Scottish politics, women and politics and post-war economic policy. She is vice-convenor of the Unit for the Study of Government in Scotland and assistant editor of the journal *Scottish Affairs*. She is a founder member of both Engender and the Women's Co-ordination Group, and was a Commissioner on the Scottish Constitutional Convention (1993–94). Her co-authored books include *Politics and Society in Scotland* (1996 and 1998) and *The Scottish Electorate* (1998).

Jim Crowther has been actively involved in research and adult and community education for 10 years. He is currently a lecturer in community education at Moray House Institute of Education, University of Edinburgh. He is a founder member of the Popular Education Forum for Scotland, a member of the editorial group of *Concept* – the Scottish journal for community education – and has published work on the educative dimension of social movements and developments in critical literacy.

Lorraine Dick was born and educated in Muirhouse, Edinburgh. She has worked in the community education field for 12 years in a variety of different city centre and community-based projects. After studying history and history of art, utilising her early experience in publishing and using outreach strategies, she has forged links with museums, design, history and popular culture as an integral part of her educational work.

John Dickie spent five years as a community development officer in Malawi, and then seven years as community relations officer with what is now Lothian Racial Equality Council. After a foray into primary school teaching brought very mixed results, he now helps his wife run their guest house, leads a group producing a local community newspaper, and researches and teaches local history.

Robert Duncan has been a Tutor Organiser with the WEA since 1980, working mainly in Lanarkshire and the west of Scotland. He is a history specialist, and the author and editor of many publications in labour and community history.

David Fisher first heard about Socialist Sunday Schools through involvement in an oral history project, and spent two years researching the movement, conducting interviews with former 'little comrades' in Edinburgh and Glasgow. He is currently an information worker in the National Health Service. He continues to do historical research when he can, his current interest being in fellow-travellers and the left during the 1940s and 1950s.

Vernon Galloway is an adult educator working with the Adult Learning Project in Edinburgh. He has worked in a range of community settings and has acted as consultant to several communities across Scotland. He has been published in the *Scotsman* and the *Edinburgh Review* and is currently at work on a manual of cultural action. He is actively involved in the Scottish Civic Assembly and a founder member of the Popular Education Forum for Scotland.

Liam Kane formerly worked as a language teacher in Latin America and as a development education worker for Oxfam in Glasgow. He is currently a lecturer in modern languages and adult education at the University of Glasgow's Department of Adult and Continuing Education, and researches and teaches on popular education in Latin America. He is a founder member of the Popular Education Forum for Scotland.

Elinor Kelly joined the University of Glasgow in 1992 as Senior Lecturer in Equality Studies in the Department of Adult and Continuing Education, where she is developing a programme of education for community development workers in the West of Scotland and Pakistan. She also organises training to challenge racism and lectures on equality issues to access, undergraduate, postgraduate and overseas students. She is currently researching community development in Pakistan, minority rights in relation to religion, and language issues in the Scottish justice system. She is co-author of the booklet *The Roads* *to Racial Equality: Challenging Racism and Developing Positive Action in the Scottish Voluntary Sector* (1995).

Elspeth King has worked as a museum curator for 25 years, with Glasgow Museums, People's Palace and Dunfermline Heritage Trust. She has an interest in people's and women's history, and is at present Director of the Stirling Smith Art Gallery and Museum.

Bashir Maan first came to Scotland in 1953 as a student, and since then has been involved in community work, race relations and politics both locally and nationally. He was the first UK Muslim to be appointed as Justice of the Peace in 1968, and to be elected as a city councillor in 1970. In 1974 he was the first Asian to contest a parliamentary constituency for the Labour Party. He has served as magistrate and judge in Glasgow District Court for the past 30 years and was appointed Deputy Lieutenant, City of Glasgow in 1982. He served as Deputy Chair of the Commission for Racial Equality from 1977 to 1980 and as Chair of Strathclyde Community Relations Council from 1986 to 1996. He is a member of the Scottish Constitutional Convention and Baillie of the City of Glasgow. He is author of *The New Scots: Asians in Scotland* (1992) and numerous newspaper articles.

Cathy McCormack is a well-known activist from the Easterhouse area of Glasgow who became involved in grassroots activity because of the effects of poor housing on her children's health. She is a founder member of PODER, a popular education resource centre in Glasgow, and the Popular Education Forum for Scotland. She is currently making a film about democracy and township life in South Africa and Scotland called 'War without bullets' and writing a book about her experience of community campaigning.

Murdo Macdonald was educated at the University of Edinburgh. He has edited a number of works by George Davie including *Crisis of the Democratic Intellect* (1986). He is a former art critic of the *Scotsman* newspaper and a former editor of the literature, art and ideas journal *Edinburgh Review*. In 1990 he was appointed to the Centre of Continuing Education of the University of Edinburgh as an advisor to the arts programme, and at present he advises on Scottish Studies. He has lectured and published widely on art and ideas in Scotland with particular reference to the traditions of generalism and visual thinking. He is currently Professor of History of Scottish Art at the University of Dundee.

Mick McGrath is Head of Management and Labour Studies at Stevenson College, Edinburgh. Originally an electrician in construction and shipbuilding, he has worked in trade union and adult residential education and in the voluntary sector in the past 20 years. He has written on politics, literature and education.

Alastair McIntosh is a Quaker who grew up in the Church of Scotland on the Isle of Lewis. He has been business advisor to the Iona Community, and chairs the Projects Committee of the Scottish Catholic International Aid Fund. He is a fellow of the Centre for Human Ecology, which in 1996 was forced to reconstitute itself outside of the University of Edinburgh (where he was previously postgraduate teaching director). His applied development work includes having established the Pacific Regional Sustainable Forestry Programme in Papua New Guinea, Vanuatu and the Solomon Islands.

Isobel MacPhail is Assistant Manager at the Assynt Field Centre and is currently writing up her PhD. She is a working crofter, living on the North Assynt Estate, and is a member of the Assynt Crofters' Trust.

Sue Mansfield is a feminist researcher and tutor in community and continuing education at Northern College, Dundee. Prior to this, she worked in both the voluntary and statutory sectors as an informal educator, particularly with women. She has published work on women's historical experience in the community education movement and her current research interests focus on matriarchal discourses in relation to the professional training of community education workers in Scotland.

Helen Martin is a mother, school cleaner and community activist in the Greater Easterhouse area of Glasgow. She was involved in a local campaign to eradicate dampness which resulted in a successful experiment in solar energy-heated housing. She is a founder member of PODER, a popular education resource centre in Glasgow.

Ian Martin teaches at Moray House Institute of Education, University of Edinburgh. He has published extensively on adult and community education and is co-editor of *Community Education: An Agenda for Educational Reform* (1987) and *Education and Community: The Politics of Practice* (1992). He is a member of the editorial board of *Concept*, a founding member of the Popular Education Forum for Scotland and co-convenor of the Edinburgh Biennial Adult Education Conference.

Jane Meagher has been a local authority community education worker for 18 years. She is now Curriculum Advisor for Community Education in the City of Edinburgh Council. She is a member of the editorial board of *Concept*, the Scottish journal for the community education field.

Lindsay Paterson is Professor of Educational Policy at Moray House Institute of Education, University of Edinburgh. He has published on many aspects of both the sociology of education (in particular on the effects of social disadvantage and on the expansion of higher education) and on Scottish politics. His most recent books are *A Diverse Assembly: The Debate on a Scottish Parliament* (1998) and *The Scottish Electorate*, with Alice Brown, David McCrone and

Paula Surridge (1998). He is vice-convenor of the Unit for the Study of Government in Scotland, and edits its quarterly journal *Scottish Affairs*.

Margaret Petrie has worked in the voluntary sector for 15 years with young parents and young unemployed and homeless people in addition to developing guidance provision in the local Community Education Service and working as a freelance adult education tutor. For the last four years she has been the co-ordinator of Access Ability Lothian, a disability-led project working to promote educational inclusion. She is a member of the editorial board of *Concept* and a trustee of the Zero Tolerance Trust.

Eurig Scandrett was an ecological scientist until he moved into community education work, since when he has worked in a range of contexts, including drugs work, second chance education and trade union studies. He was a community development worker with Edinburgh Voluntary Organisations Council and is currently Community Development Officer with Friends of the Earth Scotland and a tutor in environmental policy for the Open University. He has published in both scientific and community education journals. He is a member of the editorial board of *Concept*, the Scottish journal for the field of community education.

Mae Shaw worked as a community worker in a range of settings in the voluntary sector for 15 years. She is now a lecturer in community education at Moray House Institute of Education, University of Edinburgh. She is editor of *Concept*, the Scottish journal for the field of community education and her published work includes *Radical Community Work: Perspectives From Practice in Scotland* with Ian Cooke (1996). She is a member of the editorial board of the *Community Development Journal* and is co-editor of a special issue 'Community development and social movements' with Keith Popple (1997).

Tom Steele was Tutor Organiser for the WEA North Yorkshire District from 1973 to 1987, mainly in Leeds. Following a resting period as 'freelance' researcher during which he wrote a report on the youth service in Leeds, he was a Research Fellow in the Department of Adult and Continuing Education at the University of Leeds from 1990 to 1994 and then a lecturer. In 1996 he became Access Co-Ordinator in the Department of Adult and Continuing Education at the University of Glasgow. His books include *Alfred Orage and the Leeds Arts Club* (1990), *Learning Independence: A Political Outline of Indian Adult Education* with Richard Taylor (1995) and, most recently, *The Emergence of Cultural Studies, 1945–65: Adult Education, Cultural Politics and the 'English' Question* (1997).

Index

Fossils
Whitby coast

A photographic guide

Dean R. Lomax

Photography by Benjamin Hyde – Illustrations by Nobumichi Tamura

Siri Scientific Press

ISBN 978-0-9567795-0-2

Published by Siri Scientific Press, Manchester, UK
This and similar titles are available directly from the publisher at:
http://www.siriscientificpress.co.uk

If you are an author and would like to publish with us please contact us via our website.

This book was designed, type set and published entirely within the UK by David Penney and Siri Scientific Press. Cover design by David Penney.

© 2011, Dean Lomax and Siri Scientific Press. All rights reserved. No parts of this publication may be reproduced, stored in a retrieval system or transmitted, in any form or by any means, electronic, mechanical, photocopying, recording or otherwise, without the prior written permission of the publisher. This does not cover photographs and other illustrations provided by third parties, who retain copyright and may do with these as they wish.

Cover image: Saltwick Bay and various fossils illustrated throughout the text.

Contents

Whitby – a fossil hunter's paradise

Whitby, a small coastal town in North Yorkshire, is a name familiar to most fossil collectors in Britain and Europe. For hundreds of years, it has been well known as a source of a diverse range of fossils from the distant past. Whitby is set on a part of the Yorkshire Coast often referred to as *the dinosaur coast*, an illustrious section of coastline stretching from the mouth of the River Tees in the north to Flamborough Head in the south. Internationally significant fossils have been discovered around Whitby. The fossils range from the remnants of large and ferocious marine reptiles to common ammonites, allowing the fossil hunter to paint a vivid picture of the prehistoric ecosystem they once inhabited.

Many fossils found in and around Whitby are spread across museums and private collections throughout the world. It's not surprising that large numbers of fossils are found all year round and collectors come flocking to this coastline because it is one of the most productive Jurassic localities in the UK, perhaps even rivalling the Jurassic Coast World Heritage Site situated along the Dorset and East Devon coast.

This guide illustrates some of the most common fossil species collected around Whitby, based on images of museum authenticated specimens and those in private collections. It explains how to identify them and reconstructs how some of the extinct organisms may have appeared in life. From a practical view point, it explains where the fossils are found, how to go fossil hunting, provides an explanation of each fossil group and the likelihood that you, the collector, may be able to discover a similar specimen.

Important: do not over collect fossils and keep hammering to a minimum – it is rarely the best way to look for fossils. Your eyes are the best tool for finding specimens. The majority of this coastline is a SSSI (site of special scientific interest) and hammering of the cliffs is prohibited by law. Please protect the fossils found around this coastline; they have been here for millions of years, so deserve a considerable degree of respect.

The stunning scenery at Port Mulgrave.

Safety and equipment

Always safety first!

It's very easy when searching for fossils to forget your surroundings and become lost in an ancient world, but the fossil hunter must always be aware. The cliffs are continually eroding; this is great for fossil hunters hoping to discover that next great specimen, though the cliffs are unlike the tide and you cannot predict when they're going to collapse! However, enticing a huge landslip looks, the potential of finding something fantastic at the top is very low and it is best to let the tide do its job and slowly reduce the newly formed rock pile. Fossils are most often found in the loose shingle on the beach. Not only are the eroding cliffs dangerous but in conjunction with the tide they can be treacherous. The tide can come in quickly and cut you off as quite a few fossil hunters experience every year. Not only are the erosion of the cliff and turning of the tide dangerous but other problems can occur. Lying on all beaches around Whitby are many rocks ranging from small to huge, which can be difficult to walk across and some are deceptively unstable. Many are made slippery by algae, seaweed or water and it is very easy to fall, especially when carrying a heavy back pack. Always try to have both hands free. Two final points regarding safety: wear the correct clothing, personal protective equipment (see later) and appropriate footwear when looking for fossils,

and always make sure that somebody knows when and where you will be going to collect fossils. It is a good idea to carry a whistle to draw attention to yourself if you are unfortunate enough to have an accident!

One vital point each fossil hunter should have in mind: you should never hammer at the cliff face or beds of rock on the foreshore because it is unnecessary. If something highly important is spotted in such a location then a museum or specialist should be contacted in order to extract it appropriately and safely. Palaeontologists cannot search the entire coastline and keen amateurs have always played a key role in finding spectacularly rare fossils.

Looking across the rocky beach at Port Mulgrave towards Kettleness in the background.

You must always be aware of potential dangers while out collecting, safety is paramount. Above: landslip near Kettleness. Below: seaweed and underlying rocks cover the beach at Runswick Bay.

Equipment

When most people think of equipment what springs to mind are hammers and chisels which are an essential part of a fossil hunter's kit. Not just any old hammer or chisel though; many people make the mistake of trying to use toffee hammers and basic chisels to crack open fossil containing rocks. This is more dangerous to the collector than to the fossil as the hammer may splinter and cause injury. It is not necessary to buy expensive equipment, all you need for a successful trip is a good, strong, geological, rock or brick hammer with stone chisels, ideally with guards, small plastic bags to put your finds in, bubble wrap/cloth to wrap fragile specimens, goggles to protect your eyes from bits of rock when hammering, a hard hat (though you shouldn't venture under cliffs) and a strong backpack to carry it all, and something to eat and a drink to maintain energy levels. A camera is useful because it allows you to take images of the fossils embedded in the rock, and of the location where you are collecting. It is rare to see a fossil hunter fully equipped with geological maps, glues, compass, dental picks, notepad, pen, tape measures etc. However, once you have become fully engaged with this fascinating endeavour you can branch out into additional kit. Make sure you have an understanding of what equipment the location you are planning to visit requires, because sometimes the area may not warrant tools such as hammers, and might need only a keen eye and strong back to bend down and pick up specimens. Do remember to keep hammering to a minimum.

Some of the equipment used by fossil hunters - discussed above.

Geology

The rocks around Whitby are of Lower and Middle Jurassic age, formed between about 195 and 170 million years ago. The majority of fossils mentioned in this guide come from them. The name 'Jurassic' sparks the imagination of many, perhaps recalling the famous movie 'Jurassic Park'. However the dinosaurs which give the coastline its name are of Middle Jurassic age and are represented only by footprints in sandstone that was laid down in deltas and flood plains. The huge marine reptiles (which are not dinosaurs) for which the area is famous are from Lower (early) Jurassic rocks, also known as the Lias. These rocks were deposited on the margins of a subtropical marine basin, mostly some distance from the shore at the time. The sea level and coastline were not constant. When the water was deeper and further from the shore dark mud was deposited resulting in the grey and black shales that dominate many of the cliffs. When the water was shallower and closer to shore the deposits become sandier. Sea level was higher in the Lower and Upper Lias so dark shales predominate. In the Middle Lias (seen well at Staithes) there are shallower marine sandstones and ironstones: the iron was leached from subtropical soils on nearby land and washed into the sea.

Overlying the solid Jurassic rocks in much of the area is the Boulder Clay. This was formed during the Ice Age and contains 'derived' rocks and fossils brought by the ice from over a large area. This is why you can often find fossils, especially corals, from the Carboniferous Limestone whose nearest outcrops nowadays are in the Pennines and on the Northumberland coast. Pebbles and boulders are washing out of the Boulder Clay all the time.

Opposite: *A Jurassic lithostratigraphical chart which will be helpful for determining the specific age of certain fossils. It displays the entire geology of the Whitby area including the individual formations and members within. Numbers in parentheses = approximate age in millions of years.*

Stage	Lithostratigraphical division		
Aalenian (175–171)	Saltwick Formation		
	Dogger Formation		
Upper Toarcian (175)	Blea Wyke Sandstone Formation		Yellow Sandstone Mbr
			Grey Sandstone Mbr
	Whitby Mudstone Fm		Foxcliff Siltstone Mbr
			Peak Mudstone Mbr
			Alum Shale Mbr
Lower Toarcian (183)			Mulgrave Shale Mbr*
			Grey Shale Mbr
Upper Pliensbachian (183)	Cleveland Ironstone Fm		Kettleness Mbr
			Penny Nab Mbr
Lower Pliensbachian (189)	Staithes Sandstone Formation		
	Redcar Mudstone Fm		'Ironstone Shales'
			'Pyritous Shales'
Upper Sinemurian (189)			'Siliceous Shales'
Lower Sinemurian (196)			'Calcareous Shales'

*The Mulgrave Shale Member is a replacement name for the 'Jet Rock Member' (this Jet Rock Member' is an informal name and often used by fossil collectors) it also has 3 informal divisions - also called the 'Jet Rock *sensu stricto*', 'Bituminous Shales' and finally the uppermost section the 'Ovatum Band'.

Fossil hunting locations

This section covers the main fossil hunting locations near the coastal town of Whitby and provides access information in addition to details of the fossils that may be found. When visiting any of these locations please bear in mind the safety guidelines provided earlier and always check the tides! It is true that the best time to look for fossils is during the winter months as a result of bad weather and stormy seas which speed up erosion, however during poor weather conditions the access to certain fossil hunting locations can become more dangerous. Most of the fossils discovered will be from the cliffs and rocks at that location, although specimens may also have travelled from further along the coast, meaning that each specimen discussed in this guide from the locality mentioned could theoretically be found at almost any location. Fossil find frequency may be higher after rough weather conditions and extreme tides. The fossiliferous beds are often buried by sand and shingle, however when they are exposed (usually during scouring conditions) the fossils erode out more readily and the find frequency increases. Please note that you may have to pay for parking at some of the locations discussed.

Another productive location to find fossils along this coastline is Hawsker. Hawsker is situated between Saltwick Bay and Robin Hood's Bay. The location has yielded some great specimens, however it is an extremely dangerous site to access and so is not at all family friendly and is not discussed further in this guide. Only experienced fossil collectors should seek more information about this locality.

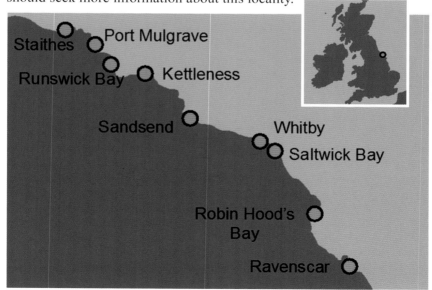

Staithes

Staithes lies 11 miles north of Whitby and is the most distant location discussed in this guide. It is a lesser known locality for fossils although it can be productive and specimens can be found on the beach to the right and left of the sea defence. The foreshore rocks, if visible, can be very fossiliferous.

Accessibility	Moderate: National grid ref: NZ 78017 18140
Fossils	Ammonites, belemnites, bivalves, brachiopods, gastropods, wood, brittle stars, crinoids, trace fossils and glacial erratics
Find frequency	Low–medium
Geology	Lower Pliensbachian to Lower Toarcian Ironstone Shales to Grey Shale Member

Access: You must park in the car park at the top of the hill and walk down a steep road through the village; either continuing straight through the village or taking a short walk left across a bridge. Be cautious when walking onto either side of the beach as slippery algae often covers the walkway, which can be dangerous. The right side of the sea defence is less dangerous. The car park has toilets.

The north side of Staithes.

13

Port Mulgrave

This locality includes some of the most beautiful scenery in Yorkshire and is perhaps the second best location to find fossils. To the general fossil collector it is a lesser known location thus the chances of finding something rarer are higher. You can find fossils once you are on the raised area with fishing boats. There is a large accumulation of shale where parts of fossils can be found, though the better specimens are found further to the right or left.

Accessibility	Difficult: National grid ref: NZ 79463 17395
Fossils	Ammonites, belemnites, bivalves, nautiloids, marine reptiles, wood, fish, crustaceans, trace fossils, plants and glacial erratics
Find frequency	High
Geology	Upper Pliensbachian to Aalenian Cleveland Ironstone Formation to Saltwick Formation

Access: Parking facilities are minimal at Port Mulgrave. You must park at the top of the cliff, and there is a very long steep walk down to the beach via hundreds of irregular steps, which can be dangerous in poor weather. Once on the beach heading left there are many large rocks to climb over, heading to the right on the beach presents easier access.

Runswick Bay

This is one of the best locations to allow all ages to get acquainted with fossils. Many specimens can be picked up from the beach shingle and from the shales on the foreshore. The majority of fossils are found further to the right in front of the cliffs or to the left past the sea defence.

Accessibility	Easy: National grid ref: NZ 80662 16138
Fossils	Ammonites, belemnites, marine reptile, glacial erratics, plants, brittle stars, bivalves, crustaceans and trace fossils
Find frequency	Medium–high
Geology	Upper Pliensbachian to Lower Toarcian Cleveland Ironstone Formation to Alum Shale Member

Access: There is a steep hill down to the beach with a well placed small car park at the bottom, only a stone's throw away from the beach, saving a long and difficult journey back up the cliff. Buses and coaches are unable to drive down the steep hill and must park at the top in another car park, from which there is a long, steep walk to the beach.

The south side of Runswick Bay.

Kettleness

The most productive location around Whitby, it has produced some of the best marine reptile fossils along the dinosaur coast. The majority of these were discovered when the cliff face at Kettleness was quarried for alum, though some interesting finds have also turned up in recent years.

Accessibility	Very difficult: National grid ref: NZ 83141 16097
Fossils	Ammonites, belemnites, bivalves, crinoids, marine reptiles, plants, wood, trace fossils and glacial erratics
Find frequency	High
Geology	Upper Pliensbachian to Lower Toarcian Cleveland Ironstone Formation to Alum Shale Member

Access: The best route is to park at Runswick Bay and walk right, away from the small village, and all the way around the cliffs; you must begin at least 2 hours before low tide. It is a long and potentially dangerous walk (roughly 1.5 miles each way) with many large rocks to climb over. This locality is recommended only to the serious fossil hunter and is not suitable for families.

The rocky shore at Kettleness towards the old alum quarry in the background.

Sandsend

This is a good locality for fossils. In recent years partial marine reptiles have been discovered here, including the skulls of ichthyosaurs. Once on the beach and facing the sea, a short walk to the left is the best location to search for fossils.

Accessibility	Very easy: National grid ref: NZ 86356 12541
Fossils	Ammonites, belemnites, bivalves, fish, marine reptiles, wood and glacial erratics
Find frequency	Medium
Geology	Lower Toarcian to Aalenian Mulgrave Shale Mb (Bituminous shales) to Saltwick Fm

Access: Parking is situated along the seafront. Although getting to the beach is very easy there are many rocks along the foreshore and these are often covered with seaweed making them slippery and dangerous. Common fossils can be found in the shingle straight onto the beach.

Whitby Beach (left and right of harbour)

Whitby beach is by far the most over collected area to look for fossils as the name 'Whitby' appears on most fossils discovered near this town that are held in museum and private collections. Naturally, visitors feel this is the place to be and spend days looking for the best fossils. It is a productive locality but given the number of collectors that visit it is unlikely that you will find particularly unusual specimens.

Accessibility	Very easy: National grid ref: NZ 89821 10870
Fossils	Ammonites, nautiloids, belemnites, bivalves, crinoids, crustaceans, fish, marine reptiles, plants, wood, trace fossils and glacial erratics
Find frequency	Medium
Geology	Lower Toarcian to Aalenian Mulgrave Shale Mb (Bituminous Shales) to Saltwick Fm

Access: Access to the beach is via gentle (sometimes slippy) slopes either side of the harbour. Fossils can be found on the foreshore in the shingle, so it is a worthwhile location for families and beginners. To the right of the harbour the beach is accessed via a short walk through the town. The beach is often littered with seaweed and moderately large rocks. Parking facilities in the town are good but can be very busy; parking at the Abbey on top of the cliff may be easier but there are a lot of steps down.

Saltwick Bay

This bay is perhaps one of the most productive localities along this coastline. It is picked over quite frequently but usually yields something and you rarely come away empty handed. Once the tide is out, searching to the right hand side (past the ship wreck) can be highly productive.

Accessibility	Easy: National grid ref: NZ 91425 10237
Fossils	Ammonites, nautiloids, belemnites, bivalves, crustaceans, fish, marine reptiles, plants, wood, trace fossils and glacial erratics
Find frequency	High
Geology	Lower Toarcian to Aalenian Mulgrave Shale Mb (Jet Rock–Bit. Shales) to Saltwick Fm

Access: Park at the top of Saltwick Bay in a small area just before the Saltwick Bay caravan site. It has toilets and a small cafe which visitors are able to use by asking at the reception. A descent down to the beach via a long set of steep steps is the best way to get to Saltwick Bay. However, these can be dangerous during poor weather conditions, especially towards the bottom. Saltwick Bay is one of the easiest locations to access and considering the find frequency is very much worth a visit.

Robin Hood's Bay

This is a famous locality for fossils. A walk through the village brings you to a picturesque bay. Fossils can be found on the foreshore but better specimens can be located further to the left and right. However, it is an over picked location so unless you know what you are looking for it can be difficult to find specimens, especially of high quality.

Accessibility	Moderate: National grid ref: NZ 95164 05331
Fossils	Ammonites, belemnites, nautiloids, bivalves, gastropods, crinoids, brittle stars, fish, marine reptiles, wood and glacial erratics
Find frequency	Low–medium
Geology	Lower Sinemurian to Aalenian Upper Calcareous Shales to Saltwick Formation

Access: Parking is at the top of the hill. Robin Hood's Bay is famous for its long and steep walk down to the beach. This is a very steep hill and is quite daunting when carrying a backpack full of fossils. Alternatively, limited parking at either Boggle Hole or Stoupe Beck allows additional points of access to the beach.

Looking towards Robin Hoods Bay from the cliff top of Ravenscar.

Ravenscar

Ravenscar, near Robin Hood's Bay is a good location to find fossils, particularly ammonites and bivalves. However, it is less productive than most sites, although this makes fossil finds particularly rewarding. Many fossils are exposed in the beds on the foreshore. When the rocks are exposed along the beach the walking conditions become difficult.

Accessibility	Very difficult: National grid ref: NZ 98003 01442
Fossils	Ammonites, belemnites, bivalves, brachiopods, crinoids, fish, marine reptiles, plants, wood and glacial erratics
Find frequency	Medium
Geology	Upper Pliensbachian to Aalenian Staithes Sandstone Formation to Dogger Formation

Access: Park in the lay-by near the National Trust Centre. It is a long walk through the Golf course of the Raven Hall Hotel down to the beach (the cliff here is 500 ft high). It takes approximately 30 minutes and can be quite dangerous in poor weather conditions. Part of the walkway down has eroded away, making access even more difficult. Heading back up the steep cliff can be very challenging after a long day of fossil hunting. It is not suitable for young children. An alternative route to this locality is to head east from Robin Hood's Bay, but this must be done with an extremely good tide. The beach is often littered with seaweed.

The high tide can quite easily cut you off if you are unaware of the tide times, ensure that you know them.

Fossil hunting is for everybody!

No matter what your age, everybody is able to participate in fossil hunting and from the instant you find your very first specimen you are likely to be hooked. Remember, you are the first person to find and see that fossil which was once a living, breathing organism many millions of years ago. Furthermore, you may have even discovered a species new to science.

There isn't really much skill to fossil hunting but naturally a planned trip tends to produce the best results in terms of fossil finds. Think about it. If you go fossil hunting armed with a basic understanding of the geology and what fossils you may be able to find in a specific area, you have a higher chance of finding fossils and indeed better, more complete specimens. Nonetheless, novice fossil hunters make some of the best and most significant new discoveries. Patience is a virtue when it comes to fossil hunting, because it can take a considerable degree of time before you get your eye in and begin to find much. Much of this comes down to noticing shapes (for example, be sure to look for rounded nodules with fossils poking out), structures and patterns that stand out from the surrounding rock. You may be able to visualise what the fossil looked like in life and catch a glimpse of planet earth when it was populated with all kinds of fascinating animals and plants that are now extinct! Many fossils along this coastline can be found in large boulders and blocks, and it is best to leave such specimens, perhaps take a photograph of the specimen as it is, rather than attempting to remove it and most probably destroying it in the process. Most fossils found here belong to organisms that lived in the sea, although some (notably dinosaur footprints and plants) are of terrestrial (lived on land) origin.

As you will discover through reading this book hundreds of fossils are found embedded in large rocks such as this chunk of lignite (coal-like material) from the sandstones (Aalenian) at Saltwick Bay. Such specimens (including footprints) are best left alone, perhaps take a photograph. Do not attempt to remove such fossils as you will destroy the individual. Unnecessary hammering is prohibited.

A group of fossil hunters at Runswick Bay.

Responsible collecting

Fossil collecting is a relaxing, rewarding and thoroughly enjoyable hobby. However, be considerate towards others – and nature – and **do not over collect specimens**. Take one fossil, leave the rest. There is no real need to collect twenty specimens of the same ammonite, leave some for others to find. A small part of an ammonite or a common bivalve may lose its value to you once you are experienced at finding fossils. However, any specimen collected or seen should always be taken with care and never intentionally destroyed! That unwanted specimen has the potential to stimulate the imagination of a beginner and even initiate a life-long passion for palaeontology – if possible, take it back to where you found it or give it to someone who will appreciate it. Always remember that each fossil you find was once part of a living thing. It is rare for any organism to preserve in the fossil record and they have been there for millions of years, so consider carefully before you attempt to remove one. Do not forget that fossils are very important. Palaeontologists around the world research and publish their findings on fossils in scientific journals. This includes fossils from Whitby and its surrounding areas.

Fossils discussed

Each fossil discussed here comes from a named locality. However, the same types of fossils can be found in the same geological outcrops at the other locations. For example, a fossil found in the Mulgrave Shale Member at Port Mulgrave could be found in the same member at Kettleness. During the course of research on this book several museum collections were examined. The provenance of some specimens was unclear, citing only Whitby as the source (common in old museum collections), when they clearly originated from other nearby localities. Their most likely origins are cited herein. This book is not intended to be a definitive guide to the thousands of fossil species that have been found in this area. It covers some of the more common species and a few of the rarer ones (relative abundance, in terms of the likelihood of finding a specimen, is indicated for each type of fossil described). This should give you a good idea of what you are likely to find and what to call it once you've found it. You can then take your interest as far as you want in investigating the plants and animals that lived here hundreds of millions of years ago. A scale bar has been placed onto each picture to give an indication of the size of each specimen.

Ammonites

Ammonites are one of the most easily recognised fossils the world over, and are perhaps the most common fossil found along this coastline. Ammonite shells are generally plano-spirally coiled (coiled in one particular orientation). They were sea creatures which resembled modern day squid and octopus (their closest living relatives), although they had a shell that was outwardly similar to some snail shells (such as those found in your garden). Ammonite fossils are so common and diverse, and evolved so quickly, that they are used to help date the rocks they are found in – these are known as index fossils. Many ammonite species are identified based on the size, shape and pattern present on the keel. Sometimes ammonite 'jaws' (aptychi) can be discovered and extremely rarely they can be found with the ammonite!

Phylloceras (opposite) is easily identified by its beautifully preserved leaf-like suture patterns. Isolated sections are most common and are often misidentified as belonging to a type of fossilised plant or seaweed.

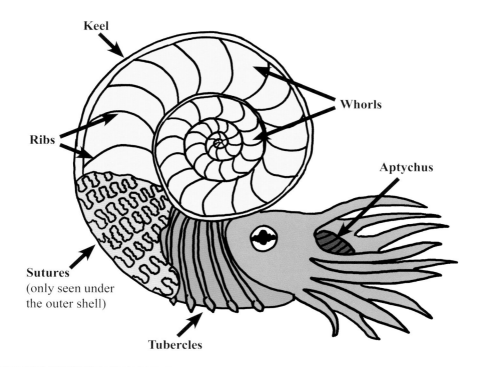

Keel

Whorls

Ribs

Aptychus

Sutures
(only seen under
the outer shell)

Tubercles

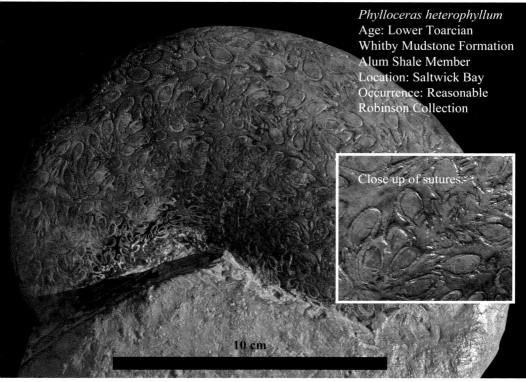

Phylloceras heterophyllum
Age: Lower Toarcian
Whitby Mudstone Formation
Alum Shale Member
Location: Saltwick Bay
Occurrence: Reasonable
Robinson Collection

Close up of sutures

10 cm

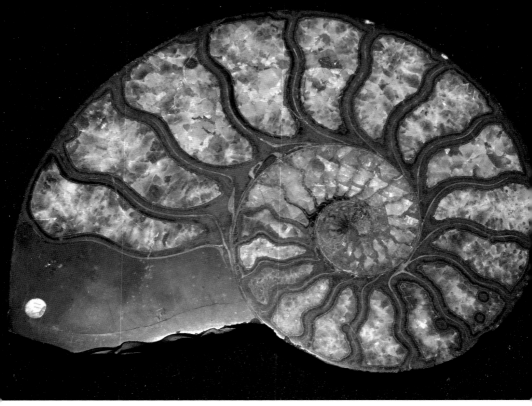

Cross section through a *Phylloceras heterophyllum* ammonite. The section has been polished to highlight the individual chambers that run through the ammonite, they are filled with the mineral calcite. In life, the chambers were filled with gas that acted as a buoyancy aid for the individual. Some ammonite fossil finds may have been extremely eroded by the sea, causing the chambers to be readily visible. Doncaster Museum: DONMG: ZG2806.

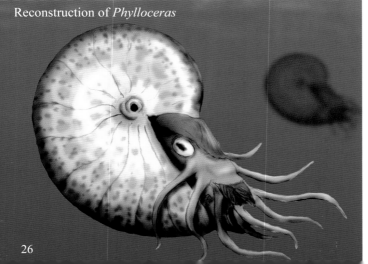

Reconstruction of *Phylloceras*

Most reconstructions of extinct animals are based on specific fossilised features. The basic shape and structure in this reconstruction of *Phylloceras* was created based upon the detailed features of the fossil. However, the head and tentacles were reconstructed through close examination of living molluscs such as the *Nautilus*.

Oxynoticeras sp.
Age: Upper Sinemurian
Redcar Mudstone Formation
Siliceous Shales
Location: Robin Hood's Bay
Occurrence: Uncommon
Manchester Museum
LL.15938.148

Smaller specimens of ammonites are often difficult to identify to species level. However the sizes of such specimens can differ greatly, this ammonite can reach lengths of up to 20 cm.

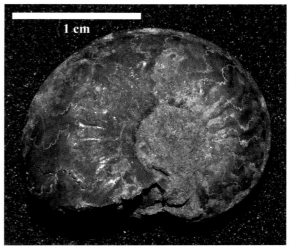

Arnioceras semicostatum
Age: Lower Sinemurian
Redcar Mudstone Formation
Calcareous Shales
Location: Robin Hood's Bay
Occurrence: Uncommon
Manchester Museum
LL.9019

Arnioceras specimens are washed down the coast as longshore drift or as glacial erratics (see page 108). Large accumulations of them have been found along the Holderness Coast.

Peronoceras fibulatum
Age: Lower Toarcian
Whitby Mudstone Formation
Alum Shale Member
Location: Runswick Bay
Occurrence: Reasonable
Manchester Museum
LL.5859

Like most ammonites around Whitby *Peronoceras* is known from several species. Most have small tubercles, the spike-like protrusions or small bumps on the ribs.

Gagaticeras gagateum
Age: Upper Sinemurian
Redcar Mudstone Formation
Siliceous Shales
Location: Robin Hood's Bay
Occurrence: Reasonable
British Geological Survey
BGS GSM 26441

Androgynoceras maculatum
Age: Lower Pliensbachian
Redcar Mudstone Formation
Ironstone Shales
Location: Robin Hood's Bay
Occurrence: Reasonable
Doncaster Museum:
DONMG: ZG418

Gagaticeras and *Androgynoceras* are easily mistaken for one another. The ribbing of *Androgynoceras* is generally much more strongly defined and spacious. In addition, *Androgynoceras* are generally larger.

Lytoceras cornucopia
Age: Lower Toarcian
Whitby Mudstone Formation
Alum Shale Member
Location: Ravenscar
Occurrence: Rare
Smith Collection

Lytoceras is a good example of an evolute ammonite. The individual whorls barely touch.

Apoderoceras subtriangulare
Age: Lower Pliensbachian
Redcar Mudstone Formation
Location: Robin Hood's Bay
Occurrence: Rare
Whitby Museum
WHITM: SIM165

This species of ammonite is the largest discussed in the guide. Large ammonites are extremely rare, however it is not impossible to find them. Usually, isolated chunks of large ammonites are discovered. Many ammonites such as *Apoderoceras* have large tubercles, the spine-like protrusions, which were most probably used for defence and display.

Dactylioceras commune
Age: Lower Toarcian
Whitby Mudstone Formation
Alum Shale Member
Location: Saltwick Bay
Occurrence: Very common
Robinson Collection

Dactylioceras is the most common ammonite that occurs along the Whitby coastline. Note the fine branching ribs, evenly spaced, and curving gently.

Dactylioceras tenuicostatum
Age Lower Toarcian
Whitby Mudstone Formation
Grey Shale Member
Location: Port Mulgrave
Occurrence: Common
Bolton Collection

Another common species of *Dactylioceras*, however the ribs are compacted tightly together, protruding outwards and curving only very slightly. Such subtle differences often indicate a different species.

Reconstruction of *D. tenuicostatum*.

Catacoeloceras perarmatum
Age: Lower Toarcian
Whitby Mudstone Formation
Mulgrave Shale Member
Location: Kettleness
Occurrence: Reasonable
Smith Collection

Grammoceras thouarsense
Age: Upper Toarcian
Whitby Mudstone Formation
Peak Mudstone and Fox Cliff
Siltstone Members
Location: Ravenscar
Occurrence: Reasonable
Manchester Museum
L.12216

A relatively small ammonite, with the
ribs spaced evenly across the whorls.

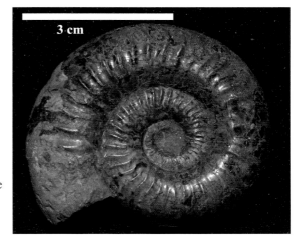

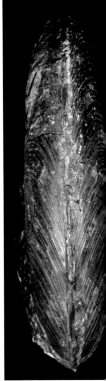

Harpoceras falciferum
Age: Lower Toarcian
Whitby Mudstone Formation
Mulgrave Shale Member
Location: Sandsend
Occurrence: Common
Whitby Museum
WHITM: SIM205

The keel is strongly defined and compacted, as seen in ventral view.

The above specimen of *Harpoceras* is one of the largest the author has viewed. However, small to medium-sized specimens are relatively common. They are best identified by the very strong sickle-like curvature of the ribbing and striking keel as seen above. Some ammonites have been discovered with stomach contents (providing evidence of the last meal before the animal died). Some are known to have fed on crustaceans.

Reconstruction of *Harpoceras*.

3 cm

Amaltheus stokesi
Age: Upper Pliensbachian
Staithes Sandstone Formation
Location: Staithes
Occurrence: Uncommon
Manchester Museum
L.9386.a

Ammonite index fossils are indicators of a specific horizon/age. *Amaltheus* is a good example, because its remains have been discovered at lots of locations across the world including Europe, North Africa and the USA .

Each ammonite has unique suture patterns, similar to finger prints. They play a key role in the correct identification of ammonite species.

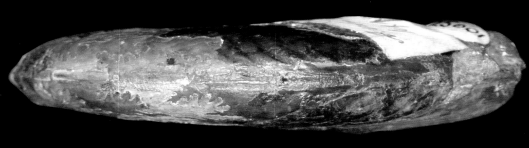

Haugia beani
Age: Upper Toarcian
Whitby Mudstone Formation
Peak Mudstone Member
Location: Ravenscar
Occurrence: Uncommon
British Geological Survey
BGS GSM 25001

Aptychus
Cornaptychus sp.
Age: Lower Toarcian
Whitby Mudstone Formation
Alum Shale Member
Location: Port Mulgrave
Occurrence: Reasonable
Whitby Museum
WHITM: 2011/16.4

Ammonite aptychi are easily mistaken for the shells of bivalves (see bivalve fossils), however they have a distinct shape and pattern as seen in the specimen illustrated, which is a complete paired aptychus. They are most often found separated from the ammonite shell and are then given their own names. An aptychus could theoretically be discovered wherever ammonites are present. Usually single, isolated valves are found. Aptychus (singular) and aptychi (plural).

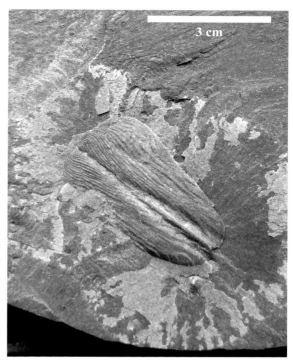

Hildoceras lusitanicum
Age: Lower Toarcian
Whitby Mudstone Formation
Alum Shale Member
Location: Saltwick Bay
Occurrence: Common
Robinson Collection

Hildoceras bifrons
Age: Lower Toarcian
Whitby Mudstone Formation
Alum Shale Member
Location: Saltwick Bay
Occurrence: Reasonable
Lomax Collection

This specimen was discovered as a positive and negative fossil. The positive of an ammonite is the actual fossil itself, whereas the negative is the impression. In most cases the negative can display just as much detail as the positive. Note the differences between this and the previous species.

The life reconstruction of a *Hildoceras* ammonite displays a dark v-shaped structure below the eyes. This is the aptychus. It was previously suggested that the aptychus functioned as an operculum (a sort of opening and closing 'door'), but in more recent years the aptychus has been considered to be part of the jaw apparatus.

Reconstruction of a *Hildoceras*.

Pseudolioceras lythense
Age: Lower Toarcian
Whitby Mudstone Formation
Alum Shale Member
Location: Port Mulgrave
Occurrence: Reasonable
Smith Collection

Often many ammonites are found together, referred to as life or death assemblages. Other fossils may be found with them, such as the small chunk of bone (probably a rib) in the specimen illustrated.

Eleganticeras elegantulum
Age: Lower Toarcian
Whitby Mudstone Formation
Mulgrave Shale Member
Location: Sandsend
Occurrence: Reasonable
Smith Collection

Some of the chambers of this ammonite are visible and display a beautiful structure. Often *Eleganticeras* is found in extremely rounded nodules termed 'cannonballs'.

Ovaticeras ovatum
Age: Lower Toarcian,
Whitby Mudstone Formation
Mulgrave Shale Member
Location: Sandsend
Occurrence: Rare
Smith Collection

Ovaticeras, *Pseudolioceras* and *Eleganticeras* have very similar ribbing, it orientates with a slight 'kink' in the pattern. Also note the prominent keel of *Ovaticeras*.

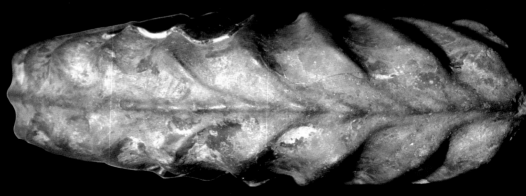

Pleuroceras hawskerense
Age: Upper Pliensbachian
Cleveland Ironstone Formation
Kettleness Member
Location: Staithes
Occurrence: Uncommon
Manchester Museum
LL.5814.b

The ribbing of *Pleuroceras* is very strong, and is particularly evident when viewed keel on. The ribs are evenly spaced and form the basis of a strong keel.

Nautiloids

The nautiloids are often misidentified as ammonites, which is an easy mistake to make because both are cephalopods that look similar to the inexperienced eye. The illustrations show their characteristic form, which consists of a larger outer whorl and smoother shell texture than most ammonites. More importantly, they have much simpler walls between the shell chambers. A living example of the nautiloids is the modern *Nautilus*, which lives today in the Pacific and Indian oceans.

Cenoceras sp.
Age: Lower Toarcian
Whitby Mudstone Formation
Alum Shale Member
Location: Port Mulgrave
Occurrence: Reasonable
Smith Collection

Incomplete, and eroded specimens such as this, which still show detail and structure are more common than the others discussed.

Reconstruction of *Cenoceras* based largely on the modern *Nautilus*. The colour of the shell is reminiscent of *Nautilus*, however, the fossilised nautiloids may have possessed similar colours and structures within their shells.

Cenoceras annulare
Age: Lower Toarcian
Whitby Mudstone Formation
Alum Shale Member
Location: Saltwick Bay
Occurrence: Uncommon
Whitby Museum
WHITM: SIM433

Differences between the two species illustrated include the general shape and size of the chambers. In *C. annulare* they are more detailed and often smaller than in *C. astacoides*.

Cenoceras astacoides
Age: Lower Toarcian
Whitby Mudstone Formation
Alum Shale Member
Location: Whitby
Occurrence: Uncommon
Manchester Museum
L.5669

Belemnites

Belemnites are one of the most commonly found fossils at Whitby. Due to their conical shape and pointed tip they are often confused for dinosaur teeth or to a lesser extent bullets, which they are aptly nicknamed. In reality, belemnites are closely related to the ammonites and are related to the modern day cuttlefish and squid. Generally the only part of a belemnite discovered is the portion of the internal 'skeleton' known as the rostrum or 'guard' which is made of calcite. Less commonly seen is the phragmocone; this is inserted into a conical cavity (the alveolus) at the front (non-pointed) end of the rostrum. These are the parts which are normally found as fossils. The apical grooves are often used to identify certain belemnite species. The pro-ostracum is very rarely preserved.

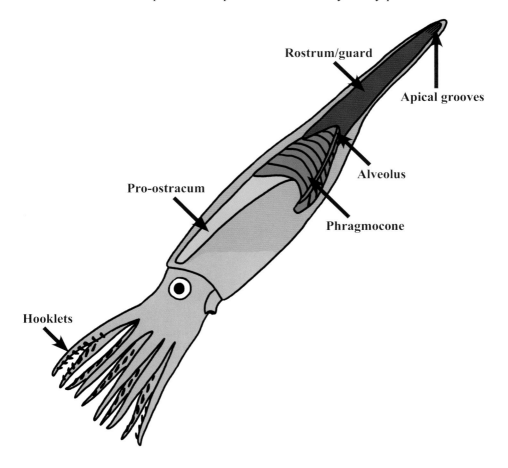

Parapassaloteuthis polita
Age: Lower Toarcian
Whitby Mudstone Formation
Mulgrave and Alum Shale Members
Location: Robin Hood's Bay
Occurrence: Reasonable
Yorkshire Museum
YORYM: 1994.1802.148

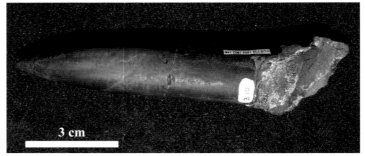

Parapassaloteuthis robusta
Age: Lower Toarcian
Whitby Mudstone Formation
Mulgrave and Alum Shale Members
Location: Saltwick Bay
Occurrence: Reasonable
Robinson Collection

A small section of phragmocone can be seen protruding from the rostrum.

Belemnite battlefield (opposite page)
Includes 2 species of belemnite:
Acrocoelites vulgaris (thick) and
Acrocoelites subtenuis (thin)
Age: Lower Toarcian
Whitby Mudstone Formation
Alum Shale Member
Location: Saltwick Bay, Whitby
Occurrence: Reasonable
Lomax Collection

Belemnite battlefields are relatively quite common along this coastline. They range from large chunks such as the specimen discussed, to smaller sections of 3-4 individual belemnites. Often complete and incomplete belemnites are found together, including separate species. It is unclear what causes these 'battlefields'. A variety of theories have been put forward some include post-spawning mortality, catastrophic mass mortality and predation (consumed by predators and then regurgitated).

42

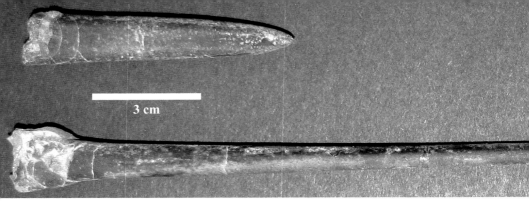

Youngibelus tubularis (long) and
Youngibelus simpsoni (short)
Age: Lower Toarcian
Whitby Mudstone Formation
Mulgrave Shale Member
Location: Saltwick Bay
Occurrence: Common
Bolton Collection

Youngibelus tubularis specimens are usually found nearly complete. However, extracting specimens is very difficult and they often break into many pieces.

Generally the only section of belemnites found is the rostrum (long pointed section heading away from the eyes). However, in very rare circumstances an entire, complete belemnite with ink sack, tentacles and hooklets intact can be found. Although this is exceedingly rare.

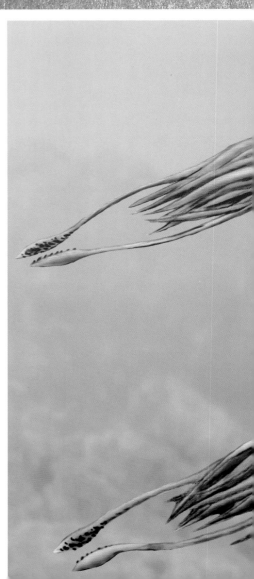

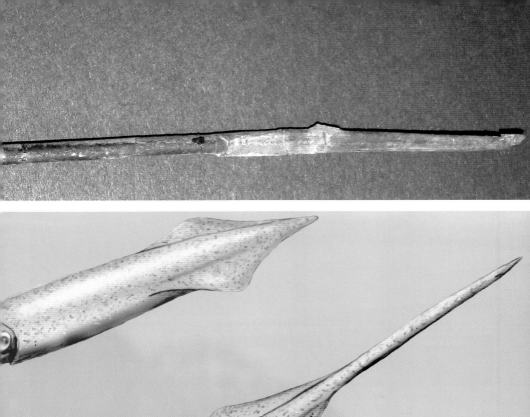

Reconstructions of *Youngibelus* belemnites.

Belemnite phragmocone (left)
Undetermined species
Age: Lower Toarcian
Whitby Mudstone Formation
Alum Shale Member
Location: Saltwick Bay, Whitby
Occurrence: Common
Lomax Collection

Nannobelus acutus (right)
Age: Upper Sinemurian
Redcar Mudstone Formation
Siliceous Shales
Location: Robin Hood's Bay
Occurrence: Common
Bolton Collection

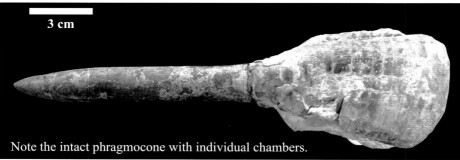

Note the intact phragmocone with individual chambers.

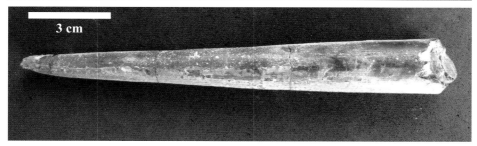

Passaloteuthis bisulcata (top)
Age: Pliensbachian to Lower Toarcian
Location: Port Mulgrave
Occurrence: Common
Bolton Collection

Acrocoelites inaequistriatus (bottom)
Age: Lower and Upper Toarcian
Whitby Mudstone Formation
Location: Saltwick Bay
Occurrence: Uncommon
Bolton Collection

Gastropods

Gastropods are molluscs, as are cephalopods and bivalves, and are found in marine, freshwater and terrestrial environments. The most familiar types are snails and slugs (on land and in water) and limpets found adhered to rocks along the coast. Gastropod fossils are relatively uncommon along the Whitby coastline, but are usually preserved showing fine details, such as individual striations. They are easily identified by their spirally-shaped structures.

Oolitcia sp. *'Turbo lineatus'*
Age: Upper Pliensbachian
Location: Staithes
Occurrence: Uncommon
British Geological Survey
BGS GSM 39977

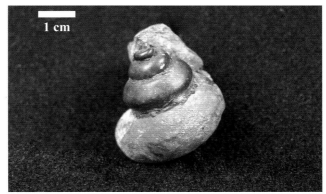

Amberleya sp.
Age: Upper Pliensbachian
Location: Staithes
Occurrence: Uncommon
British Geological Survey
BGS GSM 40028

Probably *Katosira* sp.
Age: Upper Pliensbachian
Location: Robin Hood's Bay
Occurrence: Uncommon
Whitby Museum
WHITM: SIM505

Bivalves

Bivalves are very common throughout the fossil record, but especially in the Jurassic Period. They only lived in water. Some of today's living bivalve families have changed very little over many millions of years. Common, modern bivalves include mussels and cockles. Bivalves are one of the most common fossils found around Whitby. They are often overlooked but come in various shapes and sizes, they formed an important part of the ecosystem.

Pseudopecten equivalvis
Age: Upper Pliensbachian
Cleveland Ironstone Formation
Penny Nab Member
Location: Staithes
Occurrence: Common
Robinson Collection

Pseudomytiloides is perhaps the most commonly found bivalve around Whitby. Specimens can be found compressed or inflated (bottom). They are usually found in mass accumulations. Often the original shell is preserved, sometimes specimens such as this are found with a thin layer of pyrite that coats the shell.

Pseudomytiloides dubius
Age: Lower Toarcian
Whitby Mudstone Formation
Mulgrave Shale Member
Location: Kettleness
Occurrence: Very common
Lomax Collection

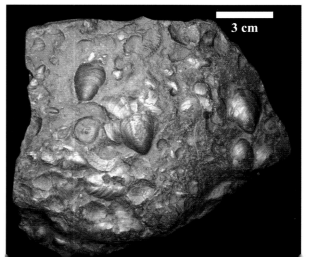

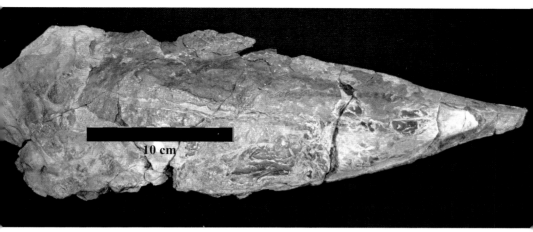

Pinna sp.
Age: Lower Pliensbachian to Upper Toarcian
Location: Ravenscar
Occurrence: Reasonable
Bolton Collection

Fossils of *Pinna* are often found as impressions. The fossilised *Pinna* differs very little from the living *Pinna* (right). They usually lie buried with their pointed ends downwards. It is highly likely the fossilised *Pinna* would have lived a very similar lifestyle. The living *Pinna* are found worldwide, this specimen was photographed in Singapore.

Pholadomya sp.
Age: Upper Pliensbachian
Location: Staithes
Occurrence: Reasonable
Whitby Museum
WHITM: SIM783

Gryphaea sp.
Age: Upper Sinemurian to Upper
Toarcian
Location: Robin Hood's Bay
Occurrence: Very common
Doncaster Museum
DONMG: ZG628

This extinct oyster is one of the most
common and iconic of the bivalves
found in the British Jurassic; it resembles a grotesque toenail, hence it's
nickname of devil's toenail.

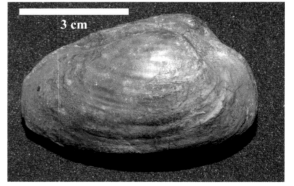

Pleuromya sp.
Age: Upper Pliensbachian to Upper
Toarcian
Whitby Mudstone Formation
Location: Whitby
Occurrence: Very common
Manchester Museum
LL.15927.4754

Most bivalves are very similar in shape
and general size; however they can be
identified from different views such
as the dorsal view seen right. Note the
two separate valves.

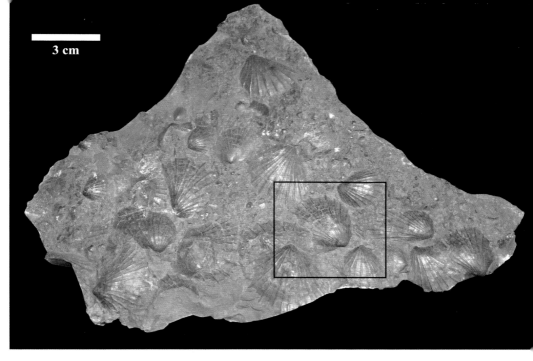

Oxytoma ?inaequivalvis
Age: Upper Pliensbachian
Cleveland Ironstone Formation
Location: Staithes
Occurrence: Reasonable
Manchester Museum
L.8019.a,b

Blocks such as this are relatively uncommon. However, small blocks containing *Oxytoma* and individual specimens are much more common. The bivalves are greatly detailed and have strong radiating ribs.

Dacryomya ovum
Age: Lower Toarcian
Whitby Mudstone Formation
Alum Shale Member
Location: Whitby
Occurrence: Very common
Doncaster Museum
DONMG: ZG2682

Cardinia listeri
Age: Upper Sinemurian
Redcar Mudstone Formation
Location: Robin Hood's Bay
Occurrence: Reasonable
Whitby Museum
WHITM: GEO3644

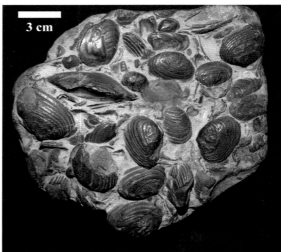

Ceromya nitida
Age: Upper Pliensbachian
Cleveland Ironstone Formation?
Location: Kettleness
Occurrence: Uncommon
Whitby Museum
WHITM: SIM343.1

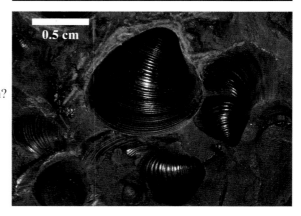

3 cm

Pseudolimea sp.
Age: Lower Toarcian
Whitby Mudstone Formation
Location: Port Mulgrave
Occurrence: Very common
Hyde Collection

These bivalves are found in mass accumulations. They are usually found
in worn nodules, which once cracked
open yield detailed individuals.

3 cm

Bositra buchi
Age: Lower Toarcian
Whitby Mudstone Formation
Alum Shale Member
Location: Saltwick Bay
Occurrence: Very common
Lomax Collection

A very common bivalve frequently
found as compressed specimens in
large numbers within the shales.
Shell material is usually present (as
seen here) but it is very fragile.

Brachiopods

Brachiopods are two-valved, marine animals that superficially resemble bivalves but they are not closely related. They were most successful in the Palaeozoic Era, but by the Mesozoic their diversity and numbers were drastically reduced and ecologically they were largely replaced by bivalve molluscs.

Lingula beani
Age: Upper Toarcian
Blea Wyke Sandstone Formation
Grey Sandstone Member
Location: Ravenscar
Occurrence: Reasonable
Yorkshire Museum
YORYM: 2007.8836.6

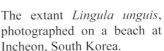

The extant *Lingula unguis*, photographed on a beach at Incheon, South Korea.

Tetrarhynchia tetraedra
Age: Upper Pliensbachian
Cleveland Ironstone Formation
Kettleness Member
Location: Staithes
Occurrence: Reasonable
British Geological Survey
BGS GSM 39510

Crinoids

Crinoids, more commonly known as 'sea lilies' or 'feather stars' resemble plants but are in actual fact animals (echinoderms). Crinoids still live today but in coral reefs and in the deep sea. Their fossils are uncommon at Whitby; some locations are more productive for crinoid fossils than others. However, it is relatively common to find parts of crinoid stems (ossicles), small star-shaped 'rocks' in the shingle at most locations. Heads of crinoids, called the calyx are rare, but if found are usually associated with the stems. In life, some crinoids would have lived attached to a substrate such as floating driftwood, and some fossil crinoid specimens have been found associated with the fossilised driftwood.

Reconstruction of *Pentacrinites*.

Crinoid calyxes
Pentacrinites dichotomus
Age: Lower Toarcian
Whitby Mudstone Formation
Mulgrave Shale Member
Location: Whitby
Occurrence: Rare
Whitby Museum
WHITM: SIM769

Note the interesting structure of the calyx with protruding stem.

3 cm

Balanocrinus ?gracilis
Age: Lower Pliensbachian
Redcar Mudstone Formation
Pyritous Shales
Location: Robin Hood's Bay
Occurrence: Rare
Bolton Collection

3 cm

Hispidocrinus scalaris
Age: Upper Sinemurian
Redcar Mudstone Formation
Siliceous Shales
Location: Robin Hood's Bay
Occurrence: Uncommon
Bolton Collection

A relatively rare crinoid at Whitby, isolated star-shaped stems (inset) and ossicles are found in the shales on the foreshore, such as in the specimen illustrated.

Balanocrinus solenotis
Age: Upper Pliensbachian
Cleveland Ironstone Formation
Location: Staithes
Occurrence: Rare
Bolton Collection

Another rare crinoid. Fragments of stems and isolated ossicles are relatively rare too. This specimen consists solely of a large stem with individual cirri (small stem-like protrusions).

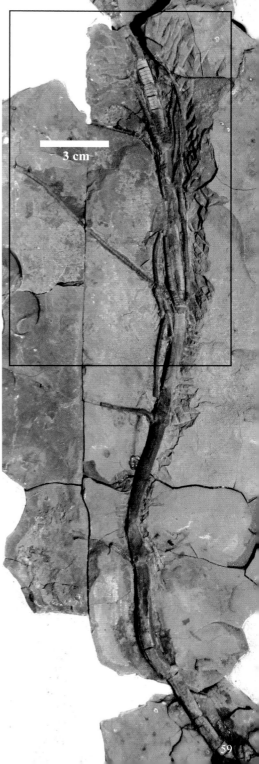

3 cm

It is understandable when looking at the specimens illustrated, why crinoids are often misidentified as plants or the roots of plants. From the photographs one can see that the crinoids consist of an individual stem with branching arms.

Echinoids (sea urchins)

The remains of echinoid fossils at Whitby are extremely rare. Very few complete specimens are known. However, the specimen illustrated has been included to show what they look like in case you do happen to find one. This specimen exhibits beautiful protruding spines and the Aristotle's lantern (chewing organ) is exquisitely preserved.

Live thorny sea urchins *Prionocidaris* sp. from Singapore.

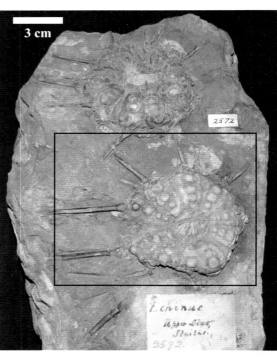

Procidaris edwardsi
Age: Upper Pliensbachian
?Staithes Sandstone Formation
Location: Staithes
Occurrence: Very rare
Whitby Museum
WHITM: SIM2572

The details preserved in echinoderm fossils are fantastic. It is understandable why echinoderms become disassociated with so many fragmentary sections. Note the similarities between the living and fossil specimens.

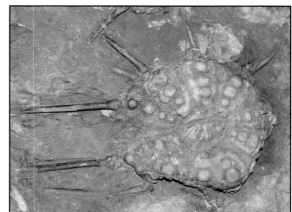

Ophiuroids (brittle stars)

Fossil brittle stars are relatively uncommon along the Whitby coastline, but if you are lucky enough to find one they are often highly detailed and beautifully preserved (see next page). The majority of specimens are discovered as partials due to their fragile nature. The oldest brittle star fossils have been dated to almost 500 million-years-old. Over the course of their history the basic shape and body plan has changed very little. Each brittle star illustrated has been identified as *Palaeocoma*. They were originally identified as *Ophioderma*, but most probably do not belong to this extant brittle star genus.

Palaeocoma milleri
Age: Upper Pliensbachian
Staithes Sandstone Formation
Location: Staithes
Occurrence: Rare
Manchester Museum
LL.12166

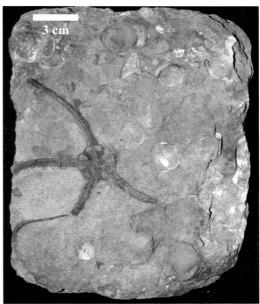

Live brittle star *Ophiomaza cacaotica* from Singapore.

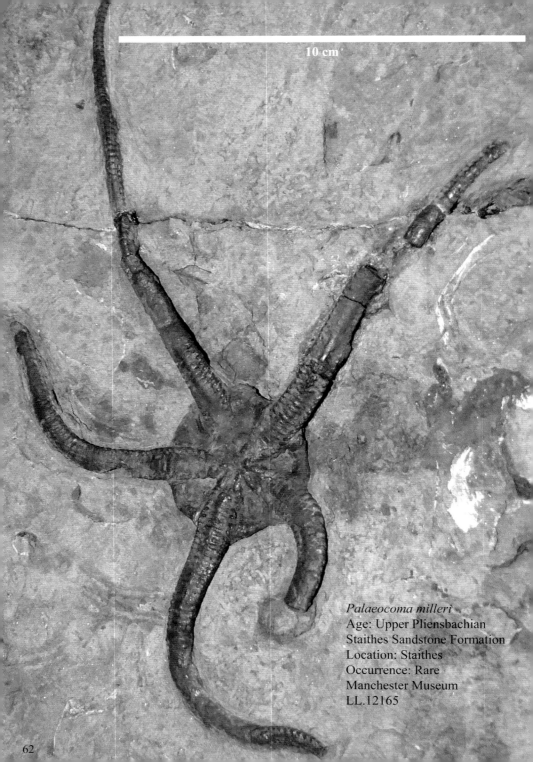

10 cm

Palaeocoma milleri
Age: Upper Pliensbachian
Staithes Sandstone Formation
Location: Staithes
Occurrence: Rare
Manchester Museum
LL.12165

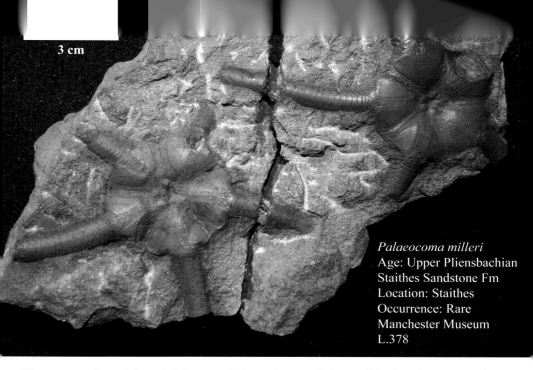

Palaeocoma milleri
Age: Upper Pliensbachian
Staithes Sandstone Fm
Location: Staithes
Occurrence: Rare
Manchester Museum
L.378

The preservation of these brittle stars differ to the rest. It is possible that the strong reddish brown colouration is due to large amounts of iron in the depositional environment.

Palaeocoma milleri
Age: Upper Pliensbachian
Staithes Sandstone Formation
Location: Staithes
Occurrence: Uncommon
Hyde Collection

Brittle star specimens can be found eroded, but the detail is still present as can be seen in this much worn specimen.

Crustaceans

Crustaceans (mainly lobsters and shrimps) occur as fossils in nodules around the Whitby area. They are quite common, but recognising the correct nodules takes time and practice. The nodules tend to be small and rounded and if cracked open with a hammer the fossil is often damaged. The alternative is to prepare them with specialised tools such as air pens. Specimens are often fragmentary but occasionally you get an easily recognisable shrimp or lobster. Determining the correct genus and species can prove very difficult because there has been insufficient research of the fossilised crustaceans found at Whitby.

Reconstruction of
Eocarcinus praecursor.

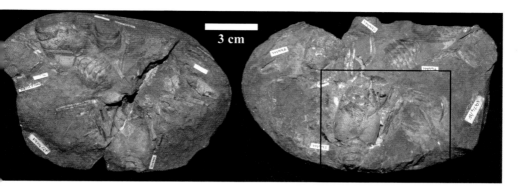

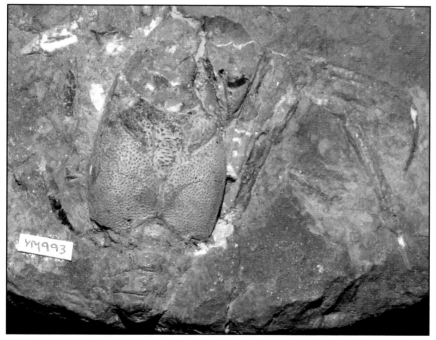

Eocarcinus praecursor
Age: ?Lower Pliensbachian
Location: Runswick Bay
Occurrence: Very rare
Yorkshire Museum
YORYM: G993–6

This is one of the oldest species of true crab, considered an evolutionary transition between lobsters and crabs. It was collected as a loose nodule on the beach, but exact horizon data are unknown. It may have come from elsewhere along the coast. The close up shows detailed patterned preservation of the pitted surface of the carapace and appendages.

Partial lobster
Undetermined species
Age: Lower Toarcian
Whitby Mudstone Formation
Location: Possibly Whitby
Occurrence: Uncommon
Manchester Museum
LL.12145

Lobster legs in nodule
Possibly *Pseudoglyphea* sp.
Age: Lower Toarcian
Whitby Mudstone Formation
Location: Whitby
Occurrence: Common
Lomax Collection

The commonly found nodules most often contain only small fragmentary remains.

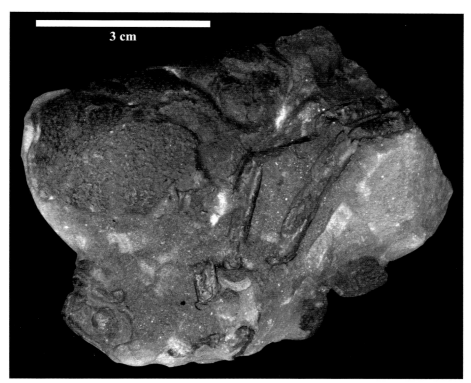

Lobster claw
Eryma sp.
Age: Lower Toarcian
Whitby Mudstone Formation
Grey Shale Member
Location: Port Mulgrave
Occurrence: Uncommon
Hyde Collection

Lobster carapace and legs
Eryma sp.
Age: Upper Toarcian
Blea Wyke Sandstone Formation
Location: Ravenscar
Occurrence: Uncommon
Manchester Museum
STR.1670.a–i

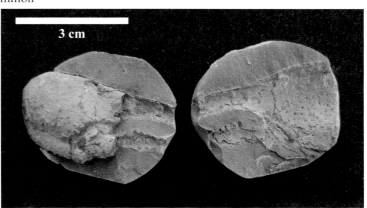

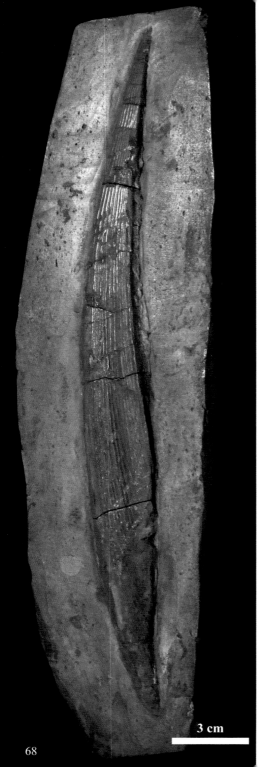

3 cm

Fish and sharks

The fossilised remains of fish at Whitby were previously found in abundance, specifically when alum quarrying was an important industry. However, complete specimens are now probably rarer than the marine reptiles. The most commonly occurring fish remains are found inside nodules as sections of bones, or as an accumulation of scales.

Shark spine
Hybodus sp.
Age: Sinemurian
Redcar Mudstone Formation
Location: Robin Hood's Bay?
Occurrence: Rare
Manchester Museum
LL.12926

This specimen has very little provenance, although it probably came from the Whitby area as specimens of this early shark have been recorded from the Lias of this coastline and further up the coast. This is a dorsal spine of the animal, see in the reconstruction overleaf (spine on back).

Reconstruction of *Hybodus* sp.

69

3D preserved fish are very rare. They are extremely interesting fossils because they give an insight into the true size and shape of what the fish was like in life. This allows for close interpretation of fossils as illustrated in the reconstruction below.

Complete 3D Fish
Lepidotes semiserratus
Age: Lower Toarcian
Whitby Mudstone Formation
Location: Whitby
Occurrence: Very rare
Manchester Museum
LL.12154
(illustrated upside-down, with head to the right)

10 cm

Reconstruction of *Lepidotes* sp.

Reconstruction of *Gyrosteus* sp.

Gyrosteus was a large sturgeon-like fish which possibly reached 17 feet in length. Isolated bones of this fish are common, but no scales or vertebrae have ever been described.

Gyrosteus mirabilis
Age: Lower Toarcian
Whitby Mudstone Formation
Mulgrave Shale Member
Location: Saltwick Bay
Occurrence: Reasonable
Lomax Collection

Scales of *L. semiserratus*
Age: Lower Toarcian
Whitby Mudstone Formation
Location: Whitby
Occurrence: Uncommon
Manchester Museum
LL.15941.923

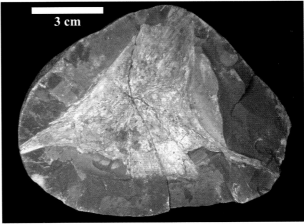

3 cm

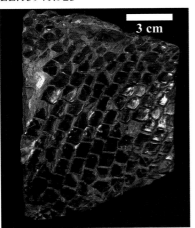

3 cm

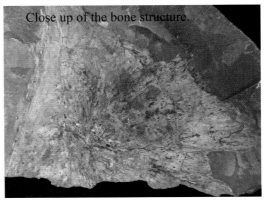

Close up of the bone structure.

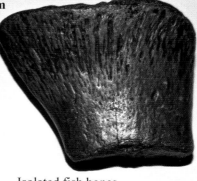

Isolated fish bones
probably *Gyrosteus mirabilis*
Age: Lower Toarcian
Whitby Mudstone Formation
Mulgrave Shale Member
Location: Saltwick Bay
Occurrence: Reasonable
Robinson Collection

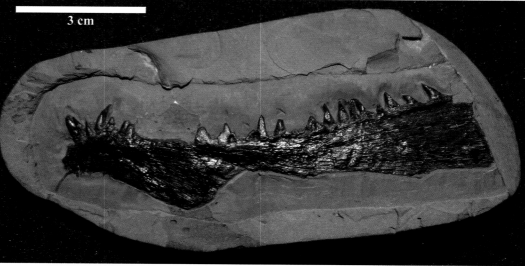

Jaw section
Undetermined species
Age: Lower Toarcian
Whitby Mudstone Formation
Mulgrave Shale Member?
Location: Port Mulgrave
Occurrence: Rare
Smith Collection

Identifying the particular type of fish this rare partial jaw belonged to is near impossible. A more complete fossil would be required to determine the correct identification, but unfortunately in this case only the jaw and teeth were found.

Fish in nodule (illustrated head end – partially eroded – uppermost)
Possibly *Dapedium* sp.
Age: Lower Toarcian
Whitby Mudstone Formation
Location: Sandsend
Occurrence: Rare
Smith Collection

5 cm

Dapedium is extremely rare from the Lias of Whitby. It is difficult
to distinguish from *Lepidotes* if insufficient material is available.

Marine reptiles

Whitby's most famous fossils are the marine reptiles. These fascinating and unusual specimens have been collected for hundreds of years. The remains have included ichthyosaurs, plesiosaurs and crocodilians. Marine reptiles are very different to dinosaurs. They swam in the ocean, whereas dinosaurs did not, although some may have paddled. The ichthyosaurs and plesiosaurs are extinct. However, the crocodilians still thrive today with several species of crocodiles, alligators, caimans and gharials. Relatively complete marine reptile remains have been discovered throughout Whitby and its surrounding areas, though such remains are very rare. Many individual marine reptile skeletons have been discovered although the commonest marine reptile finds are of isolated vertebrae which are hard to identify to species level. Correct identification usually requires a large proportion of the skeleton, including the skull.

Ichthyosaurs: A great many ichthyosaur specimens have been discovered here and the ichthyosaur holds the title of the most common marine reptile found at Whitby. Most finds are of isolated vertebrae or blocks of associated vertebrae and ribs. However, many near complete and complete specimens have been discovered, the earliest recorded example being found in 1819. Ichthyosaurs superficially resemble dolphins and sharks, but are unrelated. They thrived throughout the Triassic, Jurassic and early to mid Cretaceous, eventually becoming extinct towards the end of the Cretaceous.

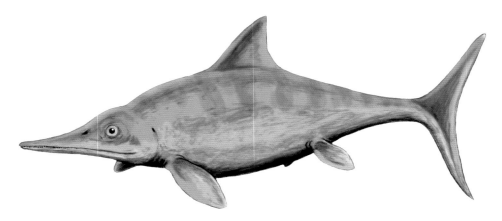

Reconstruction of an ichthyosaur.

Reconstruction of *Stenopterygius* sp.

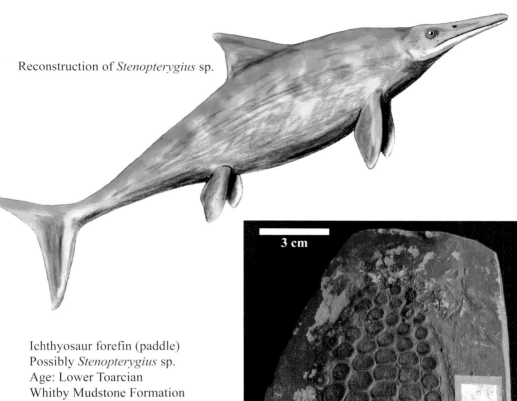

3 cm

Ichthyosaur forefin (paddle)
Possibly *Stenopterygius* sp.
Age: Lower Toarcian
Whitby Mudstone Formation
Location: Whitby
Occurrence: Rare
British Geological Survey
BGS ZK 574

Stenopterygius was a relatively medium-sized ichthyosaur, with a maximum length of no more than 13 ft (4
m). Numerous specimens of *Stenopterygius* (including those which died
during the process of giving live birth
and others which contain stomach
contents) have been found within the
Posidonia Shale at the world famous
Holzmaden lagerstätten site in Germany, the equivalent to the Lower Toarcian of Whitby.

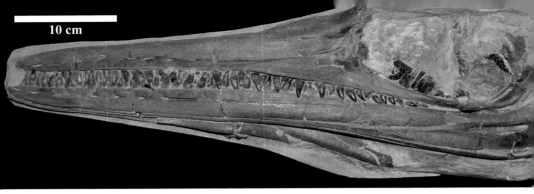

Ichthyosaur skull and close up of teeth
Stenopterygius sp.
Age: Lower Toarcian
Whitby Mudstone Formation
Location: Probably Kettleness
Occurrence: Rare
Manchester Museum
L.7543

Selection of small ichthyosaur vertebrae
Age: Lower Toarcian
Whitby Mudstone Formation
Location: Sandsend
Occurrence: Common
Smith Collection

Medium-sized ichthyosaur vertebrae
Undetermined species
Age: Lower Toarcian
Whitby Mudstone Formation
Location: Ravenscar
Occurrence: Uncommon
Manchester Museum
REP.061

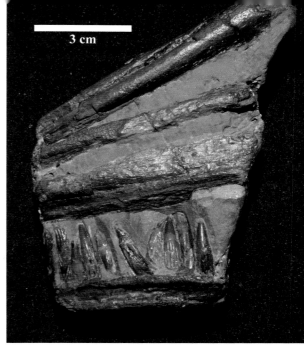

Ichthyosaur jaw section with teeth
Probably from a small
Temnodontosaurus sp.
Age: Lower Toarcian
Whitby Mudstone Formation
Location: Whitby
Occurrence: Uncommon
Smith Collection

Articulated ichthyosaur vertebrae
Undetermined species
Age: Lower Toarcian
Whitby Mudstone Formation
Location: Sandsend
Occurrence: Uncommon
Smith Collection

Worn ichthyosaur jaw section
with teeth
Undetermined species
Age: Lower Toarcian
Whitby Mudstone Formation
Location: Whitby
Occurrence: Uncommon
Manchester Museum
REP.013

This chunk of ichthyosaur jaw may not be the most visually appealing specimen seen in this book but this is what most specimens may look like due to erosion; the three teeth are highly worn, still a relatively rare find.

Ichthyosaur rib section
Undetermined species
Age: Lower Toarcian
Whitby Mudstone Formation
Mulgrave Shale Member
Location: Sandsend
Occurrence: Reasonable
Smith Collection

Reconstruction of *Eurhinosaurus* sp.

Eurhinosaurus possessed an extremely elongate snout. It somewhat resembled the modern sawfish in appearance. Numerous specimens like *Stenopterygius* have been recorded from Holzmaden, Germany.

Ichthyosaur hindfin (paddle)
Possibly *Eurhinosaurus* sp.
Age: Sinemurian to Lower Toarcian
Whitby Mudstone Formation
Location: Probably Whitby
Occurrence: Rare
Doncaster Museum
DONMG: ZG417

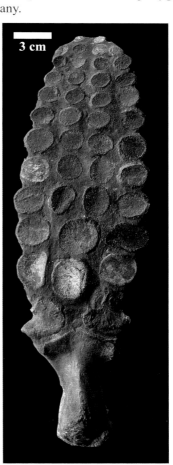

3 cm

Unfortunately the collection information available with this specimen was insufficient and simply labelled as Lias. The particular locality it derived from is unknown, though it is most likely to be the Whitby area. The specimen however was actually put back together and placed into a block matrix; we know this because the positioning of key elements of the hindfin are incorrect.

Plesiosaurs: The remains of plesiosaurs discovered along this coast have, relatively speaking, been rather good. Specimens are much rarer than their contemporaries, the ichthyosaurs, but finds have included isolated post cranial remains, to near complete specimens. Plesiosaurs like ichthyosaurs have four paddles to aid with swimming. A variety of plesiosaur species have been discovered ranging from the long necked plesiosaurs (often portrayed as the Loch Ness monster) to the short necked plesiosaurs, the pliosaurs. Pliosaurs possessed huge skulls packed with large teeth. They were the apex (top) predators that dominated the Mesozoic oceans.

Articulated plesiosaur cervical
(neck) vertebrae
Hauffiosaurus tomistomimus
Age: Lower Toarcian
Whitby Mudstone Formation
Alum Shale Member
Location: Ravenscar
Occurrence: Rare
Manchester Museum
LL.8004

An almost complete plesiosaur specimen was discovered on a field trip by the University of Manchester in the 1960s. In 2011 it was re-described as *Hauffiosaurus tomistomimus*. The vertebrae illustrated are from that specimen. Isolated plesiosaur vertebrae are quite rare and often confused with ichthyosaur vertebrae. However, they can be identified by their less concave, more robust and spherical shape.

Reconstruction of plesiosaurs.

'Isolated bone' plesiosaur partial
humerus
Undetermined species
Age: Lower Toarcian
Whitby Mudstone Formation
Location: Unclear
Occurrence: Uncommon
Whitby Museum
WHITM: GEO103

Usually isolated bones are found in large blocks and are unidentifiable.
However, small sections of bone and vertebrae can be found lying in the shales
on the foreshore. Determining the correct genus and species identification from
a single element such as a tooth or humerus can be near impossible.

Pliosaur tooth
Probably *Rhomaleosaurus* sp.
Age: Lower Toarcian
Whitby Mudstone Formation
Mulgrave Shale Member
Location: Port Mulgrave
Occurrence: Rare
Bolton Collection

Reconstruction of *Rhomaleosaurus* sp.

Crocodilians: Crocodilian remains occur in a manner similar to those of plesiosaurs; some great specimens have been discovered but they are rare. The majority of specimens found are of isolated osteoderms (dermal armour) which are easily identified by their distinct shape and pattern. A particular group of crocodilians called the thalattosuchians are the only known crocodilians from the Whitby area, with a reasonable variety described from this coast, ranging from the relatively small gharial-like species (with long and relatively slender jaws) to the medium/large-sized specimens. The fossil crocodilians have the same 'basic' structure as modern crocodiles, and have changed very little in several hundred millions of years.

Crocodilian skull and jaw
Steneosaurus ?bollensis
Age: Lower Toarcian
Whitby Mudstone Formation
Location: Whitby
Occurrence: Rare
Doncaster Museum
DONMG: ZG425

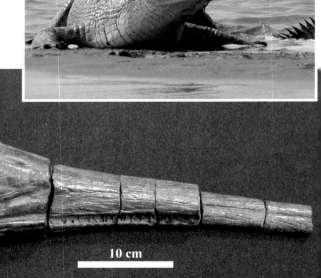

Gharial in the Chambal River, India.

10 cm

Finds such as this are rare. In this specimen the rostrum has been split into several sections. The bone can be very weak, and usually isolated sections of the rostrum are found, rather than a complete skull.

84

Reconstruction of *Steneosaurus* sp.

Section of crocodilian skull
Possibly *Pelagosaurus* sp.
Age: Lower Toarcian
Whitby Mudstone Formation
Alum Shale Member
Location: Runswick Bay
Occurrence: Rare
Smith Collection

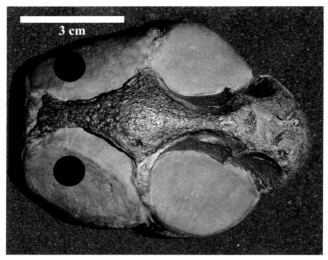

Isolated elements such as this section of skull are rare. The specimen has been prepared to help clarify where the eyes would have been situated (black circles). It is very difficult to assign the correct name to such finds when very little identifiable material is available. However, small crocodilians such as *Pelagosaurus* have been found in this area.

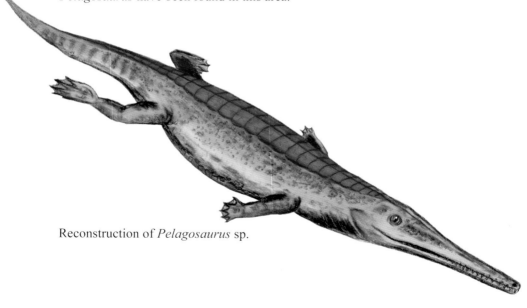

Reconstruction of *Pelagosaurus* sp.

Crocodilian osteoderm
Age: Lower Toarcian
Whitby Mudstone Formation
Alum Shale Member
Location: Kettleness
Occurrence: Uncommon
Smith Collection

Crocodilian vertebrae
Undetermined species
Age: Lower Toarcian
Whitby Mudstone Formation
Mulgrave Shale Member
Location: Sandsend
Occurrence: Uncommon
Smith Collection

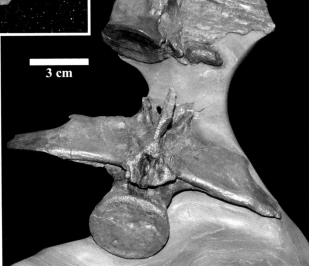

Crocodilian vertebrae are dissimilar to those of ichthyosaurs and plesiosaurs.
The shape and general structure of the processes are very different.

Dinosaurs

In reference to Whitby and the Yorkshire Coast the name *dinosaur coast* is a little misleading. Whitby has yielded some bone material tentatively identified as dinosaur but it is extremely rare. However, finding dinosaur remains is not impossible and if anything was discovered it could be of utmost importance. It is the marine reptiles that are often confused with dinosaurs and labelled 'swimming dinosaurs' which is incorrect because the marine reptiles were not dinosaurs. However, we know dinosaurs lived here during the Jurassic Period because numerous footprints have been discovered around Whitby. The footprints are preserved as natural casts; they have been attributed to theropod, sauropod, ornithopod and even thyreophoran dinosaurs. However identifying what particular dinosaur made the footprint is near impossible. Dinosaur footprints, although present in large numbers, are difficult to find and often need a bit of imagination when visualising them, as erosion has often 'deformed' specimens on the beach. Most dinosaur footprints are found in huge, impossible to carry boulders. Please do not try and remove dinosaur footprints as you will destroy them. Allow others to see and learn from such specimens.

This footprint belongs to either an ornithopod or theropod dinosaur, although it is very difficult to distinguish between the two. Note the tridactyl (three-toed) print.

The large, flattened and spherical surface indicates this print may belong to a sauropod dinosaur. Note the strong toe impression at the bottom.

Both of the above have been taken from the image opposite.

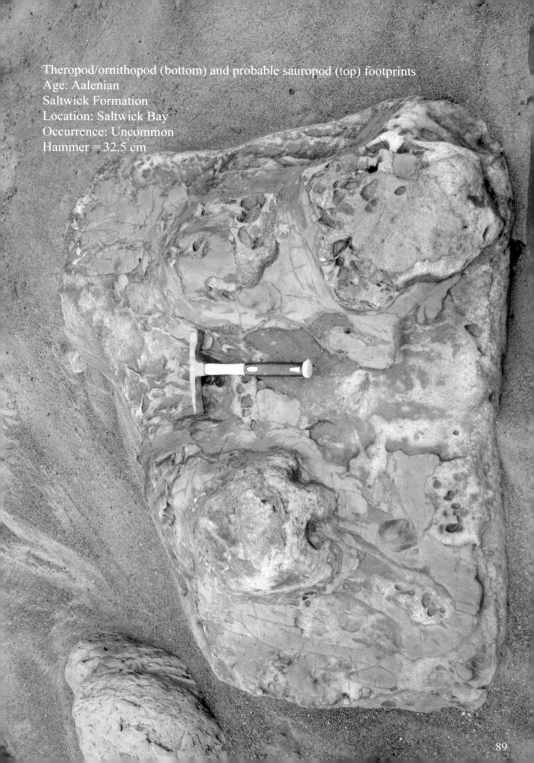

Theropod/ornithopod (bottom) and probable sauropod (top) footprints
Age: Aalenian
Saltwick Formation
Location: Saltwick Bay
Occurrence: Uncommon
Hammer = 32.5 cm

Reconstruction of a theropod dinosaur walking along the beach around 175 million years ago, leaving behind footprints.

3 cm

Theropod/ornithopod footprint
Undetermined species
Age: Aalenian
Saltwick Formation
Location: Port Mulgrave
Occurrence: Uncommon
Smith Collection

A line has been sketched over this image to highlight the footprint.

Plants

Whitby is famous for its plant beds and yields a variety of types including ferns, horsetails and cycadophytes; they are usually found in the sandstones. The fossilised plants are generally quite common in certain areas and range from small fragments of leaves to complete fronds. Most plant genera discussed are considered as 'living fossils' or they belong to groups that do not exist anymore, such as the bennettitaleans. It can be difficult to identify plant remains accurately because there are many similar types, different parts of which can carry separate names.

Horsetails: These are characterised by an alternation of nodes (bearing leaves) and internodes along the stem. The name 'horsetail' arose because the branching of these plants somewhat resembles a horse's tail. They would usually grow in wet areas such as swamps, often forming dense thickets.

10 cm

Equisetum columnare
Age: Aalenian
Saltwick Formations
Location: Port Mulgrave
Occurrence: Common
Whitby Museum
WHITM: GEO179

Modern horsetail. Compare the individual sections of the living horsetail with the fossils.

Compressions of nodes with leaves
Equisetites lateralis
Age: Aalenian
Saltwick Formation
Location: Port Mulgrave
Occurrence: Uncommon
Manchester Museum
LL.15952.637

3 cm

Ferns: The fossilised remains of ferns are perhaps the most iconic and easily recognisable plant fossils. They are often identified by their fronds, which are usually delicate. Over 12,000 extant species of fern are known.

Todites williamsonii
Age: Aalenian
Saltwick Formation
Location: Whitby
Occurrence: Uncommon
Whitby Museum
WHITM: GEO2514

Cladophlebis denticulata
Age: Aalenian
Saltwick Formation
Location: Whitby
Occurrence: Uncommon
Whitby Museum
WHITM: GEO6

The detail of the individual leaves is fantastic.

*Coniopteris
hymenophylloides*
Age: Aalenian
Saltwick Formation
Location: Whitby
Occurrence: Uncommon
Manchester Museum
L.8020

10 cm

Cycads: Cycads somewhat resemble palms; they have a large stout trunk with a crown of compound leaves. The first cycad fossils have been recorded in rocks that date back to the Permian Period and are more than 280 million-years-old. However, the Jurassic is often touted as the 'Age of Cycads' because they were so abundant. There are more than 100 extant species of cycads today.

Nilssonia compta
Age: Aalenian
Saltwick Formation
Location: Whitby
Occurrence: Uncommon
Manchester Museum
LL.15952.1476

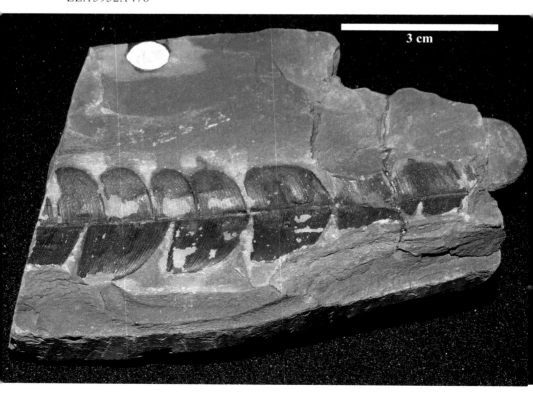

Bennettitaleans: Bennettitalean plants are often mistaken for cycads or ferns, but are neither. They had woody stems with several leaves, which resembled those of (modern) cycads. They produced the earliest flower-like reproductive structures known in the fossil record. Some of the leaves were not pinnately divided but were entire. The bennettitaleans became extinct during the Cretaceous Period.

Otozamites graphicus
Age: Aalenian
Saltwick Formation
Location: Whitby–Saltwick Bay
Occurrence: Uncommon
University of Utrecht
S.1524

Zamites gigas
Age: Aalenian
Saltwick Formation
Location: Whitby
Occurrence: Reasonable
National Centre of Biodiversity-
Naturalis
JMS 52426

Nilssoniopteris major
Age: Aalenian
Saltwick Formation
Location: Whitby
Occurrence: Reasonable
National Centre of Biodiversity-
Naturalis
JMS 52429

Left: male flower-like structure of *Ptilophyllum pectinoides*: *Weltrichia whitbiensis*
Below: *Ptilophyllum pectinoides*
Age: Aalenian
Saltwick Formation
Location: Whitby
Occurrence (left): Uncommon
Occurrence (below): Common
Manchester Museum
Left: L.8044 and below: L.8647

Reconstruction of *Ptilophyllum* sp.

Conifers: Most conifer fragments discovered are twigs carrying small leaves. The fact that these were only small fragments of conifer remains (contrary to the larger fern and cycadophyte fossils found along the Whitby coast) indicates that they probably originated from upland vegetation. The majority of fossilised wood found at Whitby (see next page) was produced by araucariaceous conifers.

Brachyphyllum mamillare
Age: Aalenian
Saltwick Formation
Location: Whitby
Occurrence: Reasonable
University of Utrecht
S.1330

Wood

Fossilised wood is one of the most common fossils found around Whitby, but can often be mistaken as just a simple 'rock'. Once the remnants of subtropical forests, most of the wood found is very fragile and encrusted with the mineral pyrite. However, some specimens are stable and have beautiful detail. The most famous fossil wood is 'Whitby jet'. Despite being considered a precious stone or mineral jet is actually a fossil. The small, and more rarely found larger sections of jet were once part of large coniferous trees similar to the modern-day *Araucaria* trees, more commonly known as the monkey puzzle. Logs of these trees were transported into the sea and then became waterlogged and sank. Jet is surprisingly very light and the colour is usually black or dark brown. Finding jet can prove quite difficult because it often occurs in seams which erode out quickly. However, jet is very light and can be washed onto the beach into the shingle rather easily. Large blocks of sandstone are found frequently lying on most beaches around Whitby. They often contain chunks of dense wood material. These blocks often fall from high in the cliffs during harsh weather conditions or landslips.

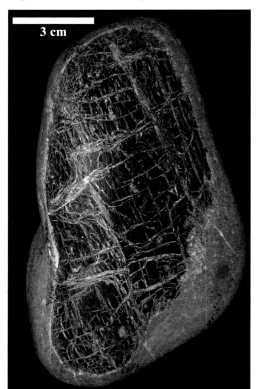

Chunk of jet on matrix
Age: Lower Toarcian
Whitby Mudstone Formation
Location: Port Mulgrave
Occurrence: Common
Lomax Collection

Araucaria angustifolia cloud forest, Itaimbezinho Canyon, Rio Grande do Sul, Brazil. Similar subtropical forests would have covered the Whitby area during the Aalenian Stage of the Jurassic Period.

Araucaria tree chunk (Whitby jet)
Age: Lower Toarcian
Whitby Mudstone Formation
Mulgrave Shale Member
Location: Whitby
Occurrence: Uncommon
Whitby Museum
WHITM: SIM419

Variety of wood
Undetermined species
Age: Lower Toarcian to Aalenian
Whitby Mudstone Formation to Saltwick Formation
Location: Saltwick Bay
Occurrence: Very common
Hyde and Lomax Collections

A large variety of fossilised wood of all shapes and sizes can be found along this coast. It is often covered with the mineral pyrite (top left).

Large block of wood
Undetermined species
Age: Aalenian
Saltwick Formation
Location: Near Kettleness
Occurrence: Very common
Hammer = 32.5 cm

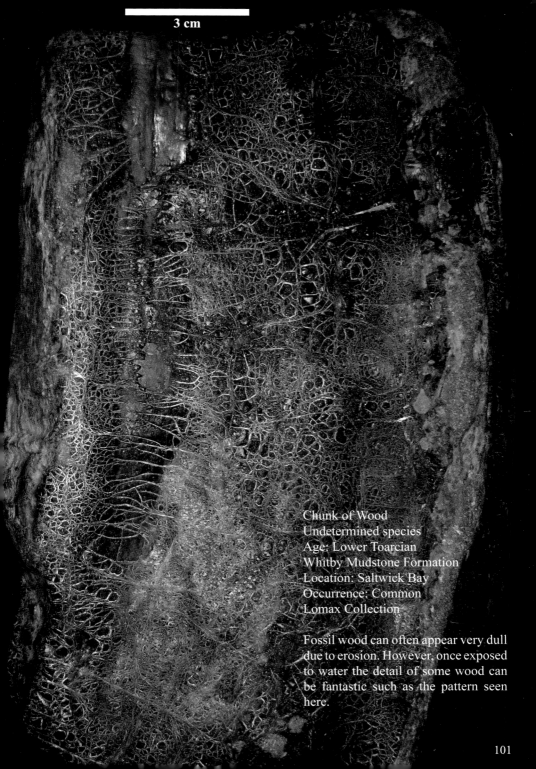

3 cm

Chunk of Wood
Undetermined species
Age: Lower Toarcian
Whitby Mudstone Formation
Location: Saltwick Bay
Occurrence: Common
Lomax Collection

Fossil wood can often appear very dull due to erosion. However, once exposed to water the detail of some wood can be fantastic such as the pattern seen here.

Trace fossils

Trace fossils are common and are important because they provide evidence of past behaviours. An excellent example of a trace fossil is a dinosaur footprint. The footprint is not actually a body fossil of the animal but represents something the animal was doing millions of years ago. Many organisms, such as burrowing bivalves, worms, crustaceans etc. form tracks and burrows which become fossilised. An important kind of trace fossil is a coprolite, which is fossil poop! Identifying which animal left its trace is near impossible, unless the animal that made it was also preserved. However, this is an extremely rare occurrence. Other interesting trace structures (not technically trace fossils) include ripple marks similar to those made by the sea today.

3 cm

The coprolites discovered along this coastline can form unusual shapes. Most coprolites are mistaken for a simple pebble, worn round by the sea. However, the specimen to the left has tiny orange coloured fish scales preserved across the surface. The coprolites were probably made by marine reptiles such as ichthyosaurs (pictured), plesiosaurs and crocodilians. However, unusually spiralled and smaller coprolites have been noted from fish and sharks.

Marine reptile coprolite
Age: Lower Toarcian
Whitby Mudstone Formation
Location: Kettleness
Occurrence: Reasonable
Manchester Museum
STR.0014.a,b

Reconstruction of an ichthyosaur.

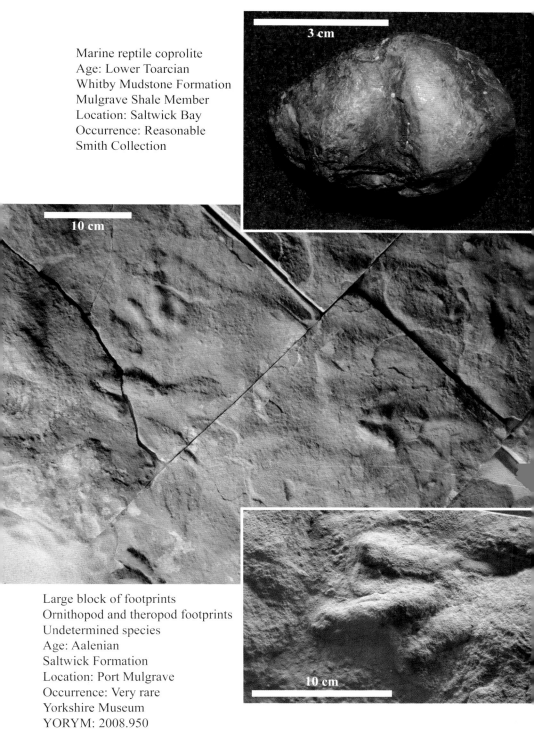

Marine reptile coprolite
Age: Lower Toarcian
Whitby Mudstone Formation
Mulgrave Shale Member
Location: Saltwick Bay
Occurrence: Reasonable
Smith Collection

Large block of footprints
Ornithopod and theropod footprints
Undetermined species
Age: Aalenian
Saltwick Formation
Location: Port Mulgrave
Occurrence: Very rare
Yorkshire Museum
YORYM: 2008.950

Ripple marks are largely seen in huge, impossible-to-move boulders. They are a great geological feature found at several localities. Large quantities of ripple marks can be seen at Staithes. The image above is of modern ripple marks made on the beach at Robin Hood's Bay.

Ripple marks (probably an erratic)
Age: Pliensbachian
Staithes Sandstone Formation
Location: Runswick Bay
Occurrence: Uncommon
Lomax Collection

Serpulid worm tubes
Age: Lower/Upper Pliensbachian
(boundary within formation)
Staithes Sandstone Formation
Location: Staithes
Occurrence: Reasonable
British Geological Survey
BGS GSM 118957

This is a secreted tube of a serpulid
worm that was originally described as
a scaphopod (mollusc with a tusk-like
shell) called *Dentalium*. The serpulid
worm tubes are not technically trace
fossils, however they are commonly
misinterpreted as such. In actual fact,
they are solid shell structures.

Modern sand tracks made by *Arachnoides placenta* an extant echinoid
from Singapore. Tracks similar to
these and burrows (below) can be
found along the Whitby coastline.
Trace fossils are quite unique because
they allow a glimpse into a moment of
the Earth's very distant past.

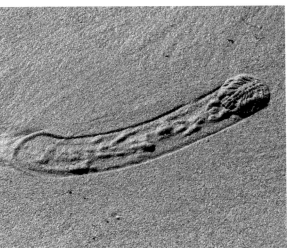

Crustacean burrow
Rhizocorallium
Age: Upper Pliensbachian
Cleveland Ironstone Formation
Penny Nab Member
Location: Staithes
Occurrence: Very common
Hammer = 32.5 cm

Pseudo fossils

When is a fossil not a fossil? When it is a pseudo fossil. Pseudo fossils are extremely common and consist of strange-shaped rocks with markings or impressions that may be mistaken for true fossils. Some of the most common pseudo fossils are unusually shaped rocks worn by the sea to form 'tooth-like' shapes or pseudo-vertebrae and other bones. Others include minerals such as pyrite (fool's gold) which can form deceptive nodules. Unruly fossil collectors may leave scratches or marks on rocks that can resemble parts of a fossil. Some pseudofossils can be very convincing and experience is necessary to distinguish them from the real thing.

Cone-in-cone
Location: Runswick Bay
Manchester Museum
M10470

The cone-in-cone structure is quite literally what it says; several cone-shaped structures placed one within the other. The cones are often orientated vertically. They are believed to form through the growth of fibrous crystals.

Pseudo fossils such as those illustrated are extremely common. Specimens such as these have in the past fooled some experts. Compare the pseudo vertebrae with the articulated ichthyosaur vertebrae in the marine reptiles section. Pyrite is an extremely common mineral and nicknamed fool's gold; it can form in a variety of shapes and sizes. Some fossils (as seen in this guide) can be fully preserved in pyrite, giving the fossil a beautiful finish. However, on the contrary some fossils can be affected by pyrite, which can lead to decay and destruction of the specimen. The first signs are usually a strong sulfur-like smell.

Pseudo vertebrae
Location: Ravenscar
Hyde Collection

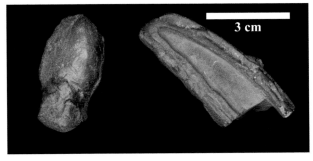

Pseudo dinosaur teeth
Location: Saltwick Bay
Robinson Collection

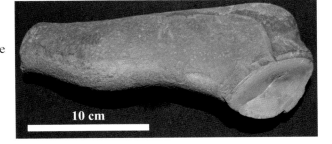

Bone-like pyrite nodule
Location: Whitby
Doncaster Museum
DONMG: ZG687

Glacial erratics 'derived fossils'

Not all fossils found at Whitby originate from the Jurassic Period. There are numerous pebbles containing corals from the Carboniferous Period (around 330 million years ago) and mammal bones and teeth from more recent times including the Pleistocene (2.5 million–12,000 years ago) and Holocene Epochs (12,000 years ago–modern day) of the Quaternary Period. These fossils and unusual rocks found with them are known as glacial erratics. The glacial erratics were transported here by glaciers during the last ice age which finished around 12,000 years ago. It is difficult to pinpoint the exact location from which the fossils originated, however it is not impossible because you may be able to link specimens from Whitby with specimens found in other more northerly locations such as Scotland!

Coral
Siphonodendron sp.
Age: Carboniferous Period (Visean–Namurian)
around 330 million-years-old
Location: Whitby
Occurrence: Very common
Lomax Collection

Coral specimens such as those illustrated are often discovered in large numbers. They may look worn and rather dull, but once you put one in water you see a completely different fossil with beautiful detail! This huge coral erratic was found lying on the beach at Kettleness. Hammer = 32.5 cm.

108

Ammonite erratic
Psiloceras erugatum
Age: Hettangian
Redcar Mudstone Formation
Location: Runswick Bay
Occurrence: Uncommon
Manchester Museum
LL.5720

Ammonite and carboniferous fossils are the most common glacial erratics to discover. Though it must be said, any fossil found further down the coast and not from its usual collection site is considered an erratic.

Isolated crinoid stem
Age: Carboniferous Period
(Visean–Namurian)
around 330 million-years-old
Location: Whitby
Occurrence: Common
Hyde Collection

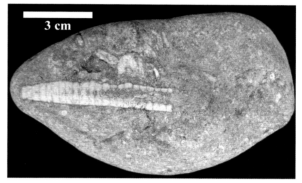

Pleurotomaria cognata
Age: Lower Sinemurian
Redcar Mudstone Formation
Location: Staithes
(originally from Redcar)
Occurrence: Uncommon
Yorkshire Museum
YORYM: 2005.813.2

Hexactinellid sponge
Hyalostelia-type root tuft
Age: Carboniferous Period
(Visean–Namurian)
around 330 million-years-old
Location: Runswick Bay
Occurrence: Uncommon
Robinson Collection

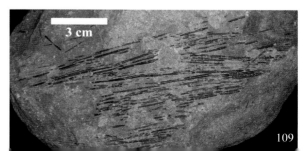

Mammoth molar tooth
Mammuthus trogontherii 'Steppe Mammoth'
Age: Pleistocene (600,000–500,000 years-old)
Location: Robin Hood's Bay
Occurrence: Rare
Whitby Museum WHITM: SIM112

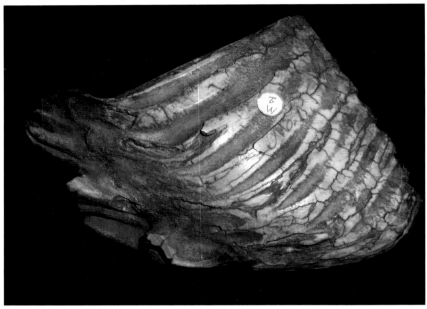

5 cm

The mammoth tooth opposite is extremely rare. It was collected during the 1800s. However, specimens such as this are not impossible to find today. During the last Ice Age, the North Sea was at certain points almost completely land and home to numerous prehistoric animals from the mammoth

Reconstruction of *Mammuthus trogontherii*

111

Auroch molar teeth *Bos* sp.
Age: Holocene (probably a few hundred to thousands of years old)
Location: Whitby
Occurrence: Uncommon
Lomax Collection

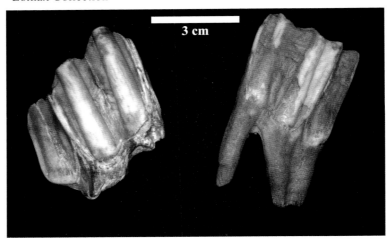

The auroch is the ancestor of domestic cattle; the last recorded specimen died in 1627.

Major finds

With such a rich source for fossil remains there is no surprise that Whitby and its surrounding areas have yielded some of the best Lower Jurassic fossils in the U.K. Some of the most famous are discussed below.

The famous 'crocodile' of Whitby: In 1824 one of the most, if not the most complete crocodilian skeleton was discovered at Saltwick Bay. It belonged to the animal *Steneosaurus bollensis* (previously *Teleosaurus chapmani*). The specimen is almost complete with only sections of both the forelimbs and the majority of the rostrum missing; it is preserved with magnificent detail including many osteoderms (bony plates along the back). The specimen is on display at the Whitby Museum in Pannet Park. It allows visitors to gain an understanding of one of the animals that once lived here and is a good resource for comparisons of crocodilian remains found by fossil hunters.

Reconstruction of *Steneosaurus bollensis*

Steneosaurus bollensis
Whitby Museum
WHITM: SIM770

10 cm

The giant 'fish-lizard': *Temnodontosaurus* sp. was found in 1893 at Kettleness. It is more than 6 metres long and has been on display in Manchester Museum since the 1890s. The ichthyosaur is relatively complete, part of which is a composite, as the forefin is from another ichthyosaur. This was common practice with alum workers who discovered such fossils and placed unassociated bones together to make specimens more aesthetically pleasing. Like all ichthyosaurs, *Temnodontosaurus* possessed enormous eyes. In fact, ichthyosaurs possessed the biggest eyes of any animal, relative to the size of their body! *Temnodontosaurus* was a large ichthyosaur and some specimens apparently reached lengths of 40 ft (12 m).

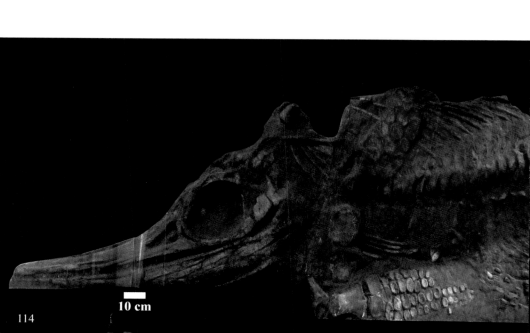

10 cm

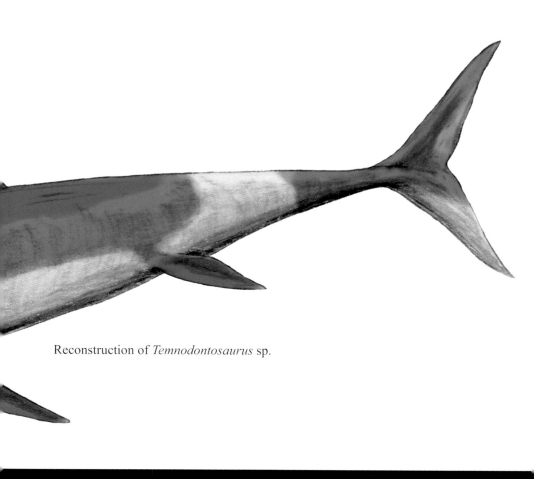

Reconstruction of *Temnodontosaurus* sp.

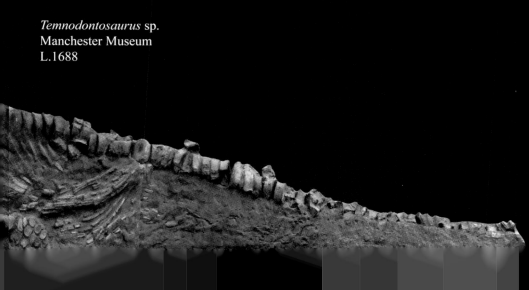

Temnodontosaurus sp.
Manchester Museum
L.1688

The mega pliosaur: This specimen was found at Kettleness during the year 1848 when the alum mining was big business. Many fossils were discovered including the remains of this huge and near complete pliosaur (short-necked plesiosaur) which included the skull. This huge 6.7 metre (22 ft) long specimen is called *Rhomaleosaurus cramptoni* and is one of the largest near complete pliosaurs ever discovered. The specimen is famously known from a cast on display in the Natural History Museum, London. However, the original is held in the collections of the National Museum of Ireland.

Reconstructions of
Rhomaleosaurus cramptoni.

Rhomaleosaurus cramptoni
National Museum of Ireland
NMING F8785 (holotype)

The tiny pterosaur: Pterosaurs, pronounced 'teh-row-sores' with a silent 'p' were some of the strangest and most fantastic animals ever to have lived. They were flying reptiles that soared in the skies around Whitby at the same time that the marine reptiles lived in the ocean. Only one pterosaur specimen has been recorded from the Whitby area and belongs to a species called *Parapsicephalus purdoni*. It is the only known specimen and consists of a partial skull with a cast of the brain cavity visible. The fossil is kept in the collections of the British Geological Survey (BGS). Pterosaur fossils are usually rare, most probably due to their fragile, hollow bones. The specimen was found at Loftus Quarry near Whitby in the 1880s, although theoretically, future discoveries could be made at any of the locations discussed in this guide! If any other pterosaur material is discovered, it should be reported to a museum.

Parapsicephalus purdoni
British Geological Survey
BGS GSM 3166 (holotype)

5 cm

Reconstruction of *Parapsicephalus purdoni*.

First time fossil hunt

Most fossil identification guides, such as this, include specimens that are considered the 'best of the best', fossils that are the largest of their type, completely prepared (with the rocks that entombed them removed) and well preserved. This guide has shown specimens at various stages, some still partly covered in matrix and others that have been fully prepared. However, most would-be fossil hunters reading such guides are led to believe that the 'best of the best' specimens can be readily found lying on the beach, such as a large 20 foot marine reptile! Unfortunately, this is not the case. Perhaps after many years of fossil hunting, that elusive big marine reptile may become a reality, but on your very first fossil hunt do not expect to find the best fossils or the biggest. Go out with an open mind and expect the unexpected. Here is a selection of fossils you may be likely to find on your first fossil hunt.

1. Being perhaps the most abundant fossil to find, ammonite partials and negatives (impressions) are very common. Masses of impressions and compressed specimens are found lying in the shales, such as *Dactylioceras* sp. illustrated.

2. Isolated crinoid stems, such as *Hispidocrinus* sp. illustrated are relatively common; they can be found worn and loose in the shingle on the beach.

3. Compacted blocks such as this are common. They are often highly pyritised and contain numerous partial ammonites and bivalves.

4. The usual glacial erratic finds consist of corals and are very common. If broken open the structure is rather detailed.

5. Small sections or parts of plants can be relatively common, such as *Otozamites* sp. illustrated.

6. Eroded, highly worn and compacted bivalves such as this are common.

7. Remains of bivalves are extremely common. They can be found in large numbers throughout the shingles and shales.

8. Highly worn parts of belemnite guards can usually be found on the beaches throughout the shingle and shales.

I've found a fossil what do I do now?

The first thing that you need to do with your fossils is to write down where you collected them. Always remember to record the location as accurately as possible and keep it with the specimen. If this information is lost it becomes just a random fossil of greatly reduced scientific interest. Many collectors just accumulate fossils for a hobby but your collection will be far more valuable and interesting if you keep a record of all your specimens in a diary or notebook.

What to record
Common name: Ammonite
Scientific name:
Dactylioceras commune
Age: Lower Toarcian
Whitby Mudstone Formation
(around 180 million-years-old)
Location: Port Mulgrave
Date found: November 2010
Smith Collection

If this guide has inspired you to go fossil hunting and you have managed to find a few fossil specimens then it has in part done its job. However, imagine a few weeks or months later, the fossils you collected are collecting dust on a shelf at home, forgotten and just another bit of clutter. Please do not let this happen! Fossils are important and were once living organisms, so cherish the specimens you find and learn more about them by visiting museums, reading books, visiting libraries, contacting specialists, further fossil hunting trips and more. Once you have become actively engaged in fossil hunting and have a collection (hopefully all labelled!) in the future it may be appropriate to donate or loan some of your specimens to a museum which may even put them on display. Always remember that the fossil specimen you have discovered could be scientifically and internationally important. If you think you have found a rarity, contact a museum or specialist!

A spectacular specimen of *Cenoceras astacoides*. The nautiloid has been highly polished which highlights the individual chambers and pyrite colouration of the specimen.

Fossil extraction and preparation

One thing people repeatedly ask is "how do you crack/get fossils out of the rocks?" The theory is relatively simple, but in reality it can be very difficult to extract specimens from the rocks that entomb them. For an ammonite specimen inside a nodule the easiest and most convenient way to remove the specimen (this is not the best way for all fossils) is to first of all secure the fossil between two strong rocks (if on the beach) so that the specimen will not roll over or move. Once secure you are ready to use your hammer and chisel to crack open the nodule. Make sure you wear your safety goggles when using these tools. Aim the chisel along the junction between the shell and the rock if the ammonite's keel is visible. Or you can just use your hammer, relying on the plane of weakness between the ammonite and the rock to allow it to 'pop' – nodules from some beds do this more easily than others. Do not worry too much if you break the specimen, about one in three Whitby ammonites split awkwardly and end up cracking. This is not necessarily the user's fault, but is due to how the ammonite was fossilised. However, remember that hammers and chisels should not be used just to hit rocks at random in the hope of finding a fossil. They need to be used properly in order to extract fossil specimens and should be used responsibly. Preparing some fossils can be a lot more difficult because it can include the use of air-powered tools such as air 'pens' and air abrasive units, which remove the surrounding rock (matrix) from the fossil. These tools are expensive and it may be better to let a specialist prepare some of the fossils for you, especially if it is something rare. Remember that every fossil is unique and that if you destroy a specimen it will be gone forever! You can improve the appearance of your fossils further by polishing them with wax, such as bees wax or similar. Although please be aware of your fossil's potential importance and make sure that it is not something unique beforehand because the use of waxes and glues can damage specimens and be difficult to remove.

Three stages to finding and extracting a fossil

1. Find a promising looking nodule.

2. Safely secure the nodule.

3. A fantastically preserved pos/neg ammonite *Hildoceras bifrons*.

Glossary

Carboniferous – The Carboniferous is a geological period of time that lasted between 360–300 million years ago.

Echinoderm – A group (phylum) of marine animals that includes echinoids, brittle stars and crinoids.

Fossil – A fossil is the remains or traces of an organism from the prehistoric past, usually considered from at least 10,000 years ago and back into the Earth's distant past.

Holotype – The single reference specimen upon which the description and name of a new species is based.

Ice age – An ice age is a period of time when glaciers covered large parts of the Earth's surface.

Invertebrate – Any animal that lacks a backbone, such as worms, molluscs and echinoderms.

Lagerstätten – A sedimentary deposit that exhibits exquisite fossil richness, detail and completeness.

Mesozoic – The Mesozoic is a geological era in Earth's history. It is made up of three periods: Triassic, Jurassic and Cretaceous. The Mesozoic era lasted around 185 million years and is known as the era of the dinosaurs.

Ornithopod – One of the most successful groups of dinosaurs, an example is *Iguanodon*.

Palaeontologist – Somebody who studies the history of life on Earth, primarily through the examination of fossils.

Palaeozoic – The Palaeozoic is a geological era in the Earth's history. It is made up of six individual periods of time. No dinosaurs existed during this time.

Post cranial – All or part of a skeleton from a single animal, apart from the skull.

Quaternary – The most recent interval of Earth's history that includes the Pleistocene and Holocene Epochs. During this time animals were much more similar to those living today than those living longer ago.

Sauropod – A group of generally quadrupedal dinosaurs that usually possessed a long neck and long tail, an example is *Diplodocus*.

SSSI – Site of Special Scientific Interest.

Terrestrial – Relating to the land rather than air or water.

Theropod – A group of bipedal carnivorous dinosaurs, an example is *Tyrannosaurus*.

Thyreophoran – A group of dinosaurs that were usually covered in 'armour' plating, an example is *Stegosaurus*.

Vertebrate – Animals that have a backbone or spinal column made up of vertebrae.

Acknowledgements and further information

I would like to give special thanks to three people in particular: Benjamin Hyde for advice and constant help with fieldwork and photography; Dr. Tarquin Bolton for advice, identification of belemnites and continual help revising the text, and Nobumichi Tamura for his artistic reconstructions and general advice.

I have benefited greatly from numerous discussions with many experts who have donated their time freely with regard to fossil identification confirmations, suggestions and general advice, and without whose kind help this book would not have been possible. They are as follows: for Marine reptiles: Dr Ryosuke Motani and Dr Adam Smith; ammonites: Andreas Schmidt; bivalves and gastropods: Dr Martin Munt and Andreas Schmidt; plants: Prof Paul Kenrick and Prof Han van Konijnenburg-van Cittert; Carboniferous fossils: Dr Joseph Botting; echinoderms: Dr Timothy Ewin, Ben Thuy and Dr Michael Simms; fish: Chris Duffin, Dr Peter Forey and Alison Longbottom; crustaceans: Dr Rodney Feldmann; mammal remains: Mark Broch, Dick Mol and Klaas Post; and dinosaurs: Dr Peter Falkingham and Dr Martin Whyte. Important thanks also go to The Western Interior Paleontological Society (WIPS: http://www. westernpaleo.org), Matthew McGrane, Renato and Julie Bonaccorsi, Andrea Marshall and my family and close friends for constant support and general advice.

I am extremely grateful to the contributing museums/institutions (and individuals therein) and to the private fossil collectors for allowing access to their collections and permitting specimens to be photographed for this guide, thus enabling others to develop an appreciation for the fossils of Whitby.

Museum and institutions acknowledgements
British Geological Survey – Paul Shepherd, Louise Neep and Dr Mike Howe
Doncaster Museum Service, Doncaster Metropolitan Borough Council – Peter
    Robinson, Laura Nugent and Carolyn Dalton
Manchester Museum – Dr David Gelsthorpe
National Centre of Biodiversity-Naturalis, Leiden, the Netherlands – Eelco
    Kruidenier and Prof Han van Konijnenburg-van Cittert
National Museum of Ireland – Nigel T. Monaghan
York Museums Trust (Yorkshire Museum) – Stuart Ogilvy and Isla Gladstone
Whitby Museum (Whitby Literary and Philosophical Society) – Mark
    Edwards, Peter Hughes and Denise Gildroy
Laboratory of Palaeobotany and Palynology, University of Utrecht, the
    Netherlands – Leonard Bik and Prof Han van Konijnenburg-van Cittert

Private collector acknowledgements
Benjamin Hyde
John Robinson
Mark, Helen, Aaron (14 years-old) and Shae Smith (10 years-old). The Smith family have been collecting fossils for five years
Dr Tarquin Bolton
Specimens from the author's private collection were also used

Picture acknowledgements – museum/institution copyrights
Images of fossils in museums/institutes assigned copyright: British Geological Survey (BGS), National Centre of Biodiversity, National Museum of Ireland, University of Utrecht and Yorkshire Museum.

©BGS NERC 2011
Haugia beani BGS GSM 25001
Turbo lineatus BGS GSM 39977
Amberleya sp. BGS GSM 40028
Tetrarhynchia tetraedra BGS GSM 39510
Serpulid worm tubes BGS GSM 118957
Parapsicephalus purdoni BGS GSM 3166
Gagaticeras gagateum BGS GSM 26441
Stenopterygius paddle BGS ZK 574

©National Centre of Biodiversity
Zamites gigas JMS 52426
Nilssoniopteris major JMS 52429

©National Museum of Ireland
Rhomaleosaurus cramptoni NMING F8785

©University of Utrecht
Brachyphyllum mamillare S.1330
Otozamites graphicus S.1524

©York Museums Trust
Parapassaloteuthis polita YORYM: 1994.1802.148
Lingula beani: YORYM: 2007.8836.6
Eocarcinus praecursor YORYM: G993–6
Large block of dinosaur footprints YORYM: 2008.950
Pleurotomaria cognata YORYM: 2005.813.2

Additional picture acknowledgements
Image of living *Pinna* bivalve – ©Ria Tan (http://www.wildsingapore.com)
Image of living brittle star – ©Ria Tan (http://www.wildsingapore.com)
Image of sand tracks (*Arachnoides placenta*) – ©Ria Tan (http://www.wildsingapore.com)
Image of living echinoid – ©Ria Tan (http://www.wildsingapore.com)
Image of living *Araucaria angustifolia* monkey puzzle trees – ©Boris Schlumpberger
Image of living horsetail – ©Jane Wilkins
Image of living *Lingula unguis* brachiopod – ©Nobumichi Tamura
Image of living gharial crocodilian – ©Charles Cuthbert

Finally, I would like to thank David Penney at Siri Scientific Press for rapid and thorough communication and for his editorial, design skills and total commitment during the preparation of this book.

Further reading
Benson, R.B.J., Ketchum, H.F., Noè, L.F. & Gómez-Pérez, M. 2011. New information on *Hauffiosaurus* (Reptilia, Plesiosauria) based on a new species from the Alum Shale Member (Lower Toarcian: Lower Jurassic) of Yorkshire, UK. *Paleontology*, 54: 547–571.

Benton, M.J. & M.A. Taylor. 1984. Marine reptiles from the upper lias (Lower Toarcian, Lower Jurassic) of the Yorkshire coast. *Proceedings of the Yorkshire Geological Society*, 44: 399–429.

Cope, J.C.W. 2006. Jurassic: the returning seas. In: *The Geology of England and Wales, 2nd edition*. Editors: P.J. Brenchley & P.F. Rawson. The Geological Society, London, 325–363.

Doyle, P. & D.I.M. Macdonald. 1993. Belemnite battlefields. *Lethaia*, 26: 65–80.

Howarth, M.K. 1962. The Yorkshire type ammonites and nautiloids of Young and Bird, Phillips, and Martin Simpson. *Palaeontology*, 5: 93–136.

Howarth, M.K. 1962. The Jet Rock Series and the Alum Shale Series of the Yorkshire coast. *Proceedings of the Yorkshire Geological Society*, 33, 381–422.

Simms, M.J., N. Chidlaw, N. Morton & K.N. Page. 2004. British Lower Jurassic stratigraphy. *Geological Conservation Review Series*, 30: 1–458.

Lomax, D.R. 2011. Fossils and fossil hunting in and around Whitby, England. *Fossil News Journal of Avocational Paleontology*, 17: 3–5.

Osborne, R. & A. Bowden. 2001. *The dinosaur coast Yorkshire rocks, reptiles and landscape*. North York Moors National Park on behalf of the Yorkshire Dinosaur Coast Project, 63 pp.

Rawson, P.F. & J.K. Wright. 2000. *The Yorkshire Coast, 3rd, revised edition*. Geologists' Association Guide no. 34, 130 pp.

Scrutton, C. 1994. The Lower Jurassic rocks between Staithes and Port Mulgrave. In: Editors, C.T. Scrutton & J.H. Powell, *Yorkshire rocks and landscapes – a field guide, 3rd edition*, Yorkshire Geological Society, pp. 150–157.

Seilacher, A. 1993. Ammonite anaptychus; how to transform a jaw into an operculum? *American Journal of Science*, 293: 20–32.

Simpson, M. 1884. *The fossils of the Yorkshire Lias; described from nature, second edition*. London and Whitby, 256 pp.

Sylvester-Bradley, P.C. 1953, A stratigraphical guide to the fossil localities of the Scarborough district. In: *The natural history of the Scarborough district, Vol, 1. Geology and botany*. Scarborough Field Naturalist's Society, Scarborough, xii + 296 pp.

Tate, R. & J.F. Blake. 1876. *The Yorkshire Lias*. Van Voorst, London.

West, I.M. 2010. *Staithes, Middle Jurassic – geological field guid*e, Appendix to Geology of the Wessex Coast. Internet site: http:\\www.soton.ac.uk/~imw/staithes.htm. National Oceanography Centre, Southampton University. Version: 19th January 2009.

Whyte, M.A. & Romano, M. 2006. Lower-Middle Jurassic sequences between Whitby and Saltwick. In: Editors, C.T. Scrutton & J.H. Powell, *Yorkshire rocks and landscapes – a field guide, 3rd edition*, Yorkshire Geological Society, pp. 158–164.

Whyte, M.A., Romano, M. & Watts, W. 2010. Yorkshire dinosaurs: a history in two parts. In: Editors, R.T.J. Moody, E. Buffetaut, D. Naish & D. Martill, Dinosaurs and other extinct saurians: a historical perspective. *Geological Society, London, Special Publications*, 343: 189–207.

Woodward, A.S. 1889. On the fossil fishes of the Upper Lias of Whitby. Part IV. *Proceedings of the Yorkshire Geological Society*, 13: 455–472.

Useful websites

http://www.palaeocritti.com – Palaeocritti is the ultimate guide to prehistoric animals! Palaeocritti allows you to look up prehistoric critters by group, period, name or location.

http://www.ukfossils.co.uk – A comprehensive guide to the UK's fossil locations. Search by region, rock unit and location.

http://www.discoveringfossils.co.uk – Introducing the palaeontology of Great Britain, learn and understand the fossils found here.

About the author

Dean Lomax (pictured in Wyoming, USA) is a palaeontologist from Doncaster, England. Dean has worked on palaeontological projects in Europe and the USA, he researches fossils and publishes articles and peer reviewed scientific papers. He can sometimes be found looking for fossils along this coastline.

UKGE
limited

* **Geological tools**
* **Beginners starter packs**
* **Fossil guides & maps**
* **Order online or by phone**
* **All major cards accepted**

Everything
you need to start
collecting fossils

- 0800 0336 002 -

www.ukge.com